Understanding Pedagogy

What is meant by pedagogy?

How does our conception of pedagogy inform good teaching and learning?

Pedagogy is a complex concept of which students and teachers need to have an understanding, yet there remain many ambiguities about what the term means, and how it informs learning. *Understanding Pedagogy* examines pedagogy in a holistic way, supporting a more critical and reflective understanding of teaching and learning. It considers pedagogy not only as a concept that covers teaching approaches and student–teacher relationships, but as one that also embraces and informs educational theory, personal learning styles, assessment, and relationships within and beyond the immediate learning context.

A detailed consideration of what it means to be a professional in the contemporary climate, *Understanding Pedagogy* challenges students and teachers to reappraise their understanding and practice through effectively linking theory and practice. Key issues explored include the importance of understanding a learning styles profile, the application of cognitive neuroscience to teaching and learning, personalised learning, assessment and feedback, and what we mean by critical reflection. Using the Personal Learning Styles Pedagogy, the authors make explicit the integration of theory and practice and the many decisions and selections that teachers and students make, their implications for what is being taught and learnt, how learners are positioned in the pedagogical process, and ultimately, how learning can be improved.

Understanding Pedagogy will be essential reading for all students and teachers in school and higher education contexts involved in the endeavour of understanding what constitutes effective teaching and learning as part of their initial teacher education and Education Studies courses at both undergraduate and postgraduate levels, and professional development activities.

Michael Waring is the Director of the PGCE/MSc (QTS) PE programmes and Senior Lecturer in the School of Sport, Exercise and Health Sciences at Loughborough University, UK.

Carol Evans is Professor of Higher Education at the University of Southampton, UK; a National Teaching Fellow and Principal Fellow of the Higher Education Academy, UK; President of the Education, Learning, Styles, Individual differences Network (ELSIN), and Associate Editor of the *British Journal of Educational Psychology*. She is also a Visiting Fellow at the Institute of Education, University of London.

Understanding Pedagogy

Developing a critical approach to teaching and learning

Michael Waring and Carol Evans

LONDON AND NEW YORK

First published 2015
by Routledge
2 Park Square, Milton Park, Abingdon, Oxon OX14 4RN

and by Routledge
711 Third Avenue, New York, NY 10017

Routledge is an imprint of the Taylor & Francis Group, an informa business

British Library Cataloguing in Publication Data
A catalogue record for this book is available from the British Library

Library of Congress Cataloging in Publication Data
Waring, Mike.
Understanding pedagogy: developing a critical approach to teaching and learning/
Mike Waring, Carol Evans.

1. Critical pedagogy. 2. Teaching—Philosophy. 3. Learning, Psychology of.
4. Cognitive styles in children. I. Evans, Carol, Professor II. Title.
LC196.W37 2015
370.11'5—dc23

ISBN: 978-0-415-57173-9 (hbk)
ISBN: 978-0-415-57174-6 (pbk)
ISBN: 978-1-315-74615-9 (ebk)

Typeset in Bembo
by Swales & Willis Ltd, Exeter, Devon, UK

In loving memory of Jean and Ron Hurley

To my wife, mum and dad without whom this book would not have been possible.

Contents

Illustrations

Figures

Tables

Acknowledgements

We are grateful for permission to print material from the following works:

Illeris, K. (Ed.) (2009). The three dimensions of learning and competence development. In *Contemporary learning theories* (p. 10). London: Routledge (Figure 3.2).

Illeris, K. (Ed.) (2007). Positions in the tension field of learning. In *How we learn. Learning and non-learning in schools and beyond* (p. 257). London: Routledge (Figure 3.3).

Kozhevnikov, M., Evans, C., and Kosslyn, S. (2014). Cognitive style as environmentally-sensitive individual differences in cognition: a modern synthesis, and applications in education, business and management. *Psychological Sciences in the Public Interest, 15*(1) (May 2014): 3–33 (Figure 5.1 and Figure 5.3).

Evans, C. (2013b). Making sense of assessment feedback in higher education. *Review of Educational Research, 83*(1): 70–120 (Figure 9.1).

Gibbs, G. (1988). *Learning by doing: A Guide to teaching and learning*, Oxford Centre for Staff and Learning Development, Oxford Brookes University, Oxford. This publication is available to download from http://www.brookes.ac.uk/ocsld/publications/ (Gibbs's learning cycle: Tool B)

Introduction

The dynamic fast-changing knowledge-rich world in which we live demands that we move beyond a reiteration of practices old and advance an evolved vision of education that promotes teachers and learners who are empowered, have a voice, and have a sense of critical awareness that allows them to deliberate, be critically reflective, and be able to make genuine choices. As part of working towards achieving this, this book is also a constructive challenge to the ideological agendas of government policy, which have created a dominant culture of compliance and regulation that has served to undermine teaching as a research-based profession in favour of an unacceptable reductionist one that sees teaching as a craft (Beauchamp *et al.*, 2013).While the implications of the changes in provision for Initial Teacher Education (ITE) and related continual professional development (CPD) activities for teachers are yet to be fully realized in the UK, it is clear that an informed outline of research-informed practice/principles supported by an understanding of pedagogy, needs to be presented to enable teachers and learners to collaboratively and critically engage with each other as part of a dynamic social process that empowers them and supports their critical judgement and the possible choices that they can make as teachers and learners in and of the twenty-first century.

Importantly, the issues raised and research-informed practices proposed in this book are relevant to everyone involved in the educational process and to the holistic concept of pedagogy which we espouse. Therefore, the challenge here is not just to schools, it is to all venues of teacher education and professional development, to make sure that the educational process continually allows the learner to develop the skills and knowledge to deliberate (as part of a collaborative critical dialogue) their critical awareness and possible choices.

As part of providing teachers with the necessary research-informed evidence to work towards achieving this evolved vision of education, in chapter one we identify what it is to be a twenty-first-century teaching professional, and address the question of what practice requires teachers to learn. How we perceive professionalism within our immediate and wider school roles, and its impact on the way we enact more sophisticated conceptions of professionalism in our practice, are examined.

In chapter two we foreground the complex concept of pedagogy, highlighting the uncertainty around the associated terminology and its numerous interpretations. A definitive definition of pedagogy is not going to be sought here; instead a holistic concept of pedagogy will be presented, key dimensions of which will be highlighted to help understand the multiple discourses that are features of all pedagogies, including the inclusive participatory pedagogy promoted throughout this book.

As part of addressing the inappropriate dichotomy between theory and practice which is evident in many manifestations of pedagogy and notions of teacher professionalism in school, in chapter three we explore what educational theory is, and its relevance, and argue for the integration of theory and practice as part of understanding the intricacies involved in the process of learning and teaching.

The application of educational theory using an integrated approach is outlined in chapter four using the Personal Learning Styles Pedagogy (PLSP) (Evans and Waring, 2009; 2015). We use the PLSP as a holistic framework to examine different aspects of practice. As part of this we highlight the essential role which teachers have to play in both their use and generation of educational theory in supporting the development of effective twenty-first-century learners.

In chapter five we explore an understanding of how people learn. We provide a state-of-the-art update on the current understandings of styles and specifically cognitive styles and related constructs from education, cognitive psychology, and neuroscience perspectives to promote a timely and necessary research-informed understanding of how we learn, and subsequently to illustrate how it can be used to inform pedagogy and enhance learning and teaching.

Reinforcing the genuine integration of theory and practice which is promoted throughout the book, chapter six will highlight key issues and provide clear guidance on how to cut through the many misconceptions about styles and related constructs and their inappropriate use in educational contexts. It will promote a focus on overarching principles involved in the application of styles rather than a focus on attempts to differentiate between different styles constructs: such an approach is vital. We introduce the concept of an enriched styles pedagogy to highlight those key parameters that practitioners should consider in the use and application of styles, and this is exemplified using the PLSP.

The question then asked in the book is how best to support the learning needs of all students. Chapter seven extends the notion of pedagogy discussed in chapter two by exploring further the concept of an inclusive participatory pedagogy and its fundamental importance in framing learning and teaching activities. As part of this chapter the meaning and differing interpretations of terms such as inclusion, personalization, individualized instruction, differentiation (which are frequently employed in discussions and application of inclusive pedagogical practice) are discussed, and important areas of development in supporting learning and teaching for students and teachers within the classroom are outlined. In chapter eight the PLSP framework, as an example of an inclusive participatory pedagogy, is employed to exemplify how learners can be empowered to take responsibility for their own learning through the implementation of overarching principles of effective learning for all students rather than a focus on individual instruction for each and every learner.

Chapter nine provides an overview of the key principles of effective assessment including feedback and demonstrates how these principles can be applied effectively within different educational contexts. We highlight the importance of supporting students to manage their own learning through enabling them to effectively self-monitor their own progress in learning. Supporting students to develop resilience in learning and especially to manage the emotional dimension of feedback is also acknowledged. Exemplification of the principles of good feedback using the PLSP is also provided.

Critical reflection is seen as the cornerstone of professional practice and an integral element of the PLSP. The PLSP has been used throughout the book to exemplify our evolved vision of education. However, there is much debate as to what critical reflection is, how it is enacted, and what it achieves. In chapter ten we define what critical reflection is and explore the use of models and tools in the teaching of critical reflection. Key principles and issues involved in supporting the critical reflection of teachers and learners using the Personal Learning Styles Pedagogy framework are highlighted as part of this.

The previous chapters have demonstrated the varied ways in which the PLSP can be used as an overarching holistic framework to guide the design and delivery of curricula including assessment in school, higher education, and workplace learning. Drawing on a rich and diverse data set including research in schools, higher education and the workplace (1999–2014), chapter eleven provides a unique synthesis of the genuine integration of theory and practice as part of an effective inclusive participatory pedagogy –the PLSP. We clearly demonstrate how each of the components of the PLSP can be realized within practice.

Highlighting future challenges, the final chapter identifies a theme which permeates the book – that of transitions. It identifies some of the challenges associated with the many transitions which we all make during our learning careers and which we need to manage. It also identifies the evolving nature of policy and practice associated with teacher education and the challenges this presents for teachers, learners and the promotion of an inclusive participatory pedagogy. Finally, the ongoing challenge for teachers to enact evidence-based practice and critical reflection is reinforced.

Chapter 1

Making sense of teacher professionalism

Overview

In this chapter we will identify what it is to be a twenty-first-century teaching professional, and address the question of what practice requires teachers to learn. How we perceive professionalism within our immediate and wider school roles affects the way we enact professionalism in our practice. Examining more sophisticated conceptions of professionalism, we will focus attention on the relationship between and the development of the following:

- teachers' conceptions of teaching: the notion of the professional teacher
- a critical professional identity
- micro-political literacy
- integrated understandings of the nature of knowledge
- professional development orientation: teacher capacity for autonomous professional development.

Defining professionalism

There are many definitions of professionalism, focusing on different aspects of the concept. Higgs and Titchen (2001, p. 5) outline a holistic view of professionalism, focusing on what teachers do both as an external and internally mediated process.

> Professional practice . . . is a rare blend of people-centred and interactive processes, accountability and professional standards, practice wisdom, professional artistry, openness to knowledge growth and practice development and engagement in professional journeys towards expertise.

Alternatively, others have focused on how individuals make sense of and enact professionalism in their practice, seeing a commitment to self and organizational development as an important dimension of this:

> Professionality [is]: an ideologically, attitudinally, intellectually and epistemologically-based stance on the part of an individual, in relation to the practice of the profession to which s/he belongs, and which influences her/his professional practice
>
> L. Evans, 2008a, p. 26

Professionalism means different things to different people depending on their specific occupational groups; it reflects the perceptions of a person's group formed by their intended purpose, status, and nature of expertise, as well as their code of practice. Professionalism can be considered socially constructed (Ifanti and Fotopoulopu, 2011): 'something which defines and articulates the quality and character of people's actions within that group' (A. Hargreaves and Goodson, 1996, p. 4); a 'consensus of the norms, which may apply to being and behaving as a professional within personal, organizational and broader political conditions' (Day, 1999, p. 13) 'subject to geographical and cultural differences in interpretation, which themselves may change over time' (Helsby, 1995, p. 317), as noted in David Hargreaves's (2000) professionalism continuum (pre-professional, autonomous, collegial, post-professional or postmodern).

Day and Gu (2007) have argued that teachers' professionalism is closely related to educational policy reforms, which have the potential to diminish or redefine teachers' professionalism, thus suggesting that professionalism is externally driven. However, this would be to overstate the power of policy reforms in impacting on teachers' sense of professionalism and positioning the teacher as a passive receiver rather than as a creative thinker and actor. Although various notions of new teacher professionalism exist, 'it is probably best to see all these various positions as *competing* versions of teacher professionalism for the twenty-first century, rather than seeing anyone as fitting an essentialist definition of professionalism and others as detracting from it' (Whitty, 2001, p. 160).

Regardless of how one defines professionalism, it is how teachers enact professionalism that is important. However, for many, professionalism is inseparable from notions of professional identity and beliefs about what it is to be a good teacher (Lasky, 2005). There is a dichotomy between perceptions of professionalism focused on externally imposed perceptions of a profession's collective remit and responsibilities (whereby professionalism is imposed from above in defining the boundaries of the profession's actual and potential authority, power and influence) and an internal perception of professionalism focused on the attitudes and behaviours of individuals in relation to their profession. Professionalism and professional culture are often seen as intertwined; however L. Evans (2008a, 2008b) has argued that professional culture is more attitudinal (the response of people towards the professionalism) whereas professionalism is more functional in that it defines how individuals operate.

In sum, notions of what it is to be a teaching professional are constantly shifting and open to individual interpretation. How teachers perceive professionalism matters in the way they enact professionalism in the construction of their professional identity, and in their teaching which impacts on students' attainment (Sammons, *et al.*, 2007). Of significance is A. Wilson *et al.*'s (2013) description of the development of professionalism as transformational rather than acquisitional, which acknowledges, thus, the importance of understanding and facilitating a more sophisticated notion of professionalism for the teacher of today. This will be discussed further in this chapter.

Key elements of professionalism

Hoyle (1975) made the distinction between professionalism and professionality, describing the former as comprising status-related elements of teachers' work and the latter as constituting the knowledge, skills and procedures that teachers use in their work. The important distinction between *being* professional (which implies the importance of training and development of specialist knowledge and skills, observance of standards, and the exercising of autonomy in decision making), and *behaving* professionally (which implies dedication and commitment) has been noted by many (e.g. Day, 1999; D. Hargreaves, 2000; Helsby, 1995). As part of being professionals, how teachers perceive themselves to be seen through others' eyes is important in framing their professional identity, or identities.

Linda Evans (2008a, 2008b) distinguished between *demanded* or *requested professionalism* (specific professional demands or requests made of an occupational group or individual workforce – usually by employers), *prescribed professionalism* (reflecting envisaged or recommended professional service levels perceived by analysts); and *enacted professionalism.* Linda Evans (2008a, 2008b) has argued the importance of *enacted professionalism* as the only meaningful conception of professionalism – that is, professional practice which is observed, perceived and interpreted. For example, professional standards for teachers and what it means to be a teacher cannot be imposed, they need to be owned and overseen by the profession itself (Sachs, 2003).

The need for more attention to be placed on becoming a teacher as part of teacher training and professional development opportunities has been identified (Wilkins, 2011). Early-career teachers in a study conducted by C. Evans (2014) found that there was little discussion about the *teacher they wanted to be and how to get there*, although such discussions – about what it was to be a teacher and specifically *how to be the teacher they wanted to be* – the student teachers felt to be highly valuable. Wilkins mirrors this finding as represented in the following quote from one of the student teachers in his study:

> It's the bit that no-one ever teaches you, about how you grow into being a teacher. On the PGCE, my Induction Mentor, it all seems a bit mechanistic. Maybe you can't teach it, you just have to grow into it. (J)
>
> Wilkins, 2011, p. 400

Traditional definitions of teacher professionalism have emphasized the role of training in providing teachers with *expert knowledge of subject, pedagogy and students* and stressed that such a position as teacher affords a degree of *autonomy* over practice and professional standards (Atkinson and Claxton, 2000; Day, 1999; Foucault, 1980; A. Wilson *et al.*, 2013), although this is increasingly contested within the context of twenty-first-century learning environments.

Drawing on Barnett's (2011) conception of *a will to offer*, teachers have the responsibility to *contribute to the knowledge base* on learning and teaching at both subject and generic levels and to exercise *expert judgement based on specialist knowledge.* A central dimension of professionalism is that of *concern for people* and a *service ethic* requiring strong relational skills and a desire to enhance, empower, and develop others. Wilkins (2011) draws on the work of Parsons (1937) and Lortie (1975) in his conception of psychic rewards, which highlights the altruistic nature of professionalism. Trust is very much a cornerstone of professional practice: 'Professionalism requires professionals to be worthy of that trust' (Evetts, 2006, p. 134). Such trust requires a shared understanding of ethical and moral dimensions of professional practice within organizational contexts along with a clear sense of individual and collective responsibility for the welfare of all.

Professionalism involves the use of *expert and wise judgement* (A. Wilson *et al.*, 2013) predicated on the development of appropriate *professional values* (Furlong, 2000b), *self-awareness*, and *responsibility for self*. 'At their best, teachers are also able to reflect on and evaluate their practices, and to make rationally and ethically defensible judgements that go beyond compliance, pragmatic constraints or ideological preferences' (Pollard, 2010, p. 2). Central to conceptions of professionalism is attention to ethical considerations.

Higgs and Titchen (2001) in their interpretation of professionalism have emphasized the importance of *teacher sensitivity to context* at local, national, and international levels and have argued that underpinning key elements of professionalism (people-centred, context-relevant, wise, and authentic practice) is the *professional artistry* of the teacher: 'the self we bring to professional practice, is a creative entity, meeting individual needs with individual solutions'(Higgs and Titchen, 2001, p. 14). A capacity for *autonomous professional development* is also identified as a key component of professionalism (Day, 1999; Ifanti and Fotopoulopou, 2011; Pollard, 2010; Webb *et al.*, 2004; Wilkins, 2011). Higgs and Titchen use the term *interactional professional* to highlight the role of the teacher in critiquing and developing his/her own practice in interaction with others:

> Interactional professionals will be equipped with generic skills (including skills in communication, problem-solving, evaluation and investigation, self-directed learning and interpersonal interaction) which will enable them to engage in lifelong learning and professional review and development, as well as responsible, self-critical autonomous practice of their professional role. They will be capable of interacting effectively with their context in a manner which is transformational, facilitative, interdependent and symbiotic (i.e. both influenced by and influencing that environment).
>
> Higgs and Hunt, 1999, p.15

Awareness, capacity, and commitment to change to enhance practice are also seen as key elements of professionalism: 'To develop professionally people need to recognise a new way of doing things as a *better* way of doing things. This recognition of a 'better way' is a key component within the process whereby people develop professionally' (L. Evans, 2010, p. 7).

Collaboration with colleagues impacts teachers' professionalism and professional development (Ifanti and Fotopoulopou, 2011). However, it is not just about collaboration with colleagues within and beyond the immediate environs of the school, it is also about teachers practicing learning with students and collaborating with outside agencies, parents and wider learning networks (e.g. government bodies; professional associations; school networks; higher education institutions (Day, 1999)).

Furthermore, increasing emphasis is being placed on the teacher as part of their professional duties not only to engage in professional development, but also to *contribute to the professional development of others* (L. Evans, 2010). *Commitment to change* is seen as key component of professionalism (Mortimore, 1999; L. Evans, 2010; Wilkins, 2011) involving a professional obligation to review and develop one's practice through both personal reflection and interaction with others stressing the *co-operative and collegial* aspects of professionalism. Being a professional means being part of a professional community and identifying with others through 'similarities in work practices and procedures, common ways of perceiving problems and their possible solutions and shared ways of perceiving and interacting with customers and clients' (Evetts, 2003, p. 401) which may be expansive, in forging collegiality, collaboration and openness to change,or restrictive, in safeguarding the interests of established groups, and being monopolistic, exploitive and not open to change.

Anna Wilson *et al.* (2013) found both commonality and variation in understandings of professionalism – commonality as expressed in three core concepts:

- exercising specialist knowledge and skills with judgement
- identifying as a member of a community based on shared practices and values, where the norms of acceptable practice and values are determined within the community rather than imposed from without
- having a sense of responsibility and service, based on a belief that what you and your professional community does is of genuine value

Variation in the level of the sophistication of understandings of professionalism has important implications for training and development of teachers.

Challenges for professionalism within twenty-first-century learning environments

Globalization, social change, technological innovation, growing cultural diversity, and the associated profusion of knowledge challenging assumptions about the what and how of teaching, along with performativity agendas (audit/target culture, regulatory mechanisms such as Ofsted in England, marketization) have had a significant impact on the work of teachers, perceptions of professionalism, and understandings of 'new professionalism' (Day *et al.*, 2007; Wilkins, 2011) as a response to increased external control. Conceptions of good teaching are changing because of an expanding knowledge base and changes in cultural and social conditions that also impinge on definitions of what competent teaching comprises.

Uncertainty is the new constant for teachers (L. Evans, 2013). That is the uncertainty of the context in which they are working given ongoing numerous policy reforms, changes in social organization and the transformative potential of e-learning. Within complex twenty-first-century learning environments teachers have a 'responsibility to prepare students fully for [a] world of uncertainty, challenge, and turbulence' (Mortimore, 1999, p.151) requiring a new type of pedagogy one where learning is a kind of *'learning-to-doubt'*and where learning affects the *'nature of being and becoming'* (Barnett, 2011).

In preparing students to manage in complex learning environments, Barnett has highlighted the need for teachers to challenge students by placing them in situations of cognitive and experiential complexity and in encouraging them to engage constructively with each other's different points of view. Teachers need to know how best to use their pedagogical skills to effectively support the self-regulatory development of their students (Kek and Huijser, 2011), to be able to keep up with changing networks, and to engage in continuous learning and relearning (Jensen, 2007).

A significant dimension in facilitating self-regulatory practice and a fundamental consideration for all teachers is the authenticity in design of learning environments (see Lombardi, 2007, pp. 3–4 for elaboration on ten elements of authentic design). Authentic learning 'focuses on real-world, complex problems and their solutions . . . [and] intentionally brings into play multiple disciplines, multiple perspectives, ways of working, habits of mind, and community' (Lombardi, 2007, pp. 2–3). Authentic learning designs include those that facilitate and empower learners to achieve learning goals. Such designs require 'not just a construction of the overall learning context, but detailed concern with the tasks, the activities of learners, and the means of knowledge representation used' (Boyle and Ravenscroft, 2012, p. 1230).

No longer can teaching be perceived as 'technically simple' (the perception that once teaching is mastered no further training is required) (D. Hargreaves, 2000); it is much more complex and academic, requiring ongoing professional development. While the autonomy and individualistic nature of how and what teachers teach in their lessons is to be celebrated, teaching in the twenty-first century is much more collegial and collaborative with constraints on autonomy (Day and Gu, 2007). However, even within the present regimes of high accountability teachers should and can hold on to their sense of autonomy and professional identity(ies) (Williams, 2011).With advances in technology such autonomy and professional identity is framed by a context in which the teacher is no longer seen as the exclusive holder of expert knowledge, with greater emphasis being placed on the importance of dialogic as opposed to a transmission mode of learning and teaching.

To enable the learners of today and tomorrow, the teachers of today have to be *'extended professionals'* (Hoyle, 1975). They are expected to expand their own knowledge by examining theory and practice, collaborate with colleagues to share and develop ideas and evaluate practice, work with students attending to student voice through negotiation of tasks, contribute to school policy-making, and collaborate with parents and external partners (Lamote and Engels, 2010).

The intensification of teachers' work (A. Hargreaves, 1994), the detailed and prescriptive nature of the curriculum, the sustained introduction into schools of various government initiatives, and the extensive bureaucratic demands to which teachers are subjected are perceived by many as eroding their professional autonomy, resulting in a technicist model of '*incorporated professionalism'* which has deprofessionalised teachers into compliant deliverers of state-imposed initiatives (see Wilkins, 2011 for further discussion of this). However, Lasky (2005) has argued that managerialism has not impacted on the identity of the teacher, with teachers feeling moral and ethical obligation to be more than just a 'deliverer of the curriculum'. Within this debate less attention has been given to the emergence of the *empowered professional* arising from changes in leadership culture within and across schools that are led by collegial professionalism rather than by top-down initiatives (Coles and Southworth, 2005).

The *transformative activist professional* is another interpretation of new professionalism where teachers are seen as able to balance the needs of public accountability with professional autonomy (Sachs, 2003). The activist professional creates new spaces to operate within rather than operating in micro-autonomous spaces as incorporated professionals do, actively challenges managerialism and creates new cultures through collegial discourses. Wilkins (2011, p. 405) found within newly qualified teachers the emergence of a type of professionalism most aligned to the notion of the empowered professional demonstrating a more relaxed approach to balancing accountability with autonomy, perhaps reflecting their own experiences within performativity-focused education systems. He noted the following characteristics of these teachers.

> They fully embrace the accountability culture of teaching, less from a sense of democratic duty as public servants than simply because it is *effective*.They have little patience for those amongst their experienced colleagues who they see as resistant to change, and are generally comfortable with the wider framework of performative management cultures – so long as they continue to enjoy the'micro-autonomy' of the classroom.

In sum, the dichotomy in contemporary views on professionalism is highlighted by Linda Evans (2013, p. 474) with one perspective, viewing professionalism as an 'externally imposed, articulated perception of what lies within the parameters of a profession's collective remit and responsibilities' and by Ailsa Kolsaker (2008, p. 522), who adopts the alternative perspective, acknowledging the role of external control and accountability in defining and preserving professional status – an approach that entails a 'commitment to ongoing professional development and a willingness to adhere to external mechanisms that assure professional practice'.

Enacting professionalism

Notions of *incorporated, empowered, and transformative* professionalism are important in informing how teachers perceive and work within the regulatory aspects of their profession. A demanded professionalism (L. Evans 2008a, 2008b) such as that set out in the new *'Teachers' Standards'* for teachers in England (DfE, 2011a) is not the same as an enacted professionalism. These new standards are the fourth reincarnation of standardized assessment of teachers, which was first introduced in 1998. In terms of practice and attitudes, they require that all teachers:

> . . . make the education of their pupils their first concern, and are accountable for achieving the highest possible standards in work and conduct. Teachers act with honesty and integrity; have strong subject knowledge, keep their knowledge and skills as teachers up-to-date and are self-critical; forge positive professional relationships; and work with parents in the best interests of their pupils.
>
> DfE, 2011a, p. 7

All teachers need to look critically at the professional standards which are used to inform their practice, and be able to articulate what these mean for their own practice. The rhetoric inherent in the *Teachers' Standards* is about providing a base line of expectations for practice, a framework for all teachers, at any career stage, to inform development of their teaching and associated professional development. Within the standards there is an emphasis on what teachers should be able to do and what they should know; they are also concerned with quality assurance and accountability and the notion of quality improvements (see Sachs, 2003).

A key issue is how standards are interpreted at individual, school, and network of schools levels, as well as the extent to which there is consensus about what constitutes 'effective', 'appropriate', 'high' teaching and professional development of teachers in situ. Furthermore, to what extent are locally derived interpretations of what is effective practice transferable across contexts? Standards also need to be flexible to the changing conditions of teaching and learning. Standards must not be interpreted in a technical–rational way:

> . . . teaching is an extremely complex endeavour and standards cannot completely provide an account of this complexity, nor encompass comprehensively what 'good teaching' might be. Any definitions of 'good teaching' are contestable and not as settled a matter as the standards might suggest
>
> Heilbronn and Yandell, 2011, p. 3

Such contestability is essential for dialogue and an essential dimension of the critical participatory pedagogy promoted within this book as part of a holistic notion of pedagogy. How the standards are enacted are important; for example, teachers define appropriate conduct rather than simply exercising it (A. Wilson *et al.*, 2013).

Linda Evans's (2008a, 2008b) depiction of *enacted* and *demanded* professionalism argues that standards can only work if teachers recognize that there are better ways of doing things and that there is a shared understanding of what *better* means within context. In so doing, attention is drawn to the importance of attitudinal rather than functional development, demonstrating the need for more attention to be focused on those intellectual/motivational change features in addition to the procedural/productive ones prominent in externally imposed models of teacher development. In order for standards to work they must have currency among teachers and the broader society itself, and any set of professional standards for teaching needs to be owned and overseen by the profession itself (Sachs, 2003). As part of professionalism, professional standards should be seen not as a straitjacket, enforcing a particular form of teaching or narrow set of teacher attributes, but as the 'necessary provocation for teachers to think about their work, classroom activities and professional identity in quite fundamentally different and generative ways', enabling internal regulation by the profession itself rather than external control (Sachs, 2003, p. 185).

Questions for reflection

- Which of these three descriptors: 'incorporated, empowered, and transformative professional' best describes how you see your own professional identity and why?
- What others way would you describe your professional identity that is not captured in the three descriptors?
- What are the affordances and constraints impacting your sense of professional identity?

Developing more sophisticated understandings of professionalism

Building on Hoyle's notion of restricted and extended professionalism, A. Wilson *et al.* (2013) identified a continuum of *less sophisticated to more sophisticated understandings of professionalism* amongst teachers in relation to

- the extent to which individuals perceived professionalism as externally or internally determined or as an integration of the two
- level of awareness of the impact of one's actions on colleagues and pupils
- degree of focus on rights versus responsibilities of a professional
- professionalism as an external persona adopted in workplace contexts versus professionalism as part of self-identity
- teaching involving a technical rationalist approach to what works versus valuing theory underpinning pedagogy and integration of rational and intuitive decision making.

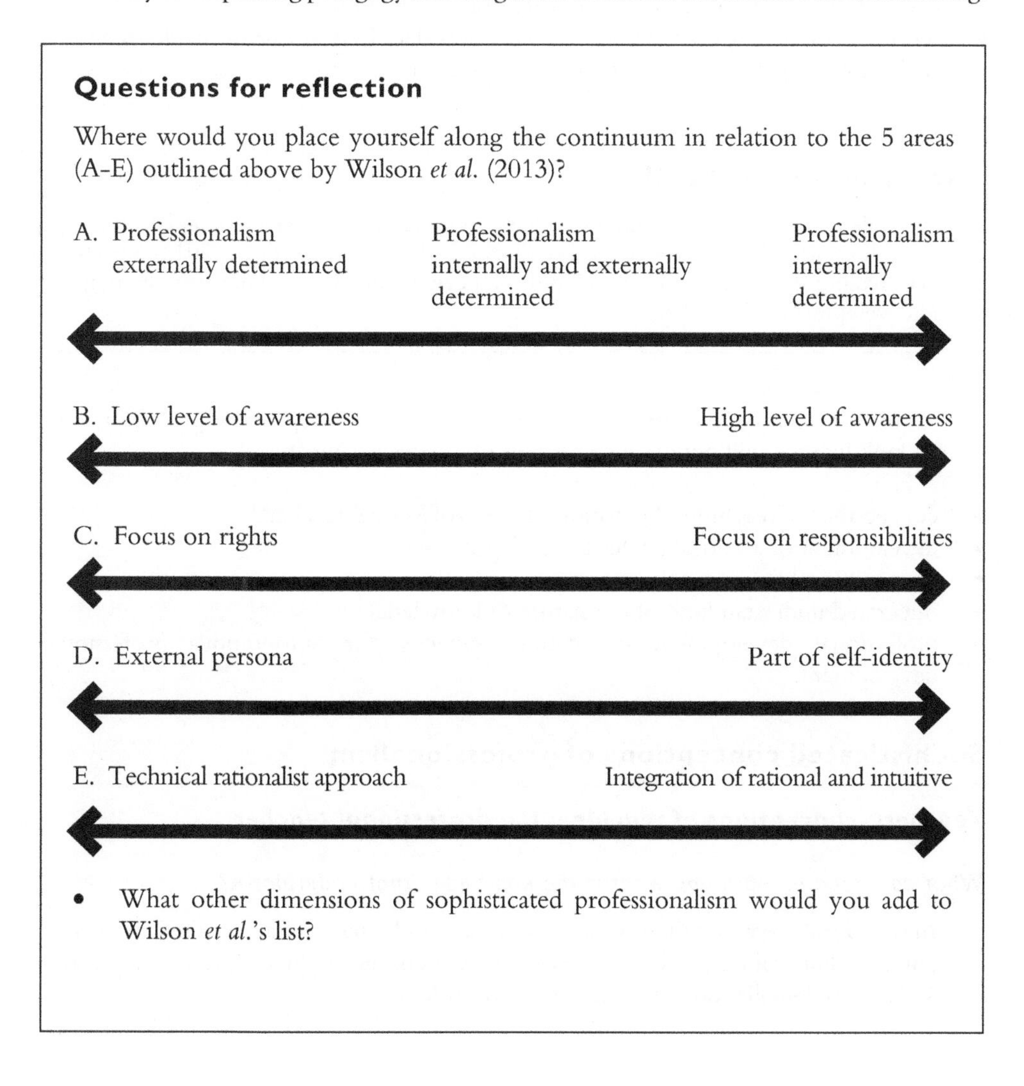

Questions for reflection

Where would you place yourself along the continuum in relation to the 5 areas (A-E) outlined above by Wilson *et al.* (2013)?

- What other dimensions of sophisticated professionalism would you add to Wilson *et al.*'s list?

Anna Wilson *et al.* (2013) have argued that attention needs to be placed on an explicit discussion of the meaning and purpose of professionalism that goes beyond a narrow interpretation of professional standards, and that to develop and promote more sophisticated understandings of professionalism teachers should be exposed to:

- multiple perspectives and areas of uncertainty in knowledge and applications of knowledge
- opportunities for student self-evaluation and exploration of personal standards for work quality
- illustrations of contextual variation in appropriate professional conduct
- opportunities to explore the relationship between external codes of ethics set by professional bodies and students' own personal codes and values
- discussions of how what might at first appear to be externally determined norms, practices, and values are the result of both explicit and implicit co-operation and negotiations among members of a professional community
- reflection on when professionals' choices and decisions are being made, together with explicit consideration of their scope of impact.

Questions for reflection

On a scale of 1–5 (with 5 meaning that the area is attended to very well and 1 representing least attention), consider the extent to which A. Wilson *et al.*'s (2013) aspects of curriculum design as outlined above (have been attended to in your own training and development as a teacher.

As part of our examination of what a more sophisticated conception of professionalism should look like we will now focus attention on the following areas:

- conceptions of teaching: the notion of the professional teacher
- development of a critical professional identity
- micropolitical literacy
- integrated understandings of the nature of knowledge
- professional development orientation: capacity for autonomous professional development.

Sophisticated conceptions of professionalism

Teachers' conceptions of teaching: the professional teacher

What do I need to learn and what is the knowledge that underpins it?

> In walking alone with others we need to understand our own frames of reference (our cultures, spirituality, professional roles), to understand other people's backgrounds and seek reconciliation between these various frames.
>
> Higgs and Titchen, 2001, p. 271

A more sophisticated conception of teaching is that of the *professional teacher* as defined by Winch *et al.* (2013): autonomous in exercising their own judgement in the classroom and making decisions about how to interpret theoretical and research-based knowledge and whether or how to adopt it in their own practice, i.e. integrating notions of the craft teacher and executive technician. Such teachers interrogate their own practice as to what works or does not, and why, and they are able to assimilate new ideas and adapt these to suit specific situations and contexts. This position is contrasted with that of the *craft view of teaching*, in which subject knowledge and situational awareness are valued but theoretical or empirical-based knowledge is dismissed as abstract or irrelevant to specific context,and the stance taken by the *executive technician*, who values research findings but adopts an instrumentalist approach, following protocols and applying rules to practice and *not* interpreting or adapting teaching to particular needs or situations

Teachers' conceptions of teaching, perceptions of the teaching context, and approaches to teaching matter (Kek and Huijser, 2011) are influenced by personal, professional and cultural factors (Ifanti and Fotopoulopou, 2011). How teachers view and enact professionalism is affected by a number of aspects: their previous experiences of learning and teaching; their training to become a teacher; how they see themselves as teachers within the school community (directly informed by their relationships with students and colleagues); and in relation to government policy initiatives. The investment in developing their expertise as a teacher informed by development opportunities which are self- and

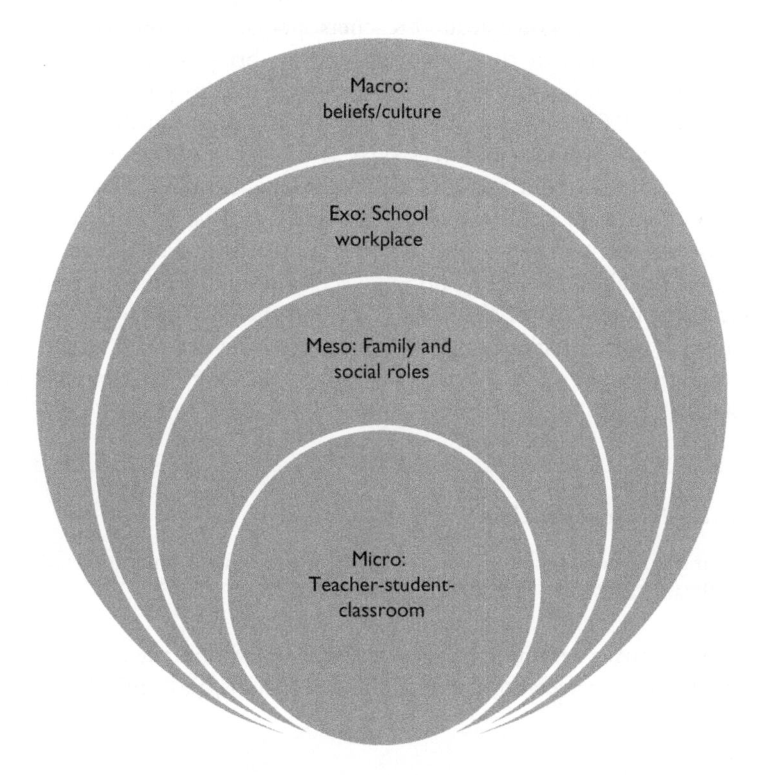

Figure 1.1 Professionalism as a nested concept using Bronfenbrenner's Ecological Theory of Human Development

institution-directed is another interrelated aspect framing teachers' interpretation and enactment of professionalism.

Bronfenbrenner's (1979) ecological framework provides a useful tool for teachers to consider their understandings and enactment of professionalism and construction of their professional identity(ies) around four interlinked systems: micro-systems (e.g. teacher, student, classroom), meso-systems (e.g. family and peers), exo-systems (e.g. institutional culture, departmental cultures, school policies, interpretation of government regulatory frameworks), and macro-systems (e.g. cultural background).

Teachers' perceptions of what they believe to be important and how they interpret their role(s) impacts on professional identity development.

A critical professional identity

There are many different meanings and interpretations of identity; some focus more on teachers' roles and others relate professional identity to self-image: how teachers perceive themselves as teachers. As Lamote and Engels (2010, p. 4) have noted, 'In an occupation where who one is as a person is so much interwoven with how one acts as a professional, both sides cannot be separated'. A teacher's professional identity is dynamic over time and space; it may consist of different sub-identities related to different contexts and relationships, for example: the person as a self-oriented active individual, a skilled professional, and a member of a professional community (Puurula and Löfström, 2003). These differing identities revolve around teachers' personal interpretation of their roles and tasks, their perception of their own efficacy (to bring about desired outcomes), their commitment (Lamote and Engels, 2010), their self-image, and future perspective (Kelchtermans, 2009). Teacher identity(ies) are important in the construction and sustaining of teachers' professional selves (Day *et al.*, 2006a, 2006b), and they impact on teachers' capacities for, and attitudes to, professional learning (Day and Gu, 2007). Teacher identity comprises the interactions between *professional* (social and policy expectations of what a good teacher is, and the educational ideals of the teacher), *situated* (located in a specific school context), and *personal* (based on life outside school and linked to family and social roles (Day *et al.*, 2006a, 2006b)) spheres. The degree to which these three dimensions of teacher identity are in balance and the extent to which the teacher can draw on internal and external support also affect teacher commitment and resilience (Day and Gu, 2007).

Questions for reflection

The following questions relate to your sense of professional orientation, task orientation, self-efficacy, and commitment to teaching.

- What is your own definition of a good teacher? How does this align and/or conflict with policy expectations, the school expectations, and familial expectations?

- What do you believe to be important in your work?
- What do you want to achieve with your students?
- What do you consider the best ways of teaching to achieve your goals?
- What has informed your personal belief system about the best ways of the teaching?
- What are the essential tasks you have to perform in order to feel that you are doing well?
- How well do you think you are doing your job as a teacher?
- On a scale of 1–10 (ten = strongest) to what extent do you feel competent in your own teaching ability? What impacts on your sense of capability?
- How well do you feel able to judge the most appropriate approaches for a specific learning context? What are your strengths and areas for development?
- To what extent do you feel committed and connected to your profession? What factors impact this?
- To what extent do you feel a valued member of your work-based community at the classroom level, departmental or faculty level, or whole school level?

A *critical professional identity* is important in the development of more sophisticated notions of professionalism. Critical professional identity development is about addressing dilemmas and conflicts; examining one's own contradicting values; reflecting on one's own belief systems, norms, and prejudices regarding students, education and teaching; and self-appreciation of the social and cultural contexts upon which these values and norms are based, along with an understanding of the cultural mechanisms that form the social structures according to which we were educated (Dvir and Avissar, 2013).

Teachers need to make their own *subjective educational theory* (their personal system of knowledge and beliefs about education – the how and the why of teaching) explicit. In this way, critical professional identity is focused on the exploration of the power relationship between individual and socially situated experience,and it is commonly framed within the literature around discussions of social justice and/or the culturally responsive teacher. It is about examining moral and political agendas in the work context, and considering how these impact on self-understanding. A critical professional identity presupposes that one will challenge the existing social order in order to reduce inequalities in the spirit of Giroux's (1988) transformative intellectual, and enable empowerment by promoting teacher and student agency.

A critical professional identity aligns with Shulman's (1999) *scholarship of teaching concept* focused on becoming public; becoming an object of critical review and evaluation of the members of that community; and members of that community beginning to use, build upon and develop those acts of mind and creation. Kelchtermans's (2009, pp. 260–261) accent on a teacher's development of a *personal interpretative framework* is relevant to discussions of teacher professional identity:

> I have argued that throughout their careers teachers develop a *personal interpretative framework:* a set of cognitions, of mental representations that operates as a lens through which teachers look at their job, give meaning to it and act in it. This framework thus guides their interpretations and actions in particular situations (context), but is at the same time also modified by and resulting from these meaningful interactions (sense-making) with that context. As such it is both a *condition for and a result of* the interaction, and represents the – always preliminary – 'mental sediment' of teachers' learning and developing over time.

Self-understanding and teacher understanding of context through the development of effective filtering skills are important in contributing to the development of positive professional identity(ies) along with assisting external support structures.

Micropoliticalliteracy

The development of teachers' *micropolitical literacy* aligns with more sophisticated understandings of professionalism and relates to how teachers develop a way of making sense of situations in terms of the working conditions they consider crucial for doing a good job and the development of effective strategies and tactics for negotiating, navigating, influencing and controlling their working conditions (Kelchtermans, 2009, p. 262). It is also about ensuring opportunities or spaces to enable critical and collaborative discourse and to expose one's ideas to the critical gaze of others (Barnett, 1997; Furlong, 2000a). As articulated by Furlong (2000a, p. 27):

> True professionalism depends on a continued commitment to hold up knowledge, from wherever it comes, to public, collaborative scrutiny. It also depends on the commitment to create and maintain those spaces within professional life . . . where critical discourse can flourish.

How an individual views their own networks (ego-centred network perspectives) contributes to an individual's identity development and is a component of micropolitical literacy. Using Wenger's (1998, 2000) concept of communities of practice it is important for professional teachers to consider the extent to which they are able to identify and develop appropriate networks, and their ability to align with specific networks; how they see their role in each of these networks (peripheral or central); their level of choice as to the nature of their role(s) within networks; and how they carry aspects of their identity from one network to another. Carmichael *et al.* (2012, pp. 220–221) highlight the value of social network analysis for individuals to consider their *position* in a network and the *role* and *prestige* this brings; the *directedness* of links (one-way, two-way or unspecified); and special network functions such as *cutpoints* (nodes which, if removed, would 'break' the network), *bridges* (links between components of the whole network) and *brokers* (bridges and bridge-builders). Other useful concepts include: *affiliation networks imported into workplace settings* (where individuals share a commitment to concepts, principles, or communities which may be more important to them than inward and formal networks), and loosely defined, self-regulating and long-lived *communities* versus managed, task-oriented *knotworks*.

Using social network analysis it is possible to examine *strong ties*, defined as proximal, frequent, reciprocal,and *weak ties* (distal, infrequent, not reciprocal). Carmichael *et al.* (2012, p. 230) noted that 'while strong links are frequent, bi-directional and proximal, it is the strength of the infrequent, distal weak links upon which an individual can draw that provides them with an advantage'. Using ego-centred network analysis, teachers and organizations can examine variations in the social capital available to them, with a view to assessing their own ability to develop and position themselves within networks, and assess how this positioning affects their learning, in order to capitalize on the networks teachers/schools have, and to be able to use them to benefit practice. Mapping of networks from individual and organizational perspectives can be a highly valuable activity in contributing to the professional development of all teachers within a school.

The proponents of more sophisticated conceptions of professionalism not only understand the power of networks and the importance of *brokerage*, defined as the ability to act as a bridge between different communities (Wenger, 1998, 2000), but also act as builders of bridges. Skilled in recognizing 'structural holes' in networks, they broker interactions between individuals or groups and may then withdraw from the interaction (Carmichael *et al.* (2012, p. 221). It is important to capitalize on the personal networks that such individuals have, and use them for the benefit of practice. This implies that schools, and teachers within a school, need to know the nature of the networks that exist in order to contribute to their development and make the best use of them.

Questions for reflection

- Draw your own diagram of your networks within and beyond school. On the diagram
  - o note the number of networks you belong to within and external to the school
  - o demonstrate the strength of the specific networks to scale
  - o show linkages between networks and directionality of links
  - o demonstrate the relevance of the networks to your role as a professional teacher.
- What does this diagram tell you about your professional self?
- How have you positioned yourself within your network diagram: which networks are you most active within? What are your roles within these networks?
- Which networks are most important to you and why?
- How do your external networks interlink with your internal ones?
- What do your networks tell you about your role(s) within school and beyond?
- To what extent would you describe your networks as enriched versus impoverished?
- To what extent is your involvement in your networks sustainable? How are you prioritizing membership and roles?
- How are you maintaining links?

Integration of knowledge

More sophisticated conceptions of professionalism acknowledge the importance of the integration of Aristotle's three types of knowledge: theoretical (*episteme*); technical (craft/art) (*techne*) and practical (*phronesis*) knowledge, and importantly include self-knowledge (self-awareness, understanding of own thinking and emotions) to enact professional artistry (Higgs and Titchen, 2001). Professionalism is understood as situated, socially and dialogically constructed. Furthermore, the importance of *reflection and rationalism* is acknowledged (Furlong, 2000a).

> To be competent authentic practitioners . . . professionals need to understand the philosophy, the knowledge generation paradigms and the truths, realities and perceptions which ground, frame and define their professions.
>
> Higgs and Titchen, 2001, p. 11

Eraut's (1994) typology of professional knowledge is relevant here in refining this notion:

- *Conceptual knowledge* (concepts, values, principles, theories which help to think about and interpret experience)
- *Process knowledge* (decision-making, leadership, management of change)
- *Knowledge of educational practice* (knowledge of alternatives in learning and teaching – 'fitness for purpose')
- *Situational knowledge* (capacity to read situations – case knowledge)
- *People knowledge* (what makes people tick).

To these we would add

- *Self-knowledge* (self-awareness, understanding of own thinking and learning, and how one operates both individually as a part of different communities).

It is the bringing together of these facets to enable an *integrated fluent performance* that is an important element of more sophisticated understandings of professionalism.

A more sophisticated conception of professionalism integrates *embrained, encoded, embodied,* and *embedded forms* of knowledge (Lam, 2000). Colluci-Gray *et al.* (2013, p. 130), define *embrained knowledge* as theoretical and usually linked to the body of knowledge acquired through professional training and education, and with the capability to draw directly on research findings; *encoded knowledge* is found typically in policy documentation, serving the purpose of standardization and professional compliance; *embodied knowledge* is individual, tacit and practical: for example, the skills teachers learn through trial and error in the classroom; *embedded knowledge* is the collective form of tacit knowledge that is shared by colleagues: the norms and routines within a school that shape the ethos of each establishment. Colluci-Gray *et al.* (2013) have argued that teachers need to have greater awareness of the encoded knowledge of policy that shapes and organizes educational discourses.

In twenty-first-century learning environments, the fact that there is an objective body of knowledge available to practitioners to guide their practice is increasingly challenged by the question as to whether objective knowledge actually exists (Barnett, 2011) and whether theoretically-based knowledge can actually guide practice. The lack of relevance of educational research to teachers has been raised by D. Hargreaves (1994) and D. Hargreaves *et al.* (2005) who have argued that educational research is largely based on theoretical rather than practical reason, and that more attention should be given to what constitutes practitioner research and to how the gap between practitioner and academic education research can be narrowed. Allied to this have been issues to do with the lack of evidence-based research within education (see BERA (2013a) for research-informed education perspectives).

At the core of more sophisticated notions of professionalism is a willingness to engage with research in order to assess its utility and ripeness for adaptation to context. It is not about an unthinking acceptance of received opinion. It involves critical scrutiny of evidence, whether that be directly from enquiry-oriented practice evident in schools, from active participation in research, and/or from examination of researcher-led studies (Bell *et al.*, 2010). Importantly, research in this context is interpreted more broadly and is not purely associated with higher education researcher-led studies. A key tension here relates to the subjectivity of knowledge and what counts as evidence. Tatto (2013) has warned about the potential limitations of a *'Big Science'* view of what counts as evidence (e.g. randomized control trials (RCTs) as advocated by Goldacre, 2013). Therefore, a more sophisticated understanding of professionalism requires teachers to carefully interpret and adapt findings to practice rather than passively to accept and apply received protocols and toolkits. It also requires balancing potential conflicts between the drive for improving quality and standards of practice and improving professional status, emphasizing scientific and technical ways as standards of knowledge and skill, and the emotional dimensions of teaching (being passionate about learning and caring for students' learning (D. Hargreaves, 2000)).

Teachers' willingness to critically engage in discourse where they explicitly critique the background consensus belief systems, norms, values, and ideologies taken for granted in everyday life is important: 'It is the commitment to engage in such discourse in relation to one's knowledge and one's values that, for critical theorists, constitutes the heart of true professionalism (Furlong, 2000a, p. 27). Critical theory is helpful and important here for its ability to critique both *positivistic* (aligned with evidence-based practice) and *interpretive* conceptions of knowledge (aligned with the subjectivity and situational nature of professional knowledge). Critical theory begins from a critique of both *positivist* and *interpretive* conceptions of knowledge. Therefore, more sophisticated notions of professionalism call on teachers to draw on and integrate different kinds of evidence, gained both *intuitively* and *rationally* (Furlong, 2000a).

Pedagogic expertise requires a combination of science, craft and art (Pollard, 2010). This includes: analytic and objective thinking to plan for learning and reflective thinking to monitor and learn from experience and intuitive skills (seeing patterns, fluency, flexibility, coping with complexity, and being holistic and self-aware (for a fuller discussion of developing intuitive capability see Eraut, 2000, p. 264).The Teaching and Learning Research Programme's (TLRP's) Ten Principles of Effective Teaching and Learning (James and Pollard, 2006; Pollard, 2010) based on a synthesis of the research findings from 22 school-based studies, provides a holistic picture of factors that enhance learning and act as a reflective tool for teachers to consider their practice (Table 1.1).

Table 1.1 TLRP's ten principles of effective teaching and learning (Pollard, 2010, p. 8)

1 **Equips learners for life in its broadest sense**
Learning should aim to help people to develop the intellectual, personal and social resources that will enable them to participate as active citizens and workers and to flourish as individuals in a diverse and changing society. This implies a broad view of learning outcomes, and that equity and social justice are taken seriously.

2 **Engages with valued forms of knowledge**
Teaching and learning should engage with the big ideas, facts, processes, language and narratives of subjects so that learners understand what constitutes quality and standards in particular disciplines.

3 **Recognizes the importance of prior experience and learning**
Teaching should take account of what learners know already in order to plan their next steps. This means building on prior learning as well as taking account of the personal and cultural experiences of different groups.

4 **Requires the teacher to scaffold learning**
Teachers should provide activities which support learners as they move forward, not just intellectually, but also socially and emotionally, so that once these supports are removed, the learning is secure.

5 **Needs assessment to be congruent with learning**
Assessment should help to advance learning as well as to determine whether learning has taken place. It should be designed and carried out so that it measures learning outcomes in a dependable way and also provides feedback for future learning.

6 **Promotes the active engagement of the learner**
A chief goal of teaching and learning should be the promotion of learners' independence and autonomy. This involves acquiring a repertoire of learning strategies and practices, developing a positive attitude towards learning, and confidence in oneself as a good learner.

7 **Fosters both individual and social processes and outcomes**
Learning is a social activity. Learners should be encouraged to work with others, to share ideas and to build knowledge together. Consulting learners and giving them a voice is both an expectation and a right.

8 **Recognizes the significance of informal learning**
Informal learning, such as learning out of school, should be recognized as being at least as significant as formal learning and should be valued and used appropriately in formal processes.

9 **Depends on teacher learning**
The importance of teachers learning continuously in order to develop their knowledge and skills, and adapt and develop their roles, especially through classroom inquiry, should be recognized and supported.

10 **Demands consistent policy frameworks with support for teaching and learning as their primary focus**
Policies at national, local and institutional levels need to recognize the fundamental importance of teaching and learning. They should be designed to make sure everyone has access to learning environments in which they can thrive.

Questions for reflection

Review the TLRP's ten principles of effective teaching and learning and consider the following questions.

- To what extent do you attend to these principles in your teaching, and what are the reasons underlying this?
- Which of these principles do you perceive to be most important in your teaching, and why?
- Are there additional principles you would add to this list, and why?
- Are there any tensions for you in aiming to attend to the TLRP principles?

Importantly, more sophisticated notions of professionalism interrogate *tacit* knowledge. Tacit knowledge (that which is known but difficult to explain), is complex and personal (Berry, 2009). Building professional knowledge involves acquiring both self-knowledge (knowledge of one's own knowledge and skills, and of how one learns), and self-awareness (ability to reflect on and assess one's behaviours and actions in a professional practice context) (Berry, 2009, p. 308):

> Reflection encompasses more than a set of skills and knowledge, it also calls on particular dispositions (personal qualities) that include: open-mindedness to seeing problems within one's own practice; willingness to open one's practice up for scrutiny; as well as preparedness to take risks and expose oneself as vulnerable.

Being able to critically reflect on practice to carefully examine what they (teachers) do is commensurate with more sophisticated conceptions of professionalism (see chapter 10). Placing more attention on *deliberative actions* (reflection-on-action) is key to this. Schön (1983) in his seminal work *The Reflective Practitioner* introduced three different levels of explicitness in thinking: *knowing-in-action* (reflection is entirely implicit, embedded in the act of doing itself); *reflection-in-action* (draws interpretive processes to the level of consciousness without stopping what you are doing – e.g. it can take place as you teach); *reflection-on-action* (takes place after the event, where you try to make sense of the processes that were going on in your actions (see Furlong, 2000a, p. 22). Elaine

Wilson and Helen Demetriou (2007) have argued that most teacher thinking is on *hot action* (reflecting in action) and far less is *cold deliberative, purposeful reflection* on practice. Deliberative actions require searching for information and taking into account values considerations (Eraut, 2004a). Reflection is an overused and abused term with reflective skills and practices often used in a predominantly instrumental and technical way (A. Hargreaves, 1995). However, they should encompass both the skill and the attitude of making one's own actions, feelings, and experiences the object of one's thinking. Reflection should be more than a rational instrumental and technical approach aimed at the development of knowledge for practice: it should also encompass moral, political and emotional dimensions. Kelchtermans (2009) in his exposition of reflective practice argues that for teachers to be genuinely critical they need breadth of content as well as depth in reflection. In relation to the latter he has argued that reflection needs to go beyond the level of action to the level of underlying beliefs, ideas, knowledge and goals –the personal interpretative framework.

> By examining and unmasking the moral and political agendas in the work context and their impact on one's self-understanding, one's thinking and actions, reflection can open up perspectives for empowerment and for re-establishing the conditions for teaching and learning that allow for pedagogical processes to take place in which people can regain the authorship of their selves.
>
> Kelchtermans, 2009, p. 263

More sophisticated notions of professionalism acknowledge the importance of a contextualized and judicious approach in which teachers question their practice within the specific context of their school and their classes, are highly sensitized to the requirements of their specific situation and their working context, and exemplify notions of professionalism. For example, in England student teachers are expected to experience two different school contexts as part of their school-based teaching placements. This creates a situation whereby they are expected to reflect within the context. However it can be particularly difficult for student teachers to do this. They are expected to be able to take such understanding of their experiences and actions within one specific context, and then reboot their thinking within another school context during their second placement, raising significant issues associated with their ability to transfer and adapt their knowledge and skills from one context to another. This is a very challenging and demanding expectation of those who are learning to teach and one where they may need considerable assistance through the provision of clear and explicit guidance and the 'tools' to frame/structure this.

Professional development orientation

A core element supporting teachers' critical professional identity and reflection as part of a more sophisticated notion of professionalism is their capacity for autonomous professional development. Linda Evans (2013) has coined the term *developmentalism* (commitment to self-organizational development) to conceptualize new understandings of professionalism – the extent to which individuals, groups and organizations are committed to professional development.

Such commitment on the part of the individual requires: *criticality* – search for meaning as opposed to passive acceptance of ideas; ongoing interrogation of the knowledge base underpinning educational practice (C. Evans, 2014; D. Hargreaves, 2000); a sophisticated *understanding of how they learn* (C. Evans, 2014); a *broad frame of reference* – the ability to draw on a wide range of sources: self-study, studying the work of others, classroom enquiry, questioning and testing ideas (Day, 1999); a *collaborative ethos* – willingness to collaborate and engaged with colleagues, students and parents in the pursuit of improved understandings of practice (D. Hargreaves, 2000); *intentionality* – emphasis on a deliberative rather than a reactive approach to reflection (Mutton *et al.*, 2010); a *willingness to interrogate one's own understandings and preparedness to offer up one's own ideas to scrutiny* (Barnett, 2011); the *ability to seek, use and apply feedback* constructively in development of practice rather than being constrained by it (C. Evans,2014); the *ability to maximize affordances* within a context in pursuit of learning rather than seeing oneself constrained by the environment (C. Evans, 2014; Mutton *et al.*, 2010); the adoption of an *aspirational* rather than a satisficing mindset (Mutton *et al.*, 2010); the *ability to access and developnet-works* of support – and to develop brokerage skills (Wenger, 1998); the *ability to prioritize and balance professional development needs* in relation to context and individual requirements (C. Evans, 2014); ability *to learn from others and integrate new understandings* while maintaining a sense of self (C. Evans, 2014).

This list is by no means exhaustive; however, underpinning all of these ideas is a strong attitudinal component – a passion and willingness to engage in ongoing learning, a commitment to enhancing practice; a desire to learn. In moving towards and promoting more sophisticated understandings of professionalism L. Evans (2002) has argued that professional development policies need to place far more attention on teachers' professionality orientation in order to enhance professional performance. On a personal level, Day (1999, p. 7) has argued that teachers need to regularly review not just '. . . the what" and the "how" of their teaching but also . . . the "why" in terms of their core "moral" purposes'.

Nevertheless, a commitment to one's own professional development and identification of self as a learner is contingent with more sophisticated conceptions of professionalism (Pedder *et al.*, 2005). Pedder *et al.* have found that even though teachers valued social networks within schools and beyond to support their learning, they did not attribute high value to research as a source for improving their learning and teaching. In addition they found that levels of pupil consultation, joint research, team teaching and peer observation were low. They subsequently highlighted the need for academic research to be more accessible to teachers; we would also argue, along with D. Hargreaves *et al.*, 2005, that more value needs to be attached to practitioner research and forging collaborative bottom-up research projects between higher education and schools – with schools leading and higher education facilitating research in relation to the school needs. Teacher learning is contingent on organizational commitment and affordances. Pedder *et al.* highlight the way in which the organizational role facilitates teacher learning by providing constructive environments and structures to enable shared enquiry and critical reflection about each other's teaching as a way of improving their practices, and learning from each other. A sophisticated understanding of professionalism requires teachers to consider not only their professional development learning requirements, but also their role(s) in developing themselves and others at a number of levels – as classroom teachers, as supporters of their colleagues' learning and role(s) in departmental and whole school learning within and beyond the parameters of the school – and how they integrate learning opportunities afforded by these differing contexts and roles. Such development is a collective endeavour and while the self-actualizing teacher committed to their own professional development can certainly be affective, affordances and constraints in relation to how schools conceive of themselves as learning communities impacts on teacher professional development; an inclusive approach advocates a distributed mentoring approach where all teachers are mentors of each other.

Questions for reflection

In defining professionalism much attention is afforded to the *'being'* and *'becoming'* a professional. The following articles examine the development of teacher identity and notions of resilience and teacher well-being, including factors supporting and impeding development. These additional resources are useful for teachers, and, particularly, early career teachers and mentors, to consider in supporting teacher development within schools.

Questions to consider include:

- What do you think teacher resilience is and why is it important?
- How are you developing your own resilience and that of your students?
- What impacts on your sense of professional identity?
- What makes you feel vulnerable within your working environment and why?
- How do you manage not knowing?
- How are you integrating into your school communities of practice?
- How are you being assisted with this?

Additional reading for this activity:

Arnon, S., and Reichel, N. (2007).Who is the ideal teacher? Am I? Similarity and difference in perception of students of education regarding the qualities of a good teacher and of their own qualities as teachers. *Teachers and Teaching: Theory and Practice,13*(5), 441–464.

Berry, A. (2009). Professional self-understanding as expertise in teaching about teaching, *Teachers and Teaching: Theory and Practice, 15* (2), 305–318.

Bruce, C. D., Esmonde, I., Ross, J., Dookie, L., and Beatty, R. (2010). The effects of sustained classroom-embedded teacher professional learning on teacher efficacy and related student achievement. *Teaching and Teacher Education, 26*, 1598–1608.

Bullock, S. M. (2009). Learning to think like a teacher educator: Making the substantive and syntactic structures of teaching explicit through self-study. *Teachers and Teaching: Theory and Practice, 15(2),* 291–204.

Cuenca, A. (2011). The role of legitimacy in student teaching: Learning to 'feel' like a teacher. *Teacher Education Quarterly*, Spring 2011, 117–130.

Hong, J.Y. (2010). Pre-service and beginning teachers' professional identity and its relation to dropping out of the profession. *Teaching and Teacher Education, 26*, 1530–1543.

Lamote, C., and Engels, N. (2010): The development of student teachers' professional identity. *European Journal of Teacher Education, 33*(1), 3–18.

Nasser-Abu Alhija, F., and Barbara Fresko, B. (2010). Socialization of new teachers: Does induction matter? *Teaching and Teacher Education, 26* (8), 1592–1597.

Pearce, J., and Morrison, C. (2011) Teacher identity and early career resilience: Exploring the links. *Australian Journal of Teacher Education, 36* (1), Article 4.

Shanks, R., Robson, D., and Gray, D. (2012). New teachers' individual learning dispositions: A Scottish case study. *International Journal of Training and Development, 16*(3), 183–199.

Wilson, E., and Demetriou, H. (2007). New teacher learning: Substantive knowledge and contextual factors.*The Curriculum Journal, 18*(3), 213–229.

Summary

How teachers perceive professionalism has important ramifications for their enactment of professionalism in their practice. The development of professional identity is internally and externally mediated to varying degrees. More sophisticated interpretations of professionalism are important for all teachers to explore, especially in relation to one's conceptions of teaching, development of a critical professional identity, micropolitical literacy, view of knowledge, and commitment to professional development. How a teacher positions him/herself as a professional within twenty-first-century learning environments and manages both individual and external affordances and constraints in the development of his/her professional identity is fundamental to how that teacher operates within a classroom, with colleagues, and within and beyond the school context, to impact on student learning.

Key readings

Higgs, J., and Titchen, A. (2001). *Professional practice in health, education and the creative arts.* Oxford: Blackwell.

This book explores the doing, knowing, being, and becoming of professional practice from a number of different perspectives. The book is important in its emphasis on the professional artistry and creativity of professional practice. The intuitive nature of teaching is also capturedin Atkinson, T., and Claxton, G. (Eds.) (2000). The intuitive practitioner. Berkshire: Open University Press.

Livingston, K. (2014). Teacher educators: Hidden professionals. *European Journal of Education, 49*(2), 218–232.

Relevant to all teacher educators, this article considers teacher educators' identities, and the importance of professional development attuned to the specific needs of this distinctive group, a group that is under-represented within the literature on professionalism.

Wilkins, C. (2011). Professionalism and the post-performative teacher: New teachers reflect on autonomy and accountability in the English school system. *Professional Development in Education, 37*(3), 389–409.

This article examines what it is to be a teaching professional, highlighting the tensions between accountability and autonomy in current educational systems, with a focus on the English context. It is important when reading this article to reflect on how competency frameworks within your own specific context influence your understanding of professionalism and how this is evoked in your practice.

Wilson, A., Akerlind, G., Walsh, B., Stevens, B., Turner, B., and Shield, A. (2013). Making 'professionalism' meaningful to students in higher education. *Studies in Higher Education, 38*(8), 1222–1238.

This article builds on the extended professional concept introduced by Hoyle and examines what a more sophisticated notion of professionalism in twenty-first-century learning environments constitutes.

Weblinks

AITSL (2012). *Professional learning or school effectiveness in Australia. What does it take?* Australian Institute for Teaching and School Leadership Ltd. Available online at http://www.aitsl.edu.au/verve/_resources/ICSEI_spread.pdf (accessed 3 January 2014).

Eraut, M. (2008). *How professionals learn through work.* Draft 1 / 22/04/08 Surrey: Surrey Centre for Excellence in Professional Training and Education. University of Surrey. Online. Available online at http://surreyprofessionaltraining.pbworks.com/f/How+Professionals+Learn+through+Work.pdf (accessed 20 November 2013).

Goldacre, B. (2013). *Building evidence into education.* Available online at https://www.gov.uk/government/publications/test-learn-adapt-developing-public-policy-with-randomised-controlled-trials (accessed 20 July 2013).

Lombardi, M. M. (2007). Authentic learning for the 21st century: an overview. ELI paper 1. Available online at http://www.educause.edu/library/resources/authentic-learning-21st-century-overview (accessed 6 September 2013).

Pollard, A.(Ed.)(2010). *Professionalism and pedagogy: A contemporary opportunity.* A commentary by TLRP and GTCE. London: TLRP. Available online at http://www.tlrp.org/pub/documents/TLRPGTCEProf&Pedagogy.pdf (accessed 10 September 2013).

Chapter 2

Making sense of pedagogy

Overview

Within this chapter we foreground the complex concept of pedagogy, highlighting the uncertainty around the associated terminology and its numerous interpretations. A definitive definition of pedagogy will not be sought, instead a holistic concept of pedagogy will be presented, key dimensions of which will be highlighted to help understand the multiple discourses that are features of all pedagogies, including the inclusive participatory pedagogy promoted within this book, and more specifically that around the Personal Learning Styles Pedagogy (Evans and Waring, 2009; Evans, 2013a; Evans and Waring, 2014 (chapter 11); Evans and Waring, 2015). Importantly by outlining our holistic notion of pedagogy we are highlighting (in an attempt to inform a transformative agenda) those decisions which are made in schools, teacher education, higher education institutions and in society more broadly regarding the nature of knowledge which is to be promoted, the position and view of the learner in the learning process, and how learning is organized and optimized.

Exploring pedagogy

A teacher's understanding of and stance in relation to pedagogy is fundamental to informing how and where they position themselves as a professional and (re)frame their vision of education and its future, including the types of learning, learners and society that they want to promote as part of that. Ask yourself what your vision for the future of education is. What types of learning, learners and society do you want to promote as a teacher? What and how are future learners' interests being acknowledged and addressed in the curricula and schooling that you want to promote? Pedagogy, and the way in which you interpret and operationalize it, plays a vital part in all dimensions of your teaching and the extent to which you can constructively shape the answers to these questions. Unfortunately, often ignored and misunderstood by many educationalists and their respective communities of practice, pedagogy and its place in a transformational agenda of education is too often lost.

We would like to join Leach and Moon (2008, p. 1) in their starting ' . . . premise that good teachers are intellectually curious about pedagogy'. However, there is a great deal of confusion, uncertainty and contestation over what pedagogy actually is and how its complexity is adequately captured within any definition (Mortimore, 1999). Pedagogy is likely to mean different things to different people, with teachers, researchers and policy makers approaching the notion of pedagogy from very different perspectives and conceptual standings. Coupled with a history of infrequent use and disregard for the place of pedagogy within the educational communities of North America and the UK (Collins, *et al.*, 2001; Leach and Moon, 1999) uncertainty over the term pedagogy is understandable.

A problematic, narrow and often misconstrued definition of pedagogy is that of 'the science of teaching' (Smyth, 1987; Watkins and Mortimore, 1999). Such a definition has commonly been used; however, it 'deserves to be discredited' (Smyth, 1987, p. 1). In the first instance, it is very much reliant on one's conception and assumptions about science and teaching respectively. For example, if one were to consider science from an interpretive perspective (as socially constructed, creative, uncertain) compared to a positivistic perspective (reductionist, deterministic, independent) the interpretations offered would be opposing. Unfortunately, historically the common interpretation of 'science' is that allied to a positivist paradigm: this would not be at all appropriate in a definition for pedagogy as it negates any notion of consciousness on the part of the teacher or learner and therefore removes any potential for them to act in a transformative capacity; however one would accept the essence of an interpretive definition. With regards to an interpretation of teaching, it has been too easily reduced to merely an association with teaching approaches, methods and related pupil–teacher relations. In an attempt to explore a more appropriate definition of pedagogy Watkins and Mortimore (1999) highlight a notion of pedagogy as a 'craft'. However, even though it might be more of an attempt to acknowledge variation and unpredictability, this remains very much lacking in its attempts to reflect the complexity of interrelationships that the term pedagogy needs to embrace, such as those between the values and assumptions associated with the learning context, the teacher, the learner, and notions of knowledge and learning. Significantly, that simplification evident in a 'craft' notion of pedagogy seriously undermines the capacity for critical reflection and the detailed interrogation of practice.

Beetham and Sharpe (2007, p. 2) consider 'pedagogy in the original sense of guidance to learn: learning in the context of teaching, and teaching that has learning as its goal.' In presenting such a relationship, they highlight an important dialogue between teaching and learning. They consider this dialogue to be at the heart of what they mean by pedagogy. Watkins and Mortimore (1999, p.3) define pedagogy as 'any conscious activity by one person designed to enhance the learning in another'.

Leach and Moon (2008, p. 6) view pedagogy as a 'dynamic process, informed by theories, beliefs and dialogue, but only realized in the daily interactions of learners and teachers in real settings'. The value of such a definition is the dynamism of the process, the expectation that it will be constantly reworked by learner and teacher in practice. This is a very important aspect of our holistic conceptualization of pedagogy (see Figure 2.1) which encapsulates and celebrates at its centre an active and critical learner who is enabled to make an informed and willing contribution to a just and democratic society. It too attempts to illustrate the dynamic reworking of those interrelationships between policy, theory, knowledge and rationale, all framed and informed by political and social agendas, cultures of practice and power relations. As Leach and Moon (2008, p. 3) highlight from Freire's work, 'pedagogy is a social process which extends to the political arena'.

Presenting such a view of pedagogy provides an opportunity to make explicit the many decisions that are made in all educational contexts and the potential consequences of them in relation to what things are taught, how they are taught and why they are taught. This is certainly not a neutral landscape – it is very much about a socially critical agenda, one in which notions of learner empowerment are framed by those power relationships that

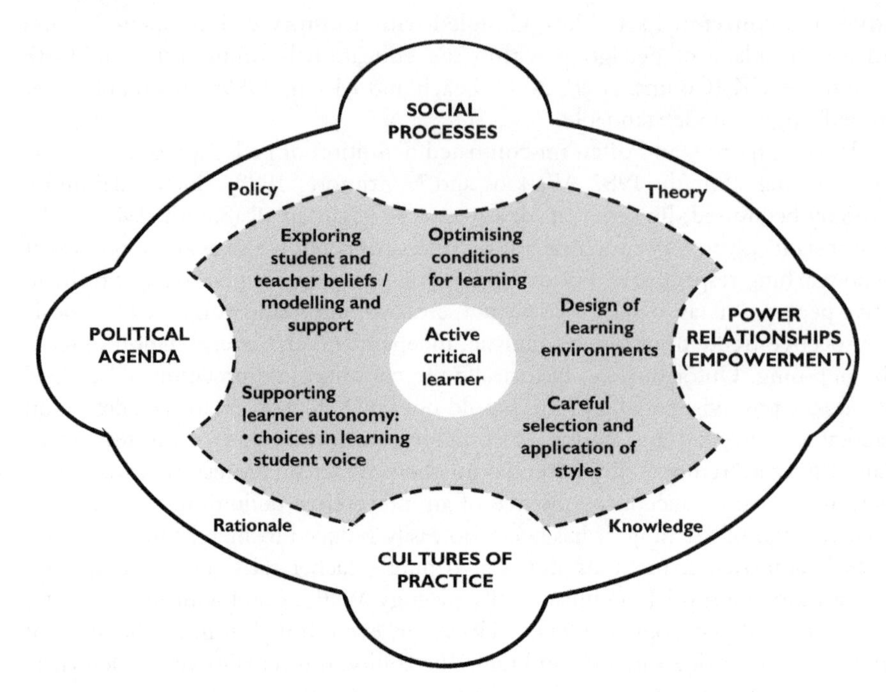

Figure 2.1 A holistic conceptualization of pedagogy
Developed from Penney and Waring, 2000

revolve around how knowledge is conceptualized and therefore what knowledge is valued, and how learners are positioned in relation to how that knowledge is created as part of the pedagogical process. As alluded to earlier, our broad and holistic conception of pedagogy has scope way beyond the school setting. It is very much about promoting and informing democracy in education and the broader society. In that sense it joins forces with notions of critical pedagogy and the promotion of critical agents (McLaren and Kincheloe, 2007) and of the idea that all issues can and should be viewed from a variety of perspectives, and it is these which students and teachers are invited to critically reflect upon (Nieto, 2001).

Importantly, our holistic notion of pedagogy is not standardized or mechanistic, and conceived as a technical or purely linear process from knowledge, to critical reflection and then action. We would align closely with Giroux's (2007, p. 3) notion that:

> Pedagogy is not about balance, a merely methodological consideration, on the contrary . . . education . . . must do everything possible to provide students with the knowledge and skills they need to learn how to deliberate, make judgments, and exercise choice, particularly as the latter is brought to bear on critical activities that offer the possibility of democratic change. Democracy cannot work if citizens are not autonomous, self-judging and independent . . .

Our holistic and integrated conception of pedagogy is very much about promoting equitable and democratic societies – which raises questions about the nature and degree of ownership that learners have as part of the learning process. It demands that as teachers we are critically reflective of the selections we make regarding: the type of society, the values and interests that we have and which we use to inform the organization and design of learning environments, the way in which we support learner autonomy through choices in learning, and the nature and extent of the student voice. It is also about how we explore and cater for student and teacher beliefs about learning and teaching and go about optimizing conditions for learning. Importantly, providing such an active critical role for the students in the learning process as part of a holistic conception of pedagogy demands that teachers develop their professional identity, and more sophisticated interpretations of professionalism, which are important for all teachers to explore, particularly in relation to their conceptions of teaching, their view of knowledge, and their commitment to professional development needs. How a teacher interprets and manages their professional identity is fundamental to how they operate within and beyond the school context to impact on student learning.

At the heart of our holistic notion of pedagogy is an interest in creating new 'possibilities for thought' (Ball, 1990, p. 18) in education; where learning is a kind of *'learning-to-doubt', which* affects the *'nature of being and becoming'* (Barnett, 2011). It is about being creative, making and taking the responsibility as teachers and students to promote and explore different possibilities as part of a critical and transparent dialogue which empowers the learner with a sense of critical awareness and reflexivity, allowing them to evolve and constructively contribute towards a just and democratic society.

Summary

In this chapter we have presented a conceptualization of pedagogy to be used to critique and inform how you position yourself as a professional and to support your critical reflections and the decisions which you make as a teacher regarding the nature of knowledge which you promote, the position and view you have of the learner in the learning process, and how learning is organized and optimized. Importantly, the holistic conceptualization of pedagogy you have been presented with celebrates the fundamental and integrated relationship between theory and practice, and certainly does not accept a split between them. It is vital that teachers value and have ownership of integrated theoretical approaches as a better way to understand the intricacies of the process of learning and teaching as part of their critical reflections and implementation of a holistic and integrated pedagogy.

Questions for reflection

- What is your vision for the future of education?
- What types of learning, learners and society do you want to promote as a teacher, and why?
- What and how are future learners' interests being acknowledged and addressed in the curricula and schooling that you want to promote?

- What role does research play in informing your vision for education and the type of learning, learners and society you promote?

Key readings

Giroux, H.A., (2011). *On Critical Pedagogy*. London: Continuum.

This book collates a number of essays from the academic career of Giroux. It is particularly pertinent because he places such great importance on the productive and deliberative nature of pedagogy, and, as he points out, so do Paulo Freire, Roger Simon and Joe Kincheloe amongst others. As part of this Giroux highlights schools and higher education as important sites in which to provide learners with alternatives, rather than more of the same as part of their futures.

Leach, J., and Moon, B., (2008). *The Power of Pedagogy*. London: Sage.

This book explores the ideas of pedagogy through the work of key figures including Freire, Montessori, and Vygotsky, and framed by holistic concept of pedagogy at its core, it conceptualizes pedagogy and its transformational influence on schools in particular.

Stainthorp, R., and Tomlinson, P. (Eds). (2005). Pedagogy – Teaching for Learning. *British Journal of Educational Psychology Monograph Series II, Number 3*. Leicester: British Psychological Society.

Looking at the psychological contributions to pedagogy and a systematic understanding of teaching and learning, this book offers various contributions which deal with issues relevant to schools.

Weblinks

The Carnegie Foundation. *Advancing Teaching – Improving Learning*. Available online at www.carnegiefoundation.org/atil (accessed 4 May 2014).

Entwistle, N. J., Tomlinson, P., and Dockrell, J. (2007). Student learning and university teaching. *British Journal of Educational Psychology Monograph* Series II, Number 4. Leicester: British Psychological Society. Available online at http://www.bps.org.uk/publications/journals/bjep-monographs/bjep-monographs

Gale, R. A. (2006). Fostering integrative learning through pedagogy. Carnegie Foundation for Advancement of Learning. Available online at http://gallery.carnegie foundation.org/ilp/uploads/pedagogy_copy.pdf

The Sutton Trust. *Improving social mobility through education website*. Available online at http://www.suttontrust.com/our-work/research/current/ (accessed 1 May 2014).

Linked resources include

Higgins, S., Katsipataki, M., Kokotsaki, D., Coleman, R., Major, L.E. and Coe, R. (2013). *The Sutton Trust – Education Endowment Foundation teaching and learning toolkit*. London, Education Endowment Foundation. Available online at http://educationendowmentfoundation.org.uk/index.php/toolkit (accessed 5 May 2014).

Higgins, S. (2011). *What works in raising attainment and closing the gap: research evidence from the UK and abroad*. Presentation for the Education Endowment Foundation. Available online at http://educationendowmentfoundation.org.uk/uploads/pdf/What_works_in_raising_attainment_and_closing_the_gap (accessed 2 May 2014).

Chapter 3

Making sense of educational theory

A critical introduction

Overview

In this chapter we will explore educational theory and its relevance, and argue that theory and practice should be seen not as separate entities but as integral to what teachers do in their everyday practice. Key educational theoretical perspectives will be identified along with the value of integrated theoretical approaches as a better way to understand the intricacies of the process of learning and teaching.

Relevance of educational theory

> Teachers should be able and willing to scrutinise and evaluate their own and others' practice in the light of relevant theories, values, and evidence. They should be able to make professional judgements which go beyond pragmatic constraints and ideological concerns, and which can be explained and defended.
>
> Pollard, *et al.*, 2010, p. 5

Educational theory is an essential element informing how teachers interpret and understand their world and their everyday teaching practices within that world, framed by their personal theories. Definitions and opinions of the meaning of the concept of educational theory are varied; Eraut's definition provides a useful starting point:

> Educational theory comprises concepts, frameworks, ideas, and principles that may be used to interpret, explain, or judge intentions, actions, and experiences in educational or educational-related settings
>
> Eraut, 1994a, p. 70

As noted by Eraut (2004a, p. 57) 'Theory is an inherent part of how we interpret and understand the world around us. The way in which we conceptualise our environment depends on our personal theories.' Our implicit theories are those that frequently determine what we actually do in practice as opposed to *espoused theories*, perceived as those that are ideologically correct and acquired during professional education (Argyris and Schön, 1974). Examining the gap between implicit and espoused theory is an important element of professional practice and is related to a teacher's personal interpretative framework described by Kelchtermans (2009, p. 260) as 'a set of cognitions, of mental representations that operates as a lens through which teachers look at their job, give meaning to it and act in it.' Importantly, this framework is seen as being interactional in that it guides a teacher's actions and is modified by interactions within learning and teaching contexts. Such a framework has also been described by Mezirow (2000) as a person's frame of reference involving a habit of mind and a point of view which are about our way of knowing and not just about what we know. It is therefore important for teachers to consider both *codified academic knowledge* (embedded within teaching practices, academic literature, policy documentation), *uncodified cultural knowledge* (acquired through participation in social activities), *personal knowledge* one brings to the workplace (personal versions of codified knowledge, knowledge of people and situations, skills and practices know-how, memories of events, self-knowledge, attitudes, emotions), and our *implicit theories* that are observable in our practice but seldom explicated by us.

To be able to use theory effectively within practice and for practice to inform theory, teachers need to be able to articulate their own intertwined knowledge and beliefs about education, defined by Kelchtermans (2009) as a teacher's *subjective educational theory* (the how and why of dealing with a situation, informed by knowledge). Such knowledge may consist of specific subject and pedagogical knowledge acquired through formal/informal training as well as that gained from experience of working with colleagues and personal experience of what works in practice. Crucially, such knowledge only becomes an integral part of a teacher's subjective educational theory if s/he has experienced that it works for them or is perceived as true for their own practice. If we do not consider our fundamental assumptions about the nature of learning, our teaching may be limited by narrow or even erroneous conceptions of learning.

In summary, our theories frame the way we act and how we justify our actions (Wenger, 2009). As part of this, our conceptions of learning impact on how we design, enact and interpret learning and teaching experiences. In order for learning to be more informed '. . . the use of concepts and theories are needed because they allow us to think about, anticipate and reflect on action and upon ourselves as acting' (Elkjaer, 2009, p. 77).

Educational theories themselves are not static but evolve in relation to changing requirements and enhanced understanding of the processes at work within specific contexts and understandings of self. 'A theory of learning for the future advocates the teaching of a preparedness to respond in a creative way to difference and otherness. This includes an ability to act imaginatively in situations of uncertainties.' (Elkjaer, 2009, p. 74). Learning is complex and multidimensional: 'any process that in living organisms leads to permanent capacity change and which is not solely due to biological maturation or ageing' (Illeris, 2007, p. 3). Learning is about increasing knowledge, memorizing what has to be learned, applying and using knowledge, understanding what has been learned, seeing things in a different way, and changing as a person according to Säljö's (1979a) and Marton *et al.*'s (1993) learning conceptions. The importance of additional conceptions of learning within twenty-first-century learning environments to include building social competence (knowing how to communicate and get on with others) (Purdie and Hattie, 2002), and reasons for learning– learning as a duty versus seeing learning as part of a continuous life-long process (Tynjälä, 1997) – have been highlighted by Peterson *et al.* (2010).

The initial interpretation of conceptions of learning as representing a developmental hierarchy with surface conceptions at one end (acquiring facts) and deep at the other (learning as understanding and seeing things in new ways) has been challenged; having deeper conceptions does not mean learners will always use a deep approach to learning. It is about selecting the most appropriate strategies for a task; memorizing can represent a deep process especially in relation to different cultural interpretations and practices (C. Evans, 2014).

The theory practice relationship: practising theory and theorizing practice

Theory and practice should be seen not as separate entities but as integral to what teachers do in their everyday practice. The importance of integrating theory (*propositional knowledge*) with *practical knowledge* has been highlighted as a key requirement of the twenty-first-century professional teacher (Eraut, 2004a; Thiessen, 2000; Verloop, Van Driel, and Meijer, 2001). A key issue is how teachers perceive theory and whether they see this as integrated in what they do on an everyday basis or whether they see practice and theory as separate. In discussions with early career teachers, most of the teachers claimed not to use theory in their practice – seeing theory as something separate, as purely academic, something they studied during their teacher training year but not something they applied to their practice (Evans and Waring, 2015). To support teacher understanding and integrated use of theory in teaching more explicit attention needs to be focused on:

- what theory is
- how teachers implement and develop theory
- the relative value teachers attach to theory in their practice
- which theories are most applicable to teachers' practice
- how theory is enacted within practice.

Eraut (2004a) has argued that in reality there are a range of situations whereby at one end of the continuum explicit use is made of theory within practice (theory that may be derived from personal experiences, acquired informally from colleagues, or more formally through specific study), and at the other end, theory is more implicit – personal theories of learning are acted upon with little reference to published theory. According to Eraut, the use of theory in practice depends on a number of interrelated factors including an individual's disposition towards wanting to use theory and experience of using theory across contexts.

> Unless the use of theory is repetitious, it will have to be reinterpreted/transferred to fit each new situation; and this will require a little or a great deal of further learning, depending on how different the new situation proves to be from those previously encountered. Thus a person's theoretical capability will depend not only on the range of theories which they 'know and understand' or even on the range of theories they have used; but also on the range of contexts in which they have used them, and their accumulated expertise in, and disposition towards, further use of those theoretical resources.
>
> Eraut, 2004a, p. 58

Furthermore, Kelchtermans (2009, p. 264) has argued that the idiosyncratic nature of any teacher's subjective educational theory which is mainly based on personal experiences is potentially incomplete, biased or wrong and that if teachers want to develop the validity of their professional know-how, or refine or extend it, they need to critically reflect on their practice, making the implicit educational theory explicit. Furthermore, using one's own theories is not about applying a set rule; it is about judging whether a specific situation warrants a particular approach. As commented on by Wenger (2009, p. 215) 'A perspective is not a recipe; it does not tell you just what to do. Rather, it acts as a guide about what to pay attention to, what difficulties to expect, and how to approach problems.' As a consequence of this, there are many different interpretations of theory (Wood, 1998).

Within education, the reconceptualization of approaches to applying theory to practice has seen the supremacy of knowledge founded in theory and the techniques of disciplines over practice knowledge being challenged (Rutter, 2009), with increased emphasis being placed on *knowledge in practice* rather than *knowledge for practice*. Knowledge in practice refers to professional knowledge comprising three components: process knowledge (skilled behaviour and deliberation), personal knowledge (impressions and experiential interpretations), and propositional knowledge (theories, concepts and propositions) (Eraut, 1994a). Within professional contexts, theory and experience are integrated, theoretical knowledge cannot be applied 'off the shelf': it has to be adapted by a teacher to suit the demands of a particular learning context by 'integrating, tuning, restructuring theoretical knowledge to the demands of practical situations and constraints' (Bromme and Tillema, 1995, p. 261). In this way the theory–practice relationship can be seen as inseparable rather than as opposing elements. Rutter (2009) referencing Thompson (1995) has argued that the question should be 'how do knowledge and thought influence or inform our actions?' rather than 'how do we apply theory to practice?'.

Critical reflection on practice involving interrogation of one's own subjective educational theory is not confined to finding answers in predefined bodies of knowledge; it is also about generating new professional knowledge and understanding, and development of theory (Kelchtermans, 2009; Rutter, 2009; Thompson, 2000). To ensure rigour, such personal knowledge needs to be tested, analysed and viewed against formal research and theory (Brookfield, 1995) and as part of this, individuals need to be aware of their own personal constructions of knowledge and the factors influencing such constructions. However, while greater emphasis is being placed on the value of knowledge in practice, traditional views favouring the superiority of explicit, scientific, and discipline-based theory over professional knowledge may act as a significant barrier to the dissemination of professional knowledge created through practice learning within and across institutions. An important consideration for schools and higher education institutions is the value attached to different forms of knowledge and how this is communicated in supporting the professional development of teachers through development of curricula including assessment and in specific training opportunities (Rutter, 2009).

Questions for reflection

- What do you see as the main purpose of education?

- Examining your own teaching, what are your personal theories on learning and teaching?

- What do you believe has informed your personal theories of learning and teaching?

- On a continuum from theory embedded in practice to theory as separate to practice where would you position yourself, and why?

Educational theory embedded in practice	Educational theory informing practice	Educational theory separate to practice

- On a continuum from using theory 'explicitly' in practice to using theory 'implicitly' in practice where would you position yourself and why?

Explicit and deliberate use of theory	Implicit use of theory

- In considering the different conceptions of learning as outlined below; to what extent is your emphasis in teaching on conceptions 1–3 as compared to conceptions 4–6? What factors affect this?

Conceptions of learning

1 Increasing knowledge
2 Memorizing what has to be learned
3 Applying and using knowledge
4 Understanding what has to be learned
5 (i) Seeing things in different ways
(ii) Building social competence
(iii) Seeing learning as part of a continuous life-long purpose rather than as a duty
6 Changing as a person

- Are there other conceptions of learning that you feel are important but are missing from this list? If so what are they and why are they important?

Different types of learning theory

> There are many different kinds of learning theory. Each emphasizes different aspects of learning, and each is therefore useful for different purposes. To some extent these differences in emphasis reflect a deliberate focus on a slice of the multidimensional problem of learning, and to some extent they reflect more fundamental differences in assumptions about the nature of knowledge, knowing, and knowers, and consequently what matters in learning.
>
> Wenger, 2009, p. 210

Some theories of learning focus on learning as individual (behaviourist and cognitive learning theories), while others are focused on a social view of learning (social and situated learning theories). Table 3.1 summarizes key features of some of the most well-known educational theories (behaviourist, cognitive constructivist, and social constructivist/ socio-cultural), mindful of the fact that such categorizations simplify the inherent complexity within the field as these broad headings encompass a range of perspectives, and also overlapping constructs. The table is not an exhaustive one in that there are many other educational theoretical positions.

Behaviourism while seen as having less utility in twenty-first-century learning environments has value in certain contexts (where correct responses are required, in the memorization of specific facts, where learners need to be able to react in predictable ways, e.g. test conditions and performance of specific skills where a level of automation is required).

'*Constructivism* is an umbrella term that groups learning perspectives with the same basic assumption about learning: the understanding that knowledge is actively constructed by the learner' (Gijbels *et al.*, 2006, p. 214); it rejects the idea that knowledge is passively received (Tynjälä, 1999). *Cognitive constructivism* emphasizes the knowledge construction of the individual, whereas *social constructivism* stresses collaborative processes in knowledge building (see Figure 3.1).

Cognitive constructivism is valuable in its emphasis on the role of the learner and the attention afforded to learners' thoughts, beliefs and values within the learning process; in its attention to learning how to learn; and in its support of the development of learner self-regulatory skills. Constructivist approaches can be very resource- and organizational-intensive and can assume autonomy and motivation on the part of the learner (Pollard,

Table 3.1 Features of behaviourist, cognitive constructivist and socio-constructivist theoretical models

	Behaviourism	*Cognitive constructivism*	*Social constructivism/Socio-culturalism*
Learning theorists	Guthrie (1935); Hull (1951); Pavlov and Anrep (1927); Skinner (1953); Thorndike (1903); Watson (1913)	Ausubel (1963); Bruner (1963); Chomsky (1957; 1995); Gagné (1985); Koffka (1922); Köhler (1939); Lewin (1935); Piaget (1952), Perry (1970; 1981); Vygotsky (1934/1962/1986)	Bernstein (1971); Bruner (1996); Dewey (1933); Lave and Wenger (1991); Merrill (1994); Rogoff (1990); Salomon (1993, 1994); Vygotsky (1934/1962/1986)
Focus	• Objectively observable behaviours • Learning is nothing more than the acquisition of new behaviour(s)	• Mental processes–internal cognitive structures • Knowledge is actively constructed by learners in response to interactions with environmental stimuli • Knowledge is considered as self-sufficient and independent of the contexts in which it finds itself • Focus on *assimilation and accommodation* (incorporate new ideas into existing framework and adapting understandings) • *Staged development* (Piaget's 3 stages: sensorimotor; concrete operational, formal operational)	• The processes by which learners build their own mental structures when interacting with the environment • Learning is more than assimilation and accommodation of new knowledge by learners – it is the process by which learners are integrated into a knowledge community • Different perspectives within this field place differing emphasis on the role of individual and social aspects in learning **Variations** • *Social constructivism* considers social and individual aspects of development, but places greater emphasis on the importance of the social environment. Learning cannot be separated from its social context. Emphasis is on the impact of collaboration, and negotiation on thinking and learning and co-construction of it • Some include the *situatedness* of learning (interaction between social and physical contexts). Knowledge is considered as

(continued)

Table 3.1 Continued

	Behaviourism	*Cognitive constructivism*	*Social constructivism/Socio-culturalism*
			situated and is a product of the activity, context and culture in which it is formed and utilized ('participation' and 'social negotiation') (e.g. Lave and Wenger's position). Within *situated cognition*, social learning is expanded to give nonsocial aspects of the environment an active role in the individual's learning as well. Effective learning occurs via interaction with and support from people and physical artefacts (Suchman, 1987) • *Distributed cognition* considers the group rather than individual as the primary unit of analysis
Key concepts Keesee (2011)	Conditioning is a universal learning process • *Classic conditioning* – when a natural reflex responds to a stimulus • *Behavioural or operant conditioning* – when a response to a stimulus is reinforced. If a reward or reinforcement follows the response to a stimulus, then the response becomes more probable in the future	How humans process and store information is very important in the learning process • *Schema* – An internal knowledge structure. New information is compared to existing cognitive structures called 'schema'. Schema may be combined, extended or altered to accommodate new information • *Three-stage information processing model* – input first enters a sensory register, then is processed in short-term memory, and then is transferred to long-term memory for storage and retrieval • *Sensory register* – receives input from senses, which lasts from less than a second to four seconds and	• *Assisted learning:* Where at least two persons try to solve a problem. The social world of a learner includes all the people and participants in all forms of activities • *The zone of proximal development* (Vygotsky, 1978) is where a more able other actively scaffolds the learning of another at a level beyond which the individual could not perform alone • *Meaning making* – the community plays a central role, and the people around the learner greatly affect the way he or she sees the world • *Tools for cognitive development* – the type and quality of these tools (culture, language, important adults to the student) determine the pattern and rate of development

	then disappears through decay or replacement. Much of the information never reaches short-term memory but all information is monitored at some level and acted upon if necessary • *Short-term memory (STM)*: sensory input that is important or interesting is transferred from the sensory register to the STM. Memory can be retained here for up to 20 seconds or more if rehearsed repeatedly. Short-term memory can hold up to 7 plus or minus 2 items. STM capacity can be increased if material is chunked into meaningful parts • *Long-term memory and storage (LTM)* – stores information from STM for long-term use. Long-term memory has unlimited capacity. Some materials are 'forced' into LTM by rote memorization and over learning. Deeper levels of processing such as generating linkages between old and new information are much better for successful retention of material • *Meaningful effects* – Meaningful information is easier to learn and remember • *Serial position effects* – It is easier to remember items from the beginning or end of a list rather than those in the middle of the list, unless that item is distinctly different to the others	• *Situated Learning Theory and Community of Practice* (Lave and Wenger) emphasizes the relational and negotiated character of knowledge and learning and the engaged nature of learning activity for the individuals involved. It is within communities that learning occurs most effectively. Interactions taking place within a community of practice (e.g., co-operation; problem solving; building trust, understanding, and relations) have the potential to foster community social capital that enhances the community members' well-being

(continued)

Table 3.1 Continued

	Behaviourism	*Cognitive constructivism*	*Social constructivism/Socio-culturalism*
		• *Practice effects* – Practising or rehearsing improves retention especially when it is distributed practice. By distributing practices, the learner associates the material with many different contexts rather than the one context afforded by mass practice • *Transfer effects* – The effects of prior learning on learning new tasks or material • *Interference effects* – Occur when prior learning interferes with the learning of new material • *Organization effects* – When a learner categorizes input such as a grocery list, it is easier to remember • *Levels of processing effects* – Words may be processed at a low-level sensory analysis of their physical characteristics to high-level semantic analysis of their meaning. The more deeply a word is processed the easier it will be to remember • *State dependent effects*– If learning takes place within a certain context it will be easier to remember within that context rather than in a new context	
View of knowledge Berkeley.edu Willis (2009)	• Knowledge is objective and verifiable • A repertoire of behavioural responses to environmental stimuli	• Knowledge is relative, subjective, constructed, problematic • Actively constructed by learners based on pre-existing cognitive structures • Knowledge is the interaction between the individual and the environment	• Knowledge is distributed • Knowledge is constructed within social contexts through interactions with communities. Mind is part of the social world and knowing and doing, thinking and social activity are not separated.

View of learning Willis (2009)	Change in behaviour	Transformation of internal cognitive structures (including insight, information processing, memory, perception)	Interaction/observation in social contexts. Movement from the periphery to the centre of a community of practice
Locus of learning Smith (1999, 2003)	Stimuli in external environment	Internal cognitive structuring	• Learning is in relationship between people and environment
View of learning process Smith (1999, 2003)	• Passive absorption of a predefined body of knowledge by the learner. Promoted by repetition and positive reinforcement • Transmission: absorbing, memorizing, and reproducing	• Active assimilation and accommodation of new information to existing cognitive structures • Individual conceptual restructuring resulting from a process of interpreting and making sense of new experiences • Discovery by learners	• Integration of students into a knowledge community. Collaborative assimilation and accommodation of new information • Identity formation of self within a community, growing from novice to expert • First, understand within social interaction before progressing to independence
View of motivation Willis (2009)	Extrinsic motivation, involving positive and negative reinforcement (reward and punishment)	Intrinsic motivation involving learners setting their own goals and motivating themselves to learn	Intrinsic and extrinsic motivation. Learning goals and motives are determined both by learners and by extrinsic rewards provided by the knowledge community
Teaching and learning process Smith (1999, 2003)	• Transmission approach • Scientific measurement	• Individuals construct their own representations • Teachers mediate activities and experience that create dilemmas and provoke new conceptions	• Interaction, negotiation and collaboration • Model and practice activities within social norms of structured interaction situated within community of practice • Meaning is created through social interaction with others, especially talking
Purpose in education	Produce behavioural change in desired direction	Develop capacity and skills to learn better	Full participation in communities of practice and effective utilization of resources

(continued)

Table 3.1 Continued

	Behaviourism	*Cognitive constructivism*	*Social constructivism/Socio-culturalism*
Learner role	Passive receiver • Memorization and repetition	Active meaning maker • Major responsibility for learning by being motivated, active, metacognitive to create and recreate sophisticated mental models • Move from novice to expert • Learners process, store, and retrieve information for later use – creating associations and creating a knowledge set useful for living. The learner uses the information processing approach to transfer and assimilate new information	Teacher and learner are co-inquirers but with teachers mediating among students' personal meanings, meanings emerging from collective thinking and discourse, and the culturally established meanings of the wider society (subject, organization). • Learning is an active process in which learners construct new ideas or concepts based upon their current/past knowledge, social interactions, and motivation. • Learning apprentice through co-operative collaboration and legitimate peripheral participation (Lave and Wenger, 1991).
Teacher role Pollard (2002) Willis (2009)	• Transmits knowledge and skills • Designs the learning environment • Shapes child's behaviour by positive/negative reinforcement • Students are assessed primarily through tests	• Teacher facilitates by providing children with opportunities to construct knowledge and skills through experience • Learning can be independent of teaching	• Teachers within communities of practice work alongside students developing whole person (behaviour, cognition, language and affective responses) assisting them to independence • Knowledge and skills constructed through experience, interaction and teacher support • Learning comes through the interdependence of teacher and student
Manifestations in adult learning (Smith, 2003)	• Behavioural objectives • Competency-based education • Skill development and training	• Cognitive development • Intelligence, learning and memory as function of age • Learning how to learn	• Socialization • Social participation • Associationalism • Conversation

Learning design/ activities Keesee (2011)	• Development of instructional objectives (predetermined outcomes/targets) • Learning controlled by the teacher • *Reinforcement* (consistent repetition of the material; small, progressive sequences of tasks; and continuous positive reinforcement/rapid feedback) • *Multiple opportunities*(drill and practice) • *Allowing pupils to learn at their own pace*	• Learning outcomes not predictable – emphasis on fostering rather than controlling learning • The teacher facilitates learning by providing an environment that promotes discovery and assimilation/ accommodation • Authentic problem-based learning using strategies derived from information processing approaches	• Collaborative learning is facilitated and guided by the teacher. The content is not pre-specified, direction is determined by the learner, and assessment does not depend on specific quantitative criteria, but rather on the process and self-evaluation of the learner • Learning design is aimed at enhancing collaboration and dialogue and engaging others (e.g. *domain experts*) to participate in certain ways • Emphasis on development of teamwork skills. Individual learning seen as essentially related to the success of group learning
	Approaches Instructional cues to elicit correct response; building fluency (get responses closer and closer to correct response); discrimination (recalling facts); generalization (defining and illustrating concepts); associations (applying explanations); chaining (automatically performing a specified procedure)	**Approaches** Explanations; demonstrations; illustrative examples; Gestalt Theory; corrective feedback; mnemonics; Dual-Coding Theory; chunking information; repetition; concept mapping; advanced organizers; analogies; summaries; interactivity; synthesis; Schema Theory; metaphor; generative learning; organizational strategies; Elaboration Theory	**Approaches** Modelling; collaborative learning; coaching Scaffolding; problem-based learning; authentic learning; cognitive flexibility; object-based learning
Assessment	Emphasis on testing. Students assessed against norms – summative and diagnostic testing	Students assessed against norms - summative and diagnostic testing	Individual assessments – emphasis on formative assessment

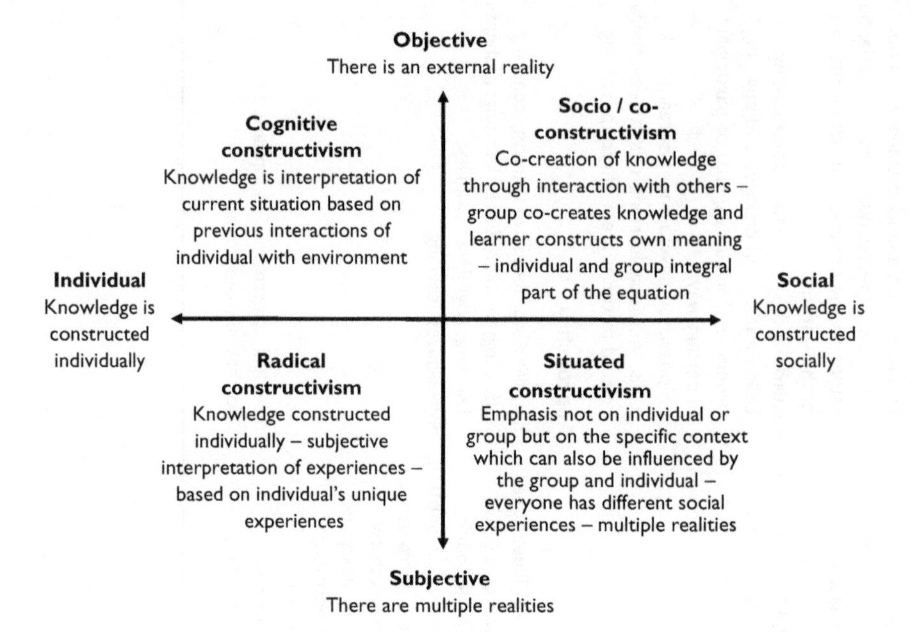

Figure 3.1 Constructivist perspectives

2002; 2014), requiring very high levels of skill on the part of the teacher (understanding of processes of learning, ability to build on learner's starting points, integration of approaches).

Social constructivism and socio-cultural approaches place emphasis on the socially constructed nature of learning, although there is a tension in the relative level of influence of individually and collectively constructed views of learning where learning is seen variably as a situated process, as a process of changing participation, as mediated by cultural tools, and as the joint construction of knowledge (de Laat and Simons, 2002).

Situated Cognition Theory views learning as only making sense within a specific context: knowledge is not something that is generalizable. Socio-cultural approaches to learning and teaching, such as *Situated Learning Theory*, suggest that learning must be understood as a process that is not solely in the mind of the learner.

Social-constructivist perspectives make a distinction between individual cognitive activities and the environment in which the individual is present, whereas the *socio-cultural perspective* regards the individual as being part of that environment. Its supporters point out that learning cannot be understood as a process that is solely in the mind of the learner (Van Boxtel, 2000). Learning takes place in a social context and is seen as a process of participating in cultural practices, a process that structures and shapes cognitive activity (Lave and Wenger, 1991). The socio-cultural perspective promotes relational perspective emphasizing the mutuality of the relations between learners and emphasizes the dialectic nature of the learning interaction (Sfard, 1998).

The following authors have been instrumental in the development of (1) cognitive constructivism, (2) social constructivism, and (3) socio-cultural approaches respectively:

1 *Piaget* (1952) emphasized the internal independent psychological development of a learner's cognition, and the learner as an active meaning maker rather than passive recipient of learning.
2 *Vygotsky* emphasized that learning and teaching are essentially social activities that take place between social actors in socially constructed situations. He was interested in what the student and knowledgeable others brought to a learning situation and what factors (cultural and historical) also impacted on such interactions (Tudge and Scrimsher, 2003). A key theme of his work was that learning is mediated by tools and signs (*semiotics*) including: language; systems of counting; mnemonic techniques; algebraic symbol systems; works of art; writing; schemes, diagrams, maps, drawings, signs, computers, calculators, paint brushes. These semiotic means act as tools that facilitate the co-construction of knowledge, and internalisation of some of these is thought to aid future independent problem-solving activity.
3 *Bruner* introduced the idea of spiralling (Bruner, 1963) which, counter to the idea of learning as a steady incremental accumulation of knowledge, incorporates the argument that the learner constantly returns to interrogate previous learning and understandings in the light of new learning and experience. Bruner took more account of the role of sociocultural factors in learning, and potential links and disconnects between learning within and beyond the school context. In doing so he placed greater emphasis on an awareness of different ways of learning, and sensitivity to student context, along with a focus on developing metacognition so that students are more aware of how they go about learning.

While much of the framework for socio-constructivist/cultural theory was put forth by Lev Vygotsky (1986 (1934/1962); 1997 (1941)), extensions, elaborations, and refinements of aspects of sociocultural theory can be found in *activity theory* (Chaiklin and Lave, 1993; Leontiev, 1981) and *cultural-historical activity theory* (Cole, 1996; Cole and Engeström, 1994; Engeström, 2009).

In sum, 'constructivism is not a unified theory, but rather a conglomeration of different positions with varying emphases' (Tynjälä, 1999, p. 363–364). It involves two key principles, first that 'knowledge is actively constructed by the learner, not passively received from the environment, [and second] *coming to know* is a process of adaptation based on and constantly modified by a learner's experience of the world' (Jaworski, 1993).

Enacting constructivism in practice is complex. While there is some consensus about what constructivist (cognitivist and social) teaching and learning environments should comprise (see Gagnon and Collay, 2006; Grennon Brooks and Brooks, 1993), Evans and Kozhevnikov (2011) have noted that translation of constructivist principles into practice is inconsistent given different interpretations by teachers and students of what is actually involved in doing so and how the different components are integrated.

Loyens *et al.* (2008) agree that constructivism is enacted in different ways, but they have argued that most forms of constructivism involve four core features:

1 knowledge construction
2 co-operative learning
3 self-regulated learning, and
4 the use of meaningful, authentic problems in education.

These four features are also evident in Gijbels *et al.*'s (2006, p. 215) discussion of seven key features of constructivist learning environments:

1 arguments, discussions, debates
2 conceptual conflicts and dilemmas
3 sharing ideas with others
4 materials and measures targeted toward solutions
5 reflections and concept investigation
6 meeting student needs and
7 making meaning, real-life examples.

A key issue for all teachers when applying constructivist principles to their practice is evaluating the efficacy of these.

Questions for reflection

- In designing constructivist learning environments, how are you
  - ascertaining students' prior knowledge and understanding
  - connecting the focus of the lesson to students' lives
  - ensuring student involvement in decision-making
  - ensuring students have sufficient knowledge and understanding in order to debate ideas
  - ensuring assessment is authentic
  - involving students in assessment and feedback
  - ensuring meaningful reflection
  - developing your own understanding of the relational dimension of teaching
  - using individual and collaborative learning activities?

> According to Vygotsky and Luria . . . systems for representing and communicating knowledge generate important transformations in the minds of those who master them. So when children learn how to read, and how to make use of mathematical symbols, they acquire new ways of thinking . . . If all this proves to be correct, then systems for representing the world are not just things that we think about; they determine how we think
>
> Wood, 1998, p. 41

- How is technology impacting on your ways of thinking and teaching?
- How is technology impacting the way your students learn?

An integrated approach

Given that 'all learning implies the integration of . . . an external interaction process between the learner and his or her social, cultural or material environment, and an internal psychological process of elaboration and acquisition' (Illeris, 2009, p. 8), an integrated approach is warranted, one that takes account of the most relevant educational theory for consideration in a specific context (Chisholm and Demetriou, 2006; Chisholm *et al.*, 2009): 'If we are to understand how the person learns to become a whole person, then we need to combine all of these theories' (Jarvis, 2009, p. 30). Indeed, as James (2006a) has argued that teachers should blend the different theoretical positions in their approaches to learning and teaching.

Constructivists might argue that sociocultural theories do not adequately account for the process of learning, and sociocultural theorists might retort that constructivist theories fail to account for the production and reproduction of the practices of schooling and the social order. The challenge of relating actively constructing students, the local microculture, and the established practices of the broader community requires that adherents to each perspective acknowledge the potential positive contributions of the other perspective (Cobb, 1994, p. 18)

However, in considering such a synthesis, a judicious approach is essential in determining what the different theories have to offer, their currency, and how they can be most usefully combined (Loftus and Higgs, 2010) relative to the specific needs and requirements of a learning situation. Teachers need to establish which areas of knowledge are relevant and what specific knowledge is required for a particular learning context. Extracting the most relevant aspects of theory from a potentially vast area is complex. Eraut (2004a) has argued that the ability to recognize what theory(ies) is/are needed in each situation is learned through participation in practice and receipt of feedback on one's actions, arguing that ' . . . most components of a practitioner's theoretical repertoire remain dormant until triggered by a very specific aspect of the situation' and that these are also contingent on the time scale available (Eraut, 2004a, p. 67). However, a holistic perspective sees theory and practice as totally integrated within a teacher's repertoire. As already alluded to, every teacher operates according to a theory or theories of learning and a philosophy of what they perceive education to be about. Sometimes these theories are conscientiously held and referenced to published theory while other theories are held and acted upon less consciously with little reference made to published theory (Moore, 2000); it is therefore important for all teachers to examine what theoretical positions underpin their practice and why.

The importance of bringing individual and social views of learning together in order to fully understand the complexity of learning processes and all the conditions that influence and are influenced by such processes of learning has been argued (Illeris, 2009; Packer and Goicoechea, 2000). Illeris acknowledged the close connection between cognitive and emotional dimensions in learning. In his model (Figure 3.2) the *content dimension* of his model concerns what is learned (knowledge, skills, opinions, attitudes, values, ways of behaving, methods, strategies,etc.), where the aim of the learner is to construct meaning and deal with learning challenges in order to develop *personal functionality*. His *incentive dimension* function represents the continuous mental balance of the learner; personal sensitivity is developed through motivation, feelings, emotions, and volition. Illeris argued that the learning content is always 'obsessed' with the *incentives at stake* (what impulses drive learning –desire, interest, necessity, compulsion, fear) and that the incentives are always influenced by the content. Illeris's view is that these two dimensions (*content and incentive*) are always initiated by impulses from the interaction processes, and integrated into the internal processes of elaboration and acquisition.

In Illeris's model (2009, p. 11), the interaction dimension (the environment) provides the impulses that initiate the learning process (e.g. perception, transmission, experience,

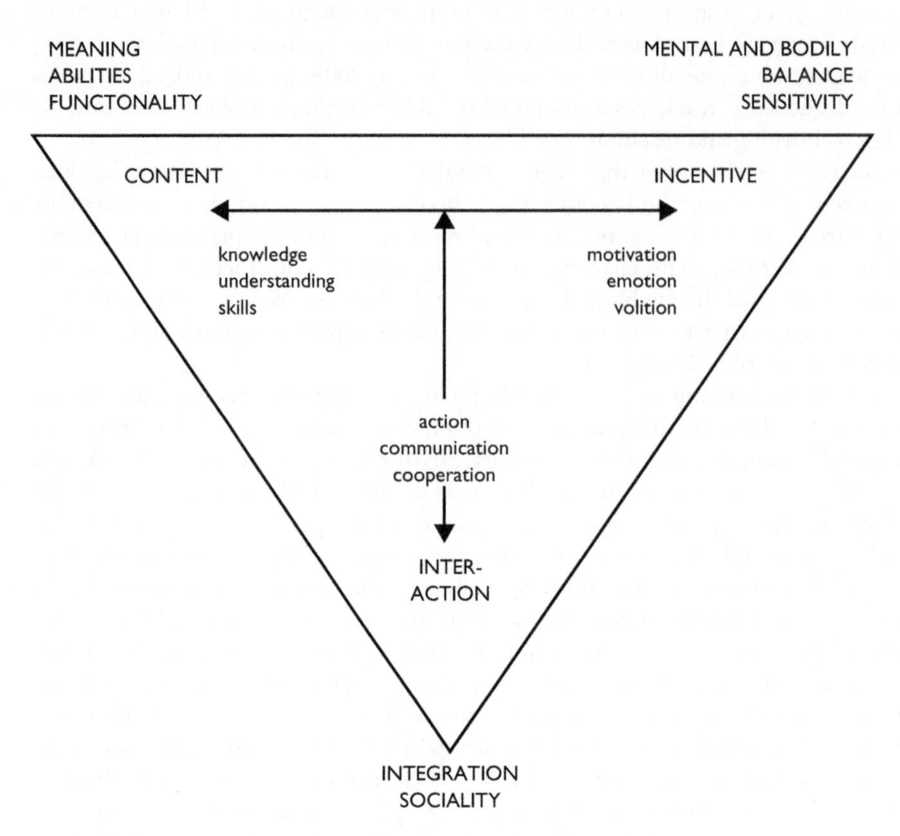

Figure 3.2 The three dimensions of learning and competence development
From Illeris (2009, p. 10)

imitation, activity, participation). 'It serves the personal integration in communities and society and thereby also builds up the sociality of the learner.' In everyday learning situations, learners need to be interacting with the learning context and making sense of information (elaboration, and acquisition). Acquisition involves both cognitive and emotional dimensions of learning – for example, whether a learner has sufficient prior knowledge to cognitively process new information, whether a learner is interested in the content and can see the value of it, along with how they feel within specific learning contexts.

The situational aspect of learning is also important and was a later addition to Illeris's model to demonstrate how the learner is interacting with the environment at a number of levels (classroom situation, materials school situation, familial, social, societal). The relationship is two-way, with the environment influencing the learner and the learner influencing the environment.

Illeris connected separate theoretical positions and located his own position at the centre of the triangle taking into consideration both cognitive and social approaches to learning (Figure 3.3).

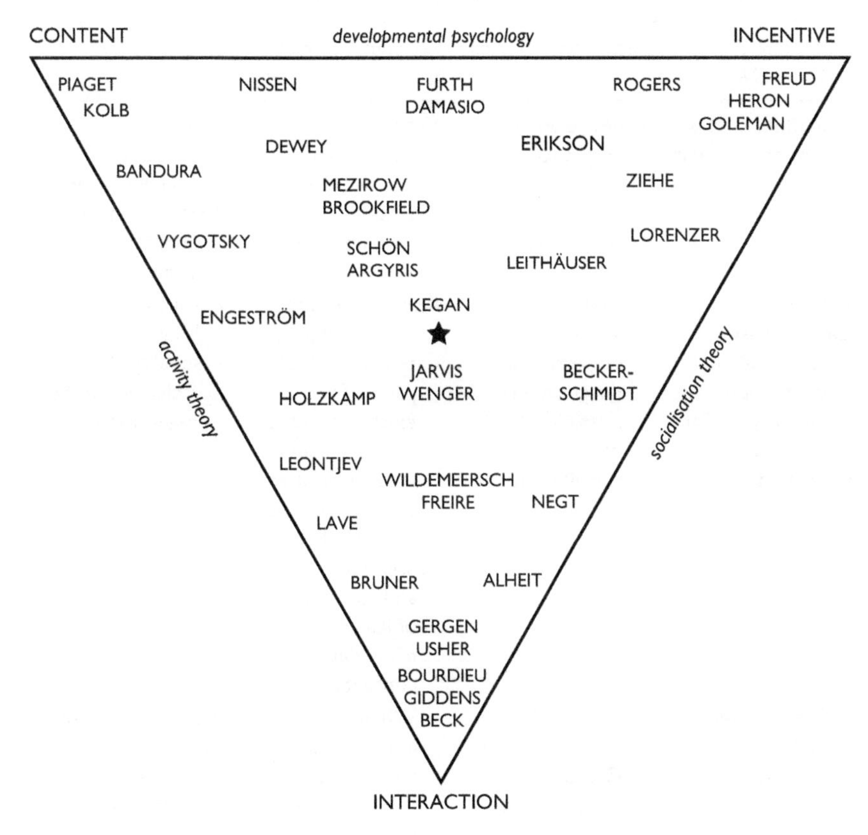

Figure 3.3 Positions in the tension field of learning

From Illeris, K. (2007, p. 257)

Conceptually, Illeris sees learning as constructivist, in which as a learner one actively builds up one's own mental schemes in order to be able to recall relevant content information (about a person, situation, issue, subject), and mental patterns (organization of motivations, emotions etc.) about how one feels about a situation or context. Significantly, although information is stored and can be retrieved effectively through the creation of schemes and patterns, such storage is constantly evolving because of new experiences or understandings, as will be discussed in chapters five and six. Understanding of the plasticity of the brain in building new connections and new patterns of storage and also in rewriting emotional memories is an important development within cognitive neuroscience that has pedagogical implications. Importantly, in different contexts, different types of learning can be activated which impact on the development of an individual's mental schemes and patterns. Building on the work of Piaget (1952), Illeris describes four different types of learning, as summarized in Table 3.2. He has argued that the greatest focus (and often an exclusive one) within education has been on assimilative learning, consequently excluding a more integrated approach which would see attention given to how all learning processes can be supported to enable learners to develop competence within twenty-first-century learning environments.

Table 3.2 Four types of learning (developed from Illeris, 2009, pp. 12–14)

Type of learning	*Cumulative or mechanical learning*	*Assimilative learning*	*Accommodative or transcendent learning*	*Transformative learning*
	Something that is new and not part of something else – isolated	A new element added to an already established scheme/pattern	Where it is not possible to connect learning to any existing scheme/pattern	Simultaneous restructuring of schemes and patterns in all dimensions of learning
Results of learning	*Automation* Only able to recall and apply in situations mentally similar to the learning context	*Achieving links* to the scheme or pattern in question – recall possible when working in the specific field	*Relinquishing and reconstruction* One breaks down parts of an existing scheme or pattern and transforms it so the new situation can be linked in. Possible to recall and apply results of learning to many different contexts	*Profound and extensive change* Personality changes or changes in the organization of the self
When it occurs	• First few years of life • Learning something new which has no context of meaning or personal significance	• Learning in school subjects • Gradual development of one's capacities	• When an individual cannot relate to or understand a situation • Requires motivation to want to acquire new understanding	Crisis-like situations where challenges are experienced as urgent and unavoidable
Parallels		Single loop learning (Argyris &Schön, 1996) Adaptation oriented (Ellström, 2001)	Double loop learning (Argyris &Schön, 1996) Development oriented (Ellström, 2001) Zone of proximal development (Vygotsky, 1978)	Expansive (Engeström, 1987) Transformative (Mezirow, 1991) Transitional (Alheit, 1994)
Importance	Most important in childhood	Everyday learning	Only occurs in special situations of profound significance to the learner	

David A. Kolb (1984, p. 38) defined learning as 'the process whereby knowledge is created through the transformation of experience'. In his experiential learning cycle Kolb did not seek to create an alternative to behaviourist or cognitive theories of learning but instead suggested that 'through experiential learning theory a holistic integrative perspective on learning . . . combines experience, perception, cognition, and behavior.' (pp. 20–21).To be successful, he argued, learners needed four different kinds of abilities: concrete experience (CE), reflective observation (RO), abstract conceptualization (AC), and active experimentation (AE). The experiential learning theory proposes that the learning cycle varies according to individuals' learning style and the learning context in which they are participating. The learning cycle stresses the importance of concrete and immediate experiences in order to create meaning in learning and for validating the learning process. While individuals may have preferences, the aim is that they should be able to use all four abilities in learning in order to involve themselves fully in new experiences, reflect and observe their experiences from different perspectives, create concepts that integrate their observations into logically sound theories, and be able to use their theories in decision making.

Questions for reflection

David A. Kolb and Jack Mezirow emphasized the importance of transformative learning, which is defined as

> . . . the process by which we transform problematic frames of reference (mindset, habits of mind, meaning perspectives) – sets of assumption and expectation – to make them more inclusive, discriminating, open, reflective and emotionally able to change. Such frames are better because they are more likely to generate beliefs and opinions that will prove more true or justified to guide action.
>
> Mezirow, 2009, p. 92

- How are you developing transformative learning experiences within your classroom and your school with students and colleagues?

- What are the assisting and limiting factors for you in the development of these transformative learning experiences?

Summary

Educational theory embodies a host of principles, concepts and frameworks (including learning theories), any combination of which are employed to reflect upon, evaluate and assess ideas, aims, activities and experiences in educational contexts. Educational theory is an essential element informing how teachers interpret and understand their context, learning and everyday teaching practices within that context.

Theory and practice should not be seen as separate entities but integral to what teachers do in their everyday practice. The integration of theory (*propositional knowledge*) with *practical knowledge* is a key requirement of the twenty-first-century professional teacher. To be able to use theory effectively within practice and for practice to inform theory, teachers need to be able to articulate their own intertwined knowledge and beliefs about education.

The theories a teacher has frame the way they act and how they justify their actions. As part of this, a teacher's conceptions of learning impact on how they design, enact and interpret learning and teaching experiences. How teachers perceive theory and the extent to which they see it as integrated into what they do on an everyday basis are framed by their critical reflections on and awareness of their own constructions of personal knowledge and the factors impacting on that, compared to more formal theory. However, regardless of the degree of consciousness of formal theory, every teacher operates according to a theory or theories of learning and a philosophy of what they perceive education to be about. A judicious approach is essential in determining what the different educational theories have to offer, their currency, and how they can be most usefully combined relative to specific needs and requirements of a learning situation. Extracting the most relevant aspects of theory from a potentially vast area is complex. Teachers also have an important role to play in the generation of new theory.

Conceding that there are certain limitations associated with the categorization of learning theories presented in this chapter, particularly regarding the simplification of the inherent complexity and overlap within and between them, it is nevertheless vital that in following an integrated approach one should take account of the most relevant learning theories and how they can be blended. To this end, the use of constructivist, socio–cultural, and socio–critical theoretical perspectives in informing the development of the Personal Learning Styles Pedagogy (Evans and Waring, 2009, Evans, 2013a; Evans and Waring, 2014; Evans and Waring 2015) is acknowledged prior to its elaboration in chapter four.

Key readings

Kelchtermans, G. (2009). Who I am in how I teach is the message: Self-understanding, vulnerability and reflection. *Teachers and Teaching: Theory and Practice, 15* (2), 257–272.

This article focuses on the self-image of the teacher and the individual and contextual factors impacting this. The messages inherent in the article are relevant to all those involved in teaching. The notion of vulnerability is an especially important one in the context of learning to teach.

Illeris, K. (2009). (Ed.). *Contemporary learning theories.* London: Routledge.

This book provides a synthesis of current learning theories and conceptual frameworks from sixteen leading theorists. For an overview of learning theories also see Moore, A. (2000). Teaching and learning. Pedagogy, curriculum and culture. London: Routledge.

Wood, D. (1998). *How children think and learn.* Malden, MA: Blackwell Publishing.
This book examines different educational theoretical perspectives (e.g. those of Bruner, Piaget, and Vygotsky) and considers the practical implications of trying to put theory and research into practice from the teacher perspective.

Weblinks

Atherton, J.S. (2013a). Learning and teaching: Cognitive theories of learning. Available online at http://www.learningandteaching.info/learning/cognitive.htm

Atherton, J.S. (2013b). Experiential learning. Available online at http://www.learningandteaching.info/learning/experience.htm#ixzz2pqbrorsw (accessed 18 January 2014).

Atherton, J.S. (2013c). Instructional Design. Available online at: http://www.instructionaldesign.org/theories/subsumption-theory.html (accessed 12 January 2014).

Perera, N. C. (2011). *Constructivism, social constructivism and situated cognition: A sliding scale.* Available online at http://nishancperera.com/2011/01/31/constructivism-social-constructivism-and-situated-cognition-a-sliding-scale-by-nishan-perera/ (accessed 17 January 2014).

Plucker, J. A. (Ed.). (2013). *Human intelligence: Historical influences, current controversies, teaching resources.* Available online at http://www.intelltheory.com (accessed 6 January 2014).

Riegler, A. (2003). *The key to radical constructivism.* Available online at http://www.univie.ac.at/constructivism/key.html (accessed 10 January 2014).

Smith, M. K. (2003). Learning theory. In *The encyclopedia of informal education.* Available online at http://infed.org/mobi/learning-theory-models-product-and-process/> (accessed 11 December 2013).

Thirteen ed online. Available online at http://www.thirteen.org/edonline/concept2class/constructivism/index_sub5.html (accessed 10 January 2014).

University of California, Berkeley. *Teaching guide for graduate student instructors.* Online. Available online at http://gsi.berkeley.edu/teachingguide/theories/learning-chapter (accessed 20 December 2013).

Chapter 4

The application of educational theory

An integrated approach using the Personal Learning Styles Pedagogy

Overview

In this chapter we will demonstrate the use of constructivist, socio-cultural and socio-critical theoretical perspectives in informing the development and implementation of the Personal Learning Styles Pedagogy (Evans and Waring, 2009, Evans, 2013a; Evans and Waring, 2014 (chapter eleven); Evans and Waring 2015). We argue that teachers have an essential role to play in both their use and generation of educational theory in supporting the development of effective twenty-first-century learners.

An integrated approach

> What is needed is a theoretical framework that has place both for the individual mind and for the larger social and cultural context that makes intellectual activity possible and meaningful.
>
> Vosniadou, 1996, p. 106

The Personal Learning Styles Pedagogy

The need for clear guidance on how to apply an understanding of cognitive styles to learning and teaching within twenty-first-century learning environments led to the development of the Personal Learning Styles Pedagogy (PLSP). The PLSP is informed by research in education, neuroscience and cognitive psychology. It demonstrates integration of cognitivist and socio-cultural theoretical perspectives (Cobb, 1994; Packer and Goicoechea, 2000; Saxe, 1991; Tynjälä, 1999) and social critical theory (Butin, 2005). The PLSP comprises five interrelated components of practice (see Figure 4.1) and provides a holistic framework in which to examine different aspects of practice (e.g. use of a PLSP in the design of learning contexts – see chapters six and eight); PLSP approach to assessment (see chapter nine); PLSP approach to critical reflection (see chapter ten), as well as providing an overarching tool to examine support for learners (students and teachers – see chapter eleven: The PLSP Framework).

Combining different educational theoretical perspectives in this way is not new and integrated approaches have been increasingly advocated (Bereiter, 1994; Cobb, 1994, 1995; Hatano, 1997; Hatano and Miyake, 1991; Jaworksi, 1993; Resnick, 1994; Tynjälä, 1999; Vosniadou, 1996). The different constructivist theoretical positions are not incompatible (Gijbels *et al.*, 2006; Tynjälä, 1999); one position does not imply rejection of the other (Bereiter, 1994). It inherently makes sense to combine these different perspectives

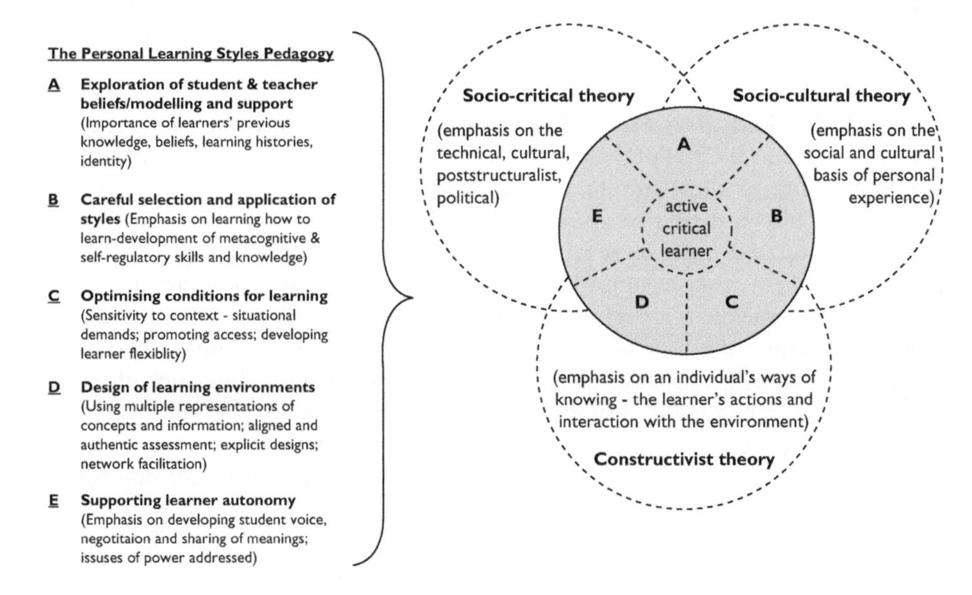

Figure 4.1 Theoretical frameworks including components of the Personal Learning Styles Pedagogy

See C. Evans and Waring, 2009; 2015; C. Evans, 2013(a). Integrated Educational Theory: see also Tables 8.1, 9.1, 10.1, and chapter eleven. Figure 4.1 is reproduced from Kozhevnikov and Kosslyn, 2014

in order to seek to 'better understand how internal representations and processes interact with external environmental variables including both the transitory aspects of the situational context and the more permanent effects of the tools and artifacts of the culture' (Vosniadou, 1996, p. 105). Salomon and Perkins (1998) also support an integrated approach arguing three key points:

(i) individual learning can be less or more socially-mediated learning;
(ii) individuals can participate in the learning of a collective, sometimes with what is learned distributed throughout the collective more than in the mind of any one individual; and
(iii) individuals and social aspects of learning can interact over time to strengthen one another in a 'reciprocal spiral relationship'.

Integrating educational theory: Supporting notions of learning and pedagogy

Approaches are needed that 'takes into consideration biological and situational factors without giving up the notion of an individual mind' (Vosniadou, 1996, p. 105). We recognize, as part of the holistic notion of pedagogy presented in chapter two, that learning is not a purely cognitive process but also a social process involving changes in values and identities. Culture(s) at a variety of levels (family, school, workplace, society, ethnicity etc.) can enhance and restrict learning. Furthermore, individuals do not passively internalize culture; the individual has the capacity to change cultural reality itself; a key aspect of education is in supporting learner cognitive flexibility to see things in different ways and to change them (Vosniadou, 1996). We support the concept of situated learning (Lave and Wenger, 1991), but, in agreement with Eraut, we are adamant about not subjugating the individual perspective on knowledge and learning:

> Individuals belong to several social groups in which they both acquire and contribute knowledge, and their experiences of multiple group membership cannot be ring-fenced. Many of these groups have changing memberships and relatively short lifetimes. Thus members of a group acquire only part of the knowledge present in that group, and interpret it within a personal context and history that has been shaped by their experiences in other groups, both prior and contemporary. There will also be aspects of a person's knowledge that have been constructed through lifelong learning and have become unique to them, i.e. outside the circle of shared cultural knowledge, because of the unique set of situations in which they have participated. For example, a single idea will acquire a distinct web of meaning for each individual user according to the sequence of situations in which they used it. The greater the range of usage, the more distinctive its personal meaning is likely to be. . . .
>
> Eraut, 2004a, p. 56

Figure 4.1 illustrates the application of constructivist and socio-cultural principles. Associated with our holistic notion of pedagogy and the development of a critical pedagogy (see Freire, 1972; Giroux, 1993) there is reference to socio-critical theory which is also important within the PLSP model. Social critical theory is concerned with the concept and practice of a critical pedagogy that is essential for teachers and student teachers within twenty-first-century learning environments (see chapter one). Social critical theory is not incompatible with socio-cultural perspectives in its examination of equity issues (Bruner, 1996). Socio-critical theorists argue that individuals have the capacity to change their circumstances although their ability to do so is constrained by various forms of social, cultural and political domination (Habermas, 1971). Carrington and Selva (2010), citing Leonardo (2004), have argued that critical theorists propose:

> '. . . that quality education is as much about teaching students the ability to read the world more critically (ideology critique) as it is imagining a better world that is less oppressive (utopian critique) (Leonardo, 2004, p. 16). These theorists support the production and application of theory that underlies a transformative approach to learning. . . . and provides the framework for a form of critical discourse that can change the pedagogical process from one of knowledge transmission to knowledge transformation (Leonardo, 2004)
>
> Carrington and Selva, 2010, p. 46

The PLSP is predicated on an understanding of how individuals process information and how this process is mediated by the cultural context at micro to macro levels. An integrated theoretical perspective that considers both how individuals conceptualize information and how participation in cultural environments impacts on such processes in the development of cognitive style is fundamental to the development of our approach.

> . . . learning involves not only becoming a member of a community, not only constructing knowledge at various levels of expertise as a participant, but also taking

> a stand on the culture of one's community, in an effort to take up and overcome the estrangement and division that are consequences of participation. Learning entails both personal and social transformation.
>
> Packer and Goicoechea, 2000, p. 228

While the PLSP approach is based on the fact that cognitive style mediates and is mediated by cultural considerations – it can be reinforced and/or developed (a sociocultural stance), it is concerned with students' cognitive self-organization and the processes by which individuals' interaction with the social environment impacts on their cognitive styles development (a cognitive stance). In line with Saxe (1991) we focus on individuals' understandings while at the same time we place emphasis on the influence of cultural practices and the use of sign forms and cultural artefacts (Vygotsky). In this way we are concerned with structural perspectives on understanding what students learn and the processes by which they do so (constructivist) as well as functional perspectives on understanding (socio-cultural) – the conditions that support or hinder learning (Hiebert *et al.*, 1996). While we acknowledge the importance of the cultural context and 'coming to know' as part of collaboration within communities of practice, this cannot be looked at in isolation without consideration of the cognitive processes and conceptual structures involved in learning. As part of our approach we argue that an understanding of information processing models is essential if teachers are to enhance student access to, and engagement in, learning. Morgan and Morris (1999) found a substantial lack of homogeneity in the vocabulary and concepts available to teachers with which they were able to describe their own teaching and the factors underpinning their approaches. Understanding how individuals process information enables a more judicious and informed approach to teaching in the selection of resources, activities and assessment options to inform curriculum design.

In the next section we will focus on key aspects of learning design that are integral to a PLSP– e.g. importance of student voice (component E), scaffolding learning (components A and D); attending to housekeeping (component D); and supporting teacher identity development within communities of practice (components C, D, and E) –and we will explicate the use of theory in attending to these within our overall PLSP design.

Student/teacher voice

A key tenet of the PLSP is the promotion of student/teacher voice; the ability to critique the status quo in order to improve learning and teaching is an important part of this. Butin's (2005) socio-cultural approach using his four lenses (*technical, cultural, political, and postmodern/poststructural*) provides a useful framework for teachers and student teachers to examine beliefs and assumptions about practice with the aim of addressing social injustice through the adoption of a critically reflective approach. Using a *technical* lens, it is possible to focus on the pedagogical effectiveness of a learning context and to consider how learning can be improved. The *cultural* lens encourages individuals to consider the meanings of the practice for themselves, from others' perspectives and at the organizational level along with consideration of their sense of self within community(ies). A *political* lens considers issues of power and is about promoting and empowering individuals by also addressing inequalities. A *postmodern/poststructuralist* lens requires learners to consider how the learning process creates, sustains and/or disrupts the boundaries and norms by which we make sense of ourselves and the world and assumes that there is no single truth, and that individuals are constructed and construct themselves in society.

Scaffolding

Integrating cognitive and socio-cultural theoretical perspectives in our design of learning activities as part of the PLSP we place emphasis on the appropriate provision and removal of *scaffolding*, incorporating Vygotsky's notion of the *zone of proximal development* which is typically interpreted as involving learner support/guidance from a more knowledgeable other (the gap between what a child can do unassisted and what the same child can achieve with the benefit of adult assistance (Vygotsky, 1962, 1978)). The notion of scaffolding in the PLSP involves cognitive, social and affective dimensions of support from others along with detailed consideration of the learning and teaching histories of the learner and teacher.

> How people respond to learning in workplace settings will vary enormously depending on the different subjectivities they bring to the interaction. If we really wish to understand how to maximise the learning that can occur, then we need to explore the complex subjectivity that people bring to the work setting.
>
> (Loftus and Higgs, 2010, p. 387)

Challenge and support from a knowledgeable other are important dimensions of scaffolding.

Challenge: the importance of challenge is highlighted from information processing, neuroscience, and motivational perspectives. Challenge is particularly important from Vygotskian perspectives; Vygotsky described pedagogy as being aimed at *ripening* rather than *ripe* functions (see Moore, 2000); this position aligns with current cognitive neuroscience perspectives on the need to challenge learners in order to develop brain capacity (Adey *et al.*, 2007).

Knowledgeable other: the notion of the *knowledgeable other* from Vygotskian socio-constructivist and from situated learning perspectives (novice – expert) is far from straightforward, requiring sensitivity to context and mindful negotiation; Butin's power lens is important here. Peer support is not unproblematic in terms of learners' perceived *readiness*, their ability to engage in peer learning activities, and the trust afforded in themselves and others. In addressing scaffolding issues, a key aspect of our approach is in teaching students/teachers to be more cognizant of the nature of scaffolding support that they require and to be more proactive in attaining this for themselves. For the teacher, the scaffolding issues revolve around knowing students sufficiently well in order to place scaffolding accordingly and, most importantly, to be able to remove it to avoid dependent learning and lack of progression on the part of the learner. Within our approach such guidance does not need to be solely in the form of dialogue from a specific person or face to face (Rogoff, 1990).

Housekeeping

In the PLSP much attention is afforded to the importance of what we have termed *housekeeping* (Component D(i)) which includes a focus on feed-forward activities such as an emphasis on the importance of directing students to appropriate resources (virtual learning environments/communities etc.), as well as guiding learners through focused tasks prior to and following a teaching activity (see chapters six to nine, and eleven). The PLSP places considerable focus on affective and motivational aspects of learning– an area often overlooked in integrative approaches (Vosniadou, 1996). Explicit discussion with learners about individual, contextual (current and historical) influences regarding beliefs about learning and specifically maladaptive and positive motivational styles (self-worth, learned helplessness, and mastery) is important, especially for those learning to teach, in considering the impact of learning design/context on both students' attitudes towards learning and their own motivation styles within teaching and learning contexts (see chapter eight for further elaboration on different motivational styles and suggested teaching strategies). Crucially we see motivational styles as a fluid construct resulting from the interaction of an individual's innate dispositions and the affordances and constraints of the environment.

Supporting teacher identity development within communities of practice

One of the central foci of the PLSP, from an individual differences perspective, is in supporting learners to make sense of, integrate with, and challenge existing conceptions of learning and work practices as part of *communities of practice* (CoPs). As part of this, individuals need to manage their levels of participation in many different communities (including formal and informal networks; physical and virtual worlds, within and beyond the parameters of their place of work). While accepting the importance of developing shared understandings as part of developing expertise within CoPs from the socio-cultural perspective, supporting the development of learner agency to navigate different CoPs effectively to enable greater autonomy rather than being subordinated to established practices is a key aim of the PLSP. Of high interest is how individuals negotiate membership of CoPs, their roles, their diverse ways of participating in them, and how this impacts on identity development (Cobb and Bowers, 1999). While identity development from a socio-cultural perspective is seen as developing through 'negotiating the meanings of our experience of membership in social communities' (Wenger, 1998, p. 145), we are in agreement with Kelly (2006, p. 513) in that:

> Teachers' identities are neither located entirely with the individual nor entirely a product of others and the social setting. They can be regarded as the ways in which practitioners see themselves in response to the actions of others towards them; that is they are the constantly changing outcomes of the iteration between how practitioners are constructed by others, and how they construct themselves, in and away from social situations.

Such a position acknowledges the agency of the learner in negotiating their sense of learning identity. In learning to teach, the ability of a teacher to develop a sense of self within a community, to both retain and develop their identities is an important aspect of developing their own capacity within a learning context; their ability to influence others and develop cultures is an important part of this, along with the capacity to remain true to the 'authentic self'.

> When we remember who we are, we bring our authentic selves forward. Many times . . . we are forced at an early age to hide our true selves in order to survive. At some point, this hiding becomes unnecessary, yet we find it hard to break the habit. Every day we choose anew whether we will support the authentic self or the false self. . . .
>
> Higgs and Titchen, 2001, p. 270, quoting Arrien, 1993, p. 80

Teacher identity: integrating the past with the present: the ability to incorporate the past and integrate this with the present is important in the development of teacher identity; this may involve addressing established schema that will no longer work successfully in specific contexts. As part of this an understanding of relational dynamics is important; as Willis (2009, pp. 1–2) quoting Lave notes, learning that leads to autonomy and fuller participation in community "cannot be pinned down to the head of the individual or to assigned tasks or to external tools or to the environment, but lie[s] instead in the relations among them-(Lave, 1993, p. 9). Wenger (2010) acknowledges that building a coherent identity is becoming more challenging within twenty-first-century learning environments. Woods and Jeffrey (2002) have noted that teachers do not simply adopt the identities which, through their affordances, social circumstances assign them. Evans (2014) highlighted the varying ability of student teachers to be able to both assimilate and adapt to different school contexts. A key attribute of those student teachers who managed their transitions more effectively was their ability to develop their identity(ies) to incorporate the ways of being and doing in the new context with established frames, without losing sight of 'who they were'; those less able to integrate into new school contexts felt established ways of working threatened their sense of identity and, unable to identify with the community, saw themselves as operating 'parallel and separate' to colleagues within the school context. From a socio-critical perspective, our approach encourages a critical pedagogical stance which requires learners to go further than recycling knowledge in an uncritical and conservative way. Becoming part of a community of practice is much more than adaptation and socialisation; it is also about creating new ways of doing and becoming; creativity and innovation are important aspects of this (Elkjaer, 2009).

Knowledge of, in, and across practice: while a cognitive constructivist perspective sees individuals being able to acquire knowledge and skills and understanding (*knowledge of practice*) in one context and being able to use this effectively elsewhere, the situated socio-cultural perspective sees this as problematic because an important part of the equation in the learning process is '*knowledge in practice.*' The socio-cultural position is that 'knowledge in practice' does not lie entirely with the individual but is distributed across teachers, students and both conceptual artefacts such as models and theories, and physical artefacts (books, computers, schemes of work etc.) (Wenger, 1998). Teacher expertise is seen as being closely linked to the particular working practices and associated ways of thinking within a school context (Lave and Wenger, 1991; Wenger, 1998), However, we would see expertise as being capable of transcending specific contexts as, within twenty-first-century learning contexts, teachers are increasingly working within and beyond the immediate context of a school as part of wider school networks. For Schön (1983, 1987) a key feature of expert teachers is an active and productive relationship with their *knowledge-in-* and *knowledge-of-practice*. Expertise in the Lave and Wenger framework is defined as being able to participate fully in the particular social practices of the teacher's areas of expertise. Teacher learning is thus seen as the movement of teachers from peripheral (novice) to full (expert) participation in the specific working practices and their associated ways of knowing and thinking which define particular school circumstances.

The importance of situational knowledge and being able to integrate different forms of the 'what and how of learning' from different contexts has been highlighted by Bruner (1996). In line with Soja's (1996) interpretation of situated learning, and as reported by Gipps (2008), within the PLSP we advocate development of a '*fourth space*' in the context of learning to teach, in which student teachers' *primary discourses* (those used in informal social interactions – Facebook/blogs/twitter, home, friends, family), *secondary discourses* (school workplace setting), *tertiary discourses* (university formal taught courses e.g. PGCE) are brought together within a *fourth space* to enable integration of perspectives and to support integrated identity development.

Negotiated entry: Wenger's concept of *legitimate peripheral participation* has been used to characterize the process by which newcomers become included in a CoP which, within the context of learning to teach, we have described as *negotiated entry*. Legitimate participation according to Wenger is about ensuring appropriate entry (support and guidance) and legitimacy in being granted 'mutual engagement with others, to their actions and their negotiation of the enterprise, and to the repertoire in use' (Wenger, 1998, p. 100). In our interpretation of *negotiated entry*, newcomers are not seen as passive; nor are they seen as empty vessels to be filled. While accepting the need to move from novice to expert in learning to understand situational knowledge and practices, we do not underestimate the amount of knowledge student teachers and experienced teachers bring to new contexts and their capacity as change agents while at the same time acknowledging the power dynamics involved in negotiating entry. While some CoPs may offer more affordances than others, the newcomer needs to be equipped to navigate landscapes of practice (Wenger, 2010) and to manage the realization that 'The heterogeneous, multifocal character of situated activity implies that conflict is a ubiquitous aspect of human existence' (Lave, 2009, p. 206).

From a cognitive constructivist perspective, the ability of an individual to be able to filter vast amounts of information is crucial within twenty-first-century learning environments. From a socio-critical perspective, what constitutes the *body of knowledge to be learnt* as part of negotiated entry is important. In our model the newcomer is not seen as solely passive in acquiring and honing skills but is also seen as creating new ways and developing new understandings as part of the CoP. In facilitating student agency as a key focus of the PLSP, levels of participation in CoPs should be seen as a conscious choice rather than as a rite of passage in the journey from novice to expert. In negotiating belonging within communities of practitioners the issue is one of developing rather than preserving identity(ies). From a political socio-critical perspective it is also concerned with ensuring teacher autonomy in terms of choice of levels of participation and not marginalization by actors within the CoP and wider cultures.

Summary

In this chapter we have elucidated how we have used an integrated theoretical framework to inform the development of the PLSP. In practice, with students and teachers we have developed new understandings that contribute to our development of theory, which remains grounded in designing and developing programmes of study and implementing teaching designs: 'theoretical constructs developed in this way do not stand apart from instructional practice, but instead remain grounded in it.' (Cobb and Bowers, 1999, p. 12). As teachers, integrating theory into practice is what we do on a daily basis; being able to demonstrate explicitly how we are using theory, what has informed such decisions and how we generate new theory from active engagement with learners and colleagues as co-learners are vital discussions to make explicit in developing a shared understanding of learning within and across contexts.

Key readings

Butin, D. (Ed.). (2005). *Service-learning in higher education: Critical issues and directions.* New York: Palgrave Macmillan.

Using a socio-critical approach it is possible for teachers to use Butin's four lenses (technical, cultural, political, and post-structural) to examine inequalities – who is privileged and who is not within educational contexts? How can teaching be adjusted to ensure greater equity and how can one's own beliefs and values shape instruction from a reflexive perspective?

Gagnon, G. W., and Collay, M. (2006). *Constructivist learning design.* California: Corwin Press.

This book takes constructivist principles and demonstrates in practical ways how these can be enacted in the classroom with the aim of increasing student engagement in learning. Also relevant is Gijbels, D., van de Watering, G., Dochy, F., and van den Bossche, P. (2006). New learning environments and constructivism: The students' perspective. Instructional Science, 34, 213–226.

Wenger, E. (2009). A social theory of learning. In K. Illeris (Ed.). *Contemporary learning theories* (pp. 209–218). London: Routledge.

In this chapter, Wenger provides an update on social theories of learning, building on his previous work on communities of practice and legitimate peripheral participation (see also Lave and Wenger, 1998).

Weblinks

The Atlantic (2013). An Atlantic Special Report. Building a better human. Available online at http://www.theatlantic.com/health/archive/2013/11/how-the-brain-creates-personality-a-new-theory/281287/ (accessed 17 January 2014).

Association for Information Systems: AIS qualitative resource site. Critical social theory. Available online at http://www.qual.auckland.ac.nz/ (accessed 8 September 2013).

Canadian Council on Learning. Lecture Series Minerva: Cultivating a flexible mind: Can you learn how to learn for life? Available online at http://www.ccl-cca.ca/pdfs/Minerva/CultivatingAFlexibleMind_Leighton.pdf. (accessed 1 May 2014).

Centre for Critical Social Theory, University of Sussex. Available online at http://www.sussex.ac.uk/spt/1–4–5 (accessed 10 January 2014).

Educational Broadcasting Corporation. Object based learning. Available online at http://schools.cbe.ab.ca/b101/pdfs/inquirybasedlearning.pdf (accessed 4 January 2014).

International Centre for Educators' Learning Styles. Available online at http://www.icels-educators-forlearning.ca/index.php?option=com_contentandview=articleandid=54and Itemid=73 (accessed 12 January 2014).

Keesee, G. S. (2012). Teaching and learning resources. Available online at http://teachinglearningresources.pbworks.com/w/page/19919565/Learning%20Theories (accessed 4 January 2014).

Nationmaster. com encyclopedia. Available online at http://www.nationmaster.com/encyclopedia/Critical-social-theory (accessed 4 January 2014).

Stanford Encyclopedia of Philosophy. Available online at http://plato.stanford.edu/entries/critical-theory/ (accessed 10 January 2014).

Transition Consciousness. Online. Available online at http://transitionconsciousness.wordpress.com/2013/11/16/guest-article-iain-mcgilchrist-replies-to-stephen-kosslyn-and-wayne-miller-on-the-divided-brain/ (accessed 17 January 2014).

Wall Street Journal: A new map of how we think: Top brain/bottom brain. Available online at http://online.wsj.com/news/articles/SB10001424052702304410204579139423079198270> (accessed 17 January2014).

Chapter 5

Making sense of styles

A critical introduction

Overview

In this chapter we will develop an understanding of how people learn. We will provide a state of the art update on the current understandings of styles and specifically cognitive styles and related constructs from education, cognitive psychology and neuroscience perspectives to promote a timely research-informed understanding of how we learn, and subsequently to illustrate how it can be used to inform pedagogy and enhance learning and teaching. Having outlined what cognitive style is, we will provide an overview of developments and different approaches within the styles field, including qualification of the dominant terminology used to describe styles, attempts at unifying styles, an integrated theoretical framework to assist in an understanding of styles, and an exploration of style constructs. We will clarify that all individuals have a styles profile and not just one single cognitive style available to them and that it is possible to identify families of styles at different levels of information processing.

The relevance of styles

An understanding of how we learn is a key requirement for teachers and learners in the context of twenty-first-century learning environments (Barnett, 2011). An understanding of styles is essential in order for students and teachers to be able to effectively manage their own learning (Evans and Waring, 2009; Sternberg, 1996). As noted by Sadler-Smith (2012, p. 168) ' . . . it is impossible to foster metacognitive approaches without an informed awareness of habitual learning and information processing preferences (styles), that is, *there can be no learner-focused and practically useful metacognition without styles*.' [Sadler-Smith's italics]. Zhang and Sternberg point to the all-pervasive nature and impact of style:

> . . . styles do matter! Styles make a difference in behavior and performance in diverse domains of our life, ranging from ways of learning and of solving problems to various aspects of development (such as affective development, cognitive development, career development and identity development . . . and from academic achievement to job performance . . .
>
> Zhang and Sternberg, 2009, p. 292

What are styles?

How individuals go about learning

The term *styles* is fairly ubiquitous and is often used indiscriminately in many aspects of life to mean different things. In defining styles, the education literature tends to focus on what people do when they are trying to learn: 'Styles do not describe what people are like: they describe what they do when they are trying to learn' (Boulton-Lewis *et al.*, 2001, p. 145). Schmeck (1988, p. ix) simply defined style as 'any pattern we see in a person's way of accomplishing a particular type of task.' In its broadest sense, style (s) are considered by Sternberg and Zhang referencing Biggs (2001, p. 250) [as] 'approaches to learning and even to life'. Styles are thus seen to focus on how individuals go about learning which is separate to abilities focusing on how well an individual does something (Blazhenkova *et al.*, 2011).

Styles are malleable (amenable to change), multidimensional (each individual has a styles profile) and pejorative (in that in many instances the use of a specific style does impact results) (Zhang *et al.*, 2012). It is, therefore, not possible to talk about someone having a single cognitive style.

What is cognitive style?

The term cognitive style was initially introduced to describe adaptive individual differences in cognition (G. S. Klein, 1951), however this initial understanding became lost within the literature and cognitive style was increasingly defined as stable attitudes, preferences, or habitual strategies that determine individuals' modes of perception, memory, thought, and problem-solving (Messick, 1976, 1984). Cognitive style was thus perceived as trait-like – inbuilt and fixed, unidimensional (single construct), and non-pejorative (one style is not better than another). However, current understandings of cognitive style suggest that cognitive style is shaped by an individual's interaction within the environment. So cognitive style can be described as individual differences in cognitive functioning that develop as a result of an individual's adaptation to external physical and socio-cultural environments. A cognitive style arises from a system of interacting processes, not a single process working in isolation (see Kozhevnikov *et al.* 2014). Thus cognitive style represents individual differences in cognition that help an individual to adapt to the learning environment. Cognitive style is in turn also shaped by an individual's interactions with an environment:

> . . . cognitive style is an adaptive system that moderates the effects of both an individual's predispositions [both innate and learned] and the external environment
>
> Kozhevnikov, *et al.*, 2014, p. 22

Individuals vary in the extent to which they can employ different styles and in their ability to regulate their choice and use of cognitive styles. A higher order flexible *meta-style* (see Kozhevnikov, 2007), incorporating metacognition, serves as a control structure for other subordinate cognitive styles (C. Evans *et al.*, 2013; Kozhevnikov *et al.*, 2014).

The notion of *cognitive style modification*, involving interplay between individual characteristics (e.g. general intelligence, personality) and external requirements operates at a number of levels or layers from micro (individual) to macro (global culture/society), as illustrated in Figure 5.1. These layers represent the following attributes:

- Familial (Witkin *et al.*, 1954): the influence of an individual's immediate surroundings on his or her cognitive style
- Educational: the influences of different educational systems and social groups on an individual's patterns of information processing
- Professional: the influence of professional environments on an individual's cognitive processing
- Socio-cultural: the influence of global cultural context on cognitive functioning.

The analogy used by Signorini *et al.* is useful in its suggestion that these layers are very much interwoven 'as a single knitted coat with different types of thread' (Signorini *et al.*, 2009, p. 258. Together the layers help to shape habitual patterns of cognitive processing that constitute a cognitive style. From an educational perspective, the contribution and dominance of particular layers in impacting on an individual's cognitive style development is important (see Evans and Waring, 2011c).

Of high interest is the relative role of these different layers on an individual's cognitive style development and what factors serve to reinforce or enable adaptation of cognitive style. Evans and Waring (2006) have noted that at certain times and in certain contexts some students are more adaptive than others, which leads to questions about the potential design of learning environments to evoke change as well as to discussions about how able and willing a student is to adjust his/her cognitive styles. The realisation that styles are modifiable and that certain styles are preferable for the successful completion of tasks (they are pejorative) (Zhang, 2013; Zhang, *et al.*, 2012) has considerable implications for educational practice and training.

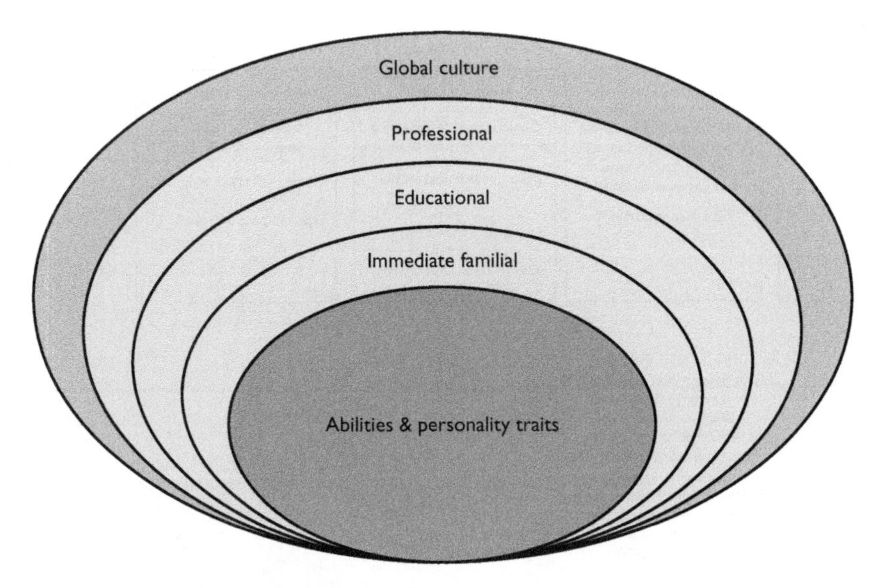

Figure 5.1 Layers affecting cognitive styles

From Kozhevnikov et al., 2014

The styles conundrum: getting to grips with styles terminology

A great deal of confusion and misunderstanding has been created by the inappropriate use of the varied terminology employed in relation to styles. In the next section we will highlight key developments in how style has been conceptualized. We will outline and distinguish between the dominant terms used to describe styles including *cognitive style, learning style, approaches to learning, learning dispositions, and learning patterns*, and outline an integrated theoretical framework that brings together different cognitive style families and levels of information processing into one model.

In tracing the evolution of style, Rayner (2000) highlighted four key areas of psychology (perception, cognitive controls, mental imagery, and personality constructs) that have been influential in contributing to an understanding of style from different perspectives (see Figure 5.2).

Kozhevnikov (2011) adds the chronology to the conceptualization of style debate in her examination of the changing conceptions of style from the 1940s to the present day. She notes that earlier conceptions of style were very much focused on individual differences in information processing, revealing that individuals differed in the way they perceived information. In the second phase in Kozhevnikov's chronology (1950s–1970s) emphasis was placed on the role of an individual's internal characteristics (abilities, personality) in preferred ways of processing, which led to the promulgation of many style constructs – and to debates regarding the differences between cognitive styles and cognitive controls. Some saw the two terms as interchangeable, whereas others perceived specific dimensions such as *impulsivity–reflectivity* and *levelling–sharpening as*being independent of one another, and representing a process available to, and used by, all individuals to categorize reality; this was in comparison to

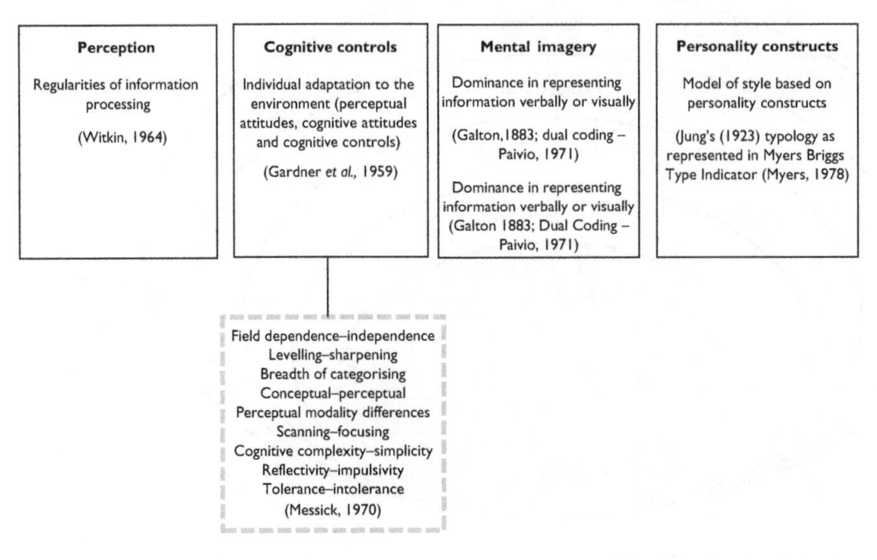

Figure 5.2 Conceptualizing style

cognitive style, which they saw as representing the extent to which control processes were exercised and organized within an individual (Gardner *et al.*, 1960). From an educational perspective it is important to consider the relevance of these constructs to teaching. Table 5.1 provides definitions for each construct and explicit reference to its relationship to teaching.

In the third phase (1970s–1980s) the acknowledgement of the influence of social and cultural factors on style became more prominent, along with the conception of cognitive styles as adapted patterns of adjustment to one's environment.

Since the 1980s greater emphasis has been placed on the neuro-cognitive basis for styles, along with attempts to develop an over-arching theory of style in order to bring different constructs together under one unifying conceptualization comprising the in-depth analysis of specific cognitive styles and the identification of style flexibility (a meta style).

Some researchers have sought to clarify the differences between cognitive styles, learning styles and strategies (Peterson *et al.*, 2009a), while others have looked at ways of integrating different style concepts (Allison and Hayes, 1996; Curry, 1983; Miller, 1987; Riding and Cheema, 1991; Sadler-Smith, 2009; Zhang and Sternberg, 2005 – see Zhang, 2011, for an overview); however none of these approaches integrate the cognitive style construct with contemporary cognitive psychology and neuroscience theories of information processing (Kozhevnikov *et al.*, 2014).

One early attempt to differentiate between cognitive style, learning style, and approaches to learning was that of Curry's (1983) influential *onion model*, whereby *cognitive personality style* was seen as the innermost layer, with a middle layer representing *information processing* and an outer layer comprising approaches to learning based on the stability of style and the relative influence of *external environment*. Therefore, in Curry's interpretation, approaches to learning were seen as more amenable to change, whereas cognitive style was seen as more trait-like, less affected by the environment, and more difficult to change. Using a similar approach Grigorenko and Sternberg (1995) classified styles into three groups: cognition, personality, and activity centred styles.

1. *Cognition-centred styles* are closely based on differences in cognitive processes and perception and resembled abilities (e.g. *reflective impulsive* (Kagan, 1965); *field dependence independence* (Witkin *et al.*, 1962))
2. *Personality-centred styles* are most similar to personality traits (e.g. Jung's personality styles, and Myers–Briggs Type Indicator (MBTI)) – for example *extraversion vs introversion*; *sensing vs intuitive*; *thinking vs feeling* (Jung, 1923); *judging vs perceiving* was added by Myers and McCaulley, 1985) to the MBTI (Myers *et al.*, 1998)
3. *Activity-centred styles* – whereby one views styles as mediators of activities from both cognition and personality approaches and places greater emphasis on the educational perspective and the role of individual differences in how an individual interacts with the environment (e.g. *surface versus deep approaches* (Biggs, 1987); *undirected, meaning-, reproduction-, and application-directed learning patterns* (Vermunt, 1998).

Peterson *et al.* (2009b, p. 11) defined *cognitive styles as* 'individual differences in people' preferred way of processing (perceiving, organising and analysing) information using

Table 5.1 Messick's nine cognitive styles and control labels (Messick, 1970, 1976

Messick's cognitive controls related to cognitive style families	*Definition*	*Relevance to teaching*
Context-dependent vs independent cognitive style family.	**Tendency to perceive events as separate versus inseparable from their physical, temporal, or . . . semantic contexts (Kozhevnikov et al., 2014, p. 23)**	
Field dependence – independence (FDI) (Witkin *et al.*, 1954)	The extent to which individuals are dependent on the structure of the prevailing visual field (e.g. being able to discern shapes within shapes- hidden forms within a picture; identify objects that are camouflaged; knowing whether a plane is level without looking out of the window)	Learners demonstrating greater field independence are less influenced by the context when performing a skill or learning, and are less reliant on being provided with a structure to the subject. A field dependence orientation implies learners are more responsive to external reinforcement, more reliant on an externally provided structure, and more likely to experience difficulty in complex learning environments. In translating FDI into style characteristics it is suggested that field independent (FI) individuals prefer tasks involving more cognitive restructuring and find spatial tasks easier to manage than their field dependent (FD) counterparts. It also suggested that FD learners tend to be more socially oriented because of their higher levels of sensitivity to external referents; they can also more easily be distracted. *It is important to consider the level of cognitive complexity and structure and how this can be differentiated for those with differing levels of FDI. It also has implications regarding the balance of individual and group work and nature of pairings of learners*
Rule-based vs intuitive processing	**An individual's tendency towards being directed / driven by rules (analytic), *versus* -driven, by salient characteristics or by relying on heuristic evidence in his/her information scanning (aleatoric – chance) (Kozhevnikov *et al.*, 2014)**	
Conceptual – perceptual (Broverman, 1960) / conceptualizing styles (Wallach, 1962)	Individual differences in the tendency to categorize perceive similarities/ differences among stimuli in terms of many differentiated concepts	Learners may group objects in different ways (e.g. analytic grouping is on the base of common features, e.g. birds and bats have wings; relational grouping – because of functional thematic relationships, e.g. turtles and whales both swim; or group them inferentially in a more abstract way where similarities are inferred but not directly observed *It is important not to close down learning by encouraging different ways of grouping and / or specifying the grouping mechanism required*

Scanning – focusing (Holzman, 1954)	It measures the intensity (active or passive) and extensiveness (narrow or broad) of scanning. Extensive scanners are meticulous, concerned with detail with extensive coverage. Also defined as the extent to which an individual attempts to verify the judgements s/he has made	Individuals vary in their ability to scan a field and cognitively record and compare visual and verbal properties from available information *It is important to allow sufficient time for learners to take on board information, for example, by providing resources prior to, and/or sufficient time during a teaching session in order for them to be able to get an overview of content and concepts* *The speed of transition and presentation of information (e.g. in power point presentations) are an important aspect associated with this* *Where detailed scanning is needed, it is important to consider strategies that may help learners to develop these skills*
Levelling–sharpening (Gardner *et al.*, 1959)	How individuals perceive and memorize images. Levellers tend to blur similar memories whereas sharpeners are less prone to confuse similar objects and may magnify small differences	Levellers may integrate information more readily into memory; however, they may also miss important information. Sharpeners may be better able to differentiate between discrete images and identify differences between them, recall structure, and remember details, and may rely more on rote memory than do levellers *It is important to consider the requirements of the task and how sharpening where required can be developed through learning and teaching activities. The development of a specific dimension like sharpening can also be directly linked to assessment objectives.*
Reflectivity–impulsivity (cognitive tempo) (Kagan *et al.*, 1964)	Individual consistencies in the speed and adequacy with which alternative hypotheses are formulated and information processed. It measures the individual's ability to reflect on the accuracy of an answer and to inhibit responding impulsively. Individuals who are more reflective have longer response times and commit fewer errors than do impulsive individuals, who answer quickly and with greater frequency of error, leading to the belief that reflectives think before they act.	Reflectivity develops over time and is responsive to training interventions. While usually seen pejoratively from a cognitive processing perspective, it is possible, although less likely, for an impulsive individual to process information quickly and also accurately. Links have been found between reflectivity–impulsivity and anxiety: with impulsive individuals demonstrating less anxiety over committing errors, lower standards for performance, and less attention to monitoring of stimuli. *Learners can be taught through questioning techniques to take time to consider their answers; provision of material and questions ahead of a lesson can also support reflective learning. Addressing learner anxiety is also important in the taking of risks. In certain contexts, learners need to be able to come to accurate decisions quickly, and reinforcement activities can support this so that key aspects of learning become automized.* *There are implications in the sharing of resources (computers, books), and possible conflicts in pairing reflective and impulsive learners, that need to be managed; the same applies for many of the cognitive controls e.g. scanning*

(continued)

Table 3.1 (Continued)

Messick's cognitive controls related to cognitive style families	*Definition*	*Relevance to teaching*
Compartmentalisation vs integration	**A tendency to prefer a compartmentalized, sequential versus an integrative, holistic approach to information processing . . . These styles reflect the degree to which people are impelled to act upon or ignore differences; acting upon differences reflects an integrative approach, whereas ignoring differences reflects a more compartmentalized approach. (Kozhevnikov et al., 2014, p. 24)**	
Breadth of categorizing (Pettigrew, 1958)	The narrow categorizer is thought to be conceptually conservative, whereas the broad categorizer is thought to be more tolerant of deviant instances (e.g. where people are asked to estimate ranges of things – such as variation in performance within a group). Wider categorizers perceive wider variation and also perceive this as permissible)	Experienced learners within a specific field are more able to categorize accurately. A certain level of knowledge of a field is necessary to be able to categorize. It is known that novice learners will make distinctions using different principles to those used by more experienced learners. Knowledge of the context is important in terms of being able to estimate category width *From a teaching perspective it is important to ensure learners have access to relevant information in making such decisions, and to consider the implications of their perceptions on category width*
Cognitive complexity–simplicity (Bieri *et al.*, 1966)	Individual differences in the tendency to construe the world, in a multidimensional and discriminating way. A complex individual's conceptual system is highly differentiated (large number of concepts), finely articulated, and flexibly integrated	The ability to be able to discriminate and integrate concepts into meaningful wholes is important. In certain contexts and for certain individuals the need to be able to deal with complexity in an integrated way is vital e.g. doctors. Some learners may go through life without considering the relationships between different concepts and events and may prefer greater cognitive simplicity *Managing complexity and building an integrative view of contexts is crucial within twenty-first-century learning environments. It is important to support learners to deal with cognitive complexity such as in problem-based learning environments. For some learners the level of cognitive complexity will need to be scaffolded to enable them to develop the skills to discern different concepts and how these are related to each other*
Tolerance–intolerance (G. S. Klein *et al.*, 1962)	The extent to which a person is willing to accept and report experiences at variance with the conventional experiencing of reality as we know it (Sternberg & Zhang, 2001, p. 12). *Tolerance* is easiness and *intolerance* is difficulty	Tolerance can support creativity development but it can also enable the learner to put themselves at risk in being too accepting of ideas (e.g. too trusting; not listening to contrary evidence) *In learning it is also important to support learners to take a leap of faith in trying out new ideas and experiencing different learning contexts, but careful scaffolding is needed.*
Possible additional cognitive style family Visual *vs* verbal	**Relative reliance on specific modalities (kinaesthetic, visual and auditory)**	
Perceptual modality differences (Messick *et al.*, 1976)	Individual consistencies in relative reliance upon the different sensory modalities available for experiencing the world	*The issue is in ensuring the most appropriate representation of material in relation to the requirements of the task and not about matching to learner's modalities. It is also important to consider the relative spatial abilities of learners when designing tasks along with the other controls listed above which impact individuals' access to information*

cognitive brain-based mechanisms and structures. They are assumed to be relatively stable and possibly innate.' The most preferred definition of *learning styles* identified from their research was: 'an individual's preferred way of responding (cognitively and behaviourally) to learning tasks which change depending on the environment or context. Therefore, a person's learning style is malleable.' (Peterson *et al.*, 2009b, p. 11). In these two definitions, there is evidence of the influence of the Curry model interpretation of styles in that the main difference between these definitions is around *stability* and the *role of the external environment* in defining whether a style is a cognitive or learning style.

The assumptions underpinning such models and definitions have recently been challenged (see Cools and Bellens, 2012; Kozhevnikov *et al.*, 2014). Evans and Vermunt (2013) have noted that stability and variability are evident in all dimensions of student learning (cognitive styles, learning styles, approaches to learning . . .), that contextual variables impact on cognitive styles, and that person-bound influences are evident in students' approaches and patterns of learning. Such findings have recently led to an increased emphasis on *overarching principles involved in the application of styles to practice* rather than on attempts to differentiate between different style constructs which may be unconstructive, and, most importantly, to an understanding of the *hierarchical nature of style* (Kozhevnikov, 2007; Nosal, 1990). Therefore styles exist at *different levels of information processing* and individuals have a *profile of styles rather* than only one style to draw on. However, some individuals may be better able to draw on higher levels of style within such a hierarchy, and able to use a wider range of styles than others. The key educational issue is the use of the most appropriate style for a given situation.

Approaches to learning

Approaches to learning 'are not characteristics of learners, they are determined by a 'relation' between a learner and a context' (Struyven *et al.*, 2006, p. 280). *Deep*, *surface*, and *strategic/achieving* approaches to learning focus on *process* and *motivation*: how students go about learning, and what drives them. They focus on the learner and the task. The acknowledgement of deep and surface approaches to learning (Marton, 1975; Marton and Saljo, 1976) has been supported over a long period of time.

> [A] deep approach is associated with students' intentions to understand and construct the meaning of the content to be learned, whereas the concept of the surface approach refers to students' intentions to learn by memorising and reproducing the factual contents of the study materials . . .
>
> Gijbels *et al.*, 2009, p. 503

The strategic/achieving approach, added later, acknowledges the impact of the demands of assessment and has been described as well-organized and conscientious study methods linked to achievement motivation, or to the determination to do well (Entwistle *et al.*, 2001), or else to how the student organizes when and where the task will be engaged, and for how long.

Students' approaches to learning are related to conceptions of learning (views about the nature of learning: mental models of learning), motivational orientations (perceptions of what one is trying to achieve in learning), cognitive strategies, and regulation of learning (Heikkilä and Lonka, 2006). Conceptions of learning develop through experiences of teaching and learning and then influence subsequent ways of studying which in turn further impact on conceptions (Evans and Kozhevnikov, 2011). Deep approaches to learning are thought to be related to higher level conceptions of learning (abstracting meaning, interpreting information to understand the world, changing as a person), with surface approaches related to lower order conceptions of learning (increasing knowledge, memorizing, acquiring facts) (Marton *et al.*, 1993; Säljö, 1979b). However, high order conceptions of learning do not necessarily imply an individual will use a deep approach, because of the range of individual and contextual variables involved. It is known that effective learners use both deep and surface approaches appropriately. This suggests there is metacognitive involvement in students being able to adopt processes and strategies which are appropriate to the requirements of a learning context.

Is a surface approach bad?

There is evidence that use of a deep approach is related to higher learning outcomes; however, this is contingent on the nature of the assessment requiring the use of a deep approach. A surface approach is often depicted as rote learning, but memorization can be a high-level skill. If assessment does not require a deep approach (this indicates an inherent flaw with the assessment design) then the use of a surface approach is appropriate.

Are approaches to learning malleable?

Yes. However, changing approaches to learning is complex given their relationship to students' beliefs, perceptions and conceptions of learning. In aiming to encourage students' use of a deep approach teachers need to be mindful of students' variable starting points, in relation to their prior knowledge and familiarity with a certain teaching format. Design considerations to take into account are summarized in Table 5.2.

What constitutes a deep approach in twenty-first-century learning environments?

Moving far beyond its initial description of how students' went about studying a specific text (searching for meaning *vs* learning by rote), today a deep approach may look very different in different contexts and in the completion of different tasks in different cultural contexts (Evans, 2014). Students use a range of strategies as part of a deep approach and it is important to examine the ways in which these are interconnected. Bi-polar descriptions of approaches are too narrow (*deep* vs *surface*) to capture how learning is enacted and what constitutes a deep approach in one discipline may be inappropriate in a different cultural and/or discipline specific context. The following three examples

Table 5.2 Encouraging a deep approach: design considerations

Teaching design issues to consider	*Managing the learning environment to promote a deep approach to learning*
Clarity of nature of task and rationale for approaching learning and teaching in a specific way	It is important to make tasks explicit and explain the relevance of the task in relation to the immediate requirements of the assessment along with clarifying the relevance of the activity to the students' learning beyond the school. Students need to see the teaching design including assessment as authentic and relevant to them
Awareness of students' different starting points	Ensure that you have undertaken baseline assessments of where the students are and that the students themselves are aware of where they are in their learning and where they need to get and how they are going to achieve this. Ongoing discussion of the learning process is important
Appropriate scaffolding	If the approach is novel and new to the students ensure sufficient time is allocated to familiarise them with the ways of working within a specific discipline/task
Guidance	Ensure appropriate time is allocated to providing sufficient structure, access to resources, and clarity about the nature of assessment, prior to engagement with learning
Degree of complexity	Ensure initial tasks are not too complex so that they do not invoke panic and a focus on surface learning among some learners. Gradually move from simple to more complex tasks and graduate according to the needs of the learner – some will be able to handle far more complexity from the outset than others
Volume of workload	Be careful to ensure the volume of work is manageable and *perceived as* manageable by the students. It is students' perception of workload that impacts their approaches to learning
Sufficient time: pace as challenge, not speed and volume of activities	Ensure sufficient time for students to be able to engage in a specific activity to be able to fully assimilate the requirements of the task and to be able to complete it before moving onto another element of work
Group considerations	• Consider the extent to which students have to participate in group work. • Clarify the features of effective group work and model these with the students. • Enable time for students to get used to working in groups and not as individuals within a group. • Ensure opportunities for students to change roles and groups to avoid the notion of the student feeling stuck with a group. • Clarify the rationale behind group choices so as to make these transparent to the learners
Ensure assessment values and rewards the type of learning the students have been asked to engage in	Assessment should require students to think more deeply. Engaging in a class discussion about understanding of a particular theme may encourage a deeper approach than asking students to purely write about a subject

demonstrate the relevance of contemporary understandings of a deep approach to learning and teaching in twenty-first-century learning environments; these comprise McCune and Entwistle's (2011) *disposition to understand;* Evans's (2014) *deep approach in learning to teach*; and Vermunt's *learning patterns*.

A DISPOSITION TO UNDERSTAND

McCune and Entwistle's (2011) concept of a disposition to understand builds on the work of Barnett (2007; 2011). Barnett has articulated the importance of specific dispositions in order to cope with complex twenty-first-century learning contexts. These dispositions include

- a will to learn
- a will to encounter strangeness
- a will to engage
- a preparedness to listen
- a willingness to be changed as a result of one's learning
- a determination to keep going.

(Barnett (2011, p. 11). Whereas a deep approach brings together motivation and learning strategies, thinking dispositions also attend to student sensitivity to the learning context. McCune and Entwistle's (2011, p. 305) *disposition to understand* comprises three components:

1. *Ability to use learning strategies* – 'relating ideas and the critical use of evidence and attention to detail'
2. '*Willingness* to put in the necessary time, effort, and concentration to apply the learning strategies effectively (using organized effort)'
3. *Alertness to the context* within which the learning is taking place, or might take place in the future, 'that monitors the learning processes and strategies in relation to the demands of the task, along with an alertness to opportunities provided by the teaching, and indeed the whole learning environment, to further one's understanding.'

McCune and Entwistle (2011) perceived disposition to understand to be a more consistent and stronger form of a deep approach to learning, in the sense of an *individual wanting to reach the fullest and most satisfying understanding possible at a particular time*. As such this is seen as a stable construct, in that once critical thinking is established it is unlikely to become reversed. However, in terms of sensitivity to context, a student's ability to notice and make best use of affordances may be comprised when s/he is facing new and unfamiliar contexts. This is something identified by Evans, who has argued that students vary in the extent and consistency to which they can activate all three elements in practice (ibid., 2014). An important dimension of the disposition to understand is the emphasis on proactivity in taking ideas forward and specifically the notion of a '*will to offer*' as a crucial element of a will to learn, which McCune and Entwistle (2011, p. 305), drawing on Barnett (2007), define as 'a readiness to put personal understanding into a public arena for critical consideration by others'.

A DEEP APPROACH IN LEARNING TO TEACH

Carol Evans (2014) has highlighted the importance of attending to the *relational dimension* of a deep approach in the context of learning to teach by identifying a student teacher's collaborative, networking, emotional self-regulation, intuitive, and boundary-crossing abilities as important. Evans noted that student teachers' ability to adopt a deep approach to learning as part of their teaching depended on their sense of self, their ability to connect with, and adapt to, the requirements of the learning environment and their perceived 'personal fit' with context; this included their ability to use a deep approach in the selection of appropriate processing and regulation strategies as part of their planning of learning activities and in their delivery. Evans (2014) identified nine characteristics of a deep approach to teaching in twenty-first-century learning environments, as summarized in Table 5.3

Questions for reflection

- Consider the role of the student teacher and mentor in facilitating the development of the nine characteristics of a deep approach, as outlined in Table 5.3.
- What other characteristics would you add to this table from both student teacher and mentor perspectives?

Table 5.3 Developing a deep approach to teaching

	Individual responsibility *How to develop student teacher perspective*	*Support from learning context* *How to support mentor perspective*
(a) student focus on meaning making • use of research-informed approaches to learning and teaching • applying theory within practice effectively • engagement with subject pedagogy • a willingness to critique own approaches to learning • ability to relate ideas and make connections • awareness of the complexity of learning • ability to develop their own theories of learning.		
(b) self-management skills • ability to self-monitor, identify priorities for development, manage the emotional dimension of learning • ability to process and filter information effectively • think on your feet • use feedback judiciously		
(c) perspective able to: • see self from others' perspectives • evaluate own performance objectively • see the bigger picture • juggle teaching and academic study		
(d) noticing • effective use of school networks of support • good understanding of school context • sensitive to the needs of others		

(e) resilience

- high levels of self-efficacy
- confidence in own ability
- good self-understanding
- ability to take risks & learn from mistakes
- repertoire of effective coping strategies

(f) managing personal response to feedback

- openness to feedback and willingness to listen
- ability to question when you do not understand
- ability to use, critique and apply feedback effectively

(g) pro-active feedback- seeking behaviour

- ability to identify good sources of feedback
- ability to seek out feedback from relevant sources and use this effectively
- ability to articulate and negotiate one's own feedback needs
- ability to engage with feedback giver in dialogue
- being prepared to challenge feedback appropriately and to justify one's own position and to modify this where necessary, based on evidence.

(h) adaptability

- ability to apply what you have learnt to the teaching of students
- being able to transfer and adapt learning from one context to another
- abilityto develop a strong sense of agency.

(i) forward thinking

- Ability to use learning to plan ahead for the future – the teacher I am going to be

---

Adapted from Evans, 2014)

LEARNING PATTERNS

This term was conceived by Vermunt (1996, 1998) to stress the malleability rather than the unchangeability of styles. Vermunt and Endedijk

> . . . conceive a learning pattern as a coherent whole of learning activities that learners usually employ, their beliefs about own learning and their learning motivation; a whole that is characteristic of them in a certain period. A learning pattern is thus a coordinating concept, in which the interrelationships between cognitive, affective and regulative learning activities, beliefs about learning and learning motivations are united . . . .
>
> 2011, p. 295

For example, a meaning orientation combines self-regulated learning, a deep approach to processing, perceived control over learning (student cognitions about learning –strong self-efficacy, constructivist learning conceptions, and attributions for academic performance).

Using the *Inventory of Learning Styles* (ILS) (Vermunt, 1994), Vermunt and colleagues discerned four *orientations/patterns* to studying, which combine a number of elements:

- *reproduction-directed* learning (students try to remember subject matter thoroughly in order to able to reproduce it in an exam)
- *meaning-directed* learning (students adopt a deep approach: they try to discover relationships within the subject matter, to get an overview, to be critical and to understand as well as possible the meaning of what they read, see, and hear)
- *application-directed* learning (students try to imagine the subject matter concretely and think about how it can be used in practice), and
- *undirected* learning (students do not know how to learn appropriately for the studies they are doing).

While acknowledging that the ILS measures a broader range of dimensions, the meaning- and reproduction-directed learning orientations echo the deep and surface approaches of Entwistle and Biggs. This suggests *a deep approach is related to self-regulation strategies.*

Exploring style constructs

While there are a vast number of styles instruments, Evans and Waring (2012) in their systematic review of styles research in education (1999–2010) identified that ten instruments were dominant; featuring in 74 per cent of the empirical articles they reviewed (n = 405). When considering the use of specific styles instruments, the *validity*, (the test is actually measuring the construct it is setting out to measure), and *reliability*, (results can be shown to be consistent if one is submitting the test several times, or through the use of an equivalent form of the test), should be taken into account. See Cassidy, 2004; Coffield *et al.*, 2005; Evans and Waring, 2012; Nielsen, 2012; Riding and Rayner, 1998; and Zhang, 2013 for overviews of instruments.)

Most frequently used styles instruments

1 The *Learning Style Inventory* (LSI) (Kolb, 1976). Kolb's model assesses four styles from a combination of two learning dimensions: *concrete experience/abstract conceptualization*

and *reflective observation/active experimentation*. The greatest contribution of the Kolb approach is in the development of the experiential learning cycle rather than specific style types.

2 The *Approaches to Studying Inventory* (ASI) (Entwistle and Ramsden, 1983). There have been many iterations of this construct (see C. Evans, 2003). There are four dimensions: *deep* (intention to understand), *surface* (intention to reproduce), *strategic* (intention to excel), and *apathetic* (lack of direction and interests).
3 The *Study Process Questionnaire* (SPQ) (Biggs, 1987), measures both strategy dimensions (*deep* vs *surface*) and motivational dimensions (*intrinsic, extrinsic,* and *achievement* orientation).
4 The *Group Embedded Figures Test* (GEFT) (Witkin *et al.*, 1962) measures *field-dependency/ independency*. It has been argued that the GEFT actually only measures degrees of field independence (C. Evans *et al.*, 2013). It does not actually measure field dependence and can be seen as more of a measure of ability, given the measurement issue.
5 The *Inventory of Learning Styles* (ILS) (Felderand Silverman, 1988) assesses learner preferences on four dimensions: *active/reflective, sensing/intuitive, visual/verbal,* and *sequential/global.*
6 The *Thinking Styles Inventory* (TSI) (Sternberg and Wagner, 1992) assesses the use of thirteen thinking styles occurring within five dimensions of mental self-government (functions, forms, levels, scopes, leanings). The thirteen thinking styles include: *legislative, judicial, hierarchic, liberal, global* comprising Type I intellectual styles; *executive, monarchic, local, conservative* comprising Type III intellectual styles; and *oligarchic, anarchic, internal, external* comprising Type III intellectual styles (see Zhang and Sternberg, 2006, p. 167 for more detail).
7 The *Learning Styles Inventory* (LSI) (Dunn *et al.*, 1975) combines five major strands called stimuli: environmental, emotional, sociological, physical, and psychological (psychological dimensions include measures of *global analytic, impulsive/reflective, and cerebral dominance*). This model mixes style and non-style dimensions.
8 The *Cognitive Styles Analysis* (CSA) (Riding, 1991), measures two orthogonal dimensions *–wholist vs analytic* and *visual vs verbal.* Questions have been raised about the reliability of the visual-verbal scale (Peterson *et al.*, 2003).
9 The *Inventory of Learning Styles* (ILS) (Vermunt, 1994) includes four styles or patterns: *undirected* (difficulty with assimilating the material), *reproduction* (information is reproduced to complete the task), *application directed* (application of learning material to concrete situations), and *meaning-directed learning* (drawing on existing and related knowledge to achieve deeper understanding).
10 The *Gregorc Style Delineator* (GSD) (Gregorc, 1982) relates to *abstract* vs *concrete* and *sequential* vs *random* styles, creating a combination of four styles: *abstract sequential, abstract random, concrete sequential, and concrete random.*

Evans's (2013a) examination of the period (2010–2013) using the same protocols as used in the Evans and Waring systematic review (2012) identified 201 relevant empirical papers and again noted the dominance of a limited number of instruments and also the increased use of the following instruments:

i *The Myers–Briggs Type Indicator* (MBTI) (Myers, 1976; Myers and McCaulley, 1985), comprising four dimensions based on four of Jung's (1923) personality types: *extraversion/introversion (EI), sensing/intuition (SI), thinking/feeling (TF), and judging/perceiving (JP).*

ii *The Cognitive Styles Index* (CSI): the original Allinson and Hayes (1996) version assesses one dimension of style: *analysis vs intuition*, whereas the modified Hodgkinson and Sadler-Smith (2003) version of the test measures *analysis* and *intuition* as two separate unipolar scales enabling four positions to be identified: *high analytic/high intuitive*; *low analytic/high intuitive*; *high analytic/low intuitive, and low analytic/low intuitive.*

iii The *Visual, Aural, Read/Write, and Kinaesthetic* (VARK), (Fleming and Mills, 1992) is based on principles of sensory perception and measures the four dimensions as per the title of the instrument.

Within this style list approaches to learning/patterns models are dominant (Biggs, 1987; Entwistle and colleagues, e.g. Entwistle and Ramsden, 1983; and Vermunt, 1994) and there is evidence of a substantial increase in their use over other models especially within higher education in recent years. Carol Evans (2013a) noted that in the period 1999–2010 approaches to learning models comprised 20 per cent of styles instruments used in education and in the period (2010–2013) they represented 52 per cent of instruments/models used in education research. Significantly, only the CSI (both versions) and Vermunt's model were deemed to have satisfactory reliability and validity by Coffield *et al.* (2004). Although the Riding, Witkin, and Fleming models assess styles at lower levels of information processing, most of the instruments are assessing higher-order information processing. Some instruments attempt to integrate cognitive style families into one instrument (e.g. Biggs) whereas others try to integrate cognitive style with other psychological variables and therefore cannot be considered as solely measures of cognitive style (e.g. Dunn *et al.*) which considers 21 constructs across a range of individual and contextual variables many of which are not style constructs).

Further style developments

Attempts to unify styles

Many of the approaches to unify styles constructs focused on simplifying styles down to one overriding dimension (e.g. analytic–holist) rested on false assumptions that the left cerebral hemisphere processes information analytically while the right cerebral hemisphere processes information holistically/intuitively. Neuroscientific evidence does not support such a view and instead demonstrates that performance in learning tasks requires both hemispheres to work together in a sophisticated parallel fashion (Howard-Jones, 2010). Furthermore, Kosslyn and Miller (2013) have argued that a better way of understanding the functioning of the brain is to look at how top brain and bottom brain systems interact rejecting the simplistic assumptions about left and right brain.

To unify style constructs Zhang and Sternberg (2006, p. 3) introduced *intellectual styles* as a general term 'that encompasses the meaning of all "style" constructs postulated in the literature, such as cognitive style, conceptual tempo, decision- making and problem-solving style, learning style, mind style, perceptual style, and thinking style'. In their generation of intellectual styles they focused on core concepts which included *high degrees of structure* vs *low degrees of structure*; *cognitive simplicity* vs *cognitive complexity; conformity* vs *non-conformity; authority* vs *autonomy*, and *for group* vs *individual work*. Thirteen thinking styles underpinned by their theory of *mental self-government* result in three intellectual styles

(Types I, II, and III). Type I styles are deemed the most preferential style demonstrating higher levels of creativity/originality, and the ability to process information in more complex ways. Type II styles are typified as requiring more structure and being more rule-bound in their processing of information, which is also at a simpler level than that of Type I. Type III style denotes style flexibility and the ability of a learner to adapt style according to the requirements of the task. Zhang *et al.* (2012) have stressed the pejorative and malleable nature of style and argued that the adoption of Type I styles is preferable in order to engage with twenty-first-century learning requirements (e.g. creative and adaptive thinking); however if the assessment does not require complex thinking, evidence suggests that Type I learners may not achieve more highly than their Type II counterparts (Zhang, 2011). A key recommendation of Zhang and Sternberg's work is to develop Type I capacity using a range of teaching approaches.

Moving forward: an integrated framework

Given that there are so many styles that an individual can draw on in his or her own learning, much attention has turned to trying to understand the relevance of using specific styles in specific contexts and to the relationships between different styles constructs and other individual learning differences. In this section we will look at one approach to integrating the vast body of literature on cognitive styles to facilitate the use of an understanding of styles in learning and teaching.

Cognitive styles differ according to the level of information processing they draw upon (Miller, 1987; Leonard *et al.*, 1999; Nosal, 1990). Bokoros *et al.* (1992) identified three dimensions of cognitive styles working at different levels of cognitive processing: information-processing, thinking–feeling, and attentional focus. Similarly, Leonard *et al.* (1999) identified pure cognitive style (processing of information), decision-making style (individual preferences for various complex decision processes), and decision-making behaviour style (reflecting how individuals approach a decision situation based on the demands of the situation or task). Nosal (1990) went further in suggesting that all styles could be located within a matrix comprising different *levels of information processing* and distinct *cognitive style families*. In developing an integrated framework of cognitive style, Kozhevnikov *et al.* (2014) have further developed the matrix concept of style, identifying *families of styles* operating at *four different levels of information processing*. The *four cognitive style families are* represented by the following:

- *context-dependency* vs *independency* (tendency to perceive events as separate *vs* inseparable from their physical, temporal, or even semantic contexts)
- *analysis* vs *intuition* (driven by rules or relying on heuristic evidence in information scanning)
- *internal* vs *external locus of control* (tendency to locate control of information processing within or outside of oneself)
- *integration* vs *compartmentalisation* (tendency to prefer a compartmentalised/sequential *vs* an integrative/synthetic approach to information processing).

These four types of *cognitive style families* are evident in each of the four *levels of information processing* which are arranged hierarchically from simple to complex, involving *perception, concept formation, higher order cognitive processing*, and at the highest level: *metacognitive processing*. Figure 5.3, adapted from Kozhevnikov *et al.* (2014), demonstrates the two axes of *information processing* (vertical axis) and *cognitive style families* (horizontal). See Kozhevnikov *et al.* (2014) for a more detailed explanation of the matrix and placement of styles within it.

In this matrix it is possible to locate styles instruments that are related to different levels of information processing and constitute specific style families (see Figure 5.3). It is also of value to consider different fields such as business and psychology to identify constructs that are being used in those domains that are also relevant in educational contexts e.g. Kagan's (1966) *reflectivity* vs *impulsivity* dimension of cognitive style and Kirton's (1976) *adaptor* vs *innovator* cognitive style.

In relation to *visual and verbal processing*, Kozhevnikov *et al.* note that different measures of verbal–visual tap different levels of information processing, supporting the possibility of an additional column in the matrix to represent a visual–verbal cognitive style family. While Ozgen *et al.* (2011) argued that spatial abilities predicted visual cognitive style, which in turn predicted visual learning preferences questions have been raised as to whether visual-verbal cognitive styles are distinct from abilities and whether it is that more visual/verbal ability gives rise to *holistic vs. sequential* cognitive style

	Cognitive styles families →			
Levels of information processing ↓	Context dependent *vs* independent	Analysis (rule based) *vs* intuition processing	Locus of processing: internal *vs* external	Integration *vs* compartmentalization
Perception	**Witkin** field in/dependence	**Kagan** reflexivity–impulsivity		**Pask** holist–serialist
Concept formation				
Higher order cognitive processing	**Gregorc** abstract–concrete **Kirton** adaptors – innovators	**Kolb** convergent–divergent **Allinson and Hayes** analysis–intuition **Gregorc** sequential–random	**Biggs** extrinsic–intrinsic motivation	**Biggs, Entwistle** deep–surface strategic approaches to learning **Vermunt** meaning – reproduction – application orientation
Metacognitive processing	**Witkin** mobility–fixity	**Hodgkinson and Sadler-Smith** High analysis – high intuition dimension		

Figure 5.3 Cognitive style matrix

For a full elaboration of the matrix see Kozhevnikov *et al.* (2014). The matrix also helps to explain why some styles which have similar nomenclature do not correlate with each other: they may be working at different levels of information processing. It also helps to identify areas where there are style gaps, such as in the area of concept formation (the ability to respond to common features of categories of objects or events). Concepts are mental categories for objects, events, or ideas that have a common set of features) this area is underrepresented in education styles constructs.

Summary

All learners (teachers and students) use a variety of styles as part of a *cognitive styles profile.* Cognitive styles are ontogenetically flexible individual differences and they are distinct from stationary individual differences (abilities, personality) that are determined primarily by genetic factors and demonstrate only limited sensitivity to ontogenetic factors (environmental and sociocultural). By integrating cognitive psychology, education and neuroscience perspectives it is possible to organize all cognitive styles into an integrated framework considering different cognitive style families and different levels of information processing.

In exploring the malleability of cognitive styles it is important to integrate such understandings with those findings from neuroscience which also suggest malleability in general cognitive ability. The concept of brain *plasticity* is fundamental. The synaptic connections within the brain change with experiences, so although there are many common neuroanatomical features, variations at the synapse level determine individual performance. Learning can change the brain (Dubinsky *et al.*, 2013). Dubinsky *et al.*, 2013, p. 319) have argued that 'teachers can view their practices as designing and providing the experiences that build students' brains so that appropriate behaviours emerge' on the basis that human capabilities (e.g. intelligence, problem-solving) all emerge from the 'complexity arising from uniquely individual histories of synaptic activation superimposed on top of genetically driven basic circuits and anatomy' (ibid, pp. 318–319). Intellectual capacity is amenable to educational influence and a change in the environment changes levels of general cognitive functioning (Adey, *et al.*, 2007; Howard-Jones, 2010). The importance of addressing both student and teacher beliefs about learning and the capacity and potential for change is an essential component of instruction.

Importantly, the use of a matrix to exemplify different levels of cognitive processing and different style families is for the very first time integrating cognitive psychology, neuroscience, and education perspectives, and in doing so provides a clear way forward in how to use styles in practice. For a teacher the question should not be: what is the difference between cognitive style and learning style? Instead, questions should be focused on *what are the specific style constructs as a teacher I need to consider in relation to specific tasks, content, and context?* It is also about knowing *what are the most effective strategies to develop the required styles for specific learning activities*? It is definitely not about categorising learners into style types.

Key readings

Hargreaves, D., Beere, J., Swindells, M., Wise, D., Desforges, C., Goswani, U., Wood, D., Horne, M., and Lownsbrough, H. (2005). *About learning: Report of the Learning Working Group.* London: DEMOS

This report highlights the importance of practitioner and researcher evidence and the value of the synthesis of the two. The need to build a common and comprehensive language of how we learn is emphasized.

Kozhevnikov, M., Evans, C., and Kosslyn, S. (2014). Cognitive style as environmentally-sensitive individual differences in cognition: A modern synthesis and applications in education, business and management. *Psychological Sciences in the Public Interest,* 15(1), 3–33.
This publication provides some of the latest thinking on cognitive styles and is significant in offering a unified conceptual framework which integrates psychology, education and neuroscience perspectives. It highlights the hierarchical nature of styles and highlights the malleability of styles through individuals' interactions with their environments. For other recent updates see Zhang (2013) and Zhang et al. (2012).

Riding, and Rayner, S. (1998). *Cognitive styles and learning strategies: Understanding style differences in learning and behaviour.* London: David Fulton.
This book provides a comprehensive overview of cognitive and learning styles and is a good entry level publication in which to explore the evolution of styles.

Weblinks

Coffield, F., Moseley, D., Hall, E., and Ecclestone, K. (2005). *Learning styles and pedagogy in post-16 learning: a systematic and critical review.* Available online at http://sxills.nl/lerenlerennu/bronnen/Learning%20styles%20by%20Coffield%20e.a.pdf (accessed 14 January 2014).

Coffield, F., Moseley, D., Hall, E., and Ecclestone, K. (2005). Thinking skills framework for post-16 learners: an evaluation. Available online at http://www.google.co.uk/url?sa=tand rct=jand q=and esrc=sand source=weband cd=1and ved=0CDIQFjAA and url=http%3A%2F%2Fvital.new.voced.edu.au%2Fvital%2Faccess%2Fservices%2FDownload%2Fngv%3A20216%2FSOURCE2andei=SYnWUsGxF4Kd7gbyw4D4CAandusg=AFQjCNEGUI5UTg-a3ji9hZsntSLcp-Cl0Q> (accessed 14 January 2014).

ELSIN: Education, Learning, Styles, Individual differences Network (ELSIN). Online. Available online at http://www.elsinnetwork.com (accessed 10 June 2013).

Higgins, S., Hall, E., Baumfield, V., Moseley, D. (2005). A meta-analysis of the impact of the implementation of thinking skills approaches on pupils. In *Research Evidence in Education Library.* London: EPPI-Centre, Social Science Research Unit, Institute of Education, University of London. Available online at https://eppi.ioe.ac.uk/cms/Default.aspx?tabid=339 (accessed 14 January 2014).

Institute for Learning. Available online at http://www.ifl.ac.uk/publications/challenging-professional-learning (accessed 14 January 2014).

Chapter 6

The application of styles

Dispelling the misconceptions

Overview

In this chapter we will highlight and reinforce the key issues and provide clear guidance on how to use styles effectively within practice. There are many misconceptions about styles and their use within learning and teaching. In seeking to address these misconceptions within the styles field we will examine some of the enduring and commonly held myths about styles and related constructs. In addition to an overview of key issues impacting on the application of styles, we will specifically examine the notions of *VAK*, consider whether or not *multiple intelligences* actually exist or matter, and reconceptualize the *style matching hypothesis*. In doing so we will identify implications for your teaching. We will argue that it is important to focus on overarching principles involved in the application of styles rather than to focus on attempts to differentiate between different styles constructs. The concept of enriched cognitive styles pedagogies will also be introduced and exemplified using the PLSP.

Key issues impacting the application of styles,

In critiquing the styles field we found 'a lack of consensual theory; confusing terminology; difficulties in identifying valid and reliable measures; and vague practical implications' (Evans and Waring, 2012, p. 295). The difficulty of making information available to practitioners to ensure the appropriate use of styles research is an issue (Goswani, 2006) and compounded by the fact that few teachers use information from the research community to inform their understanding of styles (Martin, 2010). Along with the need for clear dissemination of reliable and valid information about cognitive styles, there is a clear need for integrated professional development to establish a common framework to address the concerns raised by D. Hargreaves *et al.* (2005, p. 5):

> 'In many schools there is also no agreed vocabulary in which teachers might talk with their students about their learning, even though this is at the very heart of professional practice.'

The following list is of those key factors that have limited the effective translation of styles research into practice:

- *Lack of consensual theory:* cognitive styles models have not until now (*styles matrix*) been mapped onto contemporary psychology constructs to build a common language of individual differences; the work of Kozhevnikov *et al.* (2014) is important in seeking to address this issue having been developed in relation to current research in education, psychology and neuroscience.

- *Confusing terminology:* Evans and Waring (2012) identified the use of 84 differently named models in their review of 486 articles on the use of style in education and higher education environments which is confirmatory of other studies (Cassidy, 2004; Coffield *et al.*, 2004; Desmedt and Valke, 2004), however, they also noted the predominance of just ten models, as outlined previously. It is not just the number of styles but the inconsistent use of terms that has led to obfuscation within the field, leading to a call to rationalize the number of style instruments and to clearly demonstrate which are most relevant and in which combinations and to which specific contexts (Riding, 2000).
- *Valid and reliable measures*: Coffield *et al.* (2004, p. 141) found that only one style measure (Allinson and Hayes's CSI and its modified Hodgkinson and Sadler-Smith version) satisfied all four of their criteria (internal consistency, test–retest reliability, construct validity, and predicted validity). The report is valuable in raising questions about mis/informed use of styles. The detailed and arbitrary focus of Coffield *et al.* on only thirteen styles, including some that would not be classified as cognitive styles is a limitation of the report, but like Sharp, Bowker, and Byrne (2008) it does raise important questions about the appropriate and misappropriate use of styles. Evans and Waring (2012) in their review of styles found evidence of rigour (reliability and validity) in over 50 per cent of the articles, and highlighted the difference between styles pedagogies of *plenty* and those of *poverty* (Evans and Waring, 2009). While the importance of reliability and rigour are fundamental (Hodgkinson *et al.*, 2001), additional issues include sustainability (is the intervention enabling a student to take responsibility for their learning and it is manageable?) David Hargreaves *et al.* (2005) also draw attention to the importance of the integration of practice as well as research evidence, valuing the information gathered from practitioners.
- *Research design:* quantitative, cross-sectional and single-source designs are dominant within styles research but whether these research designs can fully capture the complexities of what is going on in the learning environment has been questioned. The need for more collaborative alternative research designs, located within practice settings, featuring expert as well as novice learners, employing more mixed methodological (qualitative and quantitative) and longitudinal designs has been advocated (Evans and Kozhevnikov, 2011); there is growing evidence of these (Evans and Waring, 2012; Gijbels *et al.*, 2014). The need to test more complete models that consider the inter-relationships between styles, other individual difference variables, and other contexts, has been highlighted (Ferla *et al.*, 2009). At the same time the need for a greater focus on evidence-based practice within education has been highlighted (Mayer, 2009; Pashler *et al.*, 2009). There are calls for more experimental studies featuring randomized control trials to properly measure the size of the effects (Pashler *et al.*, 2009), although whether such designs can fully capture the intricacies inherent in styles in education contexts is debateable. Cognitive styles also interact with other individual learning difference and contextual variables in impacting on outcomes (Renzulli and Sullivan, 2009). Clarifying the nature of the role of style in relation to other variables in impacting on performance (Furnham, 2012) is seen as crucial to the development of the field.

- *Measurement issues:* the dominant reliance on paper and pen inventories to measures styles compared to measuring observable behaviours is a criticism levelled at the field. There are also questions as to whether styles models developed for one specific context are applicable to another. Making sense of findings from different dimensions of cognitive style deduced from instruments or through observation of actual behaviours is difficult. Much research has focused on lower-order cognitive tasks (e.g. Kagan's Matching Familiar Figures Test; Witkin's field dependence (FD) and field independence (FI)) were often assessed by performance measures (error rate and response time) with simple 'right' and 'wrong' answers. Instead of measuring bipolar dimensions that represent two equally efficient ways of solving tasks, in reality these tests measure only a single pole of the dimension (e.g. EFT assesses only the level of field-independency). The result is that these tests are more like tests of spatial ability than measurements of style. As noted by Evans *et al.* (2013) most measures of field independence measure variations in FI alone: FD is not measured, it is implied. Furthermore, there are many different versions of tests that claim to measure FI, and it is highly likely that they are not measuring the same construct.
- *Focus:* much of the research on cognitive styles in education has focused on investigating the complex nature of the relationships between different style constructs (e.g. cognitive styles, learning styles, approaches to studying, thinking styles, intellectual styles, dispositions to learning, and learning patterns) along with other individual learning style difference variables (e.g. abilities, personality constructs, gender, culture). Pedagogical interventions associated with cognitive styles research in education have focused on the use of styles approaches to support students in managing their own learning transitions; the development of style flexibility; the relevance of the matching hypothesis to 21st-century learning environments; the potential of e-learning applications informed by an understanding of styles, and impacts of interventions on students' approaches to learning. In reporting findings, great emphasis has been placed on students' learning preferences and satisfaction levels: the translation of this into positive learning outcomes has been more difficult to ascertain. Clearer reporting is required regarding the precise nature of interventions and the context of studies, along with greater discussion concerning the variable impact of pedagogical interventions on different groups of students. Akbulut and Cardak's (2012) review of 70 articles on adaptive hypermedia environments (AHE) and cognitive styles found that few of the research articles addressed the effectiveness of adaptive hypermedia designs, and they identified the need for research to focus more directly on the concrete outcomes of specific designs. Carol Evans *et al.* (2013) noted a bias of emphasis in styles in education research, with greater attention being afforded to style deficits in learning and remediation of such deficits rather than looking at the potential value for all students of a more in-depth appraisal of high levels of performance. Vogel-Walcutt *et al.* (2011) also noted that the principles of learning efficiency could be examined further within the context of higher-order cognitive skills, and compared the principles with other strategies with learners on the expertise continuum from novice to expert to consider the most appropriate teaching strategies to maintain impact for a broader spectrum of learners. Along similar lines, Nosal (2009) noted that research has mainly focused on students' dominant learning preferences and has ignored 'differences in the area of aversion'; research could be enriched by a greater focus on what learners avoid.

- *Dissemination:* Evans and Waring (2012) found that less than 23 per cent of the articles they reviewed that were focused on the use of styles approaches within teaching went beyond a superficial and uncritical discussion of the use of broad range of styles within educational contexts, giving a practitioner little specific guidance to use in context. Clear guidance is required on effective ways of using styles research and related concepts in practice to inform pedagogy and curricula, along with a clear and consistent definition of what a cognitive styles pedagogy comprises within twenty-first-century learning environments. We will elaborate on what constitutes an *enriched cognitive styles pedagogy* later on within this chapter and we will explicitly discuss how to apply the Personal Learning Styles Pedagogy in chapters four, six, eight, nine, ten, and eleven).

Examining VAK, multiple intelligences, and the style matching hypothesis

The use and abuse of VAK

Evans and Waring (2012) noted the relatively poor use of styles research within schools and particularly the misuse of visual, verbal and kinaesthetic (VAK) styles. While there remain debates about whether these perceptual preferences are styles or abilities, and about how these map to other cognitive styles, we do know that it *is not possible to be visual or verbal*. The work of Blazhenkova and Kozhevnikov (2009) and their development of the Object–Spatial Imagery and Verbal Questionnaire (OSIVQ) based on cognitive psychology and neuroscience evidence demonstrates the existence of two functionally and anatomically distinct visual processing systems: visual-spatial and visual-object with verbalization forming a separate processing network.

> . . . *verbalisers,* . . . prefer to process information verbally . . . *object visualisers,*. . . . prefer to generate colourful, pictorial, high-resolution images of objects, and excel on visual-object tasks and in visual art, and *spatial visualisers,*. . . . prefer to represent schematic images and spatial relationships, and excel on visual-spatial tasks and in natural science and engineering. . . .
>
> Blazhenkova *et al.*, 2011, p. 282

Blazhenkova and Kozhevnikov (2009) found that object and spatial scales and verbal and spatial scales were negatively correlated, suggesting some negative interference between object and spatial information processing and between verbal and spatial processing but not between object and verbal processing. Thomas and McKay (2010) highlighted the importance of encouraging versatility in students given that students with high scores on all three styles (*object visualisers, spatial visualisers, verbalisers*) showed good comprehension irrespective of the design of materials they were presented with. Given that learners use both visual and verbal processing it is not surprising that trying to match instruction to a particular modality produces mixed and inconsistent findings. Kavale, Hirshorenoren and Forness (1998) found no significant learning gains from matching modalities. We do, however, know that the concept of *dual coding* is important; this assumes that visual and verbal systems are involved in all cognitive activities (Paivio, 2006). Presenting information in both visual and textual form can enhance memory (P. D. Klein, 2003;

Paivio and Csapo, 1973). Neuroscientific evidence supports this theory and has shown that *multimodal approaches* produce additional brain activity over and above that produced by experiencing each mode separately. It is also known that the use of multiple strategies by learners has led to improved memory performance (Howard-Jones, 2010).

MI (multiple intelligences): do they exist and do they matter?

Multiple intelligences are not styles. The MI theory is built around the premise that individuals have a number of separate and distinct intelligences (*linguistic, logical-mathematical, spatial, musical, bodily–kinaesthetic, intrapersonal, interpersonal, naturalistic*) rather than possessing a single all-purpose intelligence (Gardner, 1983). Evidence shows that this is simply incorrect; there is no *'convincing evidence for the independence of each of the supposed intelligences from one another'*, (Adey *et al.*, 2007, p. 79; Cooper, 2012; Visser *et al.*, 2006). As noted by Howard-Jones (2010, p. 21) 'MI theory is in direct opposition to the idea of a unitary general intelligence factor 'g', reflecting overall brain efficiency and the close interconnection of our mental skills'. Research shows that general ability, *g*, is a potent predictor of school (and work) performance – e.g. Kuncel *et al.* (2004). However, while the theoretical basis for MI does not exist, there remains much support for the application of MI in schools. Hattie (2012) referencing Gardner (2009) highlights that Gardner himself had emphasized that the most important implications of his theory were that practitioners should pay attention to individual differences and decide on what was really important in a discipline and teach it in several different ways supporting the notion of multiple ways of teaching. From a cognitive styles perspective we would argue it is more about identifying the *most appropriate way to convey and teach a specific aspect of a subject rather than multiple ways, which could lead to cognitive overload.* In explaining the possible cited benefits of MI approaches in the classroom, such benefits may derive from the following.

- Explaining things in different ways and mediums may tap into *dual coding theory*–so representations are laid down in both verbal and visual processing systems supporting conversion into long-term memory and retrieval.
- Rehearsing ideas and practising them using a variety of approaches as suggested by MI may help to reduce the load placed on working memory. In considering cognitive overload, *cognitive load theory* is relevant (CLT). This is based around the principle of reducing load on working memory. 'Working memory refers to our capacity to temporarily hold a limited set of information in our attention when we are processing it . . . .' (Howard-Jones (2010, p. 9).
- Using more imaginative approaches within the classroom and variety may stimulate student engagement in learning and also promote learner autonomy. MI applications may help promote students' ability to be active learners.
- MI approaches may be seen as empowering students with its emphasis on individuality in learning and celebration of individual talents helping to promote a more fluid interpretation of intelligence which is empowering to learners.

While MI approaches to teaching are being adopted as part of *constructivist learning design*, implementation is highly variable and a consensus on what constitutes an MI approach is lacking. Hattie (2012) argued that *there is no need to classify students into different intelligences*: the important element is to have multiple ways of teaching. An *enriched cognitive styles pedagogy* would suggest it is more about the most appropriate approaches in relation to the demands of the task, needs of the students, and context.

Should we match students' learning and teachers' teaching styles? Reconceptualization of the matching hypothesis

The traditional concept of the matching hypothesis is that people learn better when teaching is aligned to an individual's cognitive style (Mayer, 2011) and/or when styles are mismatched using the broader interpretation of the matching hypothesis (Pashler *et al.*, 2009). However, Evans and Waring (2012) have seriously questioned the utility of the matching hypothesis and have argued that the *matching hypothesis has limited value in the development of effective styles pedagogies*. The lack of evidence of positive outcomes from matching (Hattie, 2004; Pashler, *et al.*, 2009, Pham, 2012; Riener and Willingham; 2010; Scott, 2010) cannot be used to confirm the lack of relevance of styles to instruction given that the premise is fundamentally flawed (Kozhevnikov, Evans and Kosslyn, 2014). Findings from the literature are mixed with supporters (Dunn *et al.*, 1995) and detractors of style matching (see Landrum and McDuffie, 2010 for a review).

So why is the matching hypothesis concept flawed?

We argue that the existence or non-existence of styles cannot be ascertained from the mixed findings of matching studies alone. We present the following arguments that question the utility of the matching hypothesis.

- *How do I decide which cognitive style to match?* Cognitive styles as we have outlined previously are predominantly *multidimensional*. Each learner has a *cognitive styles profile* comprising different layers of the cognitive style hierarchy with styles operating at different levels of information processing. *Styles do not operate in isolation* from each other and from other individual learning differences and contextual variables (Furnham, 2012; Renzulli and Sullivan, 2009). Acknowledging the complex nature of cognitive style and the interaction of styles with other variables (person-bound and contextual), it would be very difficult to determine which style(s) to match (Evans and Waring, 2012). The existence of *style flexibility* impacts on the relevance of traditional notions of the matching hypothesis. Styles may be based on the environment and task rather than forming consistent patterns (Menaker and Coleman, 2007), with some learners being more flexible than others and with some styles being more amenable to change than others. Newcombe and Stieff (2012) noted that learners can employ multiple strategies and frequently switch strategies to problem-solve, which supports the limited utility of the matching hypothesis.
- *How do I identify style? To match a style you need to identify it.* While there are robust and valid style measures (Evans and Waring, 2012) many lack validity (see chapter five). Judicious use of styles instruments is required. We have argued that *whether one needs to use a styles instrument in teaching at all also needs to be questioned; it is more about applying principles of good practice*. In summary, if measurement is employed the judicious use of it along with careful interpretation of findings is essential.
- *Is teaching to one style possible and appropriate?* Perry Klein (2003) argued that curricular activities cannot be categorized by modality, in that most kinds of knowledge involve representations of more than one modality and engage many perceptual

> modalities. Teaching to one modality would be difficult to do. Alferink and Farmer-Dougan (2010) have argued that it is highly improbable that in any given lesson, only one style of learning would be stimulated, and that teaching to specific modalities is actually happening in reality. It is more likely that individuals are processing information across several and not one sensory modality. In addition, they argued that teaching to a student's strength and not attending to a student's less developed styles may be a disservice to students.

Much of the matching hypothesis literature has focused on the matching of perceptual cognitive styles and specifically (*verbal, visual, and kinesthetic styles* (VAK)); the relatively poor understanding of VAK especially in applications to school contexts has long been a concern for styles in education research (Sharp *et al.*, 2008). The concept of teaching to a preferred modality is not supported by neuroscience findings which have identified that *verbal and visual modalities are actually independent of one another*; in that most learners have mixed modality preferences (Blazhenkova *et al.*, 2011; P. D. Klein, 2003).

What does a reconceptualization of the matching hypothesis mean for your teaching?

> . . . A single-minded focus on style accommodation may limit the creation of tools and strategies that support the development and improvement in learning-specific cognitive functioning among students.
>
> (Rittschof, 2010, p. 110)

Increasing emphasis is now placed on developing ways to *encourage learners to adapt to different learning environments rather than to design adaptive systems* (designed to cater for individual styles) (Choi *et al.*, 2009). Styles approaches to support learning include:

- Focusing on the development of the *most appropriate cognitive styles in relation to the requirements of the task(s)* (P. D. Klein, 2003: Zhang *et al.*, 2012). Willingham (2005) and Lalley and Gentile (2009) have also argued the importance of focusing on the best modality for the specific content/context rather than focusing on individual style preferences. Kolloffel (2012) in the context of perceptual preferences, argued that learning is more influenced by the extent to which a format affords cognitive processing rather than a match between a used and preferred format, and that students should not choose on the basis of their preferences, because this might lead learners to select format(s) that are less effective for learning. Perry Klein (2003) and Menaker and Coleman (2007) have advocated that less emphasis should be placed on the matching hypothesis idea and instead greater attention should be afforded to the potential benefits of dual coding and cognitive load theories in supporting learner development.
- Supporting students to become more sensitive and proficient in using *multiple alternative strategies*,
  - working with students to develop *self-regulatory abilities* through a better understanding of how they learn, and
  - development of appropriate strategies to deploy the most appropriate styles within each given situation (Evans and Waring, 2009; 2012).

- Sadler-Smith (2012) has argued that the metacognitive capacity of learners is dependent on their understanding of learning processes, arguing for the importance of integrating an understanding of style into instruction. If students are to develop the skills to self-monitor more effectively, understanding the role of styles in relation to managing the demands of different learning contexts is vital.
- Judicious use of the matching initiative in specific contexts (e.g. when learners are facing important learning transitions and in relation to the role of specific cognitive styles in supporting access to and completion of a task). Accommodation as well as the development of learners' styles is complex. This approach requires identification of both the most appropriate means to teach a specific area of content, an analysis of which styles are most implicated in this, as well as awareness of the individual differences a learner brings to the learning context. Evans and Waring (2012) have identified that in the completion of certain tasks and in the context of certain style constructs matching can be important especially when learners are facing important learning transitions (Riding and Rayner, 1998; Snow and Lohman, 1984). Riding's work with colleagues is extensively reported in Riding and Rayner (1998), where the format of materials and interrelationships with students' cognitive style as measured by the Cognitive Styles Analysis (Riding, 1991) was found to significantly impact on student performance (e.g. size of diagrams and arrangements of images on a page impacted on certain students' access to information more than others). Within the e-learning and styles research literature there is also similar evidence of interactions between the nature of instruction, styles and context (Handal and Herrington, 2004; Rittschof, 2010).

Using styles in practice

We have highlighted the need for clear guidance on effective ways of using styles research in practice (Evans and Waring, 2012). There have been many difficulties in ensuring the effective translation of effective research into practice (e.g. complexity of the styles construct the proliferation of unreliable tools). From a practitioner-access perspective Goswani (2006) has argued the need for more effective brokers to bridge the research-practitioner divide which is paramount given Martin's (2010) finding that few teachers consulted research articles. Higher education institutions need to be looking at how networks can be developed to ensure exchange of valid and reliable information and in an accessible form. This is, however, not enough as co-ordinated and integrated continuing professional development in schools is required to develop a common language and shared understanding of learning processes including styles – which is currently lacking (E. Hargreaves, 2005). As part of this agenda D. Hargreaves *et al.* (2005) have stressed the importance of researchers and practitioners working together collaboratively to ensure research informs practice and practice informs research, highlighting the importance of valuing practitioner research in order to build a lexicon of learning to include styles especially in the context of teacher education and training.

Such collaboration has been the case with the development of the PLSP which is a genuine example of an integrated research–practice approach to enhancing learning and teaching through the informed use of styles. Central to the PLSP is the importance of supporting learners to become more metacognitively aware of their own learning processes through knowledge and understanding of cognitive styles (Evans and Waring, 2009; 2011d). As part of this, we have argued that learners need to know that

- cognitive styles are complex and are predominantly multidimensional
- different style constructs measure different aspects of style
- development of specific styles may be more or less relevant to certain contexts
- preference for one type of processing does not preclude development of alternative processing options
- cognitive styles can be developed: however style specialization may be more appropriate in certain contexts
- the range of cultural contexts that an individual inhabits impacts on individual use and development of styles
- cognitive styles interact with other variables
- greater awareness of cognitive styles can enable individuals to make more informed decisions about their learning and support the development of learner autonomy.

Enriched styles pedagogies

In trying to clarify what constitutes an effective styles pedagogy, through a synthesis of two systematic reviews of the literature Evans (2013a) has made the distinction between *enriched* and *impoverished* styles pedagogies. Table 6.1 highlights key parameters that practitioners should consider in the use and application of styles. Enriched styles pedagogies consider how styles operate within the broader context of differential psychology and include sociological and cultural factors (Moskvina and Kozhevnikov, 2011); they are holistic in their integration of ideas from different theoretical perspectives and different fields of enquiry in order to maximize learning opportunities for all learners within given contexts. They consider diverse aspects of a learner's cognitive styles profile (Zhang and Sternberg, 2006): individuality in learning is accommodated through an understanding of key principles of effective styles pedagogies rather than through individualized instruction. Enriched styles pedagogies are judicious in their use of instruments (P. D. Klein, 2003; Ritter, 2007; Yates, 2000). A key feature of enriched cognitive styles pedagogies is the challenge element in learning and the central involvement of the learner with an emphasis on self-regulatory development.

Flipping the classroom

There is other extensive evidence of the use of cognitive styles in pedagogy especially in relation to e-technologies. A key finding is that *effective use of e-technologies depends on the pedagogy underpinning it* (Gilbert *et al.*, 2011). Flipping has received much attention in the last few years. It is defined as a 'pedagogical model in which the typical lecture and homework elements of a course are reversed' (Educause, 2012). There are many different models of flipping: the main intention of all of these, however, is to increase student engagement in learning. A PLSP approach to this issue provides a critically reflective stance through which to guide decisions associated with such flipped designs. Fundamentally such an approach is about students arriving 'warmed up' to a teaching session having already engaged in the content and therefore, in theory, being more able to engage in meaningful discussions about the nature and requirements of the specific learning tasks. Using the PLSP key pedagogical decisions can be seen to revolve around:

Table 6.1 Impoverished and enriched cognitive styles pedagogies

Impoverished cognitive styles pedagogies (lacking sustainability)	*Enriched cognitive styles pedagogies (promoting autonomy in learning)*
Use of diverse learning and teaching approaches (pedagogical sheep dip approach) to promote style flexibility but without a clear rationale and understanding of the needs of the learner and requirements of the context. Too much challenge/overload, creating destructive friction	Measured use of different learning and teaching approaches aligned to curriculum goals to support development of style flexibility in relation to learner needs and the requirements of the context. Sufficient challenge to enable style development. Scaffolded approach enabling constructive friction
Lack of awareness of the pejorative nature of styles and the need to promote and develop certain styles over others in specific contexts and/or deploy appropriate strategies to manage style fixidity	Approaches focused on enhancing awareness and the development of certain styles over others for specific purposes and contexts as part of styles development. Supporting learners to manage relative levels of styles flexibility
Indiscriminate use of styles instruments. Used as labelling rather than as learning tools.	Judicious use of instruments. Focused on the metacognitive potential of styles training to support learners in managing their own learning
Accommodation of styles/styles-matching to the exclusion of the development of styles	Understanding of where styles matching may be appropriate but greater emphasis placed on the development of styles and strategies in order to support students to self-regulate their own learning
Myopic focus – narrow understanding of different styles constructs; lack of awareness of the complex nature of an individual's cognitive styles profile and the operation of styles at different levels of a cognitive styles hierarchy	Wide focus – broad understanding of different styles constructs and the multidimensional and hierarchical nature of cognitive styles comprising an individual's cognitive styles profile
Lack of attention given to the holistic experience of the learner and the inter–relationship of cognitive styles with other individual differences and contextual variables	Consideration of the holistic experience of the learner and the interrelationship of cognitive styles with other individual differences and contextual variables
One-off styles training events. Training in understanding of cognitive styles limited to induction or one-off specific training events. Lack of follow up. Training not integrated into curriculum design	Integrated and developmental approach to cognitive styles training. Understanding of styles used to underpin curriculum development and delivery including assessment as part of iterative and progressive designs
Styles 'done to learners'. Lack of discussion with students about why styles instruments are being used, what results mean, and the implications of such findings for supporting the development of learning	Working with learners to enhance self-regulatory capacity through explicit discussion of the rationale for using or not using styles instruments. Clarification of the meaning of results/training in order to support learners to consider the most appropriate use of styles and strategies in specific contexts
Learners as passive recipients of cognitive styles training.	Learners as active participants responsible for managing their own development through use of strategies aimed at enhancing their metacognitive skills

- clarifying the purpose and value of such an approach with learners who may have a product *vs* a process view of learning (PLSP Component A): stating how this is relevant and authentic to how the students are being assessed, as well as the value of such approaches to them more widely as part of an integrated pedagogy (Gale, 2006)
- in the design of online content (videos, pre-released PowerPoints, quizzes) considering overarching principles of good design (nature and volume of content: focused and specific *vs* broad; multiple resources *vs* limited resources); nature of content and how best presented (level of direction to resources (explicit/guided *vs* unguided) (PLSP components B, D)
- explicitly exploring with the students their role in the process (leader, facilitator, receiver) (PLSP components C, D, and E)
- agreeing with students the level of choice they have in participating in flipped activities and options to work individually and collaboratively (PLSP components A–E).

Experiences of flipping with students using the PLSP have suggested the importance of

- highly focused pre-lesson/session tasks
- clear direction to resources
- judicious and careful selection of resources to prevent overloading
- setting specific, structured tasks
- it being a collaborative venture between students and teacher with students as active partners
- activities scaffolded to enable progression over time
- opportunities within teaching sessions for students to demonstrate what they know and what they do not know
- ensuring an ongoing cycle of learning by following up on areas of uncertainty raised by students to feed into subsequent teaching sessions
- students taking the lead in following up on ideas with guided support
- and, most importantly
- ensuring buy-in from the students in the first place.

In attending to the heightened focus on active learning it is also important to remember the value of the didactic approach. The lecture (students passive and/or interactive) and the PowerPoint all have their place within learning; the issue is choosing the right approach to meet the demands of the learning context. Flipping is also a useful tool to be used appropriately to engage students in their learning in relation to the requirements of the context and task.

The importance of the central role of the student in the learning process is evident in McCune and Entwistle's (2011) work advocating the importance of encouraging a deep approach within teaching; increasing learner awareness of the processes of thinking and understanding; encouraging the use of authentic open-ended problems; cultivating a sense of legitimate participation, and using e-technologies in such a way as to encourage high levels of openness and interaction between multiple users. Rosenfeld and Rosenfeld (2011) have also emphasized the important role of the learner and teacher in sensitizing individuals to how they learn. There have been a number of initiatives focused on developing metacognitive, self-regulated, and motivational aspects of learning although Adey *et al.* (2007) have argued that many of these initiatives are under-theorized and short on empirical evidence of effects. One international research organization committed to the translation of evidence based approaches to styles pedagogies is that of the Education, Learning, Styles, Individual differences Network (*ELSIN*), established in 1999 to support the development of research into styles and related fields and translation into practice.

Summary

Teaching to one style is not appropriate. It is important to support the development of the most appropriate styles and strategies required for the specific learning task/context. Adey *et al.* have argued the importance of teaching for *cognitive stimulation* vs *efficient instruction* in subject matter; our PLSP approach encourages an integrated approach in that it should be possible to combine the two. Adey *et al.* note the massive challenge for all educators in ensuring the creation of sufficient (not too little and not too much for all learners in order to enhance current processing capability). To support such development they have made the following suggestions:

- Learning should be collaborative in that learners listen, argue, justify and become accustomed to changing their positions. This concurs with Dubinsky *et al.*'s (2013) emphasis on the suitability of constructivist learning environments to effect change.
- The emphasis should be on learning processes involving:
    - the need to raise awareness in students of what may be abstracted from any domain specific learning (e.g. factors in the concept-organization and quantity of information that cause difficulties in representing and processing);
    - connecting ideas to concepts already in learners'possession; and
    - development of self-regulation.
- The present learning experience needs to be connected to learning that has gone before (e.g. does it involve the mastery of similar concepts? How does the present experience relate to previous ones? How was learning handled previously?).

In considering these suggestions, addressing students' emotional experiences of learning is also essential (C. Evans, 2014) especially given the neuroscientific evidence suggesting that the emotional salience of an event influences the strength of its associated memory (Dubinsky *et al.*, 2013).

The cognitive styles field has considerable utility. It is important in contributing to our understanding of why we are more successful in some areas of learning than in others. It can be very constructive for young children as it focuses direction away from concepts of intelligence and the belief 'I'm not good enough' to considering ways in which individuals can access learning, and it is essential to ongoing learning for twenty-first-century learners. It sensitizes us to the way that others learn. It makes us think about what approach we are promoting in the classroom. It encourages us to use a variety of approaches and to open up dialogue with ourselves and other learners about the way in which we learn increasing metacognitive awareness, and provides a vocabulary to enable us to do so. As teachers and learners it demands that we use the research evidence and theory to think about our delivery, the resources that we use, the nature of the assessment, our styles of questioning, and our reactions to individual students, in a more timely and informed fashion.

Questions for reflection

- Consider the twelve statements below and indicate in each case whether you agree (A), disagree (D), or are unsure (U)

		A	D	U
1	Cognitive style is fixed and not modifiable.			
2	Cognitive style is consistent across situations and contexts.			
3	Different subject disciplines may promote different cognitive styles.			
4	If I match the style of a student s/he will do better.			
5	How I present material will impact variably on the learning of those of different cognitive styles.			
6	If students are grouped in similar styles they will do better.			
7	Those deemed to be less academic will struggle more if materials do not match their own cognitive style(s).			
8	Students vary in their style malleability.			
9	Using styles in teaching means I need to adapt my teaching to each individual student's styles.			
10	Cognitive style is influenced by cultural factors.			
11	Cognitive styles matter most when students are facing difficult learning transitions.			
12	Cognitive styles impact on how students receive, interpret and use information.			

See Appendix 6a, in this chapter, for elucidation regarding these statements

Questions for reflection

Table 6.2 asks you to consider in detail a number of elements of your teaching from a cognitive styles perspective.

Key terms referred to in the table include:

Wholist–analytic (Riding)

Wholists see the situation as a whole, and are able to have an overall perspective; analytics see the situation as a collection of parts and will often focus on one or two aspects.

Impulsivity–reflectivity (Kagan)

Impulsive students scan information quickly in order to make a decision, whereas reflective students analyse each part rationally and systematically. In lay terms, impulsivity is often judged as negative in that impulsive individuals are more prone to errors; from a cognitive styles perspective it is not a pejorative term in that impulsivity – ability to process quickly – may not necessarily imply a lack of accuracy.

Analysis–intuition (Hodgkinson and Sadler-Smith)

Analysis refers to reflectivity: rational, sequential and logical thinking, and intuition to impulsivity, creativity, thinking on one's feet.

Table 6.2 Self-review table checklist on approaches to teaching from a styles perspective

Dimension	*Key questions*
1 Volume of material	• What are the essential core concepts I need to get across? • How can this material be organized in different ways? • What is the essential information that I need to provide learners with, and what can they find for themselves or be directed to? • What can the students be given in advance so they are warmed up for the activity? • How am I assessing prior learning so that I can build on what the learner already knows?
2 Modes of presentation	• What is the best way to present and design information in relation to: o the nature of the content? o the required outcomes of the task? • How can I make information more accessible to the learner? • How do I know whether they see what I see? • What opportunities are there within lessons for students to explain your (teacher) diagrams/graphs/notes from the students' perspectives (what they see)? • Are my choices of materials/resources inclusive for all students? • To what extent do I use the resources of the students (their ideas/ invite them to bring in resources)?
3 Number of channels of information	To what extent does presenting information in different ways support and/or impede learning? • When is it best to present most of the information in one mode to support learning? When is it best to combine a variety of formats to get across an idea? • How am I encouraging learners to develop understanding by having to explain in a different mode to the one I delivered in (e.g. dual coding idea – explaining verbally – asking students to explain concept in a different medium – drawing, dance, graphically, etc.)?

4 Pace, speed and number of transitions between activities	What is the impact of pace on different types of learning and for different learners? • Are the number of activities supporting or reducing the quality of learning? • Is the speed of transitions impacting access to learning for students? • Does being busy equate to learning?
5 Holistic *vs* analytic perspectives	How does your organization of information promote holistic (wholist/ overview) *vs* analytic (detailed rational) thinking? • To what extent do you emphasize detail *vs* the overview within teaching and learning? • Do you start with an overview of a subject area (explaining how all areas fit together) and/or do you go systematically through content areas without the overview first)? • Do you regularly employ the use of overviews and summaries of key ideas? • To what extent do you involve the students in providing overviews and summaries of information and ideas? • How can you help students to take a step back in order to be able to see the bigger picture? • How do you help students to structure and organize their own work?
6 Structure and organization of lessons Design of learning sequences (tangential *vs* sequential)	• How am I structuring teaching activities to support progression in learning? • What am I doing to encourage students to think both holistically and rationally? To what extent do I explore connections between ideas between different subjects? How am I facilitating both rationality/ creativity in my curriculum/lesson design? • To what extent do I encourage thinking outside of the box?
7 Nature of questioning (open *vs* closed)	Am I using a range of question types to support learning? • What percentage of all questions are generated by my students within a lesson, compared to my questioning? • Do I allow sufficient warm-up time for students to answer questions – pre-warning them of questions coming up? • Do I allow enough waiting time once I have asked students a question?
8 Awareness of impulsive (process fast and come to decision quickly) and reflective styles (process more slowly and come to decision by considering all information	To what extent does my questioning reward impulsive or reflective learners? • If reflective and impulsive learners are paired how am I organizing their access to information given that one of the pair will scan information much more quickly than the other? • How am I supporting students to develop both reflective and impulsive cognitive styles in relation to requirements of the task?

(continued)

Table 6.2 (continued)

9 Developing student flexibility in learning	How am I supporting students to be adaptive in their learning behaviours/styles? • How am I providing sufficient constructive friction to ensure students are being challenged? • How am I also managing the learning environment to limit destructive friction?
10 Self-discovery *vs* directed teaching	• How am I supporting learners to manage their own self-regulation of their learning?
11 Classroom design involving organization of seating	• Am I using a variety of seating arrangements to support specific learning goals and to encourage students to take on different roles within different groupings?
12 Management of power relations	• To what extent am I introducing choice for learners and listening to student voice? • To what extent I am involving students in lesson design, including assessment?
13 Groupings (group, pair and individual work)	• How am I using different groupings of students to support the development of interpersonal skills? • Is the method of grouping appropriate to the requirements of the task and nature of assessment?
14 Assessment	• Am I using a range of assessment options that are aligned to the learning objectives? • Am I providing sufficient choice in assessment? • How does assessment support creativity in learning? • How authentic is the nature of assessment? • How am I teaching my students to develop effective feedback seeking and using skills?

Key readings

Dunlosky, J., Rawson, K. A., Marsh, E. J., Nathan, M. J., and Willingham, D. T. (2013). Improving students' learning with effective learning techniques: Promising directions from cognitive and educational psychology. *Psychological Science in the Public Interest, 14* (1), 4–58.

The authors discuss ten teaching techniques and their relative effectiveness in enhancing learning. The importance of teaching students to selectively choose and use the most appropriate learning strategies is highlighted.

Howard-Jones, P. (2010). *Introducing neuroeducational research.* London and New York: Routledge.

This book explores how neuroscience research findings can be used to enable a better understanding of how we learn to support enhancements in teaching. It also debunks many neuromyths that have found their way into education. Also useful within this area are the works of Adey et al. (2007); Dubinsky et al. (2013) and Blake more and Frith (2005).

Klein, P. D. (2003). Rethinking the multiplicity of cognitive resources and curricular representations: alternatives to 'learning styles' and 'multiple intelligences', *Journal of Curriculum Studies*, 35 (1), 45–81.

Klein highlights the limitations of traditional interpretations of learning styles and multiple intelligences to developing learning and teaching and instead promotes the importance of an understanding of dual coding and cognitive load theories. The importance of selecting and creating appropriate resources in relation to the requirements of the context (discipline, content of lesson, requirements of tasks etc.) is emphasized.

Weblinks

The Blakemore Lab: Peer-reviewed articles in scientific journals. Available online at https://sites.google.com/site/blakemorelab/Articles

Campaign for Learning. Available online at http://www.campaign-for-learning.org.uk/cfl/learninginschools/l2l/why_learning_to_learn.asp (accessed 12 August 2013).

Chisholm, L., Fennes, H., Kartsen, A. and Riech, K. (2009). Learning 2 learn. A method in action. Literature review synthesis report L2L. Available online at http://homepage.uibk.ac.at/~c603207/dokumente/L2L%20WP1_%LiteratureSynthesis.pdf (accessed 6 October, 2014).

Crell Centre for Research in Education and Lifelong Learning. Available online at https://crell.jrc.ec.europa.eu/?q=content/research-areas (accessed 30 July 2013).

ELSIN: Education, Learning, Styles, Individual differences Network (ELSIN). Available online at www.elsinnetwork.com (accessed 10 June 2013).

ESRC (2001–2006). Learntolearn. Economic and Social Research Council. Available online at http://www.learntolearn.ac.uk/ (accessed 30 July 2013).

L2L: Learning how to learn. Available online at http://www.open.edu/openlearn/education/learning-how-learn/content-section-0 (accessed 10 August 2013).

OECD (2010). PISA 2009 results: Learning to learn – Student engagement, strategies and practices (Volume III). Available online at http://dx.doi.org/10.1787/9789264083943-en (accessed 10 January 2012).

Research Centre for Learning to Learn. Available online at http://www.ncl.ac.uk/cflat/about/Learningtolearnresearch.html (accessed 30 September 2013).

Tertiary education research database. Available online at http://hdl.voced.edu.au/10707/69027 (accessed 12 January 2014).

TLRP: Learning how to learn – In classrooms, schools and networks 2001–2005. Teaching and learning research programme. Available online at http://www.tlrp.org/proj/phase11/phase2f.html (accessed 21 September 2013).

Appendix 6

- **Cognitive style is fixed and not modifiable.**
  Cognitive style is affected by the cultural context – styles can be reinforced or developed as a consequence of different experiences. Some styles may be more difficult to change than others and it is true that some individuals exhibit greater flexibility than others. Where style flexibility is limited, the development of strategies to surmount style inflexibility is important (see Kozhevnikov *et al.*, 2014; Zhang, 2013).

- **Cognitive style is consistent across situations and contexts.**
  Style is modifiable across situations and contexts although it is possible for styles to become habitual if the individual is not challenged by the requirements of the task or context to modify/develop their styles.

- **Different subject disciplines may promote different cognitive styles.**
  The requirements of certain discipline may attract individuals with specific styles profiles, which then reinforces style specialization. The requirements of certain disciplines may also promote the development of specific cognitive styles.

- **If I match the style of a student s/he will do better.**
  Matching is problematic as outlined within the chapter given that all individuals have a styles profile to draw on: which styles do you match? However, in certain contexts, where a specific type of knowledge/skill needs to be developed, strategies focused on supporting that specific style development might be successful. Furthermore, in situations of cognitive complexity/conflict, especially with regards to mentoring, matching individuals' dominant styles may be appropriate to support entry into a new learning environment.
- **How I present material will impact variably on the learning of those of different cognitive styles.**
  The evidence is mixed – in relation to style format matching. However, there is clear evidence of effective ways of disseminating information that is applicable to all learners regardless of style preferences.
- **If students are grouped in similar styles they will do better.**
  There is an issue as to which style attribute you use to group students. The nature of the task is also important. Where studies report positive results this has usually revolved around styles training, making students more receptive of and amenable to different ways of learning, which may be more important than the notion of style group matching and mismatching.
- **Those deemed to be less academic will struggle more if materials do not match their own cognitive style(s).**
  There is evidence that students with lower levels of ability will find it more difficult if the learning situation does not match their learning preferences (Riding and Rayner, 1998). This may reflect a lack of development of style flexibility and not knowing how to self-regulate learning in an unfamiliar context with fewer strategies to draw on.
- **Students vary in their style malleability.**
  This is true. Students do vary in the extent to which they are able to flex their style muscles and adapt their styles to suit the demands of a learning situation (see Kozhevnikov, 2007).
- **Using styles in teaching means I need to adapt my teaching to each individual student's styles.**
  A styles approach in teaching means using the most effective approaches for all students in specific situations. It is not about individualized instruction and does not necessarily involve the use of styles instruments – it requires an understanding of the core principles underpinning styles – see Personal Learning Styles Pedagogy (chapter eleven).
- **Cognitive style is influenced by cultural factors.**
  Cultural factors at a number of levels influence the development of cognitive styles (family, school, clubs, higher education, workplace, society, country) (see Eaves, 2011).

- **Cognitive styles matter most when students are facing difficult learning transitions.**
  There is evidence to suggest that when facing difficult/new learning transitions, cognitive styles matter. How students perceive the learning context and their prior experiences impact on their styles development (Balasooriya *et al.*, 2009; Balasooriya *et al.*, 2011; Evans, 2013a).

- **Cognitive styles impact on how students receive, interpret and use information**.
  True (see Zhang *et al.* 2013).

Chapter 7

Making sense of participatory pedagogies

A critical introduction

Overview

In this chapter we look at the question of how best to support the learning needs of all students. We introduce the concept of an inclusive *Participatory Pedagogy* as part of our holistic view of pedagogy, as well as identify and explore the meaning of those inter-related core concepts which serve to frame the way in which a participatory pedagogy is enacted.

Participatory pedagogies

> . . . participatory pedagogies are underpinned by explicit sets of social justice principles and ethical starting points. They comprise a particular type of pedagogical relationship between tutor and student, in which both teacher and learner work together, ethically, critically and inclusively. This might also involve a commitment to the students' life-experiences, so that different forms of knowledge and experience are drawn on and made available to help illuminate and make accessible the disciplinary or subject knowledge at the heart of the course. It also involves an explicit discussion of the different perspectives, backgrounds and forms of knowledge of the participants whilst also subjecting these to critical reflection in collaborative learning processes. These pedagogies understand concerns with curriculum and assessment as parts of pedagogical practices and relations, not as separate entities. Thus, participatory and inclusive pedagogies are concerned not only with explicit practices of teaching and learning, but also with the construction of knowledge, competing epistemological perspectives, and the ways that learning and meaning might be assessed to support pedagogical and meaning-making processes (Scott *et al.*, 2014, pp. 183–184)

In Scott *et al.*'s (2014) conception of a participatory pedagogy, a co-directed approach to learning and teaching involving student and teacher is advocated which takes account of the student's learning history. In such a pedagogy learning and teaching is framed by consideration of the holistic experience of the student, and teacher and student perspectives of learning and teaching; the beliefs of the participants matter. The focus is on both the immediate demands of the learning context and the requirements of the future through the use of critical reflection (see chapter 10).

A participatory pedagogy is based on a broad interpretation of pedagogy (see chapter 2) and notions of inclusive education, which refers to the education of all children and not just those with disabilities, and it is not about narrow definitions of individualization (i.e. specific teaching for individual students). Thomas (2013, p. 477) has argued that:

> . . . it is not diagnosis and separate treatment that are important for success at school, but rather the existence of the right conditions for learning of an understanding of what learning is, and what it can be in school.

How a participatory pedagogy is enacted will depend on an understanding of a number of interrelated core concepts which will now be explored in more detail in the following sections.

Exploring core concepts: inclusion, personalization, individualized instruction, differentiation

While government focus and educational emphasis may vary, the constant for all teachers is how best to support the learning of all students. It is, therefore, important to review developments focused on supporting all students' needs, in order to develop an understanding of effective pedagogy for twenty-first-century learning environments. Imposed national curriculum change underpinned by differing political ideologies can create uncertainty for teachers in terms of knowing what is 'best' to support the learning of their students. However, in terms of such frequent change in policy and curricula it is 'essential that the teaching profession be much better and more directly informed about the current state of knowledge about learning and the practices that best promote it (D. Hargreaves *et al.*, 2005, p. 20).

To this end we will now highlight and explore the meaning and differing interpretations of the following core concepts: inclusion, personalization, individualized instruction, and differentiation, which are frequently used in discussions about the application of a participatory pedagogy.

Inclusion

The term inclusion is a complex, contradictory and contested concept (Moran (2009, p. 46). 'Inclusion is about more than 'special needs'' (Thomas, 2013, p. 485). Learning to teach inclusively requires an understanding of oneself and one's values in relation to others, and an appreciation of the ways in which classrooms can be transformed, so that learning can be enhanced for all students. Thomas has emphasized the need for a new *'psychology of difference'*, that considers community, social capital, equality and respect and not just disability and social justice concerns. He argues that students' relative success at school can be attributed to an array of factors around which acceptance and inclusion are constructed, raising the importance of the *gradient effect* as a key consideration in the design of educational practice in schools. Building on the work of Keating and Hertzman (1999), Thomas explains the gradient effect as the extent to which social differences (e.g. income, ability) exist between members of a population. It is known that the greater such differences are, the lower the achievement at school, at national (Chiu and Khoo, 2005) and local school levels (Chudgar and Luschei, 2009). Thomas (2013) in explaining this phenomenon argued that it is not about absolute levels of income or social capital: it is about their magnitude, visibility and how in the school context students see themselves compared to others, and how this impacts on their sense of self-worth: ' . . . where they see themselves, through major differences between themselves and their peers, conspicuously excluded from the expectations, the activities, the resources, the worlds of those peers' (Thomas, 2013, p. 480). For Thomas it is about the context and creating the right conditions for learning. However, it is the way in which a student interacts with such a context that is also of fundamental importance. Moran (2009) has argued that inclusion is about educational values of equity and entitlement and primarily about cultures that are both receptive to and value diversity.

In attending to inclusion issues and specifically to the gradient effect and its potential negative impact on student identity and self-belief, there are a number of practices that schools and teachers need to consider in order to encourage what Thomas has described as *bridging activities* (approaches to learning that encourage co-operation and collaboration of all students) as opposed to *bonding activities* (tokenist approaches to inclusion which can be seen as exaggerating difference, e.g. classes solely for 'gifted' students). Thomas (2013) has argued that it is not so much absolute standards of ability but student perceptions about relative status that are important and that deliberate differentiation (ability streaming) and segregation (e.g. gifted children programmes) bring unwanted consequences for many children. We argue for the equal importance of the design and underpinning philosophy of the curriculum in supporting the creation of an inclusive learning climate. The artistry of the teacher is the key in managing the learning environment to support student individual differences in learning (informed by an understanding of concepts taken from cognitive psychology, education, and neuroscience as outlined in chapters five and six) and to include, enable, and enhance the participation of all students in education. As Moran (2009, p. 49) has noted, 'Bridging the chasm between school and life experiences and across those with and without social, cultural and economic advantages, is a challenge which requires not only sensitivity, but also a willingness to engage with matters of social responsibility and social justice.'

The importance of promoting positive mindsets has been highlighted by Dweck (2006). Teachers have the capacity to build students' brains and teachers being able to communicate to students that their brains are plastic is an important part of supporting students' sense of self in their potential to succeed.

> Given that teachers are among the best cognitive enhancers on the planet . . . rewiring students' brains on a daily basis to acquire literacy, numeracy, and reasoning skills . . . we argue that teachers benefit from additionally understanding the neuroscience of learning and memory.
>
> Dubinsky *et al.*, 2013, p. 320

The role of the social and cultural context in supporting student sense of self and performance (completion and attainment) is well known (Bliuc *et al.*, 2011a, 2011b). How students feel about themselves in communities impacts on how they learn. Thomas has also argued the importance of promoting beliefs in equal potential, in respect and recognition for all within school contexts: this applies to everyone in the school community, students and teachers.

Developing strong communities of practice to support inclusivity within education is important. Key challenges include the willingness and ability of organizations to promote integrated approaches to inclusion. Moran (2009) has argued that such practice requires more than technical competence on the part of the teacher – it requires the development of appropriate dispositions and the willingness of teachers to confront their own personal philosophies and belief systems and dominant ideologies that prevail at organizational and societal level in order to promote more culturally responsive and contextually relevant pedagogies.

Questions for reflection

Thomas (2013), drawing on Putnam's (2000) work discussed the importance of bridging activities (those that encourage co-operation, sharing, debate and collaboration of all students) in supporting inclusive practice as opposed to bonding activities (e.g. tokenist approaches to inclusion, gifted classes, certain forms of assessment) which can be seen as reinforcing exclusive identities and solidarity rather than collaboration.

- Within your own context (experiences of education as a learner and/or a teacher), what structures, policies, aspects of curriculum design, including assessment and teaching practices, encourage bridging, and why, and which ones encourage bonding, and why?
- What does this exercise tell you about your experiences of learning and practice?
- What can be done at the individual and organizational level to promote and extend inclusive bridging practices in your workplace?

Personalization

The introduction of the term 'personalization' into educational discourse in England can be attributed to the think tank DEMOS and more specifically to Leadbeater (2003) as a powerful way of reshaping public sector services (Pykett, 2010). The key strength of the approach was felt to be in leading teachers to review learning and teaching from the student perspective and to consider how individual students experienced learning (Ruddock *et al.*, 2006). However, the term personalization has always been seen as a fuzzy concept and in many respects it is one that has effectively been wiped from current English DfE documentation on learning to teach. It has been argued that the concept of personalization is not a new one and that it represents a constructivist approach to learning and teaching. There are a number of published reports on personalized learning;

these include DfES (2006); Ruddock *et al.* (2006); Sebba *et al.* (2007). For a summary of key reports on personalization, see R. J. Campbell *et al.* (2007) who in considering different perspectives on the area reviewed the following: the Nuffield review of 14–19 provision (Hayward *et al.*, 2005); the ESRC Teaching and Learning programme (Pollard and James, 2004); an NCSL special supplement (NCSL, 2004); a White Paper (DfES, 2005); and C. Gilbert, 2007.

Early examination of what personalization was or was not (DfES, 2004), were keen to emphasize that personalization is not about individualization of the curriculum: 'Personalised learning is not a matter of tailoring curriculum, teaching and assessment to 'fit' the individual but is a question of developing social practices that enable people to become all that they are capable of becoming' (Pollard and James, 2004, p. 6). Personalization is seen to be about nurturing the unique talents of every pupil (DfES, 2004). It is a collective activity that enables an individual to develop his/her own learning. 'it is social, not individualised, practice. It is also collective in another sense; the values and attitudes that teachers and students bring to learning is derived from, and embedded in, a collective organisational ethos' (R. J. Campbell *et al.*, 2007, p. 151).

Prain *et al.* (2013) have argued that personalization is about differentiation and supporting learners to develop self-regulation capability:'personalised learning depends on both effective teacher differentiation of a set curriculum to address diversity of learner needs, and the development of independent learner capacities' (p. 656), and entails ' . . . constructing a curriculum that is robust enough to meet the needs, and develop the capacities, of all students' (p. 664).

Deep personalization in the form of student and teachers as co-producers of educational knowledge should be promoted, rather than shallow personalization (better access to resources but limited student voice) (Campbell *et al.*, 2007). From our perspective a deep form of personalization is only possible if teachers' needs are identified and attended to in the form of ongoing professional development and support which includes sufficient attention to the exploring of teachers' values and beliefs and, furthermore, which ensures that school organizational structures are aligned to facilitate effective learning and teaching in the classroom.

Many have sought to identify characteristics of a personalized approach to learning as comprising a number of component parts, taking the technical perspective (Pollard and James, ESRC, 2004), whereas others have focused on the importance of an underpinning ethos permeating all aspects of school policy (DfES, 2005; Gilbert, 2007). For example, the ESRC framework incorporated assessment for learning; teaching and learning strategies that stretch pupils, curriculum entitlement and choice; student-centred organizations; and partnership beyond the school. Within such frameworks the emphasis has been on constructivist learning approaches (experiential learning, innovative use of ICT, mentoring, pupil autonomy, enrichment and extension for all) and organizational issues associated with provision beyond classroom opportunities.

There is some consensus that personalization is about equipping students to make choices about their learning (Leadbeater, 2005) although there have been many questions raised about the extent to which students within current educational systems can authentically be involved in choices about the curriculum and are able to make informed choices regardless of age, prior knowledge, abilities.

While the surface features (technical aspects), e.g. setting tasks, are important, it is the underlying values and aims of the teacher that are fundamental in ensuring a successful climate for learning for all students (R. J. Campbell *et al.*, 2007). David Hargreaves *et al.*,

(2005) also have focused on the importance of student involvement in successful personalization whereby students are seen as active collaborators within the learning process taking responsibility for their own learning. Effective personalization requires

> . . . interplay between (a) teacher expertise in identifying and addressing students' ongoing individual curricular needs, and (b) student capacity to develop, over an extended timeframe, increasing independence as learners . . . the agency of both groups as they interact is constrained by structural, cultural and pedagogical assumptions, regulations, and practices, including prescriptive curricula, and actual and potential roles and responsibilities of teachers and students in school settings.
>
> Prain *et al.* 2013, p. 661

Prain *et al.* acknowledge constraints in the implementation of effective personalization. As part of evidence- and research-informed practice, critics have argued that there is a lack of evidence that personalization has reduced the achievement gap between different groups of students (R. J. Campbell *et al.*, 2007) and there is little objective evidence of the impact of specific approaches as part of personalization agendas (Prain *et al.*, 2013). The lack of demonstrable impact is not surprising given the varied ways in which personalization has been implemented and the fact that within holistic personalized curricula designs identifying the key factor(s) impacting changes is difficult, especially as certain initiatives will have variable impact on different students for a whole host of reasons.

Personalization does require considerable resource investment (physical resources and training resources). Much attention has quite rightly been focused on the support that teachers need to develop truly inclusive personalized curricular to meet the needs of all students. Such an approach also requires mutual engagement by teachers and students. R. J. Campbell *et al.* (2007) have also argued that personalized approaches as identified by teachers require high levels of subject expertise, a whole school learning culture (participation and commitment to learning), an understanding of the contestable nature of knowledge, strong relational skills involving all those in the learning community. Importantly, they noted that a personalized pedagogy is fundamentally dependent on shared values (e.g. learning behaviour, respecting differences, attention to student voice, importance of self-motivation in learning).

What is individualized instruction?

Much is made of the fact that personalization does not advocate individualized instruction. However there is misunderstanding of this term as well. As noted by Landrum and McDuffie (2010) individualized instruction has been a defining characteristic of special education, whereas differentiation practices, as part of personalization, demand individualizing within heterogeneous classrooms. Individualization is more than a one-to-one instructional arrangement: it means matching instruction to individually identified needs which could be one-to-one, group, or whole class instruction. Although Hallahan *et al.* (2009, p. 10) drawing on the works of Itard and Séguin defined individualized instruction as that where 'the child's characteristics, rather than prescribed academic content, provide the basis for teaching techniques' it could also be argued that individualization involves consideration of both student characteristics and consideration of the most appropriate way to teach an aspect of curriculum. For Landrum and McDuffie (2010) instruction is individualized when it builds on what a student already knows and can do, puts in meaningful goals to enable further learning, and, through the design of teaching (accommodation and modification), enables all students to have full access to the curriculum. Such an approach is relevant to a broader definition of differentiation for whole class groups and not just for those with identified special learning needs.

Differentiation

As with the terms *personalization* and *individualized instruction*, there are many definitions of what differentiation is. Pham (2012, p. 18) has argued that differentiated instruction involves a combination of conceptual orientation (personalization) and practical application in order to help students 'view a subject matter from a holistic account rather than a fragmented outlook, as well as develop a critical understanding about learning principles applied in real-life settings'. We define differentiation as:

> . . . a central inclusive concept integral to a teacher's thinking, learning design and delivery. It involves the proactive creation of related learning activities that accommodate variances in the interest, readiness and learning profiles of all learners (and the teacher), allowing them to access the learning activity and work towards achieving the intended learning outcomes.
>
> Evans and Waring, 2011d, p. 152

Tomlinson defines differentiation (1999, p. 108) as a philosophy of teaching which involves consideration of students' readiness, interests and learning preferences (Tomlinson, 1999, 2003, 2005; Tomlinson *et al.*, 2003).

> Differentiating instruction is not an instructional strategy or a teaching model. It is a way of thinking about teaching and learning that advocates beginning where individuals are rather than with a prescribed plan of action, which ignores student readiness, interest, and learning profile. It is a way of thinking that challenges how educators typically envision assessment, teaching, learning, classroom roles, use of time, and curriculum.
>
> Tomlinson, 1999, p. 108

For Prain *et al.* (2013) differentiation is a vehicle for personalizing a curriculum to acknowledge and address individual differences. For Orlich *et al.* (2004, p. 17) it is 'an eclectic mix of methods combined with wisdom, logic, a sound knowledge of educational psychology and seasoned artistry'. Differentiation is, moreover, not just about dealing in the moment in managing students' immediate needs: it is also future-focused, in redesigning curricula to ensure students are prepared for the requirements of twenty-first-century learning environments (Pham, 2012).

Understanding differentiation and its application can be viewed along a continuum, at one end of which is the reductionist view (where differentiation is narrowly perceived as a reactive response to an individual experiencing difficulty), and at the other end of which is as an inclusive view (where differentiation is perceived as proactive in ensuring curriculum design is applicable and accessible to all learners (O'Brien, 2000)). We have previously argued (Evans and Waring, 2007, 2008, 2011d) the importance of placing differentiation at the centre of planning all learning and teaching activities, where an understanding of individual learning needs underpins all lesson planning, rather than seeing differentiation as an afterthought, an 'add-on' with a reductionist focus on differentiation by task, outcome, and/or support.

While all can see the value of supporting every student's needs, Prain *et al.* (2013) have argued that differentiated practice may actually increase the so-called gradient effect as noted by Thomas by reifying student differences through the creation of, for example, selective and streamed teaching. In debating this issue they also highlight that differentiation was perceived by Tomlinson as the consideration of immediate and short-term differences in content or strategies that could be applied to help students meet necessary standards. However, such an argument promotes a reductionist approach to personalization and differentiation, as it is the very structures and processes within a school that can be exclusive and limit a teacher's potential to fully meet the needs of all students.

Building on the notion of differential effectiveness, R. J. Campbell *et al.* (2003) provide a critical reflective framework to encourage teachers to consider how consistently effective they are in relation to:

(i) the application of different activities;
(ii) across subject areas;
(iii) differences in pupils' background factors (differential teacher effectiveness with children of different ages, ability, gender, socio-economic background; ethnicity etc.);
(iv) differences in pupils' personal characteristics;
(v) students' cognitive and learning styles, motivation, self-esteem, cultural and organizational contexts

Questions for reflection

Using the Campbell framework, how would you rate your effectiveness on these different dimensions of your differentiated practice on a scale of 1–10 (1=poorly developed and 10=excellent – a leader in this area).

Rating 1–10

(i) the application of different activities
(ii) across subject areas attending to differences in
(iii) pupils' background factors
(iv) pupils' personal characteristics
(v) students' cognitive and learning styles, motivation, self-esteem, cultural and organizational contexts

- In what contexts do you feel more able to differentiate and in which areas do you feel least able to? Why is this the case?

- How are you trying to develop your practice?

- What are the main barriers to the development of your practice (personal and institutional)?

Enacting differentiation

In enacting differentiation in practice, there is both consensus and difference of opinion. There is, for example, debate as to the extent to which attention to students' learning preferences and styles should be included in differentiated practice, with Pham (2012) arguing for greater attention to be placed on student readiness rather than styles. Although as we have previously argued, the request to exclude styles from differentiated practice is often based on the faulty premise of the matching hypothesis.

In Hattie's (2012) book on *visible learning,* differentiation is not explicitly mentioned. A core argument would be that differentiation is an integral part of good teaching and not an additional component. Instead, Hattie highlights the differential impact that teachers have on student learning and achievement and focuses on expert teacher characteristics that can be seen to draw on holistic interpretations of personalization and differentiation, developments in cognitive neuroscience, and cognitive styles. His expert teachers take the following steps.

(a) *Identify the most important ways in which to represent the subject that they teach* (e.g. how they: interpret and articulate with their students what a surface and deep understanding and approach to learning within their subject is; examine their own and their students' beliefs about learning and teaching; reflect on the ways in which students learn and what they have learnt). The expert teachers' aim in this process is to promote integration of knowledge, by combining new material (content and/or skills) with students' prior knowledge, and to make connections with other subjects, in so doing forming unique lessons blended to suit the needs of students and of their own teaching goals.

(b) *Create an optimal climate for learning*
(e.g. one that places emphasis on the relational dimension of learning – trust in a joint endeavour in which error is welcomed as part of the learning process).
(c) *Monitor learning and provide feedback*
(e.g. expert teachers encourage flexibility and improvisation; they are excellent feedback seekers and users of feedback).
(d) *Believe that all students can reach the success criteria*
(e.g. intelligence is seen as changeable rather than fixed; respect for students is fostered along with a passion for learning).
(e) *Influence surface and deep student outcomes*
(e.g. teachers have a holistic interpretation of learning outcomes, emphasize the development of appropriate learning strategies, and set challenging goals).

Questions for reflection

- To what extent do you agree with Hattie's description of expert teachers?
- What is your own definition of an expert teacher?
- What additional elements would you include?

From different theoretical perspectives, core principles of effective differentiated practice can be identified, and have been summarized in Table 7.1. However, Clare (2004, p. 1) argued that 'many teachers [although acknowledging differentiation as a good thing] . . . haven't a clue as to what it involves or how they might implement it in the classroom'. We would argue that differentiation should be integral to every teacher and learner interaction; that it should be seen as applying to all students and not a reactive response to a student experiencing difficulty in learning; that it needs to take account

Table 7.1 Principles of effective differentiation

Author	*Tomlinson (1999)*	*Carolan and Guinn (2007)*	*McTighe and Brown (2005)*	*Hattie (2012)*	*C. Evans, 2013a; C. Evans and Waring, 2009, 2013a, 2015)*
Principles					
Student-focused	Participation in respectful, meaningful and *challenging* work in the students' *zone of proximal development* (Vygotsky, 1934/1962/1986)	*Personalized scaffolding* to support learners in bridging the gap between what s/he can do and what s/he needs to do to complete the task	Students learn best from purposeful, *inquiry-driven* activities in which they are situated at the *centre* of the learning process	Influence surface and deep student outcomes	Supporting learner autonomy: choices in learning/student voice Exploration of *student and teacher beliefs*/ modelling and support Integrated into the learning experience *not* a one stop shop
Flexibility	Modification of content, processes and products where necessary to ensure that learners grasp key knowledge or skills Use of a wide *range of instructional strategies* in a flexible classroom environment that moves between individual, small group, and whole group activities based on need	Using *flexible means to reach defined* ends by offering multiple paths to reach defined goals	Effective instruction accommodates differences in learners' *readiness* levels, *interests* and *learning profiles*		Holistic research-informed approach Emphasis on *self-regulation* Careful selection and *application of styles* in order to support students/ teachers in developing their own strategies to manage their learning

Understanding subject	Concentration on understanding *key principles* and *critical concepts*	*Mining subject area expertise* by using *multiple ways* to navigate subject knowledge by understanding the processes of learning involved in the specific subject area	Curriculum standards need to be *unpacked and revisited multiple times* to ensure that students understand the key concepts underlying their learning	Identify the most *important ways in which to represent the subject* that they teach	Design of learning environments: *overarching principles* for all learners within context Identification of *most appropriate methods* for subject/task
Assessment	*Integration of assessment and instruction*	*Personalized scaffolding* to support learners in bridging the gap between what s/he can do and what s/he needs to do to complete the task	Assessments should require students' *explicit demonstration* of understanding in *multiple ways*	*Monitor* learning and *provide feedback*	*Authentic* assessment (*integrated* into teaching and *aligned* with curriculum goals) Emphasis on *feedforward* *Central involvement* of students in assessment process
Classroom climate	Establishment of a *collaborative* and *student-oriented* atmosphere where teachers and students plan, set goals and learn from their efforts together *Balancing of group and individual goals* to ensure personal development	Creating *caring classrooms* that acknowledge and value the unique attributes of learners		Creating an *optimal climate* for learning Believing that all students can reach the success criteria	Optimizing conditions for learning *Sensitivity* to learner context *Collaborative* Building on *learners' histories* *Balancing of group and individual goals* to ensure personal development

of pedagogical, emotional, cognitive, and social factors affecting a learner's ability to learn. Finally, for effective differentiated practice to be put in place sufficient attention should be given to teachers' needs, in terms of their own experiences of sound differentiation practices; clarity regarding what good differentiated practice constitutes as part of whole school development, along with the development of a language of learning (D. Hargreaves *et al.*, 2005).

Enactment of differentiated practice involves three related areas: *modifying the content* (what students should know and be able to do, and the materials that will support them in their learning), *the process* (the activities that help students make sense of their learning), and the *product* of instruction (the range of evidence students provide of their learning) (Tomlinson, 1999). Differentiated practice may involve all or some of these three dimensions with varying impact depending on the underpinning philosophy influencing how these dimensions are attended to in practice.

While Tomlinson (2003), Carolan and Guinn (2007), McTighe and Brown (2005), Hattie (2012), and Evans and Waring (2009, 2011d, 2015) place greater emphasis on certain aspects of differentiated practice, compared to others, it is possible to identify a number of core principles around issues to do with student voice, flexibility in approaches to learning and teaching, understanding of subject demands, holistic and authentic assessment, and classroom climate. While these principles have been clearly identified, how they are implemented in practice is highly variable which may also account for the reported variable impact of differentiated instruction on student learning outcomes (Prain *et al.*, 2013; Subban, 2006). Prain *et al.* (2013) referencing Jackson and Davis (2000) and Tomlinson (2003), highlight the challenges in implementing effective differentiated practice (teacher time, skills, resources, and parental belief that equity requires educational sameness in the treatment of students). To this list we would add the importance of a whole school ethos committed to differentiated practice and enacted through the development of supportive structures including ongoing emphasis on whole school continuing professional development. To enable this, Tomlinson (2003) has argued the importance of sustained leadership which we argue needs to be occurring at all levels within an organization. As part of this a climate where discussions are focused on what is to be a teacher of subject X, and exploring teacher and student beliefs about learning, are essential, rather than an overwhelming emphasis within meetings on the mechanics and organization of teaching. There needs to be a concerted effort across schools for every meeting to be focused on discussions about learning.

What is important in enacting those principles of effective differentiated instruction is how they are framed and combined to produce the whole experience from both learner and teacher perspectives.

Questions for reflection

Identify the distinction and relationship between personalization, individual instruction and differentiation as part of supporting the learning needs of all your students.

Summary

We have introduced the concept of an *inclusive participatory pedagogy* as an umbrella construct under which the PLSP is located, and which we acknowledge is of fundamental importance in framing learning and teaching activities as part of a holistic view of pedagogy. We have identified how the enactment of a participatory pedagogy, frequently (ab)used in discussions about the application of inclusive pedagogical practice, depends on teachers' and educational organizations' appropriate understanding of the complex and interrelated concepts of inclusion, personalization, individual instruction, and differentiation. Participatory pedagogies focus on maximizing all students' access to learning through the development of a holistic approach that considers individual and contextual variables in learning. Such an approach is certainly not about individual instruction for each and every student; it is about applying principles of good practice for all.

Key readings

O' Brien, T., and Guiney, D. (2001). *Differentiation in teaching and learning principles and practice.* London and New York: Continuum.

This book highlights the importance of understanding the principles of differentiated practice and provides examples of how to enact differentiated practice in a number of different contexts.

Prain, V., Cox, P. Deed, C., Dorman, J., Edwards, D., Farrelly, C., Keeffe, M., Lovejoy, V., Mow, L., Sellings, P., Waldrip, B., and Yager, Z. (2013). Personalised learning: Lessons to be learnt. *British Educational Research Journal, 39*(4), *654–676.*

The authors provide a critique of different conceptualizations of personalization and consider how it can be comprehended and enacted in twenty-first-century learning environments. Based on the Australian context but relevant to application more widely, Prain et al.'s conceptualization of personalization is predicated on a number of interrelated variables including differentiation of the curriculum, self-regulated learning and relational agency between teachers and between teachers and students.

Thomas, G. (2013). A review of thinking and research about inclusive education policy, with suggestions for a new kind of inclusive thinking. *British Educational Research Journal, 39*(3), 473–490.

In examining inclusive education, Thomas highlights the importance of the gradient effect (the extent to which social differences exist between members of a group) for education. The importance of perceived relative poverty is discussed along with the importance of educators' use of bridging as opposed to bonding activities to help reduce inequalities within the classroom/school context.

Tomlinson, C. A. (2003). *Fulfilling the promise of the differentiated classroom: Strategies and tools for responsive teaching.* Alexandria, VA: Association for Supervision and Curriculum Development.

Tomlinson highlights principles underpinning differentiation and a number of ways to enact this in practice. Links to resources are available online at http://mcjackson.iweb.bsu.edu/ (accessed 5 May 2014). Work utilizing Tomlinson's approach (Tomlinson hot topic, 2009) can be found on the Slide Share website: http://www.slideshare.net

Weblinks

Dahlman, A., Hoffman, P., and Brauhn, S. (nd) Classroom strategies and tools for differentiating instruction in the ESL classroom. Available online at http://minnetesol.org/journal/vol25_html_pages/17_Dahlman.htm (accessed 5 June 2014)

DfE, (2011a). Teachers' Standards. Available online at www.gov.uk/government/publications and www.gov.uk/government/publications/teachers-standards (accessed 12 June 2014)

DfES (2004). *A National Conversation about Personalised Learning*. Available online at www.standards.dfes.gov.uk/personalisedlearning (accessed 12 May 2013).

Leadbeater, C. (2005). *The shape of things to come: Personalised learning through collaboration*. Available online at http://www.innovationunit.org/sites/default/files/The%20shape%20of%20things%20to%20come.pdf (accessed 20 July 2007).

Ofsted (2012). Initial Teacher Education (ITE) inspection handbook. Manchester: The Office for Standards in Education, Children's Services and Skills. Available online at www.ofsted.gov.uk/resources/120028 (accessed 9 September 2013).

Ofsted (2013). The framework for school inspection. Manchester: The Office for Standards in Education, Children's Services and Skills. Available online at www.ofsted.gov.uk/resources/120100 (accessed 9 December 2013).

TDA (2007). Professional standards for teachers. Qualified teacher status. London: The Training and Development Agency for Schools. Available online at www.tda.gov.uk.standards (accessed 10 December 10–2013).

Chapter 8

The application of a participatory pedagogy

Using the Personal Learning Styles Pedagogy

Overview

In this chapter we discuss the Personal Learning Styles Pedagogy framework as one example of an inclusive participatory pedagogy which is focused on implementing overarching principles of effective learning for all students and not about individual instruction for each and every learner. A key premise of this pedagogical framework is the empowerment of learners to take responsibility for their own learning. Using the PLSP framework we will highlight the importance of attending to learner and teacher beliefs about learning in context and supporting student and teacher self-regulatory capacity as part of effective learning and teaching.

A Personal Learning Styles Pedagogy: an example of a participatory pedagogy

The Personal Learning Styles Pedagogy approach (PLSP) is underpinned by constructivist, socio-cultural and socio-critical perspectives. Initially the PLSP was developed from a cognitive styles perspective and then subsequently broadened to include other individual learning differences and contextual variables impacting on an individual's learning. Key themes permeating the development of a PLSP include: the importance of choice for learners; the centrality of the learner in the process; recognition of the unique starting points of learners; development of students' metawareness of their own understandings of learning processes; the importance of explicit guidance; the need for concrete and appropriate examples to contextualize learning events; the need for reinforcement and support in being able to transfer and translate ideas to suit new contexts; and opportunities to observe different ways of seeing and doing (Evans and Waring, 2009, p. 202). For practical guidance on how to use the PLSP see chapter eleven, and Evans and Waring (2009).

Key components of the Personal Learning Styles Pedagogy as previously highlighted in chapter four (Figure 4.1) include: (A) Exploration of student and teacher beliefs/ modelling and support; (B) Careful selection and application of styles to suit the requirements of the learning context; (C) Optimising conditions for learning; (D) Design of learning environments – to promote an integrated approach to the application of cognitive styles to learning and teaching; (E) Supporting learner autonomy: offering choices in learning and listening to the student voice.

Table 8.1 provides an updated version of the key aspects of each component and sub-component of the PLSP informed by practice, and by a review of over 700 academic papers concerned with the impact on learning of cognitive styles and their associated individual and contextual variables (see Evans and Waring, 2012; Evans, 2013a). The more extended version of the PLSP is also presented in Table 11.1.

Table 8.1 Components of a Personal Learning Styles Pedagogy

A. Exploration of student and teacher beliefs/modelling and support

(i) Focus on the learning histories of student and teacher
(ii) Holistic understanding: consideration of the whole experience of the learner
(iii) Exploration of learner (student and teacher) beliefs about learning (e.g. ability, self-efficacy, identity and sense of fit within learning contexts)
(iv) Enhancing learner awareness and application of styles as part of ongoing instruction on individual learning differences. Understanding of individual differences central to the design of learning environments

B. Careful selection and application of styles

(i) Judicious and informed use of instruments/styles models
(ii) Critical analysis of styles as part of instruction on individual learning differences. Appropriate application of styles models: instruments used as metacognitive tools to support understanding of the learning process
(iii) An integrated approach: awareness of the interdependence of cognitive style and other individual learning differences – role of cognitive style as a moderator variable
(iv) Development of cognitive styles as an integral element of culturally responsive pedagogies

C. Optimizing conditions for learning / sensitivity to learner context

(i) Sensitivity to needs of the learner: recognizing unique starting points. Addressing the emotional dimension of learning: working with students to ensure readiness (will and skill)
(ii) Enabling a positive learning environment: focusing on supporting students during important transition points in their learning
(iii) Care afforded to how new ideas are introduced as to the level of cognitive complexity, in order to support learner flexibility
(iv) Supporting learners' integration into communities of practice
(v) Attention given to learners' networks of support and development of identity within academic context

D. Design of learning environments

(i) Housekeeping attended to (organization of resources, information for students and lecturers, etc.)
(ii) Teaching methods informed by an understanding of cognitive styles and attuned to the requirements of the content and context (constructive alignment)
(iii) Aimed at supporting learners in developing understanding of learning to think within a specific discipline and to be become part of its community
(iv) Judicious use of accommodation of cognitive styles and the concept of matching
(v) Judicious approach in promoting development of the most appropriate cognitive styles for specific contexts
(vi) Teaching strategies aimed at stretching the student through careful addition and removal of scaffolding, and at sufficient constructive friction: aimed at developing and broadening cognitive styles and strategies as and when appropriate
(vii) Designs focused on encouraging learners to adopt deeper and more self-regulated/-directed approaches to learning (constructivist approaches with a strong emphasis on the development of metacognitive skills).
Supporting learners to reflect critically on the learning process to include self- and co-regulation. Appropriate use of tools to support process

(viii) Maximizing learning opportunities: design of learning environments focused on enhancing awareness of different learning strategies through explicit guidance and exposure to diverse learning experiences. Different ways of seeing and doing: observation, modelling, practice, application, reinforcement, and transfer
(ix) Authentic and appropriate assessment designs to support the development of deep approaches to learning
(x) Appropriate use of technology to support learning

E. Supporting learner autonomy: choices in learning / student voice

(i) Focus on the centrality of the learner as a co-constructor of knowledge
(ii) Focus on the role of the student in managing the learning process. Learners as co-designers of their learning experience(s)
(iii) Learner control afforded through design of curriculum (content, process, product) including e-learning possibilities
(iv) Flexible designs facilitated through, for example, organization of resources to maximize access; choices in pathways through programmes; nature of assessment
(v) The importance of guided/informed choice for learners
(vi) Informed and responsible use of groupings: individual and group work. Collaborative learning opportunities informed by understanding of styles (e.g. dangers/limitations of labelling, justification for groupings)

This framework has been used to design curricula with the intention of supporting student and teacher self-regulatory capacity through an enhanced understanding of learning processes. Common to the discussions in chapter seven of personalization, differentiation, and inclusion and the PLSP is the notion of providing sufficient challenge for students to attain their full potential; provision of *scaffolding* by the teacher is seen as an important way of achieving this. A relevant concept in attending to students' needs is that of Vygotsky's (1962, 1978) *Zone of Proximal Development* (ZPD) which we define loosely as the gap between what a student can achieve unassisted and what they can achieve with appropriate support, as referred to in chapters three and four. Provision of appropriate support presupposes that the teacher has a full awareness of the level the student is currently at, and an understanding of how to provide the most effective support in relation to the needs of the student and the requirements of the task. Koopman *et al.* (2011) have commented on the dangers of over-scaffolding, which can encourage learners to use surface processing strategies if they perceive that deep approaches are not necessary. Barnett (2011) has suggested the need to place learners in situations of cognitive and experiential complexity. Knowing at what level to place an intervention, and with which learners, is fundamental (Heikkilä and Lonka, 2006). Evans and Kozhevnikov (2011) and Silén and Uhlin (2008) have also noted the importance of getting the balance right to ensure constructive rather than destructive friction for learners in order to challenge existing ways of thinking without overwhelming them. Eaves (2011) has argued the importance of students and institutions adapting to each other. We have already noted the importance attached to developing student self-regulatory capacity as part of a participatory pedagogy, with the student taking increasing responsibility for their own learning. To enable students to adapt to different learning environments, the approach is not about designing adaptive systems, i.e. those designed to suit the needs of specific individual students' preferences (Choi *et al.*, 2009); it is, rather, about the critical use of evidence on effective learning from a range of domains (education, psychology, neuroscience) to inform learning and teaching designs. Using the PLSP framework to provide effective provision and removal of scaffolding, we will focus attention now on attending to learner and teacher beliefs about learning in context, and on supporting student self-regulatory capacity.

Learner and teacher beliefs about learning in context

One of the themes permeating the PLSP is the acknowledgement of the importance of the emotional dimension of learning (Evans and Waring, 2009, 2012). Empathetic awareness on the part of teachers and students that individuals learn in different ways is important (J. Campbell *et al.*, 2001). Allied to this first point is the importance of supporting learners' basic psychological needs, which are linked to intrinsic motivation (see Betoret and Artiga, 2011; Deci, 1971). Understanding students' *learning passports* is fundamental (e.g. what, how and when they learn, who they learn with, how they use their learning within and across contexts, where they access information; how they learn new skills and apply them; how they manage success and failure).

It is known that how students situate themselves in relation to their studies is associated with their perceptions of being part of a learning community and what it is to know within a specific subject discipline. Bliuc *et al.* (2011a, 2011b) have noted that if we are to further our understanding of how students learn we need to know more about how they see and think about themselves as students, and how this impacts on their learning. Research has highlighted that students' perceptions of their learning context may be more influential in determining their approaches to learning than the learning context as a lone variable (Eaves, 2011). In examining context, it is also important to consider how both students and teachers relate learning and teaching in the classroom to other contexts (different subjects; classes; roles within school, home, and the wider community); issues of authenticity and relevance are important (Boyle and Ravenscroft, 2012).

Teachers' and students' perceptions and beliefs are strong and significant predictors of individual change (Karagiannopoulou and Christodoulides, 2005; Prosser, 2004). As previously noted in this chapter and in chapters five and six, teachers' views on the malleability of intelligence have strong motivational impacts on student learning. 'It matters greatly what students believe about intelligence' (Dweck, 2007, p. 6). The growing evidence base that important parts of intelligence can be developed requires more acknowledgment within teaching. Dweck (2006; 2007; 2012) has identified that students with a *growth mindset* (i.e. they believe that their talents and abilities can be developed through passion, education, and persistence) are more resilient than students with a *fixed mindset* (i.e. they believe that their talents and abilities are fixed traits). Importantly, through training it is possible to change individual mindsets (praising the student's learning process – effort, strategies, concentration, choices, persistence rather than their intelligence). However, change at the organizational level may be more difficult to achieve (Dweck, 2007). To facilitate effective learning communities organizational and individual beliefs need to be aligned.

Building student self-regulatory capacity: a joint enterprise

Prain *et al.* (2013, p. 665) citing Boekaerts and Corno (2005) have defined self-regulated learning as 'the constructive and intentional use of personal strategies to achieve academic and well-being goals . . . [and metacognition as] gains in knowledge, awareness and control over an individual's learning, leading to purposeful improvement of performance'. While Pintrich's (2004) model of self-regulation focuses on the metacognitive element (planning, monitoring, control, and reflection, Vermunt and Verloop (1999) have highlighted the interwoven nature of cognitive, affective, and metacognitive processing activities as integral elements of self-regulation (see Table 8.2 for more explanation). These three inter-related activities involve:

- cognitive processing activities
- metacognitive processing activities
- affective processing activities

Table 8.2 Dimensions of self-regulation (adapted from Vermunt and Verloop, 1999)

Cognitive processing activities	
Relating/ structuring	Looking for connections Bringing together the different elements
Analysing	Breaking down information – serialist thinking
Concretizing/ applying	Trying to form concrete images from abstract information – looking for relevance Using knowledge in a new way. Trying to solve problems
Memorizing/ rehearsing	Rehearsing material regularly so it can be reproduced
Processing critically	Drawing own conclusions rather than accepting what is said. Actively seeking meaning and evaluating sources
Selecting	Filtering – distinguishing what is most important.
Metacognitive regulation activities	
Orienting and planning	Designing a learning process based on evaluation of requirements of the task, available resources and time
Monitoring/ testing/ diagnosing	Observing during the process whether the learning process is proceeding according to plan; monitoring –checking progress is occurring in intended direction. Testing and diagnosing – explicitly checking and diagnosing where the problem lies
Adjusting	Introducing changes to plans / asking for more support etc.
Evaluating/ reflecting	Judging extent to which outcomes achieved and reflecting about elements of the process
Affective learning activities	
Motivating/ expecting	Building up willingness to learn Process of rewarding self for attaining certain goals. Success vs failure expectations
Concentrating / exerting effort	Directing attention to ensure focus on task at hand, which sometimes can be automatic and at other times requires more constructive and mindful metacognitive regulation
Attributing / judging oneself	Ascribing learning outcomes to causal factors Judgements about oneself – general subjective competence or self-efficacy with respect to certain subjects Capacity for self-regulated learning
Appraising	The ways in which learners appraise the task relevance and relevance to personal goals
Dealing with emotions	Generating, maintaining and restoring positive feelings of well-being, self-confidence and commitment Coping with negative emotions Setting realistic learning goals Reassuring oneself Avoiding stress

The self-regulatory capacity of learners can be developed by:

- ensuring coherent programme design (K. Wilson and Fowler, 2005)
- providing explicit introduction, and induction and ongoing support for the contextual requirements of learning and purposes of specific learning activities, so that students may develop different/more appropriate frames of reference for new learning environments (Yang and Tsai, 2010)
- working with students to enhance cognitive flexibility, and
- providing meaningful modelling, and co-regulation by teachers to assist students to learn how and why to differentiate their own strategies as they engage with different learning tasks.

In developing strategies to support student learning and specifically self-regulation, Hattie (2012) has argued the importance of teachers understanding the underlying reasons for the success of strategies in order to make informed decisions about teaching methods. An understanding of concepts such as working memory capacity, cognitive load, and dual coding from an information processing perspective (Johnstone, 1997; P. D. Klein, 2003; Lalley and Gentile, 2009; Mayer and Moreno, 2003), and an understanding of the plasticity and development potential of the brain from neuroscience perspectives are important (Blakemore and Frith, 2005; Dubinsky *et al.*, 2013; Howard-Jones, 2010; Zull, 2002). In the following section we will explore ways of supporting students' cognitive regulation.

Questions for reflection

Using Table 8.2 on dimensions of self-regulation ask yourself the following questions:

- As a learner which of these areas do you see as specific strengths and which ones as areas of relative weakness? What strategies can you use to develop these?
- As a teacher, how are you seeking to support student self-regulation in your design of the learning environment?
- Which of the self-regulation dimensions are under-represented in your own teaching and why? How are you seeking to develop these?

As part of enhancing teachers' understanding of learning and the underlying reasons for the success of certain strategies in their teaching, we will now discuss why and how teachers should support the cognitive, affective and meta-cognitive processing activities that are integral elements of self-regulation.

Supporting cognitive regulation

One key strategy to enable students to have greater access to learning is to *lessen the complexity of the learning environment* in order to reduce *cognitive overload* in learners (Kyndt *et al.*, 2011; Micari and Light, 2009; Overton and Potter, 2011; Stamovlasis and Tsaparlis, 2005). How information is presented impacts on an individual's cognitive load and therefore his/her capacity to manage a task. 'CLT [Cognitive Load Theory] (van Merriënboer and Sweller, 2005) is based on the assumption that human cognitive architecture allows only a limited amount of information to be processed in WM [working memory] at a certain point in time' (Vogel-Walcutt *et al.*, 2010, p. 134). *Working memory* is a system responsible for processing and storing information during cognitive tasks (Baddeley, 1986). Working memory consists of four components: *a central executive system, a domain-general limited capacity system likened to attention*; supported by two domain-specific storage components: the *phonological loop and visuo-spatial sketchpad* that are specialized for dealing with verbal and visual and spatial information respectively, and fourth, the *episodic buffer* that is responsible for integrating information from the subcomponents of working memory and long-term memory (see Evans *et al.*, 2013; St. Clair-Thompson *et al.*, 2010).

Importantly, information exceeding working memory capacity will not be processed or encoded into *long-term memory* (LTM). LTM is not affected by the capacity issues facing working memory capacity. It is 'a relatively permanent store for a lifetime's worth of knowledge and experience' (St. Clair-Thompson *et al.*, 2012, p. 134). It is able to assimilate new information with previously acquired information in order to create chunks, or large, connected ideas otherwise known as *schemas*. Schemas are mental representations that we use to organize and simplify our knowledge of the world. As learners increase in expertise, their ability to encode, assimilate, retrieve, and apply information becomes automatic with the development of higher level schemas allowing *chunking of information* which then enables procedures to be carried out with minimal demands on working memory (van Merriënboer and Sweller, 2005). Long-term memory is known to be one of the most important characteristics influencing learning and performance; it influences the *perception filter* enabling previous ideas to be used to enable the filter to work more effectively; the importance of prior learning on subsequent performance is also well known (St. Clair-Thompson *et al.*, 2012). Linked to these concepts is learner ability to *selectively attend to information*, also known to impact performance (Howard-Jones, 2010). However, although we know the importance of the relationship between memory components and learning, little attention has been afforded to this in relation to teachers' continuing professional development.

Strategies to increase working memory capacity and reduce cognitive load

From an educational perspective it is important to acknowledge that the burden placed on working memory can be reduced by increasing its capacity or by reducing cognitive load. A number of strategies have been proffered with this in mind, as follows:

- reducing the complexity of the information being taught by focusing on the essentials –a *less is more* approach (Hattie, 2012; Pham, 2012; Vogel-Walcutt *et al.*, 2010),
- using *external memory aids* (post-its; notes; lists; journal entries) and repeating important information
- providing students with an *overview* of each lesson with *clear signposting of ideas* to develop *selective attention skills* so that they know what information is most important (e.g. image size, use of colour, time spent on a specific focus) (Santrock, 2006); or asking conceptual questions that a forthcoming lesson will answer
- using *story-telling* to develop *attention skills* and *memory recall*
- providing *pre-reading tasks* to tap into student prior knowledge as a 'warm-up' to a lesson
- *scaffolding* the information: this could involve aligning the level of complexity of information with the expertise of the learner (Vogel-Walcutt *et al.*, 2010), or organizing instruction in a logical sequence from easy to difficult, concrete to abstract, simple to complicated levels of understanding (Pham, 2012; Tomlinson, 1997; Vogel-Walcutt *et al.*, 2010)
- using *worked examples and partial solutions*, which can help by reducing the load caused by weak problem-solving methods (Sweller *et al.*, 1998)
- *presenting information in the most appropriate way* for the nature of the content and requirements of task (Kozhevnikov *et al.* 2014). Removing extraneous, or distracting, elements (Hattie, 2012); slowing dynamism of PowerPoints (rates of change between clips/pieces or segments of information (Ghinea and Chen, 2003)
- *using more than one presentation modality* (Hattie, 2012). Information can be more easily managed when divided between the two storage components of working memory (the phonological loop and visuospatial sketchpad) (see Paivio 1986; Sweller *et al.*, 1998)
- *integrating multiple sources of information into a single source*, which reduces load by reducing the need for learners to integrate the information for themselves (Rittschof, 2010; Sweller *et al.*, 1998); ideas that need to be associated with each other should be presented near to each other in space and time (Hattie, 2012).
- *enhancing chunking* by
    - increasing the amount of time spent on a task and the amount of repetition
    - segmenting the curriculum into natural components
    - restructuring multiple-step tasks into separate independent steps
- reducing processing demands by *simplifying the language used*, and *increasing the meaningfulness and degree of familiarity of material* to be processed (St. Clair Thompson *et al.*, 2012)
- reducing the *central executive* demands of a task by minimizing inhibitory demands by *exposing students to information in depth*, encouraging them to form links between existing and new knowledge and by completing one topic before moving on to the next.

Supporting metacognitive regulation

While addressing cognitive load is important and constitutes effective teaching practice, to develop *learner self-sufficiency* it is vital that students develop suitable strategies that will enable them to manage their own learning. With this in mind, appropriate addition of scaffolding and, importantly, *removal of scaffolding* need to be attended to by the teacher. Tomlinson's (1997) *equalizer framework* is a useful aid towards doing this as it considers different elements of teaching design in the context of degrees of complexity and how this can be varied in a progressive design to consider a number of important elements of learning design. For example, teachers can consider at what level to pitch their teaching in relation to:

- information, ideas, materials, and applications (e.g. foundational–transformational; simple–complex)
- representations (e.g. concrete–abstract)
- disciplinary connections (e.g. unifaceted–multifaceted)
- developing insights (e.g. small–large leaps)
- decision-making (e.g. degrees of structure: open to more structured)
- process (e.g. clearly defined to fuzzy problems
- planning (e.g. degrees of independence – less–more)
- pace of study (e.g. slower–quicker).

In chapters five and six we have already commented on the importance of working with students to enhance their general cognitive ability, however as Dunlosky *et al.* (2013, p. 46) have highlighted, many students are committed to ineffective and less effective learning strategies; a problem which is compounded by a higher premium being placed on the teaching of content compared to the teaching of skills, and a lack of professional evaluation of the most effective techniques to support specific types of learning within context.

Strategies to develop learning strategies

We know that the type of learning strategies used and the ability to use a variety of strategies impacts on levels of academic performance (Pintrich *et al.*, 1991). Elaborating, organizing, self-explanatory, and self-regulatory strategies have all been found to be beneficial to learning (St. Clair-Thompson *et al.*, 2010). Enhancing learner strategy development includes making efforts to work with students to improve, for example, the *efficiency of working memory and the development of long-term memory* (Commander and Valeri-Gold, 2001; Minear and Shah, 2006). Specifically, students can be taught how to

- use *concept maps or mind maps* to organize knowledge
- process information more quickly using *meta-cognitive strategies* and/or by *repeated practice on working memory tasks*
- use *memory strategies* such as chunking, rehearsal, visual imagery, or semantic strategies to support development and automation of schemas through deliberate practice (involving repetitive experiences with incrementally increasing complexity, immediate feedback, and the opportunity to fine-tune performance) (Ericsson *et al.* (1993). Deliberate practice encourages the development of highly organized schemas and thus the accumulated amount of deliberate practice is closely related to the attained level of performance of many types of experts (Ericsson *et al.*, 1993); forming links between existing and new knowledge, one becomes able to transfer

and adapt ideas from one context to another. The importance of attending to the subject-related requirements of a context have been demonstrated; however, context-specific instruction and styles training also needs to be able to support students to use and apply the big ideas learnt in one context to another within and across lessons, modules, and learning contexts (Solvie and Sungur, 2012)

- *critically explore and focus on the concepts to be learned* instead of on the steps involved in completing a specific task (Pham, 2012)
- *reflect on their own preconceived ideas and expectations* about learning and teaching (Rychly and Graves, 2012), through the use of appropriate tools (e.g. Dewey's (1910) framework for reflection; Brookfield's lenses (Brookfield, 1995); critical incident analysis (Tripp, 1993). Students might consider how their own approaches assist or restrict their learning and consider alternative learning approaches to assist style flexibility and development of independence and not dependence on a particular mode of delivery (Renzulli and Sullivan, 2009; Waring and Evans, 2010)
- consider *multiple ways of interacting* (multiple viewpoints that link facts, skills, procedures and deep conceptual principles; outlining, integrating and synthesizing information rather than re-reading (Dunlosky *et al.*, 2013; Hattie, 2012)
- *manage complexity and uncertainty in learning* (problem solving, simulation, modelling).
- *work collaboratively* (Nordlund, 2003) (to support both individual and collaborative assessment – self and shared understandings; collaborative critical reflection; receiving, giving and acting on feedback; identification of individual strengths and weaknesses to also maximize effectiveness at the group level through thoughtful deployment of roles and responsibilities
- use *practice testing* to enhance learning and retention involving low stakes self-assessment activities (completing practice tests; questions. It is known that this is one strategy that can be highly effective. Attempting to retrieve information involves a search of long-term memory that activates related information, and as explained by Dunlosky *et al.* (2013, p. 30), 'this activated target [information] may then be encoded with retrieved information forming an elaborate trace that affords multiple pathways to facilitate later access to that information.'
- make use of *distributed practice* – distributed learning over time has been found to aid long-term retention more than massing learning opportunities (Dunlosky *et al.*, 2013)
- make use of *interleaved practice* – where students are encouraged to learn content from many different topics or problems of different kinds. It is thought that interleaved practice helps students to discriminate between the different kinds of problems so that they will be more likely to use the correct solution for each one (Dunlosky *et al.*, 2013)

These last three strategies are derived from Dunlosky *et al.*'s (2013) review of effective learning strategies. They have argued that practice testing, distributed, and interleaved practice are among the most effective learning strategies and that it is also straightforward for a teacher to incorporate these ideas into a sequence of lessons by: using practice tests to identify student starting points; revisiting ideas and concepts from previous lessons and by using explanatory questions by getting students to consider how information is new to them, how it relates to what they already know, or why it might be true. Learner strategy development can also be attended to by using metacognitive strategies with students to consider how they learn as outlined in chapters five and six. Working with students to develop their feedback- seeking and -using skills; placing greater emphasis on feedforward rather than feedback, valuing student self-assessment as part of summative assessment, and working with students to support them in developing their own effective networks of support will be explored in chapter nine.

Supporting affective regulation

In supporting both cognitive and metacognitive self-regulation we need to consider how best to support affective self-regulation: the glue that holds the learning process together. In addressing this area, Vermunt and Verloop (1999) highlight four important dimensions: *motivation*, *attributions*, *appraisal*, and *dealing with emotions* (see Table 8.2). To maximize self-regulation capacity Scott *et al.* (2014) highlight the importance of attending to the emotional dimension of learning. The *relational dimension* of learning is of paramount importance in learning to teach. Carol Evans (2014) in reconceptualizing a deep approach to learning to teach attends to a number of affective elements which include student sensitivity to context, managing personal responses to feedback, and resilience.

Resilience can be defined in a number of ways. For Abiola and Udofia (2011) emotional resilience represents the quality that allows you to function well despite the odds against you. In C. Evans's (2014) study, resilience was linked to high levels of self-efficacy, good self-understanding, ability to take risks and to learn from mistakes, and a repertoire of effective coping strategies including the ability to detach oneself from the immediate context, demonstrate perspective, evaluate one's own performance dispassionately, and visualize oneself as the teacher one would like to be.

A promising and growing line of research in supporting learner resilience is that of mindfulness training and specifically the Mindfulness in Schools Programme (MiSP, Kuyken *et al.*, 2013). Mindfulness is about focusing attention, being aware and managing negative thinking. It is essentially about noticing and attending to negative thoughts and feelings, and acting with real awareness rather than operating in a non-thinking automatic pilot mode. It is about being in the moment, being attentively aware of what is going on, and not being distracted by invasive thoughts. Evidence suggests the efficacy of mindfulness training in altering the structure and functioning of the brain, in supporting reduced levels of multi-tasking, and in leading to greater levels of well-being among students. Positive effects have been linked to the extent to which students practice mindfulness skills (Kuyken *et al.*, 2013). As noted by Furnham (2014, p. 2), the 'aim is to challenge the tyranny of the urgent' which is exacerbated in the globalized internet world. For mindfulness training to be effective, Furnham, like Kuyken *et al.*, highlights the importance of continuity in training, along with a personal commitment and willingness on the part of individuals to incorporate mindfulness approaches into their lifestyles to support effective change: this is important from teacher and learner perspectives.

Resilience is also associated with the development of persistence and quality of effort in studying. Duckworth *et al.* (2007, p. 1087–1088) in their interpretation of resilience have focused on the notion of *grit* which they define as:

'working strenuously toward challenges, maintaining effort and interest over years despite failure, adversity, and plateaus in progress. The gritty individual approaches achievement as a marathon; his or her advantage is stamina. Whereas disappointment or boredom signals to others that it is time to change trajectory and cut losses, the gritty individual stays the course.'

Gladwell (2008, 2013) commenting on the ten-thousand-hour research (Simon and Chase, 1973) has acknowledged that cognitively complex activities take many years to master, but also focuses on the quality of effort. The 'ten-thousand-hours to become an expert' idea must be understood as an *average*, as there is a fair amount of variation behind that number: some individuals use their practice time so efficiently that they reach a high degree of excellence more quickly (Epstein, 2013: Gladwell, 2013).

The motivational dimension of learning is also of paramount importance in sustaining self-regulation. The importance of promoting mastery orientations to learning rather than self-worth and learned helplessness is well known (Leo and Galloway, 1994; Seifert, 2004). 'The adaptive ("mastery-oriented") pattern is characterized by 'challenge seeking and high, effective persistence in the face of obstacles' (Dweck, 1986, p. 1040) where an individual is concerned with achieving success, rather than avoiding failure. Whereas in the case of self-worth motivation: 'students stand to gain a great deal by not trying. The self-worth theory is based on the notion that much of a student's behaviour is designed to maintain a self-concept of high ability' (Craske, 1988, p. 153). Underpinning self-worth motivation is the concern of the individual regarding the impact of their performance of a particular task, on their self-esteem, rather than concern about the performance itself. Such students have the belief that they are capable but at the same time are uncertain about their capabilities. In the case of learned helplessness an individual attributes a lack of success to a lack of ability and 'lack[s] control in obtaining a desired outcome' (Craske, p. 1988, p. 152). In both self-worth and learned helplessness motivations, success is attributed to external factors such as luck, ease, or generosity of the teacher whereas mastery-oriented students are more likely to attribute their success to a combination of skill and effort, and their failures to a lack of proper effort.

Strategies to develop mastery orientation and achievement related learner behaviour

Specific strategies to support the development of mastery orientation advocated by Leo and Galloway (1994) include:

- for learned-helplessness-motivated students – enhance the use of *small group problem-solving situations* where children perceive that they have more control over their own learning
- to support students exhibiting self-worth motivation – develop a *classroom climate of co-operation* where *emphasis is placed on effort* and the value of incremental learning and peer support, with a focus on task rather than product
- to encourage mastery ensure *sufficient challenge* and *student self-responsibility* for learning through metacognitive skill development.

At a broader level, to support the development of achievement-related learner beliefs Stipek (1998) considers the nature of tasks, goals, evaluation, giving of help, direct statements, and classroom structure, as outlined in Table 8.3.

Table 8.3 Supporting the development of achievement-related learner beliefs

Effective classroom practice (Stipek, 1998, pp. 94–109): examples of practice
Tasks and assignments
1 Give tasks that are challenging but achievable for all students (e.g. vary the difficulty of task according to student skill level, provide tasks that are completed at different levels, ensure highest achievers are challenged)
2 Organize assignments to provide frequent opportunities to students to observe increases in their skills (order problems and assignments by difficulty level, break down difficult tasks into subunits)
Goals
3 Create short-term proximal goals
4 Vary goals among students
5 Engage students in personal goal setting (e.g. provide incentives for setting challenging goals
Evaluation
6 Give students different ways to demonstrate what they know
7 Point out what is good, right, or shows improvement
8 Provide clear, specific, and informative feedback
9 Base rewards on achieving a clearly defined standard or set of criteria or on personal improvement (ipsative)
10 Give students multiple opportunities to achieve high grades (emphasis on formative side of feedback)
11 Teach students to celebrate their classmates' successes at whatever levels they occur
12 Minimise public evaluations (e.g. limit whole class displays of results, ensure fair contests in that all students have a chance of winning, get students to monitor and record their own progress personally, ensure students have opportunities to interact with the teacher one-to-one or in small groups)
13 Teach students to evaluate their own work (e.g. encourage students to use their own judgements, provide opportunities for students to check their own work, provide students with explicit instructions on how to evaluate their own work; link evaluation criteria to instruction)
14 Be clear and consistent
Giving help
15 Encourage students to seek help (e.g. model help seeking)
16 Give no more assistance than is necessary (e.g. teach students how to access information and resources to support their own learning)
17 Encourage students to use peers for assistance (e.g. teach students how to give help)
Direct statements
18 Attribute failure to low effort of an ineffective strategy and model adaptive attributions
19 Attribute successes to effort and competence
Classroom structure
20 Differentiate tasks among students over time (e.g. different students work on several different kinds of tasks on any day, and the types of tasks students are given varies from day to day)
21 Point out 'within student' variation in skill levels
22 Involve all students productively when instructing in a whole-class format
23 Use 'ability groupings' flexibly and temporarily to address specific skill needs
24 Convey the value of many different kinds of skills
25 Give relatively poor-performing students the role of 'expert' / leader of a group

Questions for reflection

Consider the 25 areas of practice as advocated by Stipek to support positive motivational styles. To these we would add '*smart failing*' –supporting students to understand that failing is part of learning and to learn to recognize early inefficient strategies and approaches.

- Which of the 25 areas identified in Table 8.3 are most important in your practice?
- What would you add to this list?
- Are there areas of practice mentioned in Table 8.3 that you would disagree with? If so, why?

Attending to the motivational component of affective self-regulation is important, along with a consideration of the interrelated nature of cognitive, metacognitive, and affective dimensions of self-regulation. Carol Evans (2013b) has argued that too little attention has up to now been focused on the 'glue': the affective dimension that underpins the effectiveness of learner self-regulatory skills within and across learning contexts.

Summary

Central to the PLSP is student voice and supporting students to manage their own learning through focusing attention on self-regulatory development. The notion of providing sufficient challenge for students to attain their full potential and the provision and removal of scaffolding by the teacher are important ways of achieving this. As part of that challenge it is vital to strike the right balance to ensure constructive rather than destructive friction for learners in order to challenge existing ways of thinking without overwhelming them. It is important to remember that this is not about promoting and designing adaptive styles to suit the needs of specific individual student preferences. It is a matter of the critical use of evidence on effective learning from a range of domains (education, psychology, neuroscience) to inform learning and teaching designs, and, as part of this, acknowledging the emotional dimension of learning. Fundamentally it is about understanding what, how and when students learn, whom they learn with, how they use their learning within and across contexts, where they access information; how they learn new skills and apply them; and how they manage success and failure.

In examining context, it is also important to consider how both students and teachers relate learning and teaching in the classroom to other contexts (different subjects; classes; roles within school, home, and the wider community); issues of authenticity and relevance also matter.

Teachers' and students' perceptions and beliefs are strong and significant predictors of individual change. Integral and interrelated elements of self-regulation are cognitive, affective and metacognitive processing activities.

In developing strategies to support student learning and specifically self-regulation it is imperative that teachers understand the underlying reasons for the success of these strategies in order to make informed decisions about teaching methods. Therefore, an understanding of concepts such as working memory capacity, cognitive load, and dual coding from an information processing perspective and an understanding of the plasticity and development potential of the brain from neuroscience perspectives is necessary.

As part of cognitive regulation one key strategy to enable students to have greater access to learning is to lessen the complexity of the learning environment in order to reduce cognitive overload in learners. How information is presented impacts on an individual's cognitive load and therefore their capacity to manage a task. Significantly, information exceeding working memory capacity will not be processed or encoded into long-term memory. We know that long-term memory is one of the most important-characteristics influencing learning and performance. Therefore, from an educational perspective it is important to acknowledge that the burden placed on working memory can be reduced by increasing its capacity or by reducing cognitive load, and there are a number of effective strategies to achieve this.

As part of supporting metacognitive regulation and the development of learner self-sufficiency it is vital that students develop suitable learning strategies to be able to manage their own learning with the addition and removal of scaffolding. We know that the type of learning strategies used and the ability to use a variety of strategies affects levels of academic performance. Enhancing learner strategy development includes efforts to work with students to improve, for example, the efficiency of working memory and the development of long-term memory.

Affective self-regulation has four important dimensions (motivation, attributions, appraisal and dealing with emotions) and is the 'glue' that holds the learning processes together, also supporting both cognitive and metacognitive self-regulation. It is essential that the emotional regulation be attended to if self-regulatory capacity is tobe maximized. The relational dimension of learning is of paramount importance in learning to teach.

This chapter has outlined a number of strategies to support student self-regulation; it is by no means exhaustive but does demonstrate the importance of attending to self-regulation and the interrelationships between cognitive, metacognitive and emotional dimensions of learning.

Questions for reflection

Consider the two competing perspectives (outlined in the references below) on the relative importance of practice on performance and the implications of these findings for your own teaching and learning.

Macnamara, B. N., Hambrick, D. Z., and Oswald, F. L. (2014). Deliberate practice and performance in Music, Games, Sports, Education, and Professions. A meta-analysis. *Psychological Science, 25*(8), 1608–1618.

Syed, M. (2010). *Bounce: The myth of talent and the power of practice.* New York: Harper Collins Publishers.

Key readings

Hattie, J. (2012). *Visible learning for teachers. Maximizing impact on learning.* London: Routledge.

This book utilizes findings from over 900 meta-analyses to analyze what works and what does not work in the classroom that are built into the Visible Learning framework, which is essentially constructivist in nature and draws on work in education, psychology, and neuroscience. (Also see Hattie and Yates, 2014.)

Kuyken, W., Weare, K., Ukoumunee, O. C., Vicary, R., Motton, N., Burnett, R., Cullen, C., Hennelly, S., and Huppert, F. (2013). Effectiveness of the mindfulness in schools programme: Non-randomised controlled feasibility study. *The British Journal of Psychiatry, 9203 (2), 126–131.*

This article describes the effectiveness of implementing a mindfulness training programme into schools along with associated training for teachers. Further information is also available from the Exeter mindfulness network – details of which can be found in the Weblinks section of this chapter.

St. Clair-Thompson, H., Overton, T., and Botton, C. (2010). Information processing: A review of implications of Johnstone's model for science education. *Research in Scienceand Technological Education, 28*(2), 131–148.

This article focuses on the value of an understanding of information processing models in supporting student learning and achievement. It specifically looks at field independence cognitive style, working and long-term memory and how these can be developed through the use of specific learning and teaching strategies; while written within the context of science, it has applications to all disciplines.

Stipek, D. (1998). (3rd ed.) *Motivation to learn: from theory to practice.* Massachusetts: Alyn and Bacon.

This book provides a comprehensive overview of motivational theories and demonstrates how an understanding of this area can be used to support students' learning and enable learners to become more self-regulatory. Dweck's (2006; 2012) works on positive mindsets are also useful to consider.

Weblinks

Clare, J. D. (2004/6). '*Differentiation*', at Greenfield History site. Available online at http//www.johnclare.net/Teaching/Teaching_Differentiation.html (accessed 14 June 2014).

Exeter Mindfulness Network. Available online at http://www.exeter-mindfulness-network.org/ (accessed 14 May 2014).

Gladwell, M. (2013). Complexity and the ten-thousand-hour rule. Available online at http://www.newyorker.com/online/blogs/sportingscene/2013/08/psychology-ten-thousand-hour-rule-complexity.html (accessed 20 September 2013).

Huitt, W. G. (2013). Ed psych interactive. Available online at http://www.edpsycinteractive.org/materials/elecfile.html (accessed 1 May 2014).

Mindfulness in Schools website. Available online at http://mindfulnessinschools.org/ http://mindfulnessinschools.org/research/research-evidence-mindfulness-schools-project/ (accessed 14 May 2014).

OECD (2007). Understanding the brain: the birth of a learning science. Paris, OECD Publishing). Available online at http://www.oecd.org/site/educeri21st/40554190. (accessed 12 January 2014).

Schwartz, B. (2013). The paradox of choice on TED. Available online at http://www.ted.com/speakers/barry_schwartz (accessed 10 May 2014).

Chapter 9

Making sense of assessment and feedback

Overview

Framed by a holistic conception of assessment this chapter provides an overview of the key principles of effective assessment that includes feedback and demonstrates how these principles can be applied effectively within school and higher education contexts. We will argue the importance of supporting students to manage their own learning through enabling them to effectively self-monitor their own progress in learning. Students need to have a clear idea of their current standard, the standard required, and an understanding of how to bridge the gap between these positions (Sadler, 1989; 2010) as an essential part of sustainable assessment practice (Boud, 2000; Hounsell, 2007), and most importantly, a will to do so. In considering the will and desire aspect of learning, we acknowledge a need for a greater focus on the emotional dimension of feedback and associated student resilience in learning as highlighted in chapter eight.

Introduction: defining assessment and feedback

Our holistic definition of assessment sees assessment and feedback processes as integral elements of learning, whereas more narrow definitions equate assessment purely with measurement (Evans, 2013b). In fact, the failing of assessment feedback strategies has been attributed to too much emphasis being placed on the grading function of assessment and not enough attention focused on assisting students to learn (see Wiliam, 2011).

Black and Wiliam's (1998) *Inside the Black Box* galvanized interest in formative assessment with this work being taken forward by the Assessment Reform Group who as part of the publication of *Beyond the Black Box* (ARG, 1999) highlighted the importance of assessment for learning rather than assessment of learning (visit Assessment Reform Group and New Zealand's Education Ministry websites for summaries). While the ARG's (2002) ten principles of assessment for learning listed below may be well known, the manner in which they have been implemented in practice has been variable.

Assessment, according to the ARG

- should be part of effective planning
- focuses on how students learn
- is central to classroom practice
- is a key professional skill
- is sensitive and constructive
- fosters motivation

- promotes understanding of goals and criteria
- helps learners know how to improve
- develops the capacity for self-assessment
- recognizes all educational achievement.

A key problem in this regard has been the lack of consensus surrounding definitions of both *formative assessment* and *assessment for* and *of learning (AfL* and *AoL)* (see Wiliam, 2011 for an overview). Despite the best efforts of the ARG, the term *formative assessment* and the effective use of the ideas underpinning the strategy have been reduced in many instances to a limited association with measurement rather than AfL being seen as an integral part of learning. In England this has been, in no small part, due to the government's hijacking of the term AfL as part of policy and isolating it to emphasize the monitoring of pupils' progress (DfES, 2008). Eleanore Hargreaves (2005) echoes these sentiments in her exploration of teachers' conceptions of assessment for learning in that although the AfL principles place an emphasis on a *process* rather than a *performance* view involving active student engagement, in reality the *Black Box* became synonymous with a product view of assessment for learning, emphasizing measurement with teachers assuming most of the control: not what Black and Wiliam had intended. Wiliam as reported by Stewart (2012) argued that in retrospect the biggest mistake that was made was in the use of the term *assessment* rather than *better teaching*.

Such unsatisfactory interpretations that equate formative assessment to assessment for learning (AfL) and summative assessment representing assessment of learning (AoL) have also been extremely unhelpful, as in reality the picture is far more complex (for example, summative feedback can serve to inform future performance). Eleanore Hargreaves (2005, p. 224) has argued that these two approaches (AoL and AfL) are better conceived as forming two ends of a spectrum with 'a conception of knowledge as external to the learner and fixed—at one extreme [*AoL*]; and a conception of knowledge as constructed or co-constructed by the learner/s and as fluid [*AfL*] at - the other extreme.' An alternative perspective contrasts *cognitivist* approaches to assessment, which include feedback with a directive telling, and corrective approach from an expert to a passive recipient, with *constructivist* approaches, which are seen as more facilitative and dialogic. However, these should not been seen as opposite ends of a spectrum as they are not mutually exclusive (Evans, 2013b). Fundamentally, good assessment including feedback is about providing the right approach to support task, individual and contextual needs.

When considering what leads to more effective use of assessment in learning, an enhanced role for the pupil in assessment features, for example in Wiliam and Thompson's (2008) elaboration of formative assessment, building on the work of Royce Sadler (1989, 2010). Wiliam (2011) has argued that for assessment to support learning a number of conditions are required. He has urged that evidence is needed to indicate what kinds of instructional activities are likely to result in improved performance; which activities, that is, will engage learners in actions to improve learning). In this model, assessment for learning is presented as five key strategies and one cohering idea. The five key strategies are: engineering effective classroom discussions, questions, and learning tasks; clarifying and sharing learning intentions and criteria for success; providing feedback that moves learners forward; activating students as the owners of their own learning; and activating students as instructional resources for one another (Wiliam and Thompson, 2008). The cohering idea is that evidence about student learning is used to adapt instruction better to meet learning needs; in other words, teaching is adaptive to the student's learning needs and evidence from the assessments is used by teachers, learners, or their peers to improve instruction (ibid.). An important aspect of this model is the active engagement of the learner in the learning process, which is also evident in the Organisation for Economic Development and Co-operation's (OECD) (2013) identification of assessment policy priorities arising from an evaluation of assessment and evaluation practice in 28 OECD countries. Key priorities in their report include the following:

1 Integrate student assessment and school evaluation into a single framework: 'This requires a holistic approach to building a complete evaluation and assessment framework in view of generating synergies between its components, avoiding duplication of procedures and preventing inconsistency of objectives.' (OECD, 2013, summary p. 10).
2 Align student learning goals with evaluation and assessment.
3 Focus on the improvement of classroom practices and building on teacher professionalism.
4 Effectively conceive the accountability uses of evaluation and assessment results.
5 Place the student at the centre, fostering engagement in learning through using formative assessment strategies.
6 Go beyond measurement in educational evaluation. Measures of performance should be broad enough to capture the whole range of student learning objectives.
7 Build capacity for evaluation and assessment.
8 Design evaluation and assessment procedures that are fit for purpose.
9 Balance national consistency with meeting local needs.
10 Implement evaluation and assessment policy successfully.

Building on the OECD recommendations and Lord Bew's report (Department for Education (DfE), 2011b) on the uses of data derived from summative assessments, the British Educational Research Association (BERA) reconvened the UK Assessment Reform Group to emphasize the importance of the potential of the *formative* use of summative assessment (see BERA, 2013b) in response to the English DfE's proposals for assessment of primary school pupils.

In summary, both formative and summative assessment can support students' learning; the nature and role of feedback in supporting students' learning is of paramount importance. Given the confusion surrounding the nature of formative and summative assessment it is important to establish a clear and shared definition of feedback.

How feedback is defined and enacted is complex. Much depends on how the role of feedback is perceived. Hattie and Timperley (2007, p. 81) emphasize a *product* view of feedback: 'information provided by an agent (e.g. teacher, peer, book, parent, self, experience) regarding aspects of one's performance or understanding'. Boud (2000) and Hounsell *et al.* (2008) have both placed greater emphasis on feedback as an *integral part of learning* to include *feed-forward* and *feed-up* where feedback is seen as supporting learning in the immediate context as well as for future learning gains. Ramaprasad (1983) and Sadler (1989, 2005) argued that feedback is more than about the provision of information: it is about *closing the gap between where a learner is and where they need to get to* in order to make progress.

Carol Evans (2013b) in her definition of feedback emphasizes the notion of *feedback exchange*, which implies an important role for both student and teacher in supporting the development of learning. She acknowledges that feedback can be vicarious, and that it can be drawn from within and beyond the immediate learning context and from a vast array of sources, highlighting the importance of student information networks. According to Evans feedback, as an integral part of assessment, ' . . . includes all *feedback exchanges* generated within assessment design, occurring within and beyond the immediate learning context, being overt or covert (actively and/or passively sought and/or received), and importantly, drawing from a range of sources.' (2013b, p. 71).

Evans (2013b) emphasizes the importance of student agency in feedback. All assessment for learning models should include, as part of the assessment design, opportunities for students to use feedback to improve their work. The efficacy of the feedback process is highly dependent on how the role of different agents (e.g. teacher, student, peers/ colleagues, family, resource networks) is perceived by both the learner and the teacher. Are students seen as active participants in the feedback process or as passive recipients of feedback? It is interesting that although the *Teachers' standards* in England (DfE, 2011a) emphasize that the teacher's role is to '*encourage pupils to take a responsible and conscientious attitude to their own work and study*' (Standard 2), the rhetoric positions the student as a passive receiver rather than as an active agent in the assessment process. Regular feedback from the teacher matters, but so does the teacher's role in stimulating students to take greater responsibility by seeking out, interrogating, and giving feedback, all of which enhance their self-assessment and peer-assessment abilities. This prevents them from becoming passive consumers, and enables them to cope with the changing demands of 21st-century learning environments and support their own life-long learning and that of others. The need to see assessment and feedback as an *ongoing dialogue* rather than as information transmission is a key feature of sustainable assessment practice and is prominent in current effectiveness debates. It is a crucial dimension of 21st-century learning environments in which information is readily available from a variety of sources: environments in which the teacher is seen not as the font of all knowledge, but as a catalyst of a process of learning linked with a holistic notion of pedagogy.

In sum, how feedback is enacted depends on whether or not it is viewed as integral to learning and teaching. It also depends on how the purpose of feedback is perceived by the teacher and learner, for example as a tool that is challenging *vs* corrective, facilitative *vs* telling, informative *vs* reinforcing , motivational (asking what is good, and what can be better) *vs* fault-finding (pointing out what has not been done and not achieved), inquiring *vs* measuring; learning-focused *vs* performance-focused) (see Scott *et al.*, 2014).

What is sustainable feedback and why does it matter?

Sustainable assessment is about the increasing role of the student in assessment practice and the changing role of the teacher in order to facilitate student autonomy in the process (Evans, 2013b; Scott *et al.*, 2014). Boud (2000) defines it as practices that meet students' immediate assessment needs whilst not compromising the knowledge, skills, and dispositions they require to develop lifelong learning activities (see also Carless, 2011). As part of sustainable assessment, Hounsell (2007) discusses sustainable feedback and highlights the importance of three related areas of activity: feedback carrying impact beyond the immediate task; enhancing the student role in generating, interpreting and engaging with feedback; and the development of learning and teaching environments that promote dialogue about learning. Carless (2011) and Carless *et al.* (2011) in defining sustainable feedback stress the metacognitive potential of dialogic activities which can support students in generating and using feedback from self and others as part of an ongoing process of becoming autonomous self-regulating learners. In all three definitions, emphasis is on developing student self-regulatory ability; this requires training on the part of students *and* teachers to develop co-regulatory feedback practice (Price *et al.*, 2007).

While the importance of sustainable assessment has been clearly established, supporting its development within the school context has not been easy. Nicol (2008) has highlighted, for example, the extent to which students can and should be involved in all aspects of the assessment design. Inadvertently, the great emphasis placed on student monitoring and target setting has encouraged students' dependence rather than independence in their learning (e.g. *The Assessment for Learning Strategy*, DFES/AfL, 2008). Teaching to the test has led to criteria compliance: although immediate targets have been satisfied in terms of the percentage pass rate of students, preparing students to self-assess their own work in order to manage their future learning has been neglected. The lack of a strong focus on students becoming owners of their own learning is identified by Stewart (2012) quoting Wiliam, as a fundamental reason for the lack of effectiveness of such assessment for learning strategies within schools.

Reviewing the literature: signposting key themes

A considerable amount of work on assessment including feedback has been undertaken in school and higher education contexts. In supporting learner transitions from school to higher education contexts, evidence from school-based research suggests that there need to be more opportunities for oral dialogue as opposed to written feedback, a greater focus on how pedagogical strategies can create the conditions for effective learning by supporting students in taking more responsibility for their own learning, better alignment between formative and summative assessment, and an increase in the attention focused on innovative practice in summative assessment (Black and McCormick, 2010). Evans (2012a) has also commented on the need to bridge the higher education and school research and practice gap in order to enhance formative assessment and feedback practice.

Whilst acknowledging differences between the school and HEI sectors including specific contextual demands (Sadler, 2010), there are a number of overarching principles of good assessment and feedback which are relevant to all those engaged in enhancing learning and teaching. Much work being undertaken within higher education in developing assessment feedback practice is of direct relevance to schools (Evans, 2013b), and in order to facilitate student transitions from school to higher education and into the workplace it is vital to develop collaborative practice within this area. A key priority for both sectors is in supporting students to become more independent in their learning and the substantial bodies of work on self-regulation, peer feedback, and e-assessment feedback within higher education are of relevance to the school sector.

Does feedback work?

Feedback can be very powerful (Black and Wiliam, 1998; Hattie and Timperley, 2007), however its impact is highly variable (Evans, 2013b). The aim of feedback should be to enable the *gap between an actual level of performance and a desired learning goal to be bridged* (Ramaprasad, 1983; Sadler, 1989). It is the use and application of feedback to positively impact performance that is of paramount importance (Wiliam, 2011). Evans (2013b) drawing on constructivist, socio-critical and socio-cultural perspectives used a conceptual framework, *the Feedback Landscape* (see Figure 9.1) to examine affordance and barriers for learners and teachers (including individual and contextual variables) in the seeking, giving, and application of assessment feedback. The fundamental issue is that even if all the conditions for effective feedback are met, it is the *will and skill* on the part of the learner that are of paramount importance in influencing outcomes. This leads to the question of what level of investment should a teacher make given the paucity of clear research findings. In answering this question Evans (2013b), drawing on DeNisi and Kluger's (2000) work, has argued the case for the implementation of holistic assessment designs that place greater potential on feed-forward compared to feedback, and cites extensive research literature demonstrating the actual effectiveness of such initiatives.

Questions for reflection

Using the *Feedback Landscape* diagram Figure 9.1

- Map the sources of feedback that you rely on and identify which are your strongest links and which sources of support could be developed.
- Ask students to map the sources of feedback that they mainly use in order to develop their own understanding of their feedback-using patterns.
- Ask students to discuss with each other how they can develop their feedback gathering skills. (Sources can be other people within and external to school: other teachers, peers within their own class or other classes and year groups, social groups; resources can be of many different kinds, e.g. books, TV, internet, smartphone, apps, etc.).

What are holistic assessment designs?

Holistic assessment designs can be enacted in a number of different ways but they share common principles, which include:

- feedback is ongoing and an integral part of assessment
- feedback guidance is explicit
- greater emphasis is placed on feedforward compared to feedback activities
- students are engaged in, and with, the process
- the technicalities of feedback (e.g. timing and nature of feedback; availability of resources; clarity regarding assessment requirements) are attended to in order to support learning

(see Evans, 2013b, pp. 80–83 for extended discussion and additional references).

These features of design have been repeatedly identified as important in school contexts (Assessment Reform Group, 1999; Wiliam and Thompson, 2008) and in higher education settings (Boud *et al.*, 2010; Carless *et al.*, 2006; Nicol and MacFarlane-Dick, 2006). The practical application of these features is evidenced in C. Evans's (2013b) twelve key principles of effective assessment design (see Figure 9.2). These principles relate to five main interrelated areas of concern, which we will now discuss in more detail; these areas are:

- assessment design
- the role of the student
- preparation and housekeeping issues
- clarifying what is good
- the nature and design of feedback.

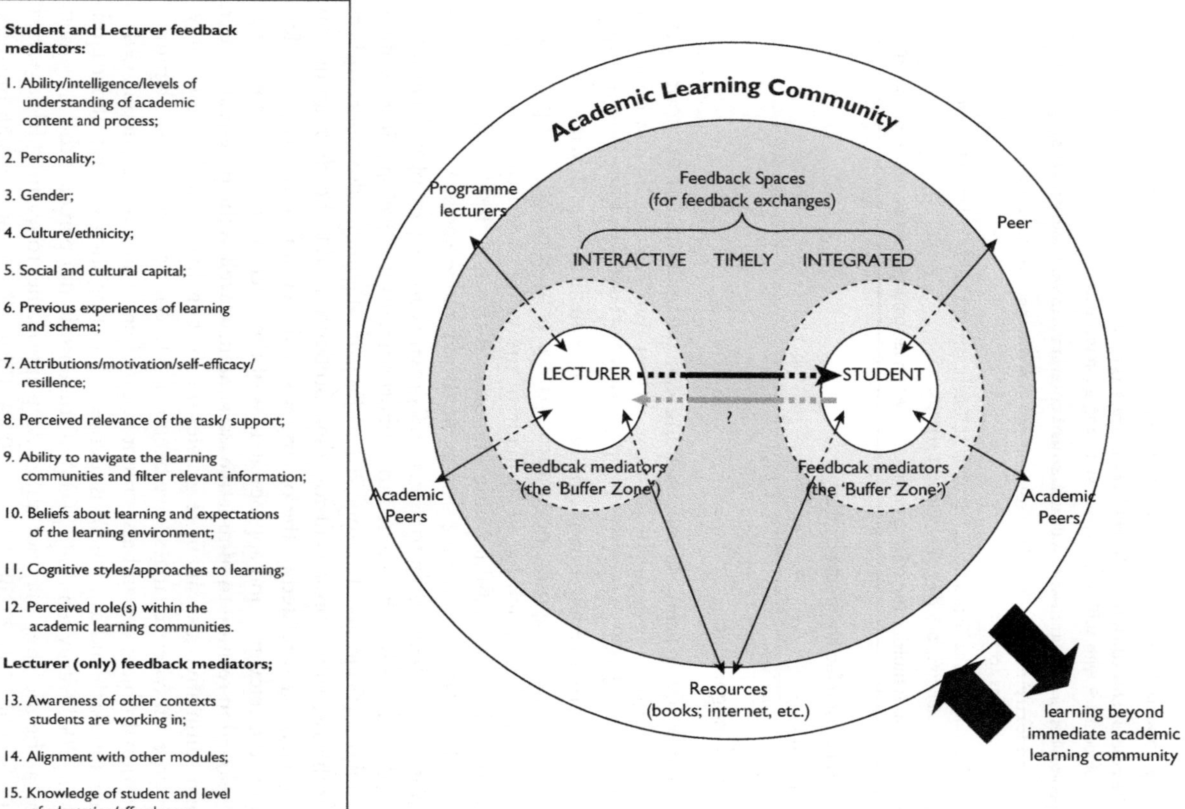

Student and Lecturer feedback mediators:
1. Ability/intelligence/levels of understanding of academic content and process;
2. Personality;
3. Gender;
4. Culture/ethnicity;
5. Social and cultural capital;
6. Previous experiences of learning and schema;
7. Attributions/motivation/self-efficacy/resillence;
8. Perceived relevance of the task/ support;
9. Ability to navigate the learning communities and filter relevant information;
10. Beliefs about learning and expectations of the learning environment;
11. Cognitive styles/approaches to learning;
12. Perceived role(s) within the academic learning communities.
Lecturer (only) feedback mediators;
13. Awareness of other contexts students are working in;
14. Alignment with other modules;
15. Knowledge of student and level of adaptation/affordances.
Academic Learning Community
Feedback Spaces
(for feedback exchanges)
INTERACTIVE
TIMELY
INTEGRATED
Programme lecturers
Peer
LECTURER
STUDENT
?
Feedbcak mediators (the 'Buffer Zone')
Feedbcak mediators (the 'Buffer Zone')
Academic Peers
Academic Peers
Resources
(books; internet, etc.)
learning beyond immediate academic learning community

Figure 9.1 The feedback landscape

Evans, 2013b, p. 98

1. Ensuring an appropriate **range and choice** of assessment opportunities throughout a programme of study.
2. Ensuring guidance about assessment is **integrated** into all teaching sessions.
3. Ensuring **all resources** are available to students via VLEs and other sources from the **start of a programme** to enable students to take responsibility for organizing their own learning.
4. Clarifying **with** students how **all elements of assessment fit together** and why they are relevant and valuable.
5. Providing **explicit guidance** to students on the requirements of assessment.
6. Clarifying with students the different **forms and sources of feedback** available, including e-learning opportunities.
7. Ensuring **early opportunities** for students to undertake assessment and obtain feedback.
8. Clarifying the **role of the student** in the feedback process as an active participant rather than merely as a receiver of feedback with sufficient knowledge to engage in feedback.
9. Providing opportunities for students to work with **assessment criteria** and to work with examples of good work.
10. Giving **clear and focused** feedback on how students can improve their work including **signposting** the most important areas to address.
11. Ensuring support is in place to help students develop **self-assessment skills** including **training in peer feedback** possibilities, including peer support groups.
12. Ensuring **training opportunities for staff** to enhance shared understanding of assessment requirements.

Figure 9.2 Key features of effective feedback design

Adapted from Evans, 2013b, p. 79

Assessment design: alignment

Assessment design really matters. Good teaching can be undermined by poor assessment design. The notion of alignment is of paramount importance and can be looked at from a number of related perspectives. First, Biggs's (1999) and Biggs and Tang's (2011) notion of constructive alignment (the extent to which there is a match between learning objectives, teaching approaches and the nature of assessment) is of paramount importance. Second, while much has been made of the value of formative assessment, it is less likely to lead to successful learning outcomes if it is not closely aligned to the requirements of the related summative *assessment* (Boud and Associates, 2010). Third, given the importance of being able to assess one's own work as part of lifelong learning, assessment design needs to be aligned to support students to develop self-assessment skills and capabilities (Boud and Lawson, 2011). Fourth, alignment also refers to how all elements of the assessment process fit together. Students need to be clear about how each assessment element is related to the others. A key dimension of this is the student being able to see the relevance and appropriateness of the teaching strategies and assessment tasks employed in relation to summative assessment, as well as the potential benefits of such beyond summative assessment (e.g. relevant to their lives, and future employment). However, even where changes have been made to ensure constructive alignment between educational objectives and assessment (e.g. where students are encouraged to develop a deep approach and assessment is focused on testing such student understanding) (Biggs *et al.*, 2001; Struyven *et al.*, 2006), if students do not perceive the assessment as relevant and authentic, they may not utilize deep approaches to learning (Balasooriya, *et al.*, 2011; Ferla *et al.*, 2009; Gijbels *et al.*, 2008). Fifth, alignment between organizational, departmental and individual teachers' enactment of assessment practices is very important (James and Pedder, 2006).

The role of the student

Fundamental to the development of holistic assessment is the increased role of the student in the assessment process (Carless, 2011), something which should permeate all decisions about assessment and feedback design. Central to such decisions about student agency and autonomy in the assessment process are notions of '*will' and 'skill'*. Students' personal histories (experiences of assessment), their levels of self-regulation, knowledge and skills vary; consequently, some students are more willing and able than others to make use of the opportunities afforded to them as part of holistic assessment design. The notion of *choice and perception of choice* in assessment, and how both teachers and students manage this, is very important. The provision of choice in the nature of assessment for a student who is low on self-regulating ability (Evans, 2013b) could be seen as negligent by the teacher given the student's relative lack of ability to choose wisely: the issue of *directed choice* is important here. The importance of supporting students to make *informed choices* as part of self-regulatory development should be a prime focus for teachers along with being explicit regarding the criteria requirements for different forms of assessment. Furthermore, students vary in their feedback seeking, feedback giving and feedback using skills. Joughin (2009) identified that some students were very *cue-conscious* and *cue-seeking* in knowing how to access feedback well. However, others he described as '*cue deaf*' in that they were not active feedback seekers and found it more difficult to utilize the feedback opportunities that were present. Similarly, Evans (2012b; 2014) identified '*savvy feedback seekers*' who were more able than others to access and filter feedback from various networks (self, peers, teachers, family, internet, books etc.). The challenge is in how best to support students to develop these life-long learning skills as part of effective assessment design so that they are best able to meet twenty-first-century learning challenges. Dweck, (1986, p. 1046) noted that 'the procedures that bring about more adaptive motivational patterns are the ones that incorporate challenge, and even failure, within a learning-oriented context and that explicitly address underlying motivational mediators'. Therefore, supporting student access to assessment and feedback requires consideration of the following areas as highlighted in the Personal Learning Styles Pedagogy (see section D (ix) of the PLSP Framework and also Tables 8.19 and 9.1):

- exploring students' previous experiences of feedback and the emotional dimension of feedback
- involving students in design of curriculum and assessment
- exploring students' networks of support
- supporting student self-regulation through the design of tools and environments to enable students to self- and peer assess providing ongoing training to students in how to give and make use of feedback opportunities
- clarifying the role of the student in the process and what sources of feedback available.

In attending to these areas the research tells us a great deal. Students' beliefs about learning impact on how they see their role in feedback (Evans and Waring , 2011a; Price *et al.*, 2010). Not enough attention has been given to the emotional dimension of feedback (Evans, 2013b). A key reason why feedback may not work is that even if feedback is given at the task level, students may interpret it at the personal level and this is connected to their levels of self-efficacy (DeNisi and Kluger, 2000). In addressing potential feedback issues, it is important to consider how the design of assessment can support students in the adoption of *mastery*, rather than *self-worth* or *learned helplessness motivations* as discussed in chapter eight. Consequently, in supporting the learning of all students, key questions for teachers to ask include:

Table 9.1 Using the Personal Learning Styles Pedagogy to support assessment design

Components of a Personal Learning Styles Pedagogy	*Examples of assessment practice*
A. Exploration of student and teacher beliefs/modelling and support	
(i) Focus on the learning histories of student and teacher (ii) Holistic understanding: Consideration of the whole experience of the learner **(iii) Exploration of learner (student and teacher) beliefs about learning (e.g. ability, self-efficacy, identity and sense of fit within learning contexts)** (iv) Enhancing learner awareness and application of styles as part of ongoing instruction on individual learning differences. Understanding of individual differences central to the design of learning environments	Foci (Example for A (iii) sub-component) • Exploration of students' experiences of assessment feedback including peer assessment and feedback • Mapping of assessment and exploration of how assessment tasks are relevant to the immediate requirements of assessment and professional practice • Examination of student aspirations and intentions regarding their aims and intentions in relation to assessment • Explication of the student role within the feedback process • Explicit attention given to the emotional dimension of feedback
B. Careful selection and application of models	
(i) Judicious and informed use of instruments/ styles models **(ii) Critical analysis of styles as part of instruction on individual learning differences. Appropriate application of styles models: instruments used as metacognitive tools to support understanding of the learning process** (iii) An integrated approach: awareness of the interdependence of cognitive style and other individual learning differences – role of cognitive style as a moderator variable (iv) Development of cognitive styles as an integral element of culturally responsive pedagogies	Foci (Example for B (ii) sub-component) • Analysis of student assessment preferences from a cognitive styles perspective, including analysis of student self-regulation strategies • Explicit discussion of strategies to manage assessment formats that students may find less preferable, and sensitivity afforded to cultural differences when planning assessment activities • Students working with teachers to design assessment rubrics to ensure access to requirements of assessment and shared understandings • Students supported in the development of seeking, receiving and acting on feedback – to develop 'savvy feedback skills'. • Peer feedback and support models negotiated and discussed with students in order for them to develop more effective networks of support
C. Optimizing conditions for learning/sensitivity to learner context	
(i) Sensitivity to needs of the learner: recognizing unique starting points. Addressing the emotional dimension of learning: working with students to ensure readiness (will and skill) (ii) Enabling a positive learning environment: focusing on supporting students during important transition points in their learning	Foci (Example for C (i) and C (iv) sub-components) • Clear mapping of all assessment within handbooks with explicit outlining of the student role in assessment • Pre-course preparation focused on tasks relevant to the level of experience of the student and on essential information that the students need to know

(iii) Care afforded to how new ideas introduced as to the level of cognitive complexity in order to support learner flexibility **(iv) Supporting learners' integration into communities of practice** (v) Attention given to learners' networks of support and development of identity within academic context	• Provision of all resources on the virtual learning environment to ensure ease of access • Timing of assessment negotiated with students in relation to academic and professional practice requirements • Clear signposting of key resources • Preparation tasks sent out in advance of taught days with subsequent reminders to ensure learners warmed up for learning. • Tasks signposted as to their level of importance. • Early diagnosis of student learning needs – e.g., requiring students to produce a two-page outline for assignments rather than full draft • Post-teaching day follow-up tasks in relation to areas identified as requiring more attention using feedback within sessions
D. Design of learning environments	
(i) Housekeeping attended to (organization of resources; information for students and lecturers etc.) (ii) Teaching methods informed by an understanding of cognitive styles and attuned to the requirements of the content and context (constructive alignment) (iii) Aimed at supporting learners in developing understanding of learning to think within a specific discipline and to be become part of that community (iv) Judicious use of accommodation of cognitive styles and the concept of matching (v) Judicious approach in promoting development of the most appropriate cognitive styles for specific contexts (vi) Teaching strategies aimed at stretching the student through careful addition and removal of scaffolding and sufficient constructive friction:aimed at developing and broadening cognitive styles and strategies as and when appropriate **(vii) Designs focused on encouraging learners to adopt deeper and more self-regulated/directed approaches to learning (constructivist approaches with a strong emphasis on the development of metacognitive skills) Supporting learners to reflect critically on the learning process to include self- and co-regulation. Appropriate use of tools to support process**	Foci (Example for D (vii) and D (viii) sub-components) • Authentic assessment opportunities of direct relevance to student learning and workplace contexts • Opportunities for dialogue within taught sessions about the nature and requirements of assessment • Explicit discussion of ideas and concepts in relation to assessment requirements • Explicit discussion of assessment criteria – students working with and developing criteria with tutors • Coaching activities whereby students give and receive feedback on their work • All materials available for learners to be able to self-manage • Explanation of the purpose and nature of feedback given to all students – students encouraged to ask specific questions of their formative assessment teacher • Focused feedback from teachers to students on key points • Feedback focused on how to improve. Prioritized and focused on specific areas for development rather than an 'overfull shopping bag of feedback' • Feedback acknowledging the strengths of performance prior to focusing on areas for development • The focus of peer feedback is made explicit – students required to clarify and agree the where and what of feedback with peers • Students required to reflect on their self-assessment skills as part of summative assessment

(continued)

Table 9.1 (continued)

Components of a Personal Learning Styles Pedagogy	*Examples of assessment practice*
(viii) Maximizing learning opportunities: design of learning environments focused on enhancing awareness of different learning strategies through explicit guidance and exposure to diverse learning experiences: different ways of seeing and doing, observation, modelling, practice, application, reinforcement, and transfer	
(ix) Authentic and appropriate assessment designs to support the development of deep approaches to learning	
(x) Appropriate use of technology to support learning	
E. Supporting learner autonomy: choices in learning / student voice	
(i) Focus on the centrality of the learner as a co-constructor of knowledge	Foci (Example for E (v) sub-components) • Choice in assessment – guided support • Choice in the use of peer assessment • Peer feedback in the hands of the learner as part of summative assessment. Students required to reflect on how they have given, received and acted on feedback
(ii) Focus on the role of the student in managing the learning process. Learners as co-designers of their learning experience(s)	
(iii) Learner control afforded through design of curriculum (content, process, product) including e-learning possibilities	
(iv) Flexible designs facilitated through, for example, organization of resources to maximize access; choices in pathways through programmes; nature of assessment	
(v) The importance of guided/informed choice for learners	
(vi) Informed and responsible use of groupings individual and group work. Collaborative learning opportunities informed by understanding of styles (e.g. dangers/limitations of labelling, justification for groupings)	

- Do methods of assessment allow all students an equal opportunity to do well?
- Are students given opportunities to redo their work and to learn from their mistakes?
- How are high-achieving as well as low-achieving students' needs addressed?
- To what extent do students collaboratively support each other in their learning?
- How are teachers collaborating with each other to support students' learning needs?
- Are teachers able to create learning contexts in their classrooms and elsewhere in which students are not afraid of failing and where making mistakes is seen as a valuable part of the learning process rather than as threatening?

Anderman and Maehr (1994, p. 297) have stressed the need to move away from ability-focused *performance goals* towards *task focused mastery goals*: 'in spite of what an individual teacher might do to stress the value of learning for its own sake, to stress the role of effort and progress, to include all within the learning community, these efforts may be undermined if the school as a whole emphasizes grades, competition, and rewards . . . '; this is very difficult in high accountability systems. However, it is essential that teachers are able to distinguish between the two maladaptive styles in order to use the most appropriate intervention: 'While it may be useful to train 'helpless' students to attribute failure to low effort, to do so with self-worth motivated students may decrease persistence further' (Craske, 1988, p. 154).

'Failure must be redefined, so that it is not seen as evidence of personal inadequacy but as a necessary part of learning' (Galloway *et al.*, 1998, p. 129). The importance of training students to develop resilience including notions of fast failing, a term borrowed from Silicon Valley which has relevance to education contexts. Dweck (2006) has argued the need for teachers to cultivate with their students a *'growth mindset'* as opposed to a *'fixed mindset'*, the former identifying success with effort, continuing learning and a belief that intelligence can change, and the latter seeing success as based on inborn abilities and the fixed nature of intelligence (see also chapter eight). However the extent to which students' can develop certain abilities and be flexible learners has been challenged (Evans, 2013b; Kozhevnikov, 2007), with greater emphasis placed on supporting students in their strategy development to enhance what they can do, and to manage effectively what they cannot do, through adept use of strategies (Evans and Waring, 2009). Provision for student choice needs to be linked to appropriate support and safeguards with the assessment design as key elements of co-regulatory practice. Scott *et al.* (2014) noted that where students were given a free choice of assessment title in one module, the less self-regulatory students often chose poorly (e.g. trying to cover too broad an area of study; choosing a focus that was not well matched to their skills set; a lack of alignment with the requirements of the assessment criteria). To address this issue all students were asked to hand in a two-page draft plan which was analysed by their lecturers at the start of the module so as to ensure all students were given appropriate support from the beginning of their engagement with the task. This is an example of sustainable assessment in that choice was provided along with scaffolding in the form of timely feedback to support the students in becoming more self-regulatory, and more aware of the areas on which they needed to concentrate.

EXPLORING STUDENTS' NETWORKS OF SUPPORT

How students identify with an academic context (Bliuc *et al.*, 2011a, 2011b) and the nature and quality of networks they have and value (Evans, 2013b) influences learning outcomes. Early assessment of students' learning needs is important and this includes working with students to address their networks of support (e.g. within and beyond the school context involving friends, family, peers, resource networks – internet) (Webb and Jones, 2009). Connected to this is addressing assumptions made about students as digital natives and their ability to use technology to access suitable resources, as well as equity issues connected to different levels of access students may have to various learning resources. Training students in how to search effectively for relevant sources of information is important and represents one relatively straightforward way to minimize inequalities in student access to information. However, it is often overlooked due to the assumptions made by teachers about the digital native generation: therefore the equity issue also has to be addressed in the design of assessment tasks to ensure that certain students are not disadvantaged. From a cognitive and social perspective the F*eedback Landscape'* (Figure 9.1) can be used to support dialogue between students and teachers around the process of learning and use of feedback.

SUPPORTING STUDENTS' SELF-REGULATORY PRACTICE

To support students in managing affect, cognitions and actions as key components of self-regulatory practice (including self-monitoring) many have argued over the importance of involving students in dialogue with teachers and peers (Black and McCormick, 2010). Focused activities/interventions (e.g. discussion of criteria; self-checking feedback sheets, rubrics, reflective writing tasks, writing frameworks, group and individual marking exercises, modelling, coaching, testing) can be successful but require ongoing development and training in how to engage with them (Parker and Baughan, 2009). However, a key issue identified by Hattie and Timperley (2007) which undermines this is the teacher assuming too much responsibility and ownership of the learning process for his/her students. So while encouraging students to take more responsibility in the assessment feedback process students, teachers do need to support students so that they may be able to share their understanding of the assessment task (Orsmond *et al.*, 2004) and students need to be genuinely involved (e.g. by being granted opportunities to use all feedback received to revise and enhance their work, to assess their own competence, to share what they know and what they do not know, and by being clear about what they can do for themselves). Students also need careful steering by the teacher in terms of scaffolding: not only in its provision, but also in its progressive rationing as appropriate to the progress of the individual student. Inability to reduce and ultimately remove scaffolding leads to student dependence rather than independence in learning.

Preparation and housekeeping issues

We have already highlighted the greater potential of feedforward compared to feedback in supporting student and teacher learning. Feedforward activities should be more dominant in supporting student/trainee teacher development of learning and teaching within the classroom. For example, when a student teacher is planning a lesson with colleagues more time and resources should be spent asking *'what can one achieve?'* and less time on feedback after the lesson (*'what has not been done?'*), to enable better learning gains; this is not to deny the importance of feedback but to place greater emphasis on focusing on what can be achieved. If students are to be encouraged to take greater responsibility for their own learning, this needs to be explicitly facilitated. Reviewing educational, cognitive and educational psychology literature and examples of pedagogical interventions aimed at enhancing student involvement in assessment design, a number of initiatives have been identified as helpful, including:

- availability of a whole programme of study and associated links to resources for students prior to commencement of teaching, and clear demonstration of how all aspects relate to each other
- reducing duplication in terms of where information is posted
- clear signposting of what is important in meeting the requirements of assessment and the setting of specific 'warm-up' tasks prior to the lesson/session to enable students to engage more fully in lessons
- integrating discussions about the nature and purpose of assessment into each teaching session (e.g. showing students how to access resources, commenting on methods of assessment)
- discussions with students as to the purposes of feedback/what constitutes effective feedback, and why
- explaining the requirements and purposes of assessment at the start of a lesson
- unpacking students' assumptions and beliefs about effective learning
- ensuring a range of assessment modes, and ongoing preparation of/support for students to manage the differing requirements of these

- training in the use of appropriate tools to enable critical reflection
- appropriate use of peer and self-assessment opportunities
- appropriate use of technology to support learning

(see Nicol and MacFarlane Dick, 2006; James *et al.*, 2001–5; Scott *et al.*, 2013;Wiliam, 2011 for further information on these.)

Particular attention within the literature has been paid to the use of e-learning to support assessment practices and the use of peer learning opportunities that require further analysis.

APPROPRIATE USE OF TECHNOLOGY TO SUPPORT LEARNING

Much has been made of the potential of e-technologies to support assessment practice. A very useful review of this area is that of Gilbert *et al.*'s (2011) *Synthesis report of assessment and feedback with technology enhancement* (*SRAFTE*), which considered 124 studies in school and higher education contexts. The key issue identified by Gilbert *et al.* was that the success of e-assessment feedback interventions (e. g. automated feedback, online discussion boards and blogs to support learning, online assessment tasks, use of clickers within teaching sessions to ascertain how many students understood specific issues to enable modifications to the teaching context in real time) was more dependent on whether the use of technology led to improved teaching methods, rather than on the technology itself (i.e. it depended on the informed use of pedagogy). In their summary, Gilbert *et al.*, 2011 (pp. 54–55) highlighted that technology-enhanced assessment methods enabled: (i) the development of learning designs that would not otherwise have been possible, (ii) enhanced student retention, inclusion and performance, (iii) teams having a shared understanding of assessment, (iv) informed data analysis to facilitate further development of assessment practice, and (v) staff training needs to be attuned to the needs of students. Given the potential of e-learning technologies to support assessment practice, more resources should be allocated to supporting teacher learning of new technologies and identifying how these can best be used to support assessment and feedback along with critical evaluation of the effectiveness of such approaches. It is not about the provision of technology per se, it is about teacher competence in being able to use such technologies effectively informed by pedagogy; this is one fruitful area where students and teachers could effectively work together to enhance assessment design.

APPROPRIATE USE OF PEER LEARNING INITIATIVES

There have been a number of reviews of peer feedback (see Falchikov and Goldfinch, 2000; Topping, 1998; Van Zundert *et al.*, 2010) in which definitions of peer feedback have varied, as well as the nature of its impact on learning. For some, peer feedback is synonymous with peer assessment (students assessment of each other), while others highlight the formative nature of peer feedback, preferring the term '*peer engagement*' (Cowan and Creme, 2005) where the role of peer feedback is to build student collaboration, confidence and autonomy. We would define peer feedback as any activity in which students engage with each other to support the learning of self and peers through their giving of feedback, use of feedback, responses to feedback and critical evaluation of it both informally and formally; we see it essentially as a formative process.

Peer feedback can be seen as motivational and enabling student self-regulatory skills (Davies, 2006); others question its effectiveness (Strijbos and Sluijsmans, 2010). Evans (2013b) has noted the current excessive emphasis on collaborative learning activities at the expense of individual independent thinking in schools; the issue is the appropriateness of the assessment design (involving collaborative and individual work) to the requirements of the task and to the learning needs of the students. Some students benefit enormously from collaborative enquiry, but others do not (Fund, 2010). It is then a question of to what extent the students should be encouraged to engage in peer feedback. For students to engage meaningfully in peer feedback they need to be convinced of its value, both in relation to their own learning and to their capacity and capability to do it.

We do know that the design of peer feedback opportunities affects student learning outcomes. This, then, highlights a training issue (for teachers and students) (Evans, 2013b). A number of contextual experiences (previous learning; nature, timing and perceived authenticity of assessment; and individual difference variables: perceived agency; trust in self and others to provide good feedback; belief in own ability linked to self-esteem and self-worth) (Evans, 2013b) impact students' attitudes to peer assessment. The following factors are important in the consideration of peer assessment design

1 The academic ability of the feedback giver and recipient impacts on the nature and quality of feedback that can be given and acted upon (Van Zundert *et al.*, 2010).
2 The roles of assessor and assessee need to be made explicit so that students are clear about their respective roles (Gielen *et al.*, 2011).
3 The nature and type of feedback peers are asked to give depends on the knowledge, understanding and skills sets of the students involved; being asked to give feedback outside one's area of expertise will undermine the quality and effectiveness of such feedback (Tseng and Tsai, 2010).
4 There is greater potential in giving feedback than in receiving it; it is what students do with feedback that is important (M. Kim, 2009).
5 Supporting students in learning to give feedback on their feedback helps to complete the feedback cycle so that students are in a position to act on feedback and to qualify points that they do not understand (Evans, 2014);
6 Developing an appropriate climate for feedback (Liu and Carless, 2006). Training students how to give feedback is important (Sluijsmans, Brand-Gruwel, and van Merriënboer, 2002), but training alone is not enough (Topping, 2010). Students need an understanding of assessment criteria, and of what constitutes good feedback, as well as an ability to reflect on their own learning as part of the giving and receiving of feedback as part of an ongoing iterative process. Understanding how to manage the emotions associated with receipt of feedback is fundamental in being able to act on feedback.

Clarifying what is good

For students to use their time productively, they need clarity about what constitutes good work and as part of this, teachers need to explain what good is and also examine with students the students' own existing schema about what they perceive to be good work, and develop effective approaches to learning within specific contexts. Students need to understand where they are now and where they need to get to in order to fully meet the requirements of assessment (Ramaprasad, 1983: Sadler, 1989). Providing clear and explicit guidance (e.g. on organization of resources, clarity about assessment criteria including using assessment criteria to mark own and others' work, exemplars of 'good' work) can open up opportunities for students to explore ideas at deeper levels as opposed to limiting sustainable assessment practice by encouraging criteria compliance and dependence (teaching to the test) (Torrance, 2007). The challenge for teachers remains one of preparing students for the immediate requirements of assessment and in supporting students to develop and value potential life-long learning skills beyond a specific assessment point as part of sustainable assessment.

Nature and design of feedback

The way in which feedback is given does matter. Hattie and Timperley (2007) identified four different types of feedback and argued that regardless of how they are employed, they vary in their effectiveness, with *self-feedback* being the least effective of the four in supporting learning gains. Their four feedback types comprise: *task feedback* – emphasizing information and activities with the purpose of clarifying and reinforcing aspects of the learning task, *process feedback* – focusing on what a student can do to proceed with a learning task, *self-regulation feedback* –focusing on metacognitive elements including how a student can monitor and evaluate the strategies he or she uses, and *self-feedback* –focusing on personal attributes, for example, how well the student has done. In reality, all types of feedback are interwoven and it is the craft of the teacher in knowing *and* the student in learning how to balance and use different types of feedback.

Questions for reflection

- We have used the PLSP to support the development of assessment practice (Evans and Waring, 2011a; 2011b; 2015). Using Table 9.1 as an example, complete Table 9.2 to review your own assessment practice and to identify your own priority areas.
- How are you supporting your students to manage their own feedback practices (seeking, receiving, and using)?
- How are you developing student self-assessment skills?
- What facilitators and barriers are there in the development of your own assessment practice?

Summary

While accepting that students have specific individual needs, there is evidence from the research literature of some core principles that should be applied in the giving of effective feedback to all students (Handley, Price, and Millar, 2008). Such principles include:

1. *Timeliness*: there needs to be sufficient time for a student to be able to use feedback to inform development of their work (Bloxham, 2008); organizationally imposed 'one size fits all' timelines may actually work in the provision of good feedback.
2. *Less may be more:* feedback should be focused on key issues to be addressed. Too much complexity may result in information overload and negative emotional regulation (Evans, 2014b).
3. *Early checks:* in supporting student learning transitions, early assessment is important to ensure students understand the requirements of assessment (Evans, 2015).
4. *Specific and generic feedback:* feedback should be appropriate to the requirements of the task (Gibbs and Simpson, 2004) and also enable feedforward (Boud, 2000).
5. *Realistic expectations:* students need to have sufficient knowledge of how to be able to use feedback effectively (Hattie and Timperley, 2007).
6. *Accessible to the learner* (Weaver, 2006): students need to receive feedback that is appropriate to their learning needs and level of understanding (Hattie and Timperley, 2007; Knight and Yorke, 2003).
7. *Feedback-seeking training* for students: this maximizes feedback opportunities (Evans, 2014).
8. *Encouragement of student responsibility in the feedback process (giving, receiving, and acting on feedback)*: students need sufficient incubation time and support to be able to process feedback and to be able to engage in equitable dialogue (written and oral) with their teacher and peers on the feedback they have received to clarify meanings, expectations, misconceptions, and future actions (Rust *et al.*, 2005). Students should be involved in developing their own feedback – in identifying actions and strategies with support from teachers as part of co-regulation (Burke, 2009) and self-regulation (Hattie and Timperley, 2007).

For assessment design to facilitate and not hinder student learning greater emphasis should be placed on feedforward compared to feedback activities. There is general agreement that:

- *feedback should be a fully integrated element of assessment* rather than perceived as a series of isolated events
- *multiple sources of feedback* should be encouraged, with the teacher not necessarily being the dominant source of feedback, but more the facilitator of student access to, and navigation and use of networks
- feedback is best viewed as *co-constructed*, involving dialogue between students and teachers
- learning can be facilitated through carefully mediated peer feedback mechanisms that allow the *individual to take control of the feedback they seek and use*
- greater emphasis should be placed on developing students' willingness to engage in and with feedback; students' *emotional regulation of feedback*, feedback relationships and feedback-seeking skills are important dimensions of this (see Boud and Molloy, 2013; Evans, 2013b; Evans, 2014; Yang and Carless, 2013 for further discussion of these areas).

Table 9.2 Enhancing feed-forward/-back

	Theme	*Things to think about*	*How could you develop this?*	*Considerations e.g. training issues / cost of resources / relative ease to implement etc.*
1	*Assessment design*			
1(a)	Constructive alignment in relation to match between objectives / teaching approaches and nature of assessment (Biggs, 1999, 2014)	• How does the *pattern and nature* of assessment enable you to assess 'deep' understanding of core concepts and practices in your subject? • Do you *over-assess?*		
1(b)	Progressive – does formative feed into summative (Boud and Associates, 2010)?	• Is assessment *suitably spaced* to enable students to use feedback and does each element *link* to the next task coherently?		
1(c)	Relevance / authenticity / fairness	• Are the tasks relevant / *appropriate to future practice?* • What is the student perception of this – how do you measure this?		
1(d)	Appropriateness in relation to student level	• Do students have *equal access* to the tasks? • Is there an appropriate *range* of assessment? • Is there *choice* in assessment? • Is *guidance* given to students on assessment choices?		
1(e)	Can the student see the value?	• How is the *nature and value* of assessment covered during induction and subsequently?		
1(f)	Is it clear to the student how the different elements of assessment fit together?	• How is organization of assessment and clarification of this managed through the virtual learning environment, documentation, and in the teaching? • How do you know students are clear about how all *elements of assessment fit together?*		

(continued)

Table 9.2 (continued)

	Theme	*Things to think about*	*How could you develop this?*	*Considerations e.g. training issues / cost of resources / relative ease to implement etc.*
2	*Role of the student*			
2(a)	Exploring previous experiences of feedback	• (How) do you get to know students' *previous experiences* of feedback? • How and when do you explore *students' beliefs* about the value of assessment and feedback?		
2(b)	Supporting self-regulation through design of tools and environments to enable students to self and peer assess	• How are you working with students to develop their *self-regulation skills*? (See 3(a)		
2(c)	Training students and teachers in how to give and make use of feedback opportunities	• What training is put in place to support students in *giving feed-back/-forward*? • What elements of feed-back/-forward should students be involved in? • What elements of feed-back/-forward do students give to each other? • What strategies are being implemented to get students to *feedback on the feedback* they have received from each other?		
2(d)	Clarification of student role in the process and sources of feedback available	• How is the student role in feed-back/-forward clarified during induction and subsequently? • How are students instructed to be more *active agents* in the feed-back/-forward process? o e.g. Are they encouraged to ask questions about their feedback? o Are they aware that they are receiving feedback when they do? • How are they being supported to develop feedback-seeking and feedback-giving skills?		

2(e)	Ownership/agency/autonomy	• To what extent are students involved in *developing assessment criteria*? • To what extent can students *choose* their mode of assessment? • What *guidance* are students given in relation to the *choices* they make? • If student self-regulation is seen as essential, to what extent does *summative assessment* allocate marks for students to explain how they have met the criteria and what areas they still need to develop in their work?		

Theme		*Things to think about*	*How could you develop this?*	*Considerations e.g. training issues / cost of resources / relative ease to implement etc.*
3	*Preparation and housekeeping*			
3(a)	Organization of resources (handbooks/VLE)	• How are resources organized to ensure *maximum student access*?		
3(b)	Availability of all resources prior to commencement of programme	• Are all resources, including *exemplars of good work*, in the virtual learning environment from the beginning of the programme?		
3(c)	Signposting of what is important	• How is the relative importance of tasks clarified with students?		
3(d)	Integrating assessment into each teaching session	• How much *time* is given *in each teaching session* to clarifying assessment requirements? How is this done?		
3(e)	Advance preparation by students so they warmed up to idea(s)	• What *early opportunities* are there for students to undertake formative assessment early on in the programme to establish needs quickly? • How can this be done effectively? • What are students expected to prepare for each session?		
3(f)	Lecturers need to have shared understandings of purposes of feedback/what constitutes feedback	• What opportunities are there for developing *shared understandings of requirements of assessment*?		

(continued)

Table 9.2 (continued)

	Theme	*Things to think about*	*How could you develop this?*	*Considerations e.g. training issues / cost of resources / relative ease to implement etc.*
4	*Clarifying what is good*			
4(a)	Students need to understand where they are now and where they need to get to	• What *tools* are you using to support student development of self-assessment skills, e.g. self-checking lists where they break criteria down to examine their own work; presentations to peers; self-reflection exercises etc?		
4(b)	Access to the rules of the game	• How does *induction* give students a clear idea of the standards they need to achieve and how elements of assessment fit together? • What resources are provided to clarify requirements?		
4(c)	Explicit direction to resources / forms of support	• How and where are different *sources of support* (peer, self, internet, journals, organizations, writing guidelines, etc.) clarified with students? • Are formalized peer support groups set up to support learning?		
4(d)	Explicit examples of good work	• Where can students access examples of good work? • What opportunities do students have to *explore each other's contributions* and how is this managed?		
4(e)	Existing schema of students need to be addressed – and early on – as to what constitutes good writing etc.	• How is *student writing* assessed from the outset? • How do you *clarify the conventions and requirements* of your discipline? How do you assess students' different starting points? • How can students support each other?		
4(f)	Clarifying assessment criteria – students using criteria	• When do students have opportunities to *mark exemplars using criteria*? What support is provided to enable this and to discuss outcomes?		

4(g)	Ownership / agency / autonomy	• Are students involved in developing their *own rubrics* in order to self-assess their own work? • Do students get the opportunity to design *and implement assessment?* • To what extent are students involved in *developing assessment criteria?* • To what extent can students *choose* their *mode of assessment?* • What guidance are students given in relation to the choices that they make? • If student *self-regulation* is seen to be essential, to what extent does summative assessment allocate marks for students to explain how they have met the criteria and what areas they still need to develop in their work?		

	Theme	*Things to think about*	*How could you develop this?*	*Considerations e.g. training issues / cost of resources / relative ease to implement etc.*
5	*Nature and design of feedback*			
5(a)	Specific *vs* generic – can it be carried forward – timing – issue of transfer and adaptation	• How does feedback enable the student to carry it forward to other assessments? • How do you ensure the balance between *generic and specific subject feedback?*		
5(b)	Most appropriate form of delivery	• What *type of feedback* is most effectively given at the group level *vs* the individual level? Oral *vs* written, electronic, via peers, via tutor, via self? • How can *summative feedback support* further work within and beyond your subject? • How is ICT being used to support the feedback process?		

(continued)

Table 9.2 (continued)

	Theme	*Things to think about*	*How could you develop this?*	*Considerations e.g. training issues / cost of resources / relative ease to implement etc.*
5(c)	Accessibility: clarifying student understanding of feedback	• What activities are devised to ensure students have understood the feedback they have received? • What have you implemented to ensure that students are *not passive receivers* of feedback?		
5(d)	Focus on higher-level outcomes, e.g. quality of argument *vs* SPAG	• How are you ensuring that *feedback focuses on critique / conceptual understandings / applications of ideas /innovation*, etc?		
5(e)	Signposted / focused	• How is *feedback focused*: how is it signposted and prioritized?		
5(f)	Realistic in expectations (learner needs sufficient knowledge of how to be able to use feedback effectively	• What *resources/support* is/are available and accessible to students to develop better understanding in order to engage with feedback? • What strategies can be taught to students so they are more able to *engage with feedback* as part of their responsibility within the learning process? • How is the *student role in feedback* clearly outlined during induction?		
5(g)	Involving students in developing own feedback as part of summative assessment?	• How can *student self-assessment be incorporated into summative assessment?*		

Key readings

Black, P., and Wiliam, D. (1998). Assessment and classroom learning. *Assessment in Education, 5*, 7–74.
This work highlighted the importance of formative assessment in supporting students' learning in the classroom and particularly the role of feedback; the value of active involvement of students in their learning, and the need for students to be able to self-assess themselves in order to improve. The emphasis on student self-regulation in assessment and feedback has been underemphasized in policy and in translation within school contexts (see also Wiliam, 2011)

Boud, D., and Molloy, E. (2012). *Feedback in higher and professional education. Understanding it and doing it well.* London and New York: Routledge.
This book promotes a learner-centred sustainable approach to assessment and feedback that sees learners more actively engaged in seeking, generating and using feedback. It looks at latest thinking on feedback and highlights key principles and implementation issues from different disciplinary and cultural perspectives. See also Merry et al. (2013) work on reconceptualizing feedback.

Evans, C. (2013b). Making sense of assessment feedback in higher education. *Review of Educational Research, 83 (1), 70–120.*
This article provides a synthesis of assessment and feedback practice within higher education; the twelve principles of effective assessment feedback design are applicable to school, higher education and workplace contexts. The 'Feedback Landscape' conceptual framework can be used to analyse the nature and quality of feedback interactions between students and teachers including other resources (peers, internet, family, societies etc.) within and beyond the immediate learning environments). The article can be downloaded free at http://rer.sagepub.com/cgi/reprint/83/1/70?ijkey=x/CimNd6vjZWI&keytype=ref&siteid=sprer (accessed 10 October 2013).

Gilbert, L., Whitelock, D., and Gale, V. (2011). *Synthesis report on assessment and feedback with technology enhancement.* Southampton, UK: Electronics and Computer Science EPrints.
This report provides an overview of how technology can support assessment practice highlighting the importance of the pedagogy underpinning the practice. It can be downloaded from http://eprints.soton.ac.uk/273221 (accessed 5 May 2014).

Weblinks

Assessment Reform Group (2002). Assessment for learning: 10 Principles. Cambridge: ARG. Available online at www.assessment-reform-group.org.uk and http://www.aaia.org.uk/afl/assessment-reform-group/ (accessed 15 August 2014) (accessed 10 June 2013).

BERA (2013b). BERA's response to the DfE consultation on primary assessment and accountability. In BERA Research Intelligence (p. 10), Issue 122. British Educational Research Association: London. Available online at http://www.bera.ac.uk/publications/Research%20Intelligence (accessed 20 December 2013).

Bloxham, S. (2008). *Guide to Assessment*, ESCalate, HEA. Available online at http://escalate.ac.uk/4148 (accessed 20 July 2009).

DFE (2011b). Independent review of key stage 2 testing, assessment and accountability: final report. Department for Education. Available online at https://www.gov.uk/government/publications/independent-review-of-key-stage-2-testing-assessment-and-accountability-final-report (accessed 12 January 2014).

DFES/AfL (2008). The *Assessment for Learning Strategy* – Department for children, schools and families. Available online at http://webarchive.nationalarchives.gov.uk/20130401151715/https://www.education.gov.uk/publications/eOrderingDownload/DCSF-00341–2008.pdf (accessed 12 January 2014).

EPPI centre. Available online at http://eppi.ioe.ac.uk/webdatabases/Intro.aspx?ID=6 (accessed 16 January 2013).

Evans, C. (2013b). Making sense of assessment feedback in higher education. *Review of Educational Research, 83 (1), 70–120.* Available online at http://rer.sagepub.com/cgi/reprint/83/1/70?ijkey=x/CimNd6vjZWI&keytype=ref&siteid=Sprer (accessed 10 October 2013).

Higher Education Academy. Available online at http://www.heacademy.ac.uk/search/search?qt=feedback&sb=relevance http://www.heacademy.ac.uk/assessment-projects-resources (accessed 10 May 2013).

Journey to Excellence Website. Available online at http://www.journeytoexcellence.org.uk/resources andcpd/research/summaries/rsassessment.asp (accessed 12 June 2013).

New Zealand Education Ministry. Available online at http://assessment.tki.org.nz/Assessment-in-the-classroom/Readings-on-formative-assessment (accessed 10 July 2013).

National Foundation for Educational Research. Available online at http://www.nfer.ac.uk/home-page.cfm (accessed 8 July 2013).

OECD (2005) *Formative Assessment: Improving Learning in Secondary Classrooms*, Paris: OECD Publishing. Available online at http://www.oecd.org/edu/ceri/35661078.pdf (accessed 10 January 2014).

OECD (2013). *'Synergies for Better Learning: an international perspective on evaluation and assessment'*. Available online at http://www.oecd.org/education/school/oecdreviewonevaluationand assessmentframeworksforimprovingschooloutcomes.htm http://www.oecd.org/edu/school/Synergies%20for%20Better%20Learning_Summary. (accessed 10 December 2013).

TES Assessment for Learning Toolkit. Available online at http://www.tes.co.uk/teaching-resource/Assessment-For-Learning-Toolkit-6020165/ (accessed 16 July 2013).

(ESRC-TLRP)Teaching and Learning Research Programme. Available online at http://www.tlrp.org/ (accessed 9 July 2013).

TLRP/ESRC Learning how to learn project. Available online at http://www.learntolearn.ac.uk http://www.tlrp-archive.org/cgi-bin/search_oai_all.pl?pn=10&no_menu=1&short_menu=1 (accessed 9 July 2013).

Chapter 10

Making sense of critical reflection

Overview

Critical reflection is seen as the cornerstone of teachers' professional practice; however, there is much debate as to what critical reflection is, how it is enacted, and what it achieves. In this chapter we will define what critical reflection is, and explore the use of models and tools in the teaching of critical reflection. Key principles and issues involved in supporting the critical reflection of teachers and learners using the Personal Learning Styles Pedagogy framework will be highlighted as part of this.

Introducing critical reflection

There is a vast body of literature on critical reflection, from many different disciplinary and theoretical perspectives (Brookfield, 1987, 1995; Ghaye and Lillyman, 2000; Johns, 2002).

Critical reflection is an important element in how we learn from experience, and it has the potential to be emancipatory. It can free learners from the implicit assumptions constraining thought and action in the everyday world and enable them to act on the forces creating inequality in professional practice and in the world (Stein, 2000, p. 2). It can help us 'make sense of the uncertainty in our workplaces' and offer us the 'courage to work competently and ethically at the edge of order and chaos' (Ghaye, 2000, p. 7). Winch *et al.* (2013) have argued that it is the capacity for critical reflection which distinguishes the best teachers from others. It is often seen as the bedrock of professional identity (Finlay, 2008). Supporting the importance of critical reflection in teaching, Larrivee (2000, p. 293) has argued that 'Unless teachers develop the practice of critical reflection, they stay trapped in unexamined judgments, interpretations, assumptions, and expectations'.

However, whether critical reflection leads to enhanced understanding or functions to reinforce or collude with existing teacher beliefs or practices is questionable (Brockbank and McGill, 1998; Stein, 2000). There is a lack of empirical research demonstrating the evidence base supporting reflective practice (J. Hargreaves, 2004). Given differences in interpretation as to what critical reflection involves, the variety of approaches and tools, and a lack of longitudinal studies examining ongoing applications of critical reflection to practice, it is very difficult to establish the effectiveness of critical reflection and critically reflective teaching. Little is known about the difficulties, practicalities and methods of critical reflection (E. Smith, 2011, p. 212). The potential uncomfortable and risky nature of critical reflection and the power dynamics associated with it have been highlighted by Brookfield (1995). Yet at the same time the potential of being able to think critically can be emancipatory for the learner. From an educational perspective, while critical reflection can be taught, a key issue remains the ability of individuals to apply what they have learnt within and across contexts (Stein, 2000).

What is critical reflection?

The term critical reflection is used widely, often thoughtlessly, and to mean different things (Lucas, 2012). Critical reflection is often conflated and used interchangeably with terms such as reflection, reflective practice, reflexivity and critical thinking (Black and Plowright, 2010; McManus, 2011). It is seen as a fairly ubiquitous activity within professional contexts and often described indiscriminately as a good thing.

> [Reflection] . . . is used as a kind of umbrella or canopy term . . . to signify something that is good or desirable . . . Everybody has his or her own (usually undisclosed) interpretation of what reflection means, and this interpretation is used as the basis for trumpeting the virtues of reflection in a way that makes it sound as virtuous as motherhood.
>
> Smyth, 1992, p. 285

Critical reflection may be intuitive, embedded in a teacher's ongoing practice enacted in tacit ways, and/or it can be approached more formally in explicit ways. The timing of reflection and the associated quality of it have been differentiated in discussions around *reflection before action*, *reflection in action*, and *reflection on action*, with far less emphasis within the literature being placed on reflection before action. Critical reflection can be a lone and/or a collaborative venture. However, the emphasis within the literature is on the solitary nature of critical reflection rather than the collaborative aspects of it. There are many different theoretical positions underpinning critical reflection; however Issitt (2000) noted that very few who claimed to be engaged in reflection had actually read anything recently about it.

Permeating themes in critical reflection

While many different definitions of critical reflection exist, a number of themes permeating such definitions can be discerned. Fundamentally, critical reflection is concerned with the *why*, the *reasons for*, and the *consequences* of what we do rather than the *how* or the *how-to* of action (Mezirow, 1990). Habermas argues that 'Critical reflective knowing is neither behavioural nor technical, not truth establishing nor captured by a discipline. It critiques all other forms of knowledge, and in so doing, it moves beyond merely reproducing what is.' (1978, p. 42). For Brookfield (1995) it is about *stance* (inquiry) and *dance* (experimentation and risk). Fook (2006, p. 10) in her definition highlights the application dimension of critical reflection alongside an understanding of context: *'the ability to understand the social dimensions and political functions of experience and meaning making, and the ability to apply this understanding in working in social context'*. In considering application and the risky nature of critical reflection, Brookfield highlights the importance of collective endeavour:

> Since our experiences as teachers are politically and organizationally sculptured, changing aspects of our individual practice often needs a collective effort . . . teachers who try to swim against the cultural and pedagogic tide that flows through institutions hostile to any questioning of the status quo had better be equipped with life preservers.
>
> Brookfield, 1995, p. 42

Challenge

Critical thinking is about challenging the validity of *presuppositions* in prior learning; as Mezirow (1990) argues, *premise reflection* more accurately captures what critical reflection is. Critical reflection addresses the question of the justification for the very premises on which problems are posed or defined in the first place. We very commonly check our prior learning to confirm that we have correctly proceeded to solve problems, but becoming critically aware of our own presuppositions involves challenging our established and habitual patterns of expectation: the meaning perspectives with which we have made sense out of our encounters with the world, others, and ourselves. To question the validity of a long-taken-for-granted meaning perspective predicated on a presupposition about oneself can involve the negation of values that have been very close to the centre of one's self-concept (Mezirow, 1990, p. 8).

Emotion

The emotional dimension of critical reflection is acknowledged in initiating the critical reflective process resulting in possible changes in the 'emotional schemas through which we perceive ourselves and relate to the world' (McManus, 2011, p. 12 referencing Mackenzie, 2002). In addition to emotions triggering critical reflection processes, they can also sustain motivation for finding meaning and continuing reflection (Fook, 2006). Emotional flexibility is linked to the capacity to critically reflect (Mackenzie, 2002). Mezirow (1990) also argues the importance of disorienting dilemmas and the role of emotions in leading to individual perspective transformations.

Transformation

Critical reflection, therefore, implies undergoing a *perspective transformation* (Mezirow, 2000). Transformational learning is about how we make meaning and make decisions to act from experiences and critical reflection is an essential part of this process.

> . . . the use of critical theory, and its development for use in critical reflection, is probably one of the major defining features of critical reflection, and therefore one of the major factors which may differentiate it from reflective practice. In this sense, critical reflection involves social and political analyses which enable transformative changes, whereas reflection may remain at the level of relatively undisruptive changes in techniques or superficial thinking
>
> Fook *et al.*, 2006, p. 9

Fook *et al.* (2006, p. 12) have argued that critical reflection involves four key dimensions and that an understanding of the technologies of power, language and practice that produce and legitimate forms of regulation is essential. The four dimensions include: (i) a process (cognitive, emotional, experiential) of *examining assumptions* (of many different types and levels) embedded in actions or experience; (ii) a *linking of these assumptions* with many different origins (personal, emotional, social, cultural, historical, political); (iii) a *review and re-evaluation* of these according to relevant criteria (depending on context, purpose, etc.); (iv) a *reworking of concepts and* practice based on this re-evaluation.

Being critical

Critical reflection requires a critical review of presuppositions from conscious and unconscious prior learning, and of their consequences (Leung and Kember, 2003, p. 69). Fundamental to critical reflection is an emphasis on examining how assumptions about power construct and restrict practice at the individual, group, and/or organizational levels.

> Critical reflection is the process by which adults identify the assumptions governing their actions, locate the historical and cultural origins of the assumptions, question the meaning of the assumptions, and develop alternative ways of acting. . . . Brookfield (1995) adds that part of the critical reflective process is to challenge the prevailing social, political, cultural, or professional ways of acting. Through the process of critical reflection, adults come to interpret and create new knowledge and actions from their ordinary and sometimes extraordinary experiences. Critical reflection blends learning through experience with theoretical and technical learning to form new knowledge constructions and new behaviors or insights.
>
> Stein, 2000, p. 1

Therefore, it is not the depth of reflective effort itself that makes it critical (Shandomo, 2010); two things make reflection critical:

> . . . reflection becomes critical when it has two distinctive purposes. The first is to understand *how considerations of power undergird, frame and distort educational processes and interactions*. The second is to *question assumptions and practices that seem to make our teaching lives easier, but actually work against our own best long term interests* – [in other words, those that are hegemonic] [italics added for emphasis].
>
> Brookfield, 1995, p. 8

Reflexivity

While some see *reflexivity* as part of critical reflection (Bolton, 2010), others differentiate between the two concepts. Finlay (2008) in distinguishing between critical reflection and reflexivity highlights the importance of self-awareness in the use of the latter term whereby emphasis is placed on questioning one's own position as well as considering contextual elements. For Bolton (2010, p. 13) 'Reflexivity is finding strategies to question our own attitudes, thought processes, values, assumptions, prejudices and habitual actions, to strive to understand our complex roles in relation to others'. Bolton in summarizing the nature of reflexivity argues it is about paying close attention to one's own actions, thoughts, feelings, values, identity, and their impact on others, situations, and professional and social structures (Bolton, 2010). Fook (2006) argues that reflexive ability is central to critical reflection in that individuals require this self-awareness in order to better understand their own role in constructing and participating in specific contexts and their knowledge of such contexts.

Theoretical frameworks used to explore critical reflection

There are many theoretical frameworks used to explore critical reflection and these are not mutually exclusive; however the particular frame(s) adopted do impact on the nature of learning achieved (Fook, 2006). From a *critical social theory* perspective critical reflection enables social change (Brookfield, 1995; 2005). From this perspective it is essential to examine how knowledge creation is directed towards political or ethical goals. Critical reflection enables an understanding of the way socially dominant assumptions may be restrictive and, in theory, frees individuals to make choices at the individual level assuming their autonomy to make such changes within specific contexts (Fook, 2006). From a *constructivist* perspective, emphasizing the socially constructed nature of learning it is important to consider how social structures, relations, and discourses impact on how individuals construct their knowledge and identities within a workplace context (Fook, 2006; Smith, 2011). A *positivist* stance would place emphasis on how in becoming aware of our personal biases we can aspire to be objective. *Feminist and emancipatory* perspectives emphasize the role of critical reflection in learning about one's own life and gaining insight into how to improve one's own situation. Critical reflection from a *reflexive modernity* perspective emphasizes how critical reflection can be used to enable individuals to examine how they engage with different contexts and construct a sense of self. Mezirow also emphasized the role of critical reflection in enabling individuals to consider how people make meaning from experience in order to inform their actions. Finlay (2008) in examining skills underpinning reflective practice advocated the use of an integrated theoretical framework to examine three interrelated areas impacting reflective practice: *self-awareness, reflection* and *critical thinking*. Using this approach self-awareness draws on phenomenology and focuses on individuals' cognitive and affective abilities to make sense of knowledge and to inform understandings. Reflection draws on existential phenomenology and critical theory to inform self-and social awareness, and critical thinking draws on scepticism and critical theory focusing on identifying and challenging assumptions about oneself and about the context in order to imagine and explore alternatives.

Teaching critical reflection

> The work required to deconstruct one's own cultural identity through reflection should . . . be included in teacher education programs of study . . . Reflection must be explicitly taught as a process and then required and assessed throughout diverse experiences in order to be meaningful.
>
> Rychly and Graves, 2012, p. 48

Key concepts

In teaching critical reflection many different approaches have been used, the majority of which draw on a number of core concepts from the works of Dewey (1897; 1910; 1916; 1933), Habermas (1971; 1972; 1974), and Schön (1983; 1987; 1991). Dewey's (1933) *pragmatic approach* focused on the processes of reflection and the interaction of thought and action in the development of practice. In this approach reflection on action is emphasized, initially stimulated by some level of conflict following an experience. For Dewey reflection was a means whereby individuals could move from routine thinking and actions towards critical reflection involving consideration of assumptions and taken-for-granted knowledge (Finlay, 2008). The Dewey (1938) five stage model typically involves (i) identifying a problem that is perplexing and 'felt'; (ii) observing and refining the identified problem to create a fuller understanding; (iii) hypothesis development or an understanding about the problem, its origins and possible solutions; (iv) subjecting the hypothesis to scrutiny and reasoning; (v) testing the hypothesis or understanding in practice. The influence of Dewey can be seen in Kolb's *experiential learning cycle* (D. A. Kolb, 1971; D. A. Kolb and Fry, 1975; D. A. Kolb, 1984; A. Y. Kolb and D. A. Kolb, 2005), suggesting that reflection is generated by experience and feeds back into the development of practice, and also in Gibbs's (1988) reflective cycle involving a description of the situation, analysis of feelings, evaluation of the experience, analysis to make sense of the experience, conclusion where other options are considered and reflection upon experience to examine what you would do if the situation arose again.

Models such as Kolb's (see Appendix: Tool A) and Gibbs's (see Appendix: Tool B) provide frameworks and questions to help structure reflection at a relatively basic level. However, Dewey suggested that in reflection many processes occur all at once, involving sequences of interconnected ideas influenced by underlying beliefs and knowledge. The Kolb model, in presenting action and reflection as separate components, is overly simplistic. However, the model's simplicity is one of the key factors affecting its use in practice, and fundamentally, the key premises underpinning it make pedagogical sense.

Boud and colleagues have been influential in contributing to ideas on experiential learning that focus attention on reflection following experience, and in offering strategies focused on *return to experience, attending to feelings, and revaluation* (Boud *et al.*, 1985). Their focus is on empowerment in relation to how individuals can both influence and learn from experience and how through *deliberate learning* (intention to learn from experience) and *meaningful learning* (intending to apply learning) learners can inform their own and others' practice (Boud and Walker, 1990). The approach is socio-constructivist in its focus on the learner's personal foundation of experience (experiences that have shaped the person), their intent that gives a particular focus to learning within a context, and the interaction of the learner with his/her resources and the external environment (*the learning milieu*). Learning is facilitated through learners noticing (what is happening both within themselves and in the external environment), *intervening*, and *reflecting in action* to continually modify their practice. The key issue is the adoption of the most appropriate strategies to support the needs of the learner, their intent, and the nature of the milieu (Segers and Van de Haar, 2011).

The influence of *Habermas's critical theory approach* (1971, 1972, 1974) is evidenced in models focused on empowerment and emancipation (Grushka *et al.*, 2005; H. S. Kim, 1999). Knowledge is perceived as socially constructed with reflection focusing on critique, evaluation, and liberation (de Cossart and Fish, 2005) in Habermas's focus on three areas of knowledge (*technical, practical, and emancipatory*).

Another key and influential player within the field of reflective practice is that of Schön (1983). For Schön (1996) critical reflection equates to *professional artistry* involving *reflection in action* (during the event) and *reflection on action* (after the event). He emphasized the importance of professional artistry in contrast to rule following technical rationality. *Reflection in action* involves being able to evaluate, assess, and act in order to shape ongoing activity in the moment. In *reflection on action*, professionals consciously review, describe, analyse and evaluate their past practice with a view to gaining insight to improve future practice. The notion of *reflection in action* builds on *knowing in action* where Schön (1983) emphasizes the intuitive grasp that practitioners have in managing teaching in the moment '*spontaneous skilful execution*' (Van den Bossche and Beausaert, 2011). When knowing in practice becomes increasingly tacit and spontaneous so that the teacher has over-learned what s/he knows, such professional specialization can limit learning and development of practice. *Reflection in action* has been interpreted in different ways. From a teacher education perspective, *reflection in action* has face validity in describing the ability to integrate both rational and intuitive thought in the moment by being able to adapt lessons in relation to ongoing formative feedback as to what is happening in the classroom at any given moment. Such *reflection in action* requires confidence, a level of expertise and available working memory capacity to be able to think in complex ways and to manage emotions as part of self-regulatory activity within the moment. However, from a phenomenological philosophy perspective Ekebergh (2007) argues that to achieve *real* self-reflection, a learner needs to be able to step out of the situation and reflect retrospectively. The issue is related to the levels of reflection involved, which is discussed by E. Wilson and Demetriou (2007) building on Eraut's work (2004c) in their discussion of three types of reflection, which they describe pejoratively. First, *hot action* (aligned to *reflection in action*) is perceived as *intuitive, tacit* and influenced by feelings, and constantly present in teachers' actions within the classroom, leading to routinization of practice. Second, *reactive/reflective actions* (aligned to *reflection on action*) focused on teachers' post lesson analysis are deemed reactive as such reflection is not necessarily aligned with enhancements in practice and reflection is seen at a more descriptive rather than analytical level. Third, *cooler deliberative learning* (aligned to reflection for action) is based on deeper understanding of the dynamics within the classroom and more widely, it is more conscious and research-informed (see E. Wilson and Demetriou, 2007, p. 224). Within the Personal Learning Styles Pedagogy we have emphasized the importance of analytical and intuitive thinking in reflection, as has Korthagen (2005) in the development of his reflection model.

In applying Schön's notion of *reflection in action* and the associated concept of inner speech (thinking through ideas and experiences using the unspoken word) Enfield and Stasz (2011) emphasize the potential of dialogic activity within communities of practice, when individuals share inner speech with others to enable articulation of ideas in order to communicate meaning and to challenge their own implicit assumptions and ideas – making the implicit explicit which may facilitate deeper levels of *reflection in action.*

There are a number of integrated holistic models informed by the work of Dewey, Habermas and Schön that integrate different levels of reflection and ensure a focus on both critical and emotional dimensions of critical reflective practice (Jay and Johnson, 2002). Johns' reflexive model of structured reflection (1994; 2000) (see Appendix: Tools C) places emphasis on the mindful self during and after experience with the goal of realizing a vision of practice as a lived reality (Finlay, 2008). Johns' ten Cs of reflection (2000) includes:

- Commitment — Accept responsibility and be open to change
- Contradiction — Note tension between actual and desired practice
- Conflict — Harness this energy to take appropriate action
- Challenge — Confront your own typical actions, beliefs and attitudes in a non-threatening way
- Catharsis — Work through negative feelings
- Creation — Move beyond old self to novel alternatives
- Connection — Connect new insights in the world of practice
- Caring — Realise desirable practice
- Congruence — Reflection as a mirror for caring
- Constructing — Building personal knowledge in practice

The ideas can be applied to individual and collaborative reflexive activities where individuals and groups can model sharing feelings and reflective practice for others as part of collaborative critical reflection practice.

Types of reflection

From a hierarchical perspective when examining the potential of reflection to impact perspective transformation, Mezirow (1991) argued that in considering three types of reflection: *Content reflection* (thinking about the actual experience itself), *process reflection* (problem-solving strategies), and *premise reflection* (examining long-held, socially constructed assumptions, beliefs and values about the experience or problem), only *premise reflection* led to transformational learning.

Smith (2011, p. 216) differentiates between forms and domains of reflection in discussing personal, interpersonal, contextual and critical reflection. The *self-level* is reflexive in its exploration of personal thoughts and actions, the quality of which depends on individual awareness, receptivity, and abilities. It is introspective, involving the learner in self-dialogue. The *interpersonal level* is focused on examining interactions with others and group dynamics to ascertain and question practice norms and decision-making processes. It is intersubjective by being focused on the relational dimension and associated with a participatory dialogical approach. *Contextual reflection* is deliberative in examining how concepts, theories and methods inform and influence practice and how these relate to one's own implicit theories. *Critical reflection* examines issues of power and raises social justice questions about which ways of thinking have been privileged by whom and for what reasons? For Finlay (2008) this is also about managing power imbalances within context as part of *social critique and ironic deconstruction* involving examination of the ambiguity and multiplicity of meanings in specific contexts.

The nature of reflection is also linked closely to the requirements of the task. Zeichner and Liston (1996) differentiated between five different levels of reflection within teaching:

1 Rapid reflection – immediate, ongoing and automatic action by the teacher (*reflection in action*)
2 Repair – involving teachers' decisions to alter their behaviour in response to students' cues (*reflection before, in, and on action*)
3 Review – exploration of an aspect of teaching through thinking, discussing and writing (*reflection on action*)

4 Research – teacher engagement in more systematic and sustained thinking over time, individually or collectively (*reflection before, in, or on action*)
5 Retheorizing and reformulating – the process by which a teacher/group/school critically examines their own practices and theories in the light of academic theories (reflection before, in, or on action).

Much of the educational literature focuses on the personal level of critical reflection but critical reflection at the organizational level of analysis has much potential with examples of approaches including

- *public reflection*, involving open discussion of the inter-personal and political complexities of organizational life (Raelin, 2001)
- *productive reflection* examining productivity and quality of working life and the potential of reflection in addressing work practices (Boud *et al.*, 2006)
- *organizing reflection* focusing on how emotions in organizations contribute to the power relations that can constrain emotional responses or define the contextually specific nature of emotional work (Reynolds andVince, 2004).

Critical reflection processes

Models of critical reflection typically involve to varying degrees a focus on *retrospection* (thinking about a situation or experience); *self-evaluation* (critically analysing and evaluating actions, assumptions and feelings from different theoretical perspectives that up to that point have been uncritically accepted as representing common sense wisdom), and *reorientation* (adopting alternative perspectives and applying what has been learnt to new learning in order to effect change) through an increased awareness of recognition, and understanding of the power dynamics within specific contexts and the variable impact of these on different members of the organization (Burns, 2002; Quinn, 2000).

Brookfield (1988) argued the importance of four key processes in learning how to become critically reflective: (i) *assumption analysis* (making explicit our taken-for-granted notions of reality); (ii) *contextual awareness* (how assumptions are a product of a specific historical and cultural context); (iii) *imaginative speculation* (imagining alternative ways of thinking about phenomena); (iv) *reflective scepticism* (ability to question universal truths or patterns of interaction and working). The ability of an individual to engage in critical reflection will vary over time and space dependent on both individual and contextual affordances and the interrelationships between the two.

In summary, a number of themes permeate different theorizations and enactments of reflective practice involving the use of models and tools. First, there is an emphasis on different forms of reflection from a *timing perspective* (*reflection before action; reflection in action; reflection on action*) with less emphasis being afforded to *reflection before action*. Second, it is suggested that it is possible to differentiate lower and higher order levels of reflection with some models incorporating all stages of reflection from descriptive to critical and others focusing solely on a specific level of reflection. While emphasis is on the greater value of *double loop* learning (learning which questions values) compared to *single loop* learning (regarding accepted values) (Argyris and Schön, 1974), not all reflection needs to be critical and it would be difficult to achieve this given the emotional investment involved and the emphasis on transformational change. From a pedagogical perspective it is about using the appropriate level of reflection for any given context. Third, as part of differentiating levels of reflection, reflection is often seen as a hierarchical staged process moving from description of practice events to analysis of situations and intentions and finally to critique of practices regarding conflicts and inconsistencies to enable emancipation and change processes (H. S. Kim, 1999); alternative cyclical models are also offered. Fourth, models place varying influence on the role of cognitive and affective dimensions. Lastly, much emphasis is placed on individual reflection compared to collaborative and organizational reflective practices.

Promoting effective critical reflection practice

Practices to support effective critically reflective practice have been aligned to the principles underpinning the PLSP and are summarized in Table 10.1. Factors impacting

Table 10.1 Critically reflective practice within the Personal Learning Styles Pedagogy framework

Promoting critical reflection practice within a Personal Learning Styles Pedagogy

A. Exploration of student and teacher beliefs / modelling and support

- Place emphasis on an examination of learners underlying beliefs and assumptions that affect how learners make sense of the experience (Segers and DeGreef, 2011)
- Explore learner's emotional learning histories (the notion of contextual space is important in relation to individual and organizational affordances and limitations (Van der Zwet *et al.*, 2011)). (Contextual space refers to how learning/training is organized and assessed; how learners are supported – e.g. mentoring support for trainee teachers; length of student placements; opportunities for feedback; access to resources; opportunities to work independently; opportunities to take on the responsibilities of a teacher; mix of classes allocated to a teacher.)
- Centre reflective practice on the learner: *'about you and your work'* (Ghaye and Lillyman, 2000).
- Focus on learning from experience as an integral part of teaching (Ghaye and Lillyman, 2000).
- Explore with learners what they value, what they do, and *why* they do it (Ghaye and Lillyman, 2000).
- Emphasize as part of reflection the links between values and actions (Ghaye and Lillyman, 2000).
- Ensure critical reflective practices are authentic and attuned to learners' professional working contexts – *'reflection in the context of practice'* (Boud, 2010).

B. Careful selection and application of styles

- Ensure critical reflection is not used as an unthinking tool (Brookfield, 1995).
- Use a range of models/tools (Finlay, 2008; Fook, 2006; Ixer, 2003; E. Smith , 2011).
- Explore critical reflection from different theoretical perspectives (Fook, 2006).
- Ensure theory and practice are integrated (Ghaye and Lillyman, 2000)
- Ensure reflective practice is research-informed – *'respecting and working with evidence'* (Ghaye and Lillyman, 2000; Rychly and Graves, 2012).
- Clarify with learners that different reflective models and tools engage different levels of complexity and therefore need to be used selectively and judiciously.
- Examine with learners the strengths and weaknesses of different approaches in relation to the value of each model in supporting the learner to meet requirements (self, task, context).
- Support learners to think flexibly and not dualistically (Rychly and Graves, 2012).

C. Optimizing conditions for learning / sensitivity to learner context

- Encourage a joint commitment on part of learner and teacher to engage in rigorous reflection (de Cossart and Fish, 2005).
- Recognize the proficiency of each learner to use reflective tools and their individual capacity for growth (Stein, 2000).
- Allocate sufficient time to support critical reflection (de Cossart and Fish, 2005; Ixer, 2003).
- Develop learner ability to perceive classroom practice from own and others' points of view (Rychly and Graves, 2012).
- Promote and develop a supportive environment (Finlay, 2008).
- Ensure critical reflection approaches are sensitive to specific cultural and social contexts.
- Scaffolding should be used to ensure appropriate use of tools from simpler to more sophisticated models.
- Ensure learners are aware of the broad range of critical reflection models from the outset. Different models are needed, at different levels, for different individuals, disciplines and organizations, to use in different contexts (Finlay, 2008).
- Facilitate learners to try out models/tools safely in practical/experiential ways (Hobbs, 2007).
- Give learners choice in their chosen method(s) of critical reflection.

D. Design of learning environments

- Use critical reflection models as tools to stimulate reflection rather than as ends in themselves; they should not be prescriptive (Lucas, 2012). They should be used to enhance practice (Ghaye and Lillyman, 2000).
- Expose learners to different models and approaches to critical reflection to inform *their* choices as to what is most suitable for them (C. Evans and Waring, 2009, 2015; Finlay, 2008).
- Reflection before, during and after action should be considered, with increased emphasis being placed on reflection prior to learning.
- Learners should be provided with opportunities to use a variety of tools to support critical reflection (logs, diaries, critical incident analysis, autobiographical and narrative approaches (de Cossart and Fish, 2006; Ixer, 2003; Smith, 2011).
- Sufficient support should be provided through critically reflective partners (peers) and tutors and through supporting the learner to become autonomous in their critical reflection.
- Structured critical reflection should be facilitated to ensure higher levels of reflection are tapped (Rychly and Graves, 2012; Smith, 2011).
- The reflective conversation is at the heart of the process. Facilitate opportunities for discourse for learners to expose their own meanings to critical reflection.
- (Ghaye and Lillyman, 2000; Mezirow, 2000).
- Use reflective practice to help learners make sense of their thoughts and
- actions (Ghaye and Lillyman, 2000).
- Encourage a more collective emphasis on reflection at work (Hoyrup and Elkjaer, 2006) through the use of dialogue, collaborative reflection opportunities, lesson study.
- Use action learning groups to help learners associate, integrate, validate, and appropriate new meanings (Graham, 1995).
- To support learner perspective transformation there should be: (a) a process for diagnosing existing conceptual frameworks and revealing them to the learner; (b) a period of disequilibrium and conceptual conflict which makes students dissatisfied with existing conceptions; (c) a reconstruction or reforming phase in which a new conceptual framework is formed (Leung and Kember, 2003).

(continued)

Table 10.1 continued

E. Supporting learner autonomy: choices in learning / student voice

- Ensure the value of critical reflection is mirrored in assessment practices. Critical reflection should be integrated into assessment so that students are able to demonstrate critical reflection as part of formative and summative assessment (Evans, 2015).
- Learners should be given opportunities to engage in critical reflection as a solo activity and as a group process (Evans, 2015; Finlay, 2008; Ixer, 2003).
- Learners should identify for themselves areas of opportunity for further learning (Rychly and Graves, 2012).
- Critical reflection should be used as an empowerment tool to support the generation of locally owned knowledge (Brookfield, 1995; Ghaye and Lillyman, 2000).
- Ensure reflective practice is systematic and rigorous (Ghaye and Lillyman, 2000).
- Ensure critical reflection is authentic and related to the development of learners'
- own knowledge as an integral part of professional practice.
- Place emphasis on developing facilitative cultures that promote and support collaborative critical reflection practice (Boud, 2010; Brookfield, 1995).

Note: learner = teacher and student

on the efficacy of reflective practice relate to the level of reflection required, the context, the individual and the interrelationship between these variables. Given that critical reflection takes place within social contexts the nature of such contexts is of great importance (Fook *et al.*, 2006). Climates encouraging critical acceptance (Fook) and reflective discourse (Mezirow) are essential. Such climates are characterized as being: open to different perspectives and ideas; valuing reflective practice; information rich; encouraging of dialogue and transparency; open to innovation; respectful of individual differences, and supportive of distributed leadership.

At the individual level, critical reflection may be affected by a learner's cognitive ability, willingness to engage in the reflective process, orientation to change, commitment to self-enquiry and readiness to change practice, and self-awareness (Stein, 2000). At the interaction level, the commitment of learner and teacher to devote time to engage in sustained critical reflection is of paramount importance. Issues of trust and power are important in this dynamic, along with the expertise of the teacher to appropriately scaffold critical reflection practice to enable learner autonomy through the judicious choice and application of models and tools.

Tools to develop critical reflection

There are a wide variety of tools that can be used to support the development of individual and collaborative critical reflective practice. Such tools can be used both informally or formally, in different mediums (written, diagrammatic or verbal forms), and to focus on different stages of reflection (de Cossart and Fish, 2006; Fook *et al.*, 2006). Such approaches, for example, include the use of Brookfield's lenses (1995) to examine ideas from different perspectives (learner, peers, pupils, research); frameworks for reflection on action (Greenwood, 1998; Smyth, 1989 – see Tools D1, D2); critical incident analysis (Flanagan, 1954 – see Tool E1); DeBono techniques (Tripp, 1993); narratives, diaries, stories, poems, pictures, objects, concept maps (de Cossart and Fish, 2005; E. Smith, 2011); use of drama (Boal technique – Boal, 1993; 1996); videos, blogs, portfolios and diaries (Evans and

Waring, 2015; Fowler, 2013; Stein, 2011); feedback and self-evaluation forms (Boud *et al.*, 1985); rubrics to examine different dimensions of reflective practice (Evans and Waring, 2015); assessment practice rewarding critical reflection as part of formative and summative assessment (Evans and Waring, 2015); use of action learning groups – e.g. lesson study techniques (Davies and Dunnill, 2008); peer discussion (Brookfield, 1987); problem-based learning (Fyrenius *et al.*, 2007). The critically informed use of such tools places emphasis on the key purpose of reflection (which layers of reflection are being tapped) in relation to the requirements of the learner within context, and to the underpinning theoretical framework, and not on an exclusive focus on the tool itself (E. Smith, 2011).

Summary

Not all reflection is critical and nor does it necessarily need to be. Different contexts will demand different sorts and combinations of reflection. The pedagogical concern from the teachers' perspective is about ensuring the appropriate level of reflection within a given context. Underpinning the concept of critical reflection is an emphasis on transformation informed by social and political analyses of contexts. A key question is the extent to which engagement in critical reflection enables teachers and their students to become successful change agents. Critical reflection is about undergoing a perspective change, which Brookfield has argued is best done collaboratively given the emotional investment involved.

> Questioning the assumptions on which we act and exploring alternative ideas are not only difficult but also psychologically explosive . . . [it] is like laying down charges of psychological dynamite. When these assumptions explode and we realise that what we thought of as fixed ways of thinking and living are only options among a range of alternatives, the whole structure of our assumptive world crumbles. Hence, educators who foster transformative learning are rather like psychological and cultural demolition experts.
>
> Brookfield 1990, p. 178

Critical reflection is not without risk (Brookfield, 1994; 1995). It should not be undertaken lightly given its potential impact to destabilize both individuals and organizational systems. Done badly it can leave individuals feeling helpless if the opportunities to change are not there and it can reinforce dominant cultural assumptions that may work against challenges to power. Given the ethical issues involved, Finlay (2008) questions whether teachers and students are obliged to take part in critical reflection. Even when organizational climates are supportive, there is a danger that critical reflection can become unthinking, routinized, mechanical, and inauthentic when models and tools are used as an end in themselves without critical reflection being seen as an integral part of professional practice. The characteristics of the individual learner are one of the most important factors influencing critical reflective working behaviour (Fook, 2006). However, as already noted, learners will vary in their readiness and ability to engage in critical reflective practice (Stein, 2000): features that may be compounded by lack of time and other work pressures. Furthermore, unearthing the more tacit elements of practice concerned with professional artistry, relational and ideological dimensions may be problematic as these are hard to quantify.

Mindful of concerns about the ways in which critically reflective practice is enacted, there is a substantial body of work articulating aspects of best practice in developing critical reflective practice, as summarized in Table 10.1. These emphasize ensuring authenticity of practice; opportunities for learners to observe and to experiment with different approaches in safe environments; and opportunities for learners to have choice in their use of approaches and agency in managing the process.

A key issue for teachers is to support learners to transfer the skills acquired from one context to another. Related to this is the challenge for teachers to ensure rigorous evaluation of approaches used to inform future practice, in order to address concerns about the lack of evidence which suggests that critically reflective learners become change agents and that the skills learnt in the development of critical reflective practice can easily be applied to different contexts (Stein, 2000). Evidence on the effectiveness of collaborative critical reflection activities is also lacking, although findings from lesson study where critical reflection has been employed are promising (Ylonen and Norwich, 2013). In moving critically reflective practice forward Boud (2010) has emphasized the importance of seeing critical reflection not as an individual venture but as a collective one.

> Productive reflection . . . picks up concerns about the need for new ways of considering reflection in workplaces that are not focused on the individual independent learner . . . reflection in such settings cannot be an individual act if it is to influence work that takes place with others.
>
> Boud, 2010, p. 32

A key issue in the development of collaborative critical reflection is the ability of organizations to maintain an 'outside looking in approach' and one that encourages the *dance* (experimentation and risk) (Brookfield, 1995). Questions arise as to which constellation of factors enables the most effective practices and what critical mass is needed to initiate and sustain initiatives; the nature of leadership is important here.

Where critical reflection is seen as an integral part of one's own teaching practice with the motivational aim of enhancing one's own and others' teaching it can be emancipatory, as evidenced in our work with early career teachers using the PLSP framework where assessment of the teachers' learning depended on their identification and development of an area of their own teaching using a critical reflective approach (Evans, 2015; Evans and Waring, 2015).

> The course [PLSP framework] provided me with a connection to theory, policy and practice which gave me the confidence during my NQT [newly qualified teacher] year to teach in the way I wanted to and enabled me to develop a 'voice' in the busy context of my school. It gave me the opportunity to explore an area of interest and a way of working which has enriched my teaching and developed my skills as a reflective practitioner.
>
> NQT 1

> The course helped me to see the bigger picture in my first year of teaching, and to delve deeper into my chosen area of interest with the support . . . I felt that I needed to keep a toe dipped in theory to inform my practice. This has enabled me to continue thinking about how I can improve and share good practice with others. The course has given me the incentive to carry on with my studies, as just being a classroom teacher isn't enough. It's good to be on the outside looking in
>
> NQT 2

Supporting teachers to be ready and equipped to critically reflect on their own practice is an essential element of teacher professional development if teachers are to manage their own learning, support the learning of their colleagues, and most importantly support their own pupils' ability to critically reflect in order to develop greater independence in learning.

Questions for reflection

Having reviewed the different approaches and conceptions of critical reflective practice, please consider the following:

- What is your perception of the value of critical reflection in learning and teaching?
- How do you reflect on your current professional practice?
- What are the main types of reflective practice that you have engaged in during the last year?
- Can you describe any examples of perspective transformation where your thinking has changed? What triggered your personal change?
- From a changed perspective were you able to develop your practice and put your ideas into practice? What factors facilitated and/or hindered this from individual and organizational perspectives? How could you further develop your use of critical reflection?
- How do you encourage students to reflect on their practice and to use higher levels of reflection? What are the facilitators and barriers in enabling you to do this?
- What approaches and tools do you use to facilitate critical reflection, and what informs their use?

- To what extent are you able to apply the principles and approaches to critical reflective practice as highlighted in Table 10.1?

- To what extent are you involved in collaborative reflective practice and what does this involve? What do you see as the advantages and limitations of collaborative approaches to reflection?

- How are you supporting your students to be able to apply critical reflective practice beyond the classroom?

Borton's (1970) framework (see Table 10.2) focuses on reflection on action. Develop a template to enable you to use this to reflect before and in action.

Table 10.2 Borton's (1970) framework guiding reflective activities

What?	*So what?*	*Now what?*
Description and *self-awareness level*	*Analysis and evaluation level*, looking deeper at what was behind the experience	*Synthesis level*, considering alternative courses of action and choices
• What happened? • What did I do? • What did others do? • What was I trying to achieve? • What was good or bad about the experience?	• So what is the importance of this? • So what more do I need to know about this? • So what have I learnt about this?	• Now what could I do? • Now what do I need to do? • Now what might I do? • Now what might be the consequences of this action?

See Tools E (in Appendix)

1 How can critical incident analysis support understanding of self and interaction with others?

2 Is critical incident analysis best done alone or in discussion with others?

3 How can you use the critical incident technique in your teaching?

4 How does change come about?

Key readings

Bolton, G. (2010). *Reflective practice*. London: Sage.

Different ways of exploring and facilitating reflective practice and reflexivity are exemplified from a variety of contexts. A companion website accompanies the book at www.sagepub.co.uk/bolton.

Brookfield, S. (1995). *Becoming a critically reflective teacher*. San-Francisco: Jossey-Bass.

This book integrates theory, research and practice in its exposition of critically reflective practice. Brookfield's four lenses (self, peers, students, and theoretical literature) provides a framework through which to examine and reflect on our own practice. The notion of criticality in reflection is explored from individual and collaborative reflective perspectives. See also Brookfield (2005).

Poulson, L. and Wallace, M. (2004). (Eds), *Learning to read critically in teaching and learning*. London: Sage.
This book and the follow up by Wallace and Wray (2011) provide clear guidance on critical reading and writing and in so doing provide tools and frameworks to support the analysis and synthesis of research.

Wallace, M., and Wray, A. (2011). *Critical Reading and writing for postgraduates* (2nd ed.). London: Sage.)

Tripp, D. (1993). *Critical incidents in teaching: Developing professional judgement.* Oxford: RoutledgeFalmer.
Tripp highlights what makes a critical incident critical is the way in which we analyse it; the event itself does not need to be critical. The book provides useful frameworks in which to explore ones' own practice and provides many examples from the school context.

Weblinks

Beddoe, L., and Healy, K. (2011). (Eds), Advances in social work and welfare education. Special issue: *Critical reflection: Method and practice, 13* (1), May 2011, 1–153. School of Social Work and Human Services. The University of Queensland: Australian Association of Social Work and Welfare Education. Available online at http://www.anzswwer.org/advances/Advances_Vol_13_No_1.pdf (accessed 3 March 2014).

Fowler, E. (2013). Changing the learning landscape. Using blogs to support reflection. Available online at www.heacademy.ac.uk/resources/detail/cll/Workshop_materials (accessed 19 March 2014).

Hawkins, R., and Woolf, H. (n.d.). Available online at http://www2.wlv.ac.uk/celt/Projects/historians_reflect/Greater_Manchester_AHP-HCS_Life_Long_Learning_Project_Team.pdf (accessed 10 December 2013).

Hay, D. B. (2010). Prizewinning essays (vol. 1). Higher Education Research Network. London: King's Learning Institute, King's College, London. Available online at https://www.kcl.ac.uk/study/learningteaching/kli/research/hern/hernjvol1.pdf (accessed 19 March 2014).

Hill, D. (n.d.) Critical reflection in early childhood education: a framework for personal and professional empowerment. University of Auckland. New Zealand. Available online at https://www.google.co.uk/#q=Hill+critical+reflection (accessed 19 March 2014).

McClure, P. (2004). Making practice-based learning work: Reflection on practice. School of Health Sciences, University of Ulster: FDTL Phase 4, project no 174/02. Available online at http://cw.routledge.com/textbooks/9780415537902/data/learning/8_Reflection%20in%20Practice.pdf (accessed 3 March 2014).

Sharp, P., Ainslie, T., Hemphill, A., Hobson, S., Merriman, C., Ong, P., and Roche, J. (2006). Making problem-based learning work: Mentoring. A resource for those who facilitate placement learning. School of Health and Social Care, Oxford Brookes University. Available online at http://www.inclentrust.org/uploadedbyfck/file/compile%20resourse/new-resourse-dr_vishal/Practice-Based%20learning.pdf (accessed 3 March 2014).

Boal

The Forum Project. What is Theatre of the Oppressed? *Tree of the Theatre of the Oppressed.* The Forum Project. Available online at http://theforumproject.org/whatisto/> (accessed 15 March 2014).

See also Boal, A. (1974). From 'Theatre of the Oppressed'. In N. Wardrip-Fruin and N. Montfort (Eds.) (2003). *The New Media Reader.* Cambridge, MA: MIT.

Brookfield

Brookfield, S. Article and interviews. Available online at http://www.stephenbrookfield.com/Dr._Stephen_D._Brookfield/Articles_and_Interviews.html (accessed 19 March 2014).

Brookfield, S. (2004). The getting of wisdom: What critically reflective teaching is and why it's important. Online. Available online at http://nlu.nl.edu/academics/cas/ace/facultypapters/StephenBrookfield.cfm

Brookfield, S. (2006). The skilful teacher: On trust, technique and responsiveness in the classroom. San Francisco: Jossey Bass.

Kolb

Kolb, D. A. (n.d.). On experiential learning. Available online at http://infed.org/mobi/david-a-kolb-on-experiential-learning/ (accessed 3 March 2014).

APPENDIX

Tool A

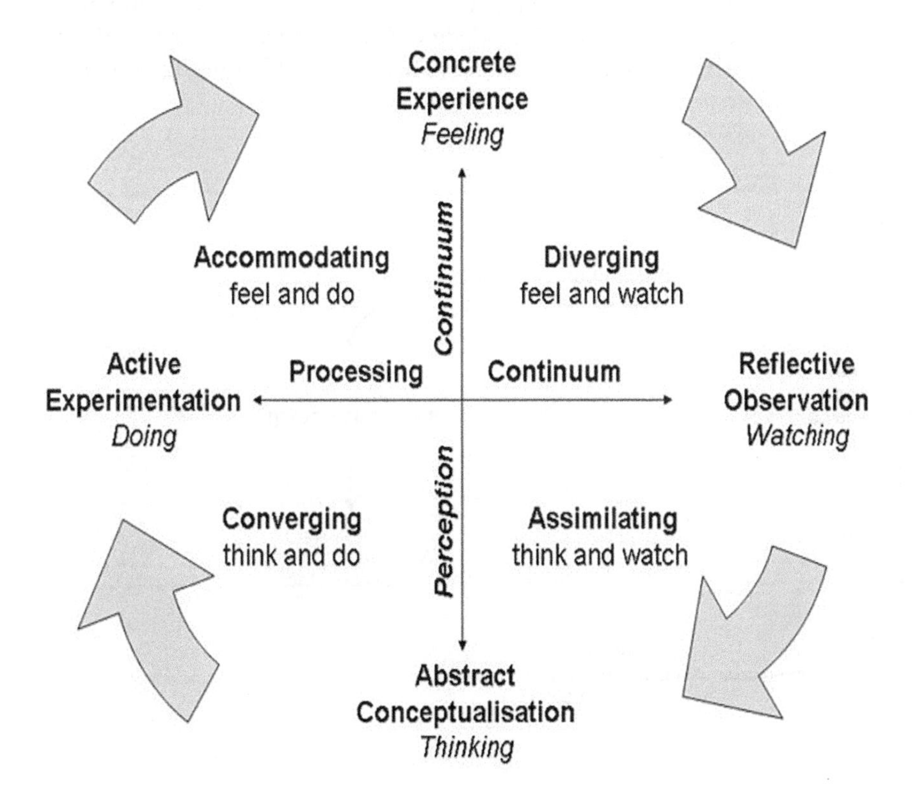

Tool A Kolb's experiential learning model

The model, from Kolb and Fry, 1975, comprises four elements: concrete experience, reflective observation, abstract conceptualization and active experimentation. These elements form a cycle of learning. Learning can start with any one of the four, but it typically begins with a concrete experience.

Key ideas (Kolb and Kolb, 2005, p. 194; Segers and Van de Haar, 2011, p. 55)

1 Learning is best understood as a process, not in terms of the outcomes; feedback is a very important part of the learning process.
2 Learning is best facilitated by a process that draws out students' beliefs and ideas about a topic, so that they can examine, test and integrate these with new, more refined ideas.
3 Learning requires the resolution of conflicts between dialectically opposed modes of adaptation to the world. Conflict, differences and disagreement drive the learning process. In the process of learning, one is called upon to move back and forth between opposing modes of reflection, action, feeling and thinking.
4 Learning is a holistic process of adaptation to the world. It is not just the result of cognition, but involves the integrated functioning of the total person: thinking, feeling, perceiving and behaving.
5 Learning results from synergetic transactions between the person and the environment.
6 Learning is the process of creating knowledge. The experiential learning theory represents a constructivist theory of learning, whereby social knowledge is created and recreated in the personal knowledge of the learner.

Tool B

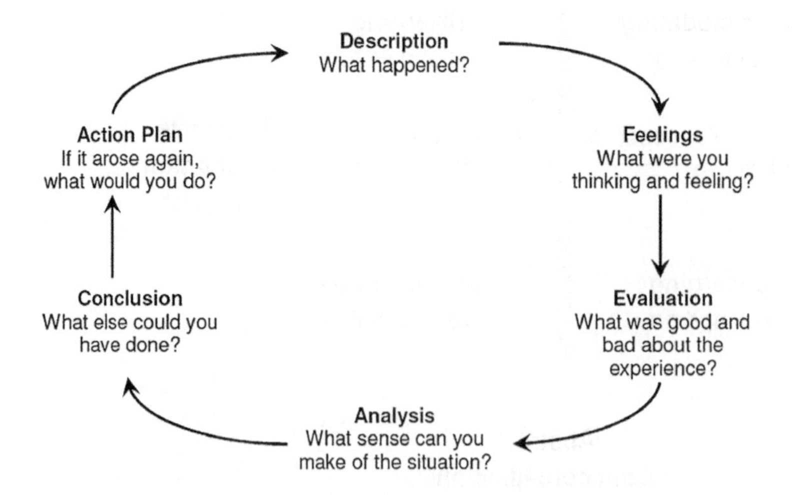

(Gibbs 1988)

Tool B Gibbs's model of reflection

Gibbs's learning cycle is reproduced with permission from Gibbs G. (1988), *Learning by Doing: A Guide to Teaching and Learning*, Oxford Centre for Staff and Learning Development, Oxford Brookes University, Oxford. This publication is available to download from http://www.brookes.ac.uk/ocsld/publications/

Gibbs's (1988) pragmatic reflective cycle encourages a description of the situation, analysis of feelings, evaluation of the experience, making sense of the experience through analysis, arriving at conclusions where other options are considered, and reflection upon experience for the learner to consider what they would do if the situation arose again.

Tools C

Johns' model of structured reflection (1994) was developed for medical contexts but can easily be applied to practice in schools. The framework uses five cue questions which are then divided into more focuses to promote detailed reflection *(substitute patient with pupil).*

Tool C.1 Johns' (1994) model of structured reflection

1 Description of the experience	• Phenomenon – describe the here and now experience • Casual – what essential factors contributed to this experience? • Context – what are the significant background factors to this experience? • Clarifying – what are the key processes for reflection in this experience?
2 Reflection	• What was I trying to achieve? • Why did I intervene as I did? • What were the consequences of my actions for: o myself? o the patient/family? o the people I work with? • How did I feel about this experience when it was happening? • How did the patient feel about it? • How do I know how the patient felt about it?
3 Influencing factors	• What internal factors influenced my decision making? • What external factors influenced my decision making? • What sources of knowledge did / should have influenced my decision making?
4 Evaluation: could I have dealt with the situation better?	• What other choices did I have? • What would be the consequences of these choices?
5 Learning	• How do I now feel about this experience? • How have I made sense of this experience in light of past experiences and future practice? • How has this experience changed my ways of knowing o Empirics – scientific o Ethics – moral knowledge o Personal – self awareness o Aesthetics – the art of what we do, our own experiences?

Tool C.2 Ways of knowing (Johns, 2006, informed by Carper, 1978)

Personal	*Aesthetics*	*Empirical*	*Ethics*	*Reflexivity*
Bring the mind home	Focus on a description of an experience that seems significant in some way	What knowledge informed me or might have informed me?	To what extent did I act for the best and in tune with my values?	How does this situation connect with previous experiences?
How was I feeling, and what made me feel that way?	What issues are significant for me to pay attention to?			How might I respond more effectively given this situation again?
What factors influence the way I was/am feeling, thinking and responding to this situation?	How are people feeling, and why do they feel that way? (empathic inquiry)			What would be the consequences of alternative actions for the patient, others and myself?
What factors might constrain my responding in new ways?	What was I trying to achieve, and did I respond effectively?			Am I better able to support myself and others as a consequence?
How do I now feel about this experience?	What were consequences of my actions on the patient, others and myself?			What insights have I gained through this reflection? (framing perspectives)

The development of Johns' *model of structured reflection* (1994; 2006) is informed by Carper's (1978) ways of knowing developed specifically for nursing, which again can be adapted for use within education. The four fundamental *patterns of knowing* in Carper's original conception include: (i)*Personal:* knowledge and attitudes derived from personal *self-understanding* and *empathy*; (ii) *Aesthetic* – in relating to the here and now: awareness of the immediate situation, seated in immediate practical action, including awareness of the patient and their circumstances as uniquely individual, and of the combined wholeness of the situation; (iii) *Empirical* – factual knowledge that can be empirically verified; (iv) *Ethical* – attitudes and knowledge derived from an *ethical* framework of professional practice, including an awareness of *moral* questions and choices. Finlay (2008) highlights the reflexive nature of Johns' approach as highlighted in the additional column in Tool C.2 (again, substitute *pupil* for *patient*).

Tools D

Tool D.1 Smyth's (1989) framework for reflection on action

Activity	*Cues*
Describe	What did I do?
Inform (analysis)	What does this mean?
Confront (self-awareness)	How did I come to be like this?
Reconstruct (evaluation and synthesis)	• What do my practices say about my assumptions, values and beliefs? • Where did these ideas come from? • What social practices are expressed in these ideas? • What is it that causes me to maintain my theories? • What views of power do they embody? • Whose interests seem to be served by my practices? • What is it that acts to constrain my views of what is possible in my practice?

Tool D.2 Smyth's (1993) six principles underpinning reflective practice

Reflection:

1 should not only be concerned with *technical skills* – it should be concerned with the *ethical, social,* and *political* context within which teaching occurs;
2 should not be restricted to teachers *reflecting individually* on their teaching; there should also be a *collective* and *collaborative* dimension;
3 is a process that is centrally concerned with *challenging the dominant myths, assumptions and hidden message systems* implicit in the way teaching and education is organised;
4 is about *creating improvements in educational practice and the social relationships* that underlie those practices;
5 is founded on the belief that *knowledge about teaching is in a tentative and incomplete state,* and as such, is continually being modified as a consequence of practice;
6 occurs best when it *begins with the experiences of practitioners* as they are assisted in the process of *describing, informing, confronting* and *re-constructing* their theories of practice.

Tools E

Tool E.1 Critical incident analysis (based on Flanagan, 1954)

Key points:

1 Any event can be analysed to create a critical incident (CI): 'incidents appear to be "typical" rather than "critical" at first sight, but are rendered critical through analysis' (Tripp, 1993, p. 25).
2 '[Critical incident analysis] does not consist of a single rigid set of rules governing such data collection. Rather it should be thought of as a flexible set of principles which must be modified and adapted to meet the specific situation at hand' (Flanagan, 1954, p. 335).

3 The analysis should focus on eliciting the beliefs, opinions and suggestions that formed part of the critical incident rather than concentrating solely on a description of the incident itself (Cheek *et al.*, 1997).
4 Critical incidents include commonplace events occurring in the everyday life of the classroom (Tripp, 1994, p. 69). In teaching, importantly, 'critical incidents are created. Incidents happen, but critical incidents are produced by the way we look at a situation: a critical incident is an interpretation of the significance of an event' (Tripp, 1993, p. 8). Critical incidents are 'not at all dramatic or obvious: they are mostly straightforward accounts of very common place events that occur in routine professional practice which are critical in the rather different sense that they are indicative of underlying trends, motives and structures' (Tripp, 1993, p. 24–25).

APPROACHES TO CRITICAL INCIDENT ANALYSIS

- Describe the event.
- Provide a contextual explanation of the incident.
- Identify your position.
- Find a more general meaning:
    - Was it related to the learning environment?
    - Was it behavioural?
    - Was it subject related?
    - Was it pedagogical?
    - Other:
        - Articulate a position.

The *surgical strands of reflection* (de Cossart and Fish, 2005) can be adapted to educational contexts and used within critical incident analysis (substitute *pupil* for *patient*).

Tool E.2 Surgical strands of reflection (adapted from de Cossart and Fish, 2005)

Surgical strands of reflection	*Prompts*
Factual strand Give a descriptive narrative of the event	• What happened? • What you felt like, thought and did? • What were the key moments of the event? • How do you see these? (Consider them critically)
Retrospective strand Look at the event as a whole. What patterns and possible new meanings can you see (this is still about surface performance)?	• What are the main patterns of, (for example) reason and/or motive, activities, failures, successes, emotions, frustrations, limitations, constraints, coercions? • How might others (patients/fellow team members/observers) have seen it overall? • Analyse the oral language used between self and fellow professionals.

Sub-stratum strand What assumptions, beliefs, values, reasoning and judgements underlay the events (probing deeper)?	• What have you learnt about being a member of a profession? • What beliefs, assumptions, theories, and values, shaped your conduct? • What customs, traditions, rituals, beliefs, dogmas, prejudices, were brought to/endemic in the situation? Where did they come from? • What knowledge was used or created during the event? • What beliefs are emerging about knowledge and how it is gained/used/created? • What perspectives from formal theory and personal experience and theory shaped the event? • What does the event (and these reflections) tell us about how you view theory and practice? • What key thinking processes did you engage in? • What key professional judgements were made during practice? • What moral and ethical issues were raised for you by this experience? • How do you regard these now?
The connective strand Relate what you have learnt in the above strands to the wider world – of practice ideas, reflections, theories and actions of other professionals, and (via reading) to formal theory	• How does it relate to past experiences, and how will it relate to future ones? • What issues and practices in your own work will you now explore further? • What theories might you develop for/about future action? • What do you need to find out more about and why? How will you do this? • What explorations/investigations of future practice might you plan?

Tool E.3 Tripp (1993, p. 44) advocates the use of thinking strategies to support critical reflection. His framework includes consideration of the following:

- *Non-events:* why what did not happen did not happen.
- *Plus, minus and interesting:* what was good, bad or neutral about an event.
- *Alternatives, possibilities and choices:* thinking about alternative things that could have happened and devising ways to make them happen.
- *Other points of view:* seeking out views of participants and non-participants to question assumptions and opinions.
- *Parts and qualities:* looking at something as a collection of parts or as a set of qualities – examining our attitudes, values, and judgements.
- *Reversal:* looking at something from the opposite point of view.
- *Omissions:* what have we left out? Have we considered all possible ideas that we can generate.

Tool F

Brookfield (1995) proposes four lenses that teachers can use in a process of critical reflection:

1 autobiographical
2 the students' eyes
3 colleagues' experiences
4 theoretical literature.

Chapter 11

The Personal Learning Styles Pedagogy implementation framework

Overview

The PLSP framework was developed in 2009 to clarify how an understanding of cognitive styles could be used within the initial teacher education context. Further analysis of over 700 full papers (articles, reports) including qualitative and quantitative studies (Evans, 2013a; Evans and Waring, 2012) led to further development of the Personal Learning Styles Pedagogy (PLSP) framework as outlined below and its application to learning and teaching contexts more broadly (across disciplines; professions; levels of study – school, higher education and beyond).

Throughout the book we have demonstrated different ways in which the PLSP framework can be used (e.g. to support assessment design and development, support critical reflection, etc). The PLSP is a flexible framework. It can be used in the implementation of specific innovations (e.g. the flipped classroom) and most importantly it can be used as an overarching holistic framework guiding the design of curricula including assessment to encompass school, higher education, and other workplace learning. The PLSP emphasizes the importance of supporting students in order for them to be able to manage their own learning both now and in their future. An implementation framework demonstrating how each of the components of the PLSP can be realized within practice will now be presented in Table 11.1; it draws on a rich and diverse data set including research in schools, higher education and the workplace (1999–2014).

While Table 11.1 highlights the closest links between sub-components of the PLSP with the Teachers' Standards (DfE, 2011) and the UK Professional Standards (HEA, Guild HE, Universities UK, 2011) it should be acknowledged that all of the components / sub-components of the PLSP interrelate in some way shape or form to all of the Teachers' Standards and UK Professional Standards (an outline of the dimensions of each of these sets of standards are presented after Table 11.1).

Table 11.1 The Personal Learning Styles Pedagogy implementation framework (Evans and Waring, 2014)

PLSP component: A. Exploration of student and teacher beliefs / modelling and support
Overarching theme: Integrated into the learning experience and ***not a*** one stop shop
All learning cycles begin with a focus on beliefs and values which are constantly revisited

Sub components of component A	*Application to teaching and learning contexts. (Learner = student and/or teacher)*	*Closest links to:*		
		Sub-components of the PLSP	*UK Professional Standards Framework (HEA, Guild HE, Universities UK, 2011)*	*Teachers' Standards (DfE, 2011a)*
A (i) Focus on the learning histories of student and teacher	• Explore with learners their *learning histories* – emotional geographies / significant learning events (A. Hargreaves, 2001): the '*learning passport*' and '*emotional stamp*', (positive and negative); the life journey or biography (Bloomfield, 2010) • Ascertain learners' *prior knowledge and skills* and build on these from the outset, – building on the notion of the *Zone of Proximal Development* (Heikkilä and Lonka, 2006; Vygotsky, 1986) • Build on *strengths and qualities* the learner brings to the context and not just the deficit view of learner as '*diminished self*' (Ecclestone, 2007). Get learners to map what they bring to the learning context and to identify both their strengths and the areas that they feel less confident about • Establish a *learning climate* where it is comfortable to discuss '*what I do not know*', and the art of '*knowing what to do when one does not know*' (Barnett, 2011) • Using flipped classroom techniques to encourage student engagement (Educause, 2012)	C (i) C (ii)	A1 A2 A3 K2 K3 K4 V1	1 2 5 6 7

A (ii) Holistic understanding: consideration of the whole experience of the learner	• Consider *cognitive, metacognitive,* and *affective* dimensions of learning (Vermunt and Verloop, 1999) • Ensure attention to the affective/emotional dimension of learning and teaching (Demetriou and Wilson, 2009; Hinton *et al.*, 2008; Lovatt *et al.*, 2011) • Ensure learning activities including assessment are *authentic* (Evans, 2013a, b) • Develop *integrated pedagogies* that consider the relevance of what is to be learnt by the learner beyond the immediate learning context (Allcock and Hulme, 2010; Huber *et al.*, 2007; Shulman, 2005) • Look at ways of developing *interdisciplinary collaboration* beyond immediate subject/ department/ year group/school/HEI (Carmichael *et al.*, 2012) • Use an *integrated approach* considering students' and teachers' processes of learning (Vermunt, 2013)	A (iii) B (iii) C (i) D (vii) D (ix) E (vi)	A1 A2 A4 A5 K2 K3 V1 V3	2 4 5 6 8
A (iii) Exploration of learner (student and teacher) beliefs about learning (e.g. ability, self-efficacy, identity and sense of fit within learning contexts)	• Explore with learners their *conceptions of learning, their beliefs and what they value* (Vermunt, 1996). Explore learner attitudes using scenarios; role play/drama; narrative; concept mapping; images; objects (Ellis *et al.*, 2006); with emphasis on a values pedagogy (Lovat *et al.*, 2011) • Focus instructional methods on those that nurture conceptual change, starting first with identifying students' naive conceptions so that they can be addressed in learning and teaching (Demetriou and Wilson, 2009)	C (ii) C (iii) D (ii) D (vi) D (vii)	A1 A2 A4 A5 K2 K3 K5 K6 V1	1 2 3 4 5 6

(continued)

Table 11.1 (continued)

Sub components of component A	*Application to teaching and learning contexts. (Learner = student and/or teacher)*	*Closest links to:*		
		Sub-components of the PLSP	*UK Professional Standards Framework (HEA, Guild HE, Universities UK, 2011)*	*Teachers' Standards (DfE, 2011a)*
	• Clarify with learners the *values and principles* underpinning the learning design to examine conflicts and areas of agreement with the aim of achieving greater alignment of values (Evans and Waring, 2015) • Explicitly address the *goals* of the learning design and explore learners' goals and factors impacting goals (Evans and Waring, 2015) • Encourage explicit discussions of learners' *implicit and subjective educational theory(ies)* (Kelchtermans, 2009) • Promote *'positive mindset'*, (Dweck, 2006) and share the knowledge that challenge in learning can develop brain capacity (Adey *et al.*, 2007) • Explore the concept of *the authentic self* (Higgs and Titchen, 2001) as part of discussions about identity development and the need for individuals to manage their different identities within and across contexts • Examine learners' *sense of fit* within contexts and get learners to *map their networks of support* and the relative strength of these within the learning context and beyond (Bliuc, 2011a, 2011b)			

A (iv) Enhancing learner awareness and application of styles as part of ongoing instruction on individual learning differences. Understanding of individual differences central to the design of learning environments	• *Promote awareness and instruction in styles* to develop a *shared lexicon of learning* in order to discuss the process of learning and development of appropriate styles (Cassidy, 2004; Cools and Evans, 2009; Desmedt and Valcke, 2004; Coffield *et al.*, 2005; Evans and Waring, 2012; Nielsen, 2012; Zhang *et al.*, 2012) • Share and discuss *principles of effective cognitive styles pedagogies* with learners (Evans, 2013a; Evans and Waring, 2012) • Promote the understanding that each individual has a *learning profile* – a hierarchy of styles – and that *styles are relatively flexible*: they can be developed (Kozhevnikov, 2007; Kozhevnikov *et al.*, 2014) • *Demonstrate* the use of specific style constructs with learners in authentic contexts (M. Rosenfeld and S. Rosenfeld, 2011) • Encourage learners *to model how they can use an understanding of styles* in the development of their own practice (Evans and Waring, 2006; Kek and Huijser, 2011)	B (i) – B (iv) D (ii) D (viii)	A1 A2 A4 A5 K3 K5 V1 V3	1 2 4 5 7

(continued)

Table 11.1 (continued)

PLSP component: B. Careful selection and application of styles
Overarching theme: Holistic research-informed approach

Sub components of component B	*Application to teaching and learning contexts. (Learner = student and/or teacher)*	*Closest links to:*		
		Sub-components of the PLSP	*UK Professional Standards Framework (HEA, Guild HE, Universities UK, 2011)*	*Teachers' Standards (DfE, 2011a)*
B (i) Judicious and informed use of instruments/styles models	• *Clarify* with learners how styles can be used effectively in practice. Students as *active participants* who are fully informed (as to reasons for using instruments, what results mean, and how such information can be used to support their learning): a second person perspective (M. Rosenfeld and S. Rosenfeld, 2011) • *Use styles instruments and associated learning and teaching tools judiciously* – Need for selectivity as to which models are used and also whether they need to be used at all (Evans and Sadler-Smith, 2006; Evans and Waring, 2012; Yates, 2000) • *Use instruments appropriately* – there is a need to ensure they are administered appropriately and their results are interpreted accurately (Evans and Vermunt, 2013)	A iv D (ii) D (iv) D (v)	A2 A3 K2 K6 V2 V3	2 6

B (ii) Critical analysis of styles as part of instruction on individual learning differences. Appropriate application of styles models: instruments used as metacognitive tools to support understanding of the learning process	• Ensure that you use instruments that demonstrate satisfactory levels of *reliability and validity* (Riding and Rayner, 1998). (e.g. informed use of object–visual, spatial–visual and verbalization (Kozhevnikov *et al.*, 2013) • Use styles instruments as *pedagogical tools* to support development of knowledge and skills in clearly identified areas (Evans and Waring 2011c, 2011d, 2012) • *Use styles instruments transparently (*be clear on what was done and how to enable replication across contexts) – follow protocols for reporting results (Des Jarlais *et al.*, 2004) • *Carefully explain the results of styles tools with learners* (e.g. learners are not 'wholists' or 'deep' – they may exhibit a preference for wholistic and deep processing within certain contexts). Encourage learners to explore the strengths and weaknesses of instruments and their relevance for practice within specific contexts (Evans *et al.*, 2013). • *Encourage learners to look at overarching principles of styles* (e.g. to consider overarching style dimensions such as degree of conformity, degree of authority, cognitive complexity, structure, and groupings of learners (Zhang and Sternberg, 2006); along with overarching principles of style constructs (e.g. Evans and Vermunt's concept of Styles, Approaches and Patterns (SAP), 2013) • Clarify what an *enriched cognitive styles pedagogy* involves as opposed to impoverished models (Evans 2013a; Evans and Waring, 2014)	B (i) D (ii) D (iv) D (v)	A1 A2 K2 K5 K6 V2	4 5 6 7 8

(continued)

Table 11.1 (continued)

Sub components of component B	*Application to teaching and learning contexts. (Learner = student and/or teacher)*	*Closest links to:*		
		Sub-components of the PLSP	*UK Professional Standards Framework (HEA, Guild HE, Universities UK, 2011)*	*Teachers' Standards (DfE, 2011a)*
B (iii) An integrated approach: awareness of the interdependence of cognitive style and other individual learning differences – role of cognitive style as a moderator variable	• Consider the *interrelationships of cognitive styles with other variables* (e.g. awareness of cognitive styles may enhance design of learning environments which might lead to greater focusing of attention which then may impact on learning outcomes) (Donche et al., 2013) • Consider *individual and contextual variables in learning* (e.g. can a styles model developed in a specific context be usefully applied to learners of a specific age, cultural background etc.?) (Eaves, 2011) • Use models that adopt a *holistic approach* (e.g. the PLSP considers relationships between cognitive style, gender, age, culture, and personality constructs; links between cognitive styles and learning strategies (PLSP: Evans and Waring, 2009, 2015; Vermunt and Endedijk, 2011)	A (ii) A (iv) D (ii)	A2 A4 A5 K3 V1 V4	5 7
B (iv) Development of cognitive styles as an integral element of culturally responsive pedagogies	• Closely examine with learners how an individual's different *cultural associations impact their styles and approaches to learning* (Eaves, 2011) • Do *not make assumptions about learners' cultural makeup* (e.g. socio-economic; ethnic) (Cheng *et al.*, 2011) • Stress the importance of developing *appropriate teaching strategies* to address the *needs of all learners* and not matching styles to typologies of learners which may not be valid (Eaves, 2011) • Take care in *grouping* students according to perceived cultural groupings – importance of *ensuring integration and not enhancing separation*	C (ii) D (iv) D (vi) D (viii) E (vi)	A2 A4 A5 K2 K3 K4 K5 K6 V2 V3 V4	5 7

	based on simplistic understandings of culture (Evans and Waring, 2011c) • Take care in *inducting learners* into new learning environments in ensuring access to the terminology and acronyms used within contexts throughout the programme of learning and not just during induction (Evans and Waring, 2015) • *Critically analyse* the *cultures* of departments, year groups, schools, HEIs /workplaces as to what types of learning are being promoted and what styles of teaching are favoured (Evans and Waring, 2011c)			

PLSP component: C. Optimising conditions for learning / sensitivity to learner context
Overarching theme: Overarching theme: Autonomy and agency

Sub components of component C	*Application to teaching and learning contexts. (Learner = student and/or teacher)*	*Closest links to:*		
		Sub-components of the PLSP	*UK Professional Standards Framework (HEA, Guild HE, Universities UK, 2011)*	*Teachers' Standards (DfE, 2011a)*
C (i) Sensitivity to needs of the learner: recognizing unique starting points Addressing the emotional dimension of learning: working with students to ensure readiness (will and skill)	• Examine with learners how they *attribute their successes and failures*. Explore strategies to support development of *mastery motivational orientations* (Seifert, 2004; Stipek, 1998) • Explore with learners *how emotions impact learning* and how they can use such information to support their own learning/teaching (Scott *et al.*, 2014) • Explore with learners notions of *resilience* (personal, workplace, global) (Duckworth *et al.*, 2007; Kelchtermans, 2009) • Explicitly explore the *impact of emotions on learning* (Evans, 2012b; 2013a; 2013b; 2014)	A (i) A (ii) A (iii) D (ii) E (vi)	A2 A5 K2 K3 V1 V2	1 2 3 4 5 6 7

(continued)

Table 11.1 (continued)

Sub components of component C	*Application to teaching and learning contexts. (Learner = student and/or teacher)*	*Closest links to:*		
		Sub-components of the PLSP	*UK Professional Standards Framework (HEA, Guild HE, Universities UK, 2011)*	*Teachers' Standards (DfE, 2011a)*
	• Encourage discussion with learners (individually and in groups) about how they manage the *emotional dimension* of learning and teaching in order to support strategy development and shared understandings (Evans, 2014; Dias and Sá, 2014) • Examine notions of *smart failing* and how to establish learning environments where a fear-of-failing mindset is replaced with *failing as a pathway to learning mindset* (Dweck, 2006) • Support *learners in sharing their ideas* and opening them up to scrutiny *'will to offer'*, (Barnett, 2011) • Model strategies to *support learner antecedent emotion regulation* (before onset or at early stages of the emotion response) along with training teachers to assist learners with the regulation of their emotions (Fried, 2011) • Explicitly train students to manage emotions through the use of: o volitional control strategies (Jakhelln, 2011; Keller and Deimann, 2012); o control-value theory to support student emotional development (Pekrun, 2006); o emotional regulation strategies (Gross, 2001)			

C (ii) Enabling a positive learning environment: focusing on supporting students during important transition points in their learning	• Ensure appropriate support throughout a programme of study – *induction* reconceptualized as an *ongoing and developmental process* and not as one stop shop (Karagiannopoulou and Christodoulides, 2005) • Promote the value and importance of *distributed mentoring systems* (responsibility of the group to support induction and not just the responsibility of a single person/mentor) (Evans, 2014) • Support learners in the development of *peer support groups as part of peer engagement rather than assessment strategies* (formal and informal). Explicit discussion of roles and support mechanisms) (Van der Pol *et al.*, 2008) • Work with learners to ascertain *sense of fit* / association with new community and in the devising of strategies to support assimilation, adaptation and influence within new contexts. Learners to reflect on facilitators and barriers to their access to communities of practice (CoPs) (Bliuc *et al.*, 2011a; 2011b; Evans, 2014)	A (i) A (ii) A (iii) C (i) C (iv) D (vi) D (iii) E (ii) E (iii) E (vi)	A2 A4 K2 K3 V1 V2	1 2 6 7
C (iii) Care afforded to how new ideas introduced as to the level of cognitive complexity in order to support learner flexibility	• *Reduce cognitive load (e.g. focus on core concepts)* (Rittschof, 2010) (e.g. paring down the curriculum to focus on what *learners most need to know* in learning to teach (Kosnik and Beck, 2009)) • Work with learners on strategies to increase *working memory capacity* (Overton and Potter, 2011) • Provide *staged learning opportunities* (Ure, 2009)	A (iii) D (vi) D (vii) D (viii) D (ix) E (vi)	A1 A2 K1 K2 V2 V4	2 3 4 6 7

(continued)

Table 11.1 (continued)

Sub components of component C	*Application to teaching and learning contexts. (Learner = student and/or teacher)*	*Closest links to:*		
		Sub-components of the PLSP	*UK Professional Standards Framework (HEA, Guild HE, Universities UK, 2011)*	*Teachers' Standards (DfE, 2011a)*
C (iv) Supporting learners' integration into communities of practice	• Use *collaborative practice* (peer learning / teaching) to assist in the development of cognitive insights about elements of teaching through shared action and discussion with more experienced others (Evans and Waring, 2009) • Support learners in *meaningful learning incidents* and '*approximations of practice*', – simulating learning/teaching contexts (Grossman et *al*., 2009) • Promote *responsible risk-taking* and trying out of new ideas; reward *innovation in modes of assessment* (Evans, 2013b) • Supporting learners in developing *noticing and filtering skills* (Evans, 2014; Sadler-Smith and Shefy, 2004) • Examine with learners *levels of fit at all levels* within an organization (subject, year group, faculty, whole school) and *availability of distributed mentoring* (support structures beyond immediate context) (Evans and Waring, 2009, 2011a) • Examine with learners their *contributions to the organization* beyond their immediate roles and the impact of membership of different groups on practice (Kek and Huijser, 2011)	A (iii) D (ii) D (vi) D (vii) D (viii) E (vi)	A1 A2 K2 K3 V1 V4	2 5 7 8

C (v) Attention given to learners' networks of support and development of identity within academic context	• Place emphasis on supporting learners' *network building* (access to resources, to other learners, and to relevant individuals, groups, and societies beyond immediate context) (Carmichael *et al.*, 2012; Evans, 2014) • Give explicit attention to discussions of the *'person / teacher I want to be'*, (Evans, 2014; Scott *et al.*, 2014)	A (ii) A (iii)	A1 A2 A4 K3 V1 V2	2 5 8

PLSP component: D. Design of learning environments
Overarching theme: General principles: adaptive rather than adapted practice

Sub components of component D	*Application to teaching and learning contexts. (Learner = student and/or teacher)*	*Closest links to:*		
		Sub-components of the PLSP	*UK Professional Standards Framework (HEA, Guild HE, Universities UK, 2011)*	*Teachers' Standards (DfE, 2011a)*
D (i) Housekeeping attended to (organization of resources; information for students and lecturers etc.)	Place emphasis on *feedforward curriculum designs:* • Ensure that learners have an *overview / plan* of content, modes of teaching and assessment, modes of working face to face and virtually as part of blended learning environments for specific programmes of study. Ensure that: o *all learning partners have access to a bank of resources* and exchange is facilitated between partners o important information / assessments are clearly *signposted* o pre-session *warm up tasks* are set to increase learner readiness and contributions (Educause, 2012) o *post-session tasks* are used to support consolidation and development of new learning	C (i) C (ii) D (ix) D (x) E (i)	A1 A2 K2 K4 K6 V2 V4	2 4 5 6

(continued)

Table 11.1 (continued)

Sub components of component D	*Application to teaching and learning contexts. (Learner = student and/or teacher)*	*Closest links to:*		
		Sub-components of the PLSP	*UK Professional Standards Framework (HEA, Guild HE, Universities UK, 2011)*	*Teachers' Standards (DfE, 2011a)*
	o *content is accessible* to all learners o the *role of the learner in the learning process* is clarified – what they can do for themselves and what is to be guided o issues of *power and agency* relating to the nature of knowledge and dialogue dynamics are openly discussed (Evans and Waring, 2009; 2015)			
D (ii) Teaching methods informed by an understanding of cognitive styles and attuned to the requirements of the content and context (constructive alignment)	• Teaching is focused on implementing *overarching principles of effective learning* for all students and not about individualized instruction for each student (Evans and Vermunt, 2013; Zhang *et al.*, 2012) • Focus on the development of the *most appropriate styles* in relation to the requirements of task and context (Fan *et al.*, 2010) • Teaching approaches based on what is the *best approach* for the context and not on student preferences (Kolloffel, 2012) • Examine how one's own learning preferences and styles impact on *teaching style* (Evans, 2004) • Teaching of thinking strategies situated in the subject domain and promoting transfer of learning and thinking strategies (Vermunt, 1996)	B (i) B (ii) B (iii) B (iv) D (iii) D (v)	A1 A2 A4 K1 K2 K3 K5 K6 V2 V3 V4	2 4 5

D (iii) Aimed at supporting learners in developing understanding of learning to think within a specific discipline and to be become part of that community	• Clarify with the learner the *key concepts* to be learnt within a specific discipline and explore the relationship of these to learning beyond the immediate academic community (Solvie and Sungur, 2012) • Use a *range of approaches and strategies* to develop understanding within a specific field (Courey et. al., 2013; Riding and Rayner, 1998; Zhang *et al.*, 2013) • Explicitly encourage discussions about *what it is to think within a specific discipline* (e.g. what does a deep approach constitute within geography?) (Zhang, 2013) • *Explicit discussion of what a deep approach in learning to teach is* (Evans, 2014; McCune and Entwistle, 2011) • Encourage *collaboration and contributions* from all in the learning community (Evans, 2013a; 2014; 2015) • Support learners to *seek out, use, and adapt* (personalize) existing *resources* (Evans, 2013a; 2014; 2015) • Support learners in taking responsibility for *developing, sharing and critically evaluating resources* (Evans and Waring, 2009) • Use a range of *presentation and delivery formats* to support student access to learning (Courey *et al.*, 2013)	C (ii) C (iv) D (ix) E (vi)	A4 K1 K3 V2 V3 V4	2 3 4 5 6
D (iv) Judicious use of accommodation of cognitive styles and the concept of matching	• Teaching is informed by an understanding that a learner has a *profile of styles* (Kozhevnikov, 2007) and that trying to match to one style is of questionable value (Zhang, 2013) • Encourage learners to consider how the following factors may affect an individual's access to learning (from own and others' perspectives):	A (iv) B (iv) D (ii) D (v) D (vi) D (viii) D (viii)	A1 A2 A5 K2 K3 V1	2 5 7 6

(continued)

Table 11.1 (continued)

Sub components of component D	*Application to teaching and learning contexts. (Learner = student and/or teacher)*	*Closest links to:*		
		Sub-components of the PLSP	*UK Professional Standards Framework (HEA, Guild HE, Universities UK, 2011)*	*Teachers' Standards (DfE, 2011a)*
	o volume of material to be delivered o modes of presentation o classroom organization (tight *vs* loose) o structured versus unstructured o variety and nature of resources used; o pace o speed and nature of transitions o range of activities o discovery versus directed teaching o classroom design o management of power relations (facilitator *vs* director of learning) o design of learning sequences (tangential *vs* sequential) o nature of questioning (open *vs* closed) o impulsivity versus reflectivity o the use of groupings	D (x) E (ii) E (vi)	V3	
D (v) Judicious approach in promoting development of the most appropriate cognitive styles for specific contexts	• Increase *awareness of style constructs* and their utility and promote the use of the most appropriate styles (Fan *et al.*, 2010) • *Ensure principles of enriched styles pedagogies are fully integrated into the curriculum* (Evans and Waring, 2009, 2015) • Develop *ongoing conversations* via teaching, face-to-face and online about the *use of styles in practice* (Evans and Waring, 2009)	B (i) B (ii) D (iii)	A1 A2 A5 K2 V1 V3	all

	• Demonstrate through specific interventions *how styles can change*. Stage 1: observe learners tackle specific task; stage 2: training in alternative approaches; stage 3: set similar task in different context to ascertain whether learners have taken on board new learning; stage 4: embed new approaches through reflection and reinforcement activities (Evans and Waring, 2011d) • Support learners in learning to *deploy the most appropriate styles for themselves* : o Set up cross-subject/year groups to *research and feedback* to their peers on key questions arising from the styles literature o Encourage learners to plan for the same learning outcomes using the same content but to deliver it in very different styles; evaluate with all (Evans and Waring, 2009)			
D (vi) Teaching strategies aimed at stretching the student through careful addition and removal of scaffolding and sufficient constructive friction: aimed at developing and broadening cognitive styles and strategies as and when appropriate	• Use *early needs analysis* to identify the precise nature of the support that is required by the learner (e.g. knowledge/ metacognitive strategies/ specific skill sets) (Evans, 2013a) • Provide additional support in the classroom and manage the retreat of support to enable learners to function independently – ensuring *constructive rather than destructive friction* (Micari and Light, 2009; Vermunt, 2007) • Ensure appropriate *removal of scaffolding* to promote learner independence (Balassoriya *et al.*, 2009) • Increase *student awareness and discernment* of knowledge sources to promote self-access (Evans and Waring, 2015) • Provide *training in learning strategies* to support learner *self-judgement* skills (Archer, 2010; Evans and Waring, 2015)	C (i) C (iii)	A1 A2 A5 K2 K3 V1	1 5 6

(continued)

Table 11.1 (continued)

Sub components of component D	*Application to teaching and learning contexts. (Learner = student and/or teacher)*	*Closest links to:*		
		Sub-components of the PLSP	*UK Professional Standards Framework (HEA, Guild HE, Universities UK, 2011)*	*Teachers' Standards (DfE, 2011a)*
D (vii) Designs focused on encouraging learners to adopt deeper and more self-regulated/directed approaches to learning (constructivist approaches with a strong emphasis on the development of metacognitive skills). Supporting learners to reflect critically on the learning process to include self- and co-regulation. Appropriate use of tools to support process	• Explicitly explore *self-regulatory skills* with learners in order for them to devise strategies to develop areas of relative weakness (Evans and Waring, 2009, 2015) • *Teach emotional regulation skills* (Hinton *et al.*, 2008) • Focus attention on an examination of *how we learn* (M. Rosenfeld and S. Rosenfeld, 2011) • *Employ meaningful critical reflection* – use a variety of tools (self and 360 degree analyses) to support learners in coming to a better understanding of their own learning and that of others (Rychly and Graves, 2012) • Actively encourage learners to consider alternative approaches by: o examining teaching episodes directly or via video o analysing lesson planning and through learner reflection on learning using critical incidents analysis o reflecting on the benefits and limitations of different strategies and approaches to learning within specific contexts by using reflective journals/discussion boards (synchronous and asynchronous) o working with learners to make sense of self/peer/student / 360 degree evaluations of their learning and teaching o explicitly discuss with learners their *volitional strategies* for maintaining effort and motivation (Turner and Husman, 2008)	A (i) A (ii) A (iii) A (iv) B (ii) B (iii) B (iv) C (i)	A1 A2 A5 K2 K5 K6 V1 V3 V4	2 5

D (viii) Maximising learning opportunities: design of learning environments focused on enhancing awareness of different learning strategies through explicit guidance and exposure to diverse learning experiences. Different ways of seeing and doing, observation, modelling, practice, application, reinforcement, and transfer	• Exemplify in your own teaching *integration of theory and practice* (Eraut, 1994a; 2004a) • Explicitly demonstrate *alternative approaches to learning and teaching* – model alternative ways of doing (Courey *et al.*, 2013; A-L de Boer et al., 2013; Ellis *et al.*, 2006; Zhang *et al.*, 2013) and identify strategies to overcome learning barriers – for example, through instruction that enables learners to *remodel information* into more accessible forms. Use a range of approaches to increase accessibility of ideas o *Co-teaching:* in a variety of forms (with a more experienced other/ as the experienced other, etc.) o *Microteaching:* out of context and within context (e.g. with small group / focusing on one idea or one aspect of teaching) o *Spiral approach:* new concepts are introduced and subsequently reinforced and developed in follow-up sessions – for example, new ideas demonstrated and learners asked to describe and model how they would use these in alternative contexts o *Range of experiences*: role play; scenarios; provision of diverse opportunities across subjects; schools etc. o *Simulations* examining aspects of practice: (highly structured versus loosely structured; sequential versus tangential questioning; directive versus facilitative teaching approaches; individual versus various forms of grouping; individual versus group assessment etc.) • Provide *opportunities for learners to argue and discuss their ideas* to enable understanding rather than regurgitation (Niaz *et al.*, 2002)	D (ii) D (vi) D (vii)	A1 A2 A5 K2 K3 V2	3 4 8

(continued)

Table 11.1 (continued)

Sub components of component D	*Application to teaching and learning contexts. (Learner = student and/or teacher)*	*Closest links to:*		
		Sub-components of the PLSP	*UK Professional Standards Framework (HEA, Guild HE, Universities UK, 2011)*	*Teachers' Standards (DfE, 2011a)*
D (ix) Authentic and appropriate assessment designs to support the development of deep approaches to learning	• See Evans (2013b). *Principles of effective feedback* • Ensure *assessment is aligned to curriculum goals* (e.g. potential of assessment to promote a deep approach to learning) (Biggs, 1999; Diseth, 2011) • *Clarify the requirements* of assessment and what *constitutes good* (Sadler, 2010) • *Encourage learners to explore their understandings and beliefs about different forms of assessment* (Segers *et al.*, 2008) • *Involve students in assessment design* (developing assessment criteria; giving feedback; agreeing timelines for assessment; developing rubrics; self-assessing) (Evans, 2013b) • Ensure assessment is *authentic* and relevant to learner needs now and in the future (Boud, 2000; Boud and Molloy, 2012, 2013; Courey *et al.*, 2013; Hounsell, 2007) • Work with learners to develop *feedback seeking and using skills and self-assessment skills* (Evans, 2015; Joughin, 2009) • Provide *training* in the development of peer assessment and feedback skills and self-assessments; manage issues of trust, competency, and expectations with students (Carless, 2011, 2013)	A (i) A (iii) E (i) E (ii) E (iii) E (iv) E (v) E (vi)	A1 A2 A3 A4 K5 K6 V2 V3 V4	6

- Place emphasis on *feedforward* rather than feedback (3:1 rule) (e.g. three times more time spent discussing/planning a lesson / piece of work than on feedback after a lesson / submission of work: front load mentoring support – greater potential to effect change); early assessment of student need (Evans, 2013b)
- Consider *various approaches to the giving of feedback* (written, oral, demonstration); timing of feedback; involvement of learners in giving feedback (and the collaborative generation of assessment criteria by learners, their peers and tutors)
- *Solicit learner feedback* on *what they want feedback on*; and also on their *feedback on the tutor feedback* (Evans and Waring, 2015)
- Develop *focused feedback skills* (e.g. focus on most important areas of feedback to prevent overloading – what was done well, what requires most attention, and how the learner can get there (*realistic, personalized, focused* and *'opening the door'*, strategies)
- *Encourage flexible approaches: Train* learners to be able to cope with *different forms of assessment* (Cano-Garcia and Hughes, 2000)
- Offer *multiple/alternative forms of assessment* (oral presentations, posters, written assignments, reports, debate) with various weightings to promote development of specific skills and promotion of flexible styles in the classroom

(continued)

Table 11.1 (continued)

Sub components of component D	*Application to teaching and learning contexts. (Learner = student and/or teacher)*	*Closest links to:*		
		Sub-components of the PLSP	*UK Professional Standards Framework (HEA, Guild HE, Universities UK, 2011)*	*Teachers' Standards (DfE, 2011a)*
D (x) Appropriate use of technology to support learning	• Place emphasis on developing ways to encourage students *to adapt* to different learning environments rather than designing *adaptive systems* (Choi et *al*., 2009). *Adaptable* systems rather than *adaptive* ones should in their design promote access through an *inclusive approach* (range of navigational tools; size of viewing window etc.; design of tasks; interactive opportunities / organization of materials (Akbulut and Cardak, 2012) • Attend to *housekeeping* – ensuring all resources *available and updated* • *Ensure that a coherent understanding of pedagogy in relation to the needs of the subject and tasks informs the technological design* and not the other way round (Jones and McLean, 2012) • *Ensure key elements of good design are incorporated into designs* (Chen and Liu, 2012). *For example:* o Make sure cognitive overload is addressed o Ensure a clear *baseline of entitlement* for all students o Clarify *learner and teacher roles* within online environments o Ensure the *rationale underpinning online tasks* is explained and clarified o Ensure learners understand the *purpose of e-learning facilities* and tasks o Ensure ongoing *monitoring and feedback* of online usage (teacher and peer feedback – distributed practice – monitoring contributions to ensure equal access and contributions to learning) • *Provide training for all learners* (teachers and students in best practices) (J. De Boer et *al*., 2011)	C (iii) D (i) D (ii) D (vii)	A1 A2 A5 K2 K4 V2	2 4

PLSP component: E. Supporting learner autonomy: choices in learning / student voice
Overarching theme: Informed choice

Sub components of component E	*Application to teaching and learning contexts. (Learner = student and/or teacher)*	*Closest links to:*		
		Sub-components of the PLSP	*UK Professional Standards Framework (HEA, Guild HE, Universities UK, 2011)*	*Teachers' Standards (DfE, 2011a)*
E (i) Focus on the centrality of the learner as a co-constructor of knowledge	• Genuinely *involve learners in curriculum design* decisions – be clear about the breadth and limits of their potential involvement from the outset • *Explicitly discuss power and agency* issues (Butin, 2005) • *Teach students how to use language to communicate difficulties* (Noddings, 1992)	D (i) D (ix)	A1 A2 V2	2 3
E (ii) Focus on the role of the student in managing the learning process. Learners as co-designers of their learning experience(s)	• *Clarify learner roles* – and regularly review/redefine. Encourage learners to take responsibility for *negotiating roles* within different learning communities (Evans, 2014; 2015) • Encourage *learner self-management* through development of self-regulatory skills • Ensure *gradual transfer of control* to the learner (Vermunt, 1996) • Ensure curriculum design enables *flexibility*: o opportunities for the learner to proceed through the course at appropriate pace; for individuals and groups: clear and alternate pathways identified o opportunities for learners to specialize or generalize within specific learning contexts (Evans and Waring, 2009)	D (vii)	A1 A2 K2 K3 V1	2

(continued)

Table 11.1 (continued)

Sub components of component E	*Application to teaching and learning contexts. (Learner = student and/or teacher)*	*Closest links to:*		
		Sub-components of the PLSP	*UK Professional Standards Framework (HEA, Guild HE, Universities UK, 2011)*	*Teachers' Standards (DfE, 2011a)*
E (iii) Learner control afforded through design of curriculum (content, process, product) including e-learning possibilities	• Ensure *curriculum design is inclusive* (e.g. learners have contributed to curriculum design; they have *full access to resources, assessment* etc.) • Ensure learners *receive and contribute to training* in how to make best use of resources and opportunities • Ensure learners' *contributions to resource development* • Review *assessment requirements* in relation to *learners needs within context* and ensure that *timelines are aligned carefully to not overload the learner* and *make sense in terms of progression and what the learner needs to know at that specific time.* (Evans and Waring, 2009; Renzulli and Sullivan, 2009) • Ensure teaching is *autonomy supportive* rather than controlling by encouraging learners to think for themselves (Fried, 2011) • Provide training in '*understanding discourse*' – to understand how individuals produce and are produced by discourses and how teachers can engage in teacher identity discourses (Hastings, 2010) • Focus attention on *clarity, structure and quality of presentation* of instruction and tasks to increase learners' sense of control (Pekrun, 2006)	C (ii) D (i) – D (x) E (i) E (ii) E (iv)	A1 A2 A4 A5 K2 K3 K4 V2 V3 V4	1 4 5 6 7

E (iv) Flexible designs facilitated through, for example, organization of resources to maximize access; choices in pathways through programmes; nature of assessment	• *Provide multiple/alternative forms of presentation* of materials and resources where appropriate (mindful of not overloading) – for example, visual, audio, mixed mode in virtual and hardcopy form (Courey *et al.*, 2013; Evans and Waring, 2009) • *Negotiate with all those involved* in the training and support of the learner regarding *priorities for development* and how best each learner can be supported in relation to agreed priorities (agreed by learner and support team)	D (i) E (ii) E (iii)	A1 A2 A3 A5 K2 K3 V1 V2	4
E (v) The importance of guided/informed choice for learners	• Support learners to make informed choices through their development of *self-regulatory skills* (Sadler, 2012) • *Ensure early assessment of learners* to enable appropriate support and choices from the outset. Full feedback on outlines and proposals but not on full drafts of work (Evans and Waring, 2015) • Ensure *level of difficulty of tasks is aligned* to the capabilities of the learners (Pekrun, 2006) • Support learners to develop a *sense of confidence and self-determination* – focus on perceptions of competence and autonomy (Seifert, 2004)	A (i) D (vii) D (ix)	A1 A2 A3 K2 V1	1 6 7

(continued)

Table 11.1 (continued)

Sub components of component E	*Application to teaching and learning contexts. (Learner = student and/or teacher)*	*Closest links to:*		
		Sub-components of the PLSP	*UK Professional Standards Framework (HEA, Guild HE, Universities UK, 2011)*	*Teachers' Standards (DfE, 2011a)*
E (vi) Informed and responsible use of groupings individual and group work. Collaborative learning opportunities informed by understanding of styles (e.g. dangers/limitations of labelling, justification for groupings)	• Use *individual, group,* and *whole class organization as appropriate to the requirements of the task*. Explicitly address the importance of *matching the learning task to the organizational unit* (individual, pair, or group) by the learner reflecting on collaborative planning activities as to why a particular organizational grouping is most appropriate for the learning task (Courey *et al.*, 2013; Evans and Waring, 2009) • *Clarify roles within group situations* • *Take care to ensure possibilities for individual work* • *Vary groupings and roles within groups* • Train learners in *how to develop effective groups* – model and encourage experimentation and sharing of insights • Ensure sufficient time is allocated to explore the *relational dynamic of group work* • Ensure informed use of groupings taking account of *individual and cultural sensitivities* and avoid assumptions about certain groups/types of learners (Hendry *et al.*, 2005)	C (i) C (iv) D (vii)	A1 A2 A4 A5 K2 V1 V2	4 5 7

Teachers' Standards (DfE, 2011a)

Part 1: Teaching

A teacher must:

1 Set high expectations which inspire, motivate and challenge pupils
2 Promote good progress and outcomes by pupils
3 Demonstrate good subject and curriculum knowledge
4 Plan and teach well structured lessons
5 Adapt teaching to respond to the strengths and needs of all pupils
6 Make accurate and productive use of assessment
7 Manage behaviour effectively to ensure a good and safe learning environment
8 Fulfil wider professional responsibilities

Part 2: Personal and Professional Conduct

The UK Professional Standards Framework for teaching and supporting learning in higher education 2011 (The Higher Education Academy, Guild HE, Universities UK, 2011)

Areas of Activity:

A1 Design and plan learning activities and/or programmes of study
A2 Teach and/or support learning
A3 Assess and give feedback to learners
A4 Develop effective learning environments and approaches to student support and guidance
A5 Engage in continuing professional development in subjects/disciplines and their pedagogy, incorporating research, scholarship and the evaluation of professional practices

Core Knowledge:

K1 The subject material
K2 Appropriate methods for teaching, learning and assessing in the subject area and at the level of the academic programme
K3 How students learn, both generally and within their subject/ disciplinary areas
K4 The use and value of appropriate learning technologies
K5 Methods for evaluating the effectiveness of teaching
K6 The implications of quality assurance and quality enhancement for academic and professional practice with a particular focus on teaching

Professional Values:

V1 Respect individual learners and diverse learning communities
V2 Promote participation in higher education and equality of opportunity for learners

V3 Use evidence-informed approaches and the outcomes from research, scholarship and continuing professional development
V4 Acknowledge the wider context in which higher education operates recognising the implications for professional practice

Key readings

Courey, S. J., Tappe, P., Siker, J., and LePage, P. (2013). Improved lesson planning with universal design for learning (UDL). *Teacher Education and Special Education, 36* (1), 7–27.
The authors use universal design for learning (UDL) principles to support teacher learning. UDL principles include presenting information in multiple formats to facilitate student access, provision of student choice in assessment, stimulating student motivation through authentic learning designs and encouragement of collaborative activities.

Evans, C., and Waring, M. (2009). The place of cognitive style in pedagogy: realizing potential in practice. In L. F. Zhang and R. J. Sternberg (Eds), *Perspectives on the nature of intellectual styles* (pp. 169–208). New York: Springer.
In this chapter the original conceptualization of the PLSP framework is outlined and its use in initial teacher education practice is demonstrated. Principles underpinning the PLSP are highlighted informed by substantial research and practice evidence. The updated framework was reported by Evans (2013a). The application of the PLSP to early teacher career development is reported in Evans and Waring (2015).

Hardaker, G., Jeffery, A., and Sabki, A. A. (2011). Learning styles and personal pedagogy. In S. Rayner and E. Cools (Eds), *Style differences in cognition, learning, and management: Theory, research and practice* (pp. 207–223). New York, NY: Routledge.
Hardaker and colleagues demonstrate the use and value of the Personal Learning Styles Pedagogy approach in higher education in virtual worlds where attention is also focused on the importance ofculturally inclusive pedagogies, the PLSP providing a styles lens through which to view and develop teaching approaches and resources.

Jones, M. M., and McLean, K. J. (2012). Personalising learning in teacher education through the use of technology. *Australian Journal of Teacher Education, 37*, (1), 75–92.
The Technology for Personalizing Learning model (TPL) emphasizes an integrated and holistic understanding of learning to drive technological developments in teaching. An enriched e-learning pedagogy is about more than matching pedagogical preferences (adaptivity) or increasing awareness of different styles. It is about an integrated understanding drawing on research about deep learning, diversity, authentic learning with IT and the relationship of these elements with the personalizing learning process to support learners to become adaptable.

Weblinks

Carnegie Foundation: Gale, R. A. (2006). Fostering integrative learning through pedagogy. Integrative Learning Project. Carnegie Foundation for the Advancement ofTeaching and the Association of American Colleges and Universities. Available online at http://www.gallery.carnegiefoundation.org/ilp/ (accessed 6 May 2014).

DfE (2011a). *Teachers' Standards*. Department for Education. Available online at http://www.education.gov.uk/publications (accessed 11 November 2013)

Educause (2012) Educause 7: Things you should know about ... flipped classrooms. Available online at http://net.educause.edu/ir/library/pdf/eli7081.pdf (accessed 3 May 2014).

HEA (2011). The UK Professional Standards Framework (UKPSF) for teaching and supporting learning in higher education. The Higher Education Academy, Guild HE, Universities UK 2011. Available online at https://www.heacademy.ac.uk/sites/default/files/downloads/UKPSF_2011_English.pdf

Chapter 12

Making sense of future challenges

Overview

As identified in this book there are many challenges associated with the ongoing and fast-changing educational landscape in which teachers and students now exist, and as part of the critical (re)vision of education that is required to ensure that it is most suitable for coping with the changing demands placed on twenty-first-century learners, both now and in their futures. This chapter will highlight two particular areas of challenge. The first challenge is that associated with the many transitions which we all make during our learning careers and which need to be managed and to remain faithful to the principles underpinning the PLSP. The second challenge is that presented for teachers by the evolving nature of policy and practice associated with teacher education.

Transitions in learning

A key theme permeating this book is that of *transitions*. We will all make many transitions during our learning careers. It is evident that with certain transitions and at certain times in our lifelong learning journeys our ability to manage such transitions may be variable; that is, there are spatial and temporal aspects of transitions and our ability to cope with these may also depend on our personal histories and geographies of managing change that we carry with us. It is also evident that some individuals appear better equipped to manage transitions compared to others: Evans (2012b) identifies '*savvy feedback-seekers*'– trainee teachers who are able to make the most of affordances in placement schools.

As identified in this book, challenge supports brain development, and boundary crossing (experience of new and different contexts) supports the development of creative thinking and cognitive style flexibility (Zhang, 2013). A key educational issue is how we can enable learners to make the most of the potential affordances available to them as a result of crossing boundaries; how can the experience be transformative? How can an individual acquire the disposition to do something conceptually different from what they could do before? (Scott *et al.*, 2014).

Furthermore, as part of twenty-first-century complex learning environments, where the potential number of transitions one will engage within one's learning career is likely to significantly increase, Barnett (2011) has argued the importance of teaching and supporting learners to cope with uncertainty and of *knowing what to do when one does not know* in supporting the transformative learning process. It is about learning to be comfortable about what one does not know – managing vulnerability. Along these lines,

Kelchtermans (2009) has argued the importance of addressing the issue of powerlessness in the context of teaching.

Therefore, a key issue for all educators must be that of enhancing our understanding of the transition process. Specifically we need to examine why some individuals cope so much better with transitions than others, and why at certain points in our lives we are more or less equipped to manage the affordances and barriers that certain transitions present us with. Better understanding of transitions is needed in order to facilitate and enable easier and more productive transitions for all learners (including teachers) (Scott *et al.*, 2014).

There are a number of ways that learners can be supported to effectively manage learning transitions, as we have identified throughout this book and framed within the Personal Learning Styles Pedagogy framework. The development of self-regulatory capacity with special attention afforded to emotional regulation is a fundamental part of this. In fostering dispositions to enable effective boundary crossing (Wenger, 2000), and in being able to support learners to transfer and adapt learning from one context to another, we have highlighted the importance ofsupporting learners in the development of a number of abilities to include, for example: understanding the self in context (managing identity development); noticing (as part of relational skill development); filtering information (developing effective cognitive processing capacities); developing effective networks of support (boundary initiating and crossing); integrating rational and intuitive thinking (cognitive style flexibility); self-assessment (self-monitoring); critically reflecting and reflexive practice (in relation to oneself and to others – see also Evans, 2014a).

An inclusive participatory pedagogy as articulated in the Personal Learning Styles Pedagogy is about supporting all learners so that they can access the rules of a particular context, inform them, and incorporate them into their repertoires of thought and action without losing sense of themselves. It is about promoting the development of creativity and the *will to offer* (innovating and offering ideas up for scrutiny from others – McCune and Entwistle, 2011) in order to enable learners and teachers to become central to the practice in which they are working and to be able to effectively choose affiliations that are appropriate to their immediate and future learning needs as part of sustainable life-long learning.

Policy and practice in teacher education

Fullan (1993, p. 7) noted that teacher education 'has the honour of being the best solution and the worst problem in education today.' This remains true today in many ways; the evolving nature of policy and practice associated with teacher education in the UK, particularly in England, presents a number of challenges for teachers and for those attempts to enact a vision of education which promotes teachers and learners who are empowered, have a voice, are critically reflective, and are able to make genuine choices.

There are many challenges created by a number of interrelated factors associated with policy and practice within teacher education. Policy and practice within teacher education is subject to many challenges (see BERA (British Educational Research Association), 2014 for a fuller explication of these), particularly that associated with the potential shift away from the notion of teaching as a research-based profession and the dominance of the perspective of teaching as a craft-based occupation. As part of the increasingly dominant culture of compliance and regulation imposed by statutory requirements on initial teacher education, there is clear evidence of a reductionist view of and assumptions about teaching:

> The English Standards and current Government policy now indicate a decisive shift away from the idea of teaching as research-based profession and towards the construction of teaching as a craft.
>
> Beauchamp, Clarke, Hulme & Murray, 2013, p. 1

We have demonstrated throughout this book the importance of research-informed practice/practice-informed research and the essential integration of theory and practice as part of understanding the intricacies involved in the process of teaching and learning as part of developing its quality. To undermine such integration is to limit the capacity for critical reflection. Therefore, in the absence of a research-integrated approach, the process by which teachers interrogate their practice individually and collaboratively, to make explicit those values and assumptions that underpin their teaching, is diminished if not removed (Winch, Orchard and Oancea, 2013). This is also part of the seriously inadequate, oversimplified notion of teaching as a 'craft-based occupation' that is permeating teacher education policy (BERA, 2014). Awareness of this pernicious trend is important in being able to counter it as part of more sophisticated notions of professionalism as articulated in chapter one.

To help teachers and those involved in teacher education to address these increasing challenges (and others) posed by the evolving nature of policy and practice within teacher education, we have argued throughout this book the importance of a critical participatory pedagogy to enable both research and practice to be transformative in relation to both individual learners (student and teacher) and the social world (Scott and Usher, 2011). Such a pedagogy encourages questioning of the status quo in order to promote inclusivity, it is about taking action on the basis of informed knowledge and understanding, and in so doing enabling individuals to see themselves differently and to be able to effect social change to ensure greater equity for all in accessing and participating in learning whether that be in schools, higher education, the workplace, and/or society more broadly.

We have highlighted, from the very start of the book, the importance of a critical professional identity, which is very much about teachers being prepared to question their own beliefs and values as well as the context in which teaching takes place at a micro level (classroom/individual), meso level (whole school policies), and macro level (broader education/policy debates). It is certainly not about the unthinking acceptance of received opinion: it requires teacher scrutiny of the evidence (integrating theory and practice) and engagement in multiple discourses with colleagues, students, policy and theory, to explicitly critique the background consensus about the nature and purposes of education. We have continually stressed the importance of an integrated approach where attention is placed on the relevance of all types of learning (cumulative, assimilative, transcendent, and transformative – see chapter three) with a particular emphasis on encouraging the transformative forms of learning to support learners to become effective boundary-crossers.

A critical pedagogy is manifested and advocated throughout this book in critiquing what learning tools are used, how they are used, and why. Specifically, Table 6.1 provides a framework to enable an informed use of cognitive styles in learning, Table 9.1 demonstrates the application of principles of good assessment practice within the PLSP framework, and Table 10.1 demonstrates a principled use of critical reflection in practice. It is essential that we as teachers and teacher educators continuously critique the why and how of what we are doing. Using practice and research evidence to enhance agency and autonomy in being able to stand up for what works is an essential part of being a teacher in the twenty-first century.

Our conceptualization of an integrated holistic pedagogy requires all those in education to draw on practice evidence, research evidence, and theory to think about the design of curricula, the resources we use, the nature of assessment, and, crucially, how we are using these to empower learners, including teachers, now and throughout their lives. It requires teachers to be able to justify their use of learning and teaching approaches and ensure that teaching approaches are adapted to the requirements of the context: it is about informed application. Informing choices, and ensuring a critical participatory pedagogy, the PLSP provides a secure framework around which to discuss pedagogical decisions. As highlighted in chapters seven and eight, a critical pedagogy requires teachers to understand the underlying reasons for the success of strategies in order to make informed decisions about teaching methods and to be able to articulate these with colleagues to make the implicit explicit. It requires the informed use of ICT in the design of individual and collaborative peer learning activities within e-learning and face-to-face contexts.

Summary

Using the PLSP framework we have emphasized the importance of cultivating sustainable learning practices by supporting students to become independent in managing their own learning (developing metacognitive capacity – e.g. self-assessment abilities; understanding requirements of different contexts – ability to transfer and adapt to new learning contexts). This requires an education focus that is forward thinking – working with colleagues and students to manage the immediate requirements of assessment and ensuring learners are also prepared for the next stages of their learning journeys (Boud, 2000).

One cannot ignore the importance of critical reflection in the transformation of education. We have highlighted the role of teachers in supporting learners (and themselves) to be able to use critical reflection to enable successful individual and organizational change. As teachers our aim must be to support learners (colleagues and students) in the *stance* (inquiry) and in learning to *dance* (experimentation and risk) (Brookfield, 1995) if we are to continue to play more enriched roles within twenty-first-century learning environments and in society more broadly.

Key readings

Connor, L., and Sliwka, A. (2014). Implications of research on effective learning environments for teacher education. *European Journal of Education, 49* (2), 165–177.

This article highlights the importance of applying the OECD's (2010) Nature of Learning seven learning principles (pp. 14–17) to initial teacher education (see Weblinks section in this chapter). The relevance of the seven principles of learning (as outlined on pages 165–166 of Connor and Sliwka article) are worth reflecting on from both student and teacher learning perspectives.

Oblinger, D. G. (Eds) (2012). Game changes. Education and information technologies. Educause.
The aim of this book is to explore the tools and processes that can improve the quality of postsecondary education with a particular focus on the role of online tools. The focus is on preparing students for the future through the design of effective learning environments both face to face and virtual. The book can be downloaded from Educause's website: http://www.educause.edu

Scott, D., Hughes, G., Evans, C., Walter, C., and Watson, D. (2014). *Learning Transitions in Higher Education*. London:Palgrave
This book provides a research informed perspective of the different learning transitions that students undertake within higher education and the role of assessment and feedback in supporting such transitions; the book has relevance to the school sector. The notion of a participatory pedagogy is outlined. Understanding the barriers and facilitators to learning are important in supporting students to manage their own learning journeys throughout the lifecourse.

Zuljan, M. V., and Požarnik, B. M. (2014). Induction and early-career support of teachers in Europe. *European Journal of Education, 49 (2), 192–205.*
This article provides an overview of support for early career teachers in 12 European countries and highlights features of effective practice (p. 200).

Weblinks

BERA (2014). *The role of research in teacher education: Reviewing the evidence.* Interim report of the BERA-RSA inquiry. London: BERA. Available online at http://www.bera.ac.uk/project/research-and-teacher-education (accessed 4 May 2014).

Educause. Available online at http://www.educause.edu/ (accessed 4 January 2014).

OECD (2010). The nature of learning: Using research to inspire practice. Paris: OECD Publishing. Available online at www.keepeek.com/Digital-Asset-Management/oecd/education/the-nature-of-learning_9789264086487-en#page1 (accessed 6 May 2014).

Bibliography

Abiola, J., and Udofia, O. (2011). Psychometric assessment of the Wagnild and Young's resilience scale in Kano, Nigeria. *BMC Research Notes, 4,* 509.

Adey, P., Csapó, B., Demetriou, A., Huatamäki, J., and Shayer, M. (2007). Can we be intelligent about intelligence? Why education needs the concept of plastic general ability. *Educational Research Review, 2,* 75–97.

AITSL (2012). *Professional learning or school effectiveness in Australia. What does it take?* Australian Institute for Teaching and School Leadership Ltd. Available online at: http://www.aitsl.edu.au/verve/_resources/ICSEI_spread.pdf (accessed 3 January 2014).

Akbulut, Y., and Cardak, C. S. (2012). Adaptive educational hypermedia accommodating learning styles: A content analysis of publications from 2000 to 2011. *Computers* and *Education, 58*(2), 835–842.

Alferink, L. A., & Farmer-Dougan, V. (2010). Brain-(not) based education: Dangers of misunderstanding and misapplication of neuroscience research. *Exceptionality: A Special Education Journal, 18,* (1), 42–52.

Alheit, P. (1994). The biographical questions as a challenge to adult education. *International Review of Education, 40*(5), 293–298.

Allcock, S. J., and Hulme, J. A. (2010). Learning styles in the classroom: Educational benefit or planning exercise? *Psychology Teaching Review, 16*(2), 67–79.

Allinson, J., and Hayes, C. (1996). The Cognitive Style Index, a measure of intuition-analysis for organizational research. *Journal of Management Studies,* 33, 119–135.

Allport, G. W. (1937). *Personality—A psychological interpretation.* New York: Henry Holy and Company.

Anderman, E. M., and Maehr, M. L. (1994). Motivation and schooling in the middle grades. *Review of Educational Research, 64*(2), 287–309.

Archer, J. C. (2010). State of the science in health professional education: Effective feedback. *Medical Education, 44,* 101–108.

Argyris, C., and Schön, D. A. (1974). *Theory in practice: increasing professional effectiveness.* San Francisco: Jossey-Bass.

Argyris, C., and Schön, D. A. (1996). *Organizational learning 11– Theory, method, and practice.* Reading, MA: Addison-Wesley.

Armstrong, S. J., Cools, E., and Sadler-Smith, E. (2012). Role of cognitive style in business and management: Reviewing 40 years of research. *International Journal of Management Reviews,* 1–14, 238–262.

Arnon, S., and Reichel, N. (2007). Who is the ideal teacher? Am I? Similarity and difference in perception of students of education regarding the qualities of a good teacher and of their own qualities as teachers. *Teachers and Teaching: Theory and Practice, 13*(5), 441–464.

Arrien, A. (1993). *The four-fold way.* San Francisco: Harper.

Assessment Reform Group (1999). *Assessment for learning. Beyond the black box.* University of Cambridge School of Education, Cambridge: ARG.

Assessment Reform Group (2002). Assessment for learning: 10 Principles. Cambridge: ARG. Available online at www.assessment-reform-group.org.uk and http://www.aaia.org.uk/afl/assessment-reform-group/ (accessed 15 August 2014) (accessed 10 June 2013).

Atherton, J. S. (2013a). Learning and teaching; Cognitive theories of learning. Available online at http://www.learningandteaching.info/learning/cognitive.htm

Atherton, J. S. (2013b). Experiential learning. Available online at http://www.learningandteaching.info/learning/experience.htm#ixzz2pqbrorsw (accessed 18 January 2014).

Atherton, J. S. (2013c). Instructional Design. Available online at: http://www.instructionaldesign.org/theories/subsumption-theory.html (accessed 12 January 2014).

Atkinson, T., and Claxton, G. (Eds) (2000). *The intuitive practitioner.* Berkshire: Open University Press. Available online at: http://www.aitsl.edu.au/verve/_resources/ICSEI_spread. (accessed 3 January 2014).

Atlantic (2013). An Atlantic Special Report. Building a better human. Available online at http://www.theatlantic.com/health/archive/2013/11/how-the-brain-creates-personality-a-new-theory/281287/ (accessed 17 January 2014).

Argyris, C., and Schön, D.A. (1974). *Theory in practice: Increasing professional effectiveness.* San Francisco, CA: Jossey Bass.

Association for Information Systems: AIS qualitative resource site. Critical social theory. Available online at http://www.qual.auckland.ac.nz/ (accessed 8 September 2013).

Ausubel, D. (1963). *The psychology of meaningful verbal learning.* New York: Grune and Stratton.

Baddeley, A.D. (1986). *Working memory.* Oxford: Oxford University Press.

Balasooriya, C.D., Tetik, C., and Harris, P. (2011). Why is my design not working? The role of student factors. *Research Papers in Education, 26*(2), 191–206.

Balasooriya, C. D. Toohey, S., and Hughes, C. (2009). The cross-over phenomenon: Unexpected patterns of change in students' approaches to learning. *Studies in Higher Education, 34*(7), 781–794.

Ball, S., (1990). *Politics and policy making in education: Exploration in policy sociology.* London: Routledge.

Barnett, R. (1997). *Higher education. A critical business.* Buckingham: SRHE/Open University Press.

Barnett, R. (2007). *A will to learn.* Buckingham: Open University Press.

Barnett, R. (2011). Learning about learning: A conundrum and a possible resolution. *London Review of Education, 9*(1), 5–13.

Beauchamp, G., Clarke, L., Hulme, M., and Murray, J. (2013). *Policy and practice within the United Kingdom.* Research and Teacher Education: The BERA-RSA Inquiry.

Beddoe, L., and Healy, K. (2011). (Eds) Advances in social work and welfare education. Special issue: *Critical reflection: Method and practice, 13* (1), May 2011, 1–153. School of Social Work and Human Services. The University of Queensland: Australian Association of Social Work and Welfare Education. Available online at http://www.anzswwer.org/advances/Advances_Vol_13_No_1.pdf (accessed 3 March 2014).

Beetham, H., and Sharpe, R. (Eds) (2007). *Rethinking pedagogy for a digital age: Designing and delivering e-learning.* London: Routledge.

Bell, M., Cordingley, P., Isham, C., and Davis, R. (2010). *Report of professional practitioner use of research review: Practitioner engagement in and/or with research.* Coventry: CUREE, GTCE, LISI and NTRP.

BERA (2013a). Challenge and change in teacher education. *Research Intelligence.* London: BERA.

BERA (2013b). BERA's response to the DfE consultation on primary assessment and accountability. *BERA Research Intelligence, 122*: 10. British Educational Research Association: London. Available online at http://www.bera.ac.uk/publications/Research%20Intelligence (accessed 10 January 2014).

BERA (2014). *The role of research in teacher education: Reviewing the evidence.* Interim report of the BERA-RSA inquiry. London: BERA

Bereiter, C. (1994). Constructivism, socioculturalism, and Popper's World. *Educational Researcher, 23*(7), 21–23.

Bernstein, B. (1971). *Class, codes and control (Volume 1).* London: Routledge and Kegan Paul.

Berry, A. (2009). Professional self-understanding as expertise in teachingabout teaching. *Teachers and Teaching: Theory and Practice, 15*(2), 305–318. Betoret, F. D., and Artiga, A. G. (2011). The relationship among student basic need satisfaction, approaches to learning, reporting of avoidance strategies and achievement. *Electronic Journal of Research in Educational Psychology, 9*(2), 463–496.

Bieri, J., Atkins, A. L., Scott, B., Leeman, R. I., Tripodi, T., and Miller, H. (1966). *Clinical and social judgement: The discrimination of behavioural information*. New York: John Wiley and Sons.

Biggs, J. B. (1987). *Student approaches to learning and studying*. Hawthorn, Victoria: Australian Council for Educational Research.

Biggs, J. (1999). *Teaching for quality learning at university*. Buckingham: SRHE and Open University Press.

Biggs, J. (2014). Constructive alignment in university teaching. *HERDSA Review of Higher Education, 1*, 5–22.

Biggs, J., Kember, D., and Leung, D.Y.P. (2001). The revised two-factor study process questionnaire: R-SPQ-2F. *British Journal of Educational Psychology, 71*(1), 133–49.

Biggs, J., and Tang, C. (2011). *Teaching for quality learning at University*. Buckingham: Open University Press/McGraw Hill.

Black, P., and McCormick, R. (2010). Reflections and new directions. *Assessment and Evaluation in Higher Education, 35*, 493–499.

Black, P. E., and Plowright, D. (2010). A multi-dimensional model of reflective learning for professional development. *Reflective Practice, 11*(2), 245–258.

Black, P., and Wiliam, D. (1998). Assessment and classroom learning. *Assessment in Education, 5*, 7–74.

Blakemore, S-J., and Frith, U. (2005). *The learning brain*. Malden, MA: Blackwell Publishing.

Blakemore Lab. Available online at https://sites.google.com/site/blakemorelab/Articles

Blazhenkova, O., and Kozhevnikov, M. (2009). The new object-spatial-verbal cognitive style model: Theory and measurement. *Applied Cognitive Psychology, 23*, 638–663.

Blazhenkova, O., Becker, M., and Kozhevnikov, M. (2011). Object-spatial imagery and verbal cognitive styles in children and adolescents: Developmental trajectories ain relation to ability. *Learning and Individual Differences, 21*(3), 281–287.

Blazhenkova, O., and Kozhevnikov, M. (2012). Intellectual styles in members of different professions. In Zhang, L-F., Sternberg, R. J., and Rayner, S. (Eds), *Handbook of intellectual styles: Preferences in cognition, learning and thinking*. New York: Springer.

Bleakley, A. (1999). From reflective practice to holistic reflexivity. *Studies inHigher Education*, 24(3), 315–330.

Bliuc, A-M., Ellis, R.A., Goodyear, P., and Hendres, D. M. (2011a). Understanding student learning in context: Relationships between university students' social identity, approaches to learning, and academic performance. *European Journal of Psychology Education, 26*, 417–433.

Bliuc, A-M., Ellis, R. A., Goodyear, P., and Hendres, D. M. (2011b). The role of social identification as university student in learning: Relationships between students' social identity, approaches to learning, and academic achievement. *Educational Psychology, 31*(5), 559–574.

Bloomfield, D. (2010). Emotions and 'getting by': A pre-service teacher navigating professional experience. *Asia-Pacific Journal of Teacher Education, 38*(3), 221–234.

Bloxham, S. (2008). *Guide to assessment*, ESCalate, HEA. Available online at http://escalate.ac.uk/4148 (accessed 20 July 2009).

Boal, A. (1974). From 'Theatre of the Oppressed'. In N. Wardrip-Fruin and N. Montfort (Eds) (2003). *The New Media Reader*. Cambridge, MA: MIT.

Boal, A. (1993). *Theater of the oppressed*. New York: Theatre Communications Group.

Boal, A. (1996). *The rainbow of desire: The Boal method of theatre and therapy* (reprinted ed.). London: Routledge.

Boekaerts, M., and Corno, L. (2005). Self-regulation in the classroom: A perspective on assessment and intervention. *Applied Psychology: An International Review, 54*(2), 199–231.

Bokoros, M. A., Goldstein, M. B., and Sweeney, M. M. (1992). Common factors in five measures of cognitive style. Current Psychology: Research and Reviews, 11, 99–109.

Bolton, G. (2010). *Reflective practice*. London: Sage.

Borton, T. (1970). *Reach, teach and touch*. London: Mc Graw Hill.

Boud, D. (2000). Sustainable assessment: Rethinking assessment for the learning society. *Studies in Continuing Education, 22*, 151–167.

Boud, D. (2010) Relocating reflection in the context of practice. In Bradbury, Frost, Kilminster and Zukas (Eds), *Beyond reflective practice* (pp. 25–36). Abingdon: Routledge.

Boud, D., and Associates (2010). *Assessment 2020: Seven propositions for assessment reform in higher education.* Sydney, Australia: Australian Learning and Teaching Council.

Boud, D., Cressey, P., and Docherty, P. (Eds) (2006). *Productive reflection at work.* Routledge, London and New York.

Boud, D., Keogh, R., and Walker, D. (Eds) (1985). *Reflection: Turning experience into learning.* London: Kogan Page.

Boud, D., and Lawson, R. (2011, September). *The development of student judgement: The role of practice in grade prediction.* Paper presented at the 14 Biennial EARLI Conference, Exeter, UK.

Boud, D., and Molloy, A. (Eds.) (2012). *Feedback in higher and professional education. Understanding it and doing it well.* Abingdon, Oxon; New York, NY: Routledge.

Boud, D., and Molloy, A. (2013). Rethinking models of feedback for learning: The challenge of design. *Assessment and Evaluation in Higher Education, 38*(6), 698–712.

Boud, D., and Walker, D. (1990). Making the most of experience. *Studies in Continuing Education, 12*(2), 61–80.

Boulton-Lewis, G., Marton, F., and Wilss, L. (2001). The lived space of learning; An enquiry into indigenous Australian university students' experiences of studying. In R. J. Sternberg and L. F. Zhang (Eds), *Perspectives on thinking, learning, and cognitive styles* (pp. 137–164). Mahwah, NJ: Erlbaum.

Boyle, T., and Ravenscroft, A. (2012). Context and deep learning design. *Computers and Education, 59*, 1224–1233.

Brockbank. A., and McGill, I. (1998). *Facilitating reflective learning in higher education.* Buckingham: Society for Research into Higher Education and Open University Press.

Bromme, R., and Tillema, H. (1995). Fusing experience and theory: The structure of professional knowledge. *Learning and Instruction, 5*(4), 261–267.

Bronfenbrenner, U. (1979). *The ecology of human development.* Cambridge, MA: Harvard University Press.

Brookfield, S. Article and interviews. Available online at http://www.stephenbrookfield.com/Dr._Stephen_D._Brookfield/Articles_and_Interviews.html (accessed 19 March 2014).

Brookfield, S. (1987). *Developing critical thinkers: Challenging adults to explore alternative ways of thinking and acting.* Milton Keynes: Open University Press.

Brookfield, S. (1988). T*raining educators of adults.* New York: Routledge.

Brookfield, S. (1990). Using critical incidents to explore learners' assumptions. In J. Mezirow (Ed.), *Fostering critical reflection in adulthood* (pp. 177–193). San Francisco: Jossey-Bass.

Brookfield, S. (1994). The getting of wisdom: What critically reflective teaching is and why it's important. Available online at http://web.ics.purdue.edu/~reid21/CDM/supporting/Brookfield%20Critically%20Reflective%20Teaching.pdf (accessed 4 March 2014).

Brookfield, S. D. (1995). *Becoming a critically reflective teacher.* San Francisco: Jossey Bass. CA: Jossey-Bass.

Brookfield, S. (2005). *The power of critical theory.* Jossey Bass: San Francisco.

Brookfield, S. (2006). *The skilful teacher: On trust, technique and responsiveness in the classroom.* San Francisco: Jossey Bass.

Broverman, D. M. (1960). Dimensions of cognitive style. *Journal of Personality, 28*, 167–185.

Bullock, S. M. (2009): Learning to think like a teacher educator: Making the substantive and syntactic structures of teaching explicit through self-study, *Teachers and Teaching: Theory and Practice, 15*(2), 291–304.

Bruce, C. D., Esmonde, I., Ross, J., Dookie, L., and Beatty, R. (2010). The effects of sustained classroom-embedded teacher professional learning on teacher efficacy and related student achievement. *Teaching and Teacher Education, 26*, 1598–1608.

Bruner, J. (1963). *The process of education.* New York: Vintage Books.

Bruner, J. (1996). *The culture of education.* Cambridge, MA: Belknap Press.

Burke, D. (2009). Strategies for using feedback students bring to higher education. *Assessment and Evaluation in Higher Education, 34*, 41–50.

Burns, R. (2002). *The adult learner at work* (2nd ed.). Sydney: Allen and Unwin.

Butin, D. (Ed.) (2005). *Service-learning in higher education: Critical issues and directions.* New York: Palgrave Macmillan.

Campaign for Learning. Available online at http://www.campaign-for-learning.org.uk/cfl/learningin-schools/l2l/why_learning_to_learn.asp (accessed 12 August 2013).

Campbell, R. J., Kyriakides, L., Muijs, R. D., and Robinson, W. (2003). Differential teacher effectiveness: Towards a model for research and teacher appraisal. *Oxford Review of Education, 29*(3), 347–362.

Campbell, R. J., Robinson, W., Neerlands, J., Hewstin, R., and Mazzoli, L. (2007). Personalised learning: Ambiguities in theory and practice. *British Journal of Educational Studies, 55*(2), 135–154.

Campbell, J., Smith, D., Boulton-Lewis, G., Brownlee, J., Burnett, P C., Carrington, S., and Purdie, N. (2001). Students' perceptions of teaching and learning: The influence of students' approaches to learning and teachers' approaches to teaching. *Teachers and Teaching: Theory and Practice,* 7(2), 173–187.

Canadian Council on Learning. Lecture Series Minerva: Cultivating a flexible mind: Can you learn how to learn for life? Available online at http://www.ccl-cca.ca/pdfs/Minerva/CultivatingAFlexibleMind_Leighton.pdf. (accessed 1 May 2014).

Cano-Garcia, F., and Hughes, E. H. (2000). Learning and thinking styles: An analysis of their interrelationship and influence on academic achievement. *Educational Psychology, 20*(4), 413–430.

Carless, D. (2011). Sustainable feedback and the development of student self-evaluative capacities. EARLI symposium, University of Exeter, Exeter, UK.

Carless, D. (2013). Trust and its role in facilitating dialogic feedback. In D. Boud and L. Molloy, *Effective feedback in higher and professional education* (pp. 90–103). London: Routledge.

Carless, D., Joughin, G., and Mok, M. C. (2006). Learning-oriented assessment: Principles and practice. *Assessment and Evaluation in Higher Education, 31,* 395–398.

Carless, D., Salter, D., Yang, M., and Lam, J. (2011). Developing sustainable feedback practices. *Studies in Higher Education, 36*(4), 395–407.

Carmichael, P., Fox, A., McCormick, R., Procter, R., and Honour, L. (2012). Teachers' networks in and out of school. *Research Papers in Education, 21*(2), 217–234.

Carnegie Foundation for Advancement of Teaching. Available online at http://www.carnegiefoundation.org/ (accessed 10 January 2014).

Carolan, J., and Guinn, A. (2007). Differentiation: Lessons from master teachers. *Educational Leadership, 64*(5), 44–47.

Carper, B. A. (1978). Fundamental patterns of knowing in nursing. *Advances in Nursing Science, 1*(1), 13–24.

Carrington, S. B., and Selva, G. (2010). Critical social theory and transformative learning : evidence in pre-service teachers' service learning reflection logs. *Higher Education Research and Development, 29*(1), 45–57.

Cassidy, S. (2004). Learning styles: An overview of theories, models, and measures. *Educational Psychology, 24*(4), 419–444.

Centre for Critical Social Theory, University of Sussex. Available online at http://www.sussex.ac.uk/spt/1-4-5.html (accessed 10 January 2014).

Chaiklin, S., and Lave, J. (1993). *Understanding practice: Perspectives on activity and context.* Cambridge: Cambridge University Press.

Chase, W. G., and Simon, H. A. (1973). Perception in chess. *Cognitive Psychology, 4,* 55–81.

Cheek, J., O'Brien, B., Ballantyne, A., and Pincombe, J. (1997) Using critical incident technique to inform aged and extended care nursing. *Western Journal of Nursing Research, 19*(5), 667–82.

Chen, C-J., and Liu, P-L. (2012). Comparisons of learner-generated versus instructor-provided multimedia annotation. *Turkish Online Journal of Educational Technology*– TOJET, 11(4), 72–83.

Cheng, H., Andrade, H. L., and Yan, Z. (2011). A cross-cultural study of learning behaviours in the classroom: From a thinking style perspective. *Educational Psychology, 31*(7), 825–841.

Chisholm, L., and Demetriou, A. (2006). *Learning to learn: Towards complementary perspectives.* Centre for Research in Education and Lifelong Learning (CRELL), Ispra, Italy.: unpublished working paper.

Chisholm, L., Fennes, H., Kartsen, A., and Reich, K. (2009). L2L: Learning to learn. A method in action. Centre for Research in Education and Lifelong Learning. Available online at http://www.demokratie-dialog.de/work/learningtolearn_synthesisreport.pdf (accessed 30 July 2013).

Chiu, M. M., and Khoo, L. (2005) Effects of resources, inequality and privilege bias on achievement: Country, school and student level analyses. *American Educational Research Journal, 42,* 575–603.

Choi, I., Lee, S. J., and Kang, J. (2009). Implementing a case-based e-learning environment in a lecture-oriented Anaesthesiology class: Do learning styles matter in complex problem solving over time? *British Journal of Educational Technology, 40*(5), 933–947.

Chomsky, N. (1957). *Syntactic structures.* The Hague: Mouton.

Chomsky, N. (1995). A dialogue with Noam Chomsky.' *Harvard Educational Review, 65,* 127–144.

Chudgar, A., and Luschei, T. F. (2009). National income, income inequality and the importance of schools: a hierarchical cross-national comparison. *American Educational Research Journal, 46*(3), 626–658.

Clare, J. D. (2004). '*Differentiation*', at Greenfield History site. Available online at http://www.greenfield.durham.sch.uk/differentiation.htm (accessed 10 May 2011). Available online (2004/6) at http//www.johnclare.net/Teaching/Teaching_Differentiation.htm. (accessed 14 June 2014).

Cobb, P. (1994). Where is the mind? Constructivist and sociocultural perspectives on mathematical development. *Educational Researcher, 23*(7), 13–20.

Cobb, P. (1995). Continuing the conversation: A response to Smith. *Educational Researcher, 24*(6), *25–27.*

Cobb, P., and Bowers, J. (1999). Cognitive and situated learning perspectives in theory and practice. *Educational Researcher, 28*(2), 4–15.

Coffield, F., Moseley, D., Hall, E., and Ecclestone, K. (2004). Learning styles and pedagogy in post-16 learning: A systematic and critical review. London: Learning and Skills Research Centre.

Coffield, F., Moseley, D., Hall, E., and Ecclestone, K. (2005). Thinking skills framework for post-16 learners: an evaluation. Available online at http://www.google.co.uk/url?sa=t and rct=j and q= and esrc=s and source=web and cd=1 and ved=0CDIQFjAA (accessed 14 January 14–2014).

Cole, M. (1996). *Cultural Psychology.* Cambridge, MA: Harvard University Press.

Cole, M., and Engeström, Y. (1994). Introduction. Mind, culture and activity. *An International Journal, 1*(4), 201.

Coles, M. J., and Southworth, G. (2005). *Developing leadership: creating the schools of tomorrow.* Buckingham: Open University Press.

Collins, J., Insley, K., and Soler, J. (Eds) (2001). *Developing pedagogy: Researching practice.* London: Paul Chapman Publishing and OU Press.

Colluci-Gray, L., Das, S., Gray, D., Robson, D., and Spratt, J. (2013). Evidence-based practice and teacher action-research: A reflection on the nature and direction of 'change'. *British Educational Research Journal, 39*(1), 126–147.

Commander, N. E., and Valeri-Gold, M. (2001). The learning portfolio: A valuable tool for increasing metacognitive awareness. *Learning Assistance Review, 6,* 5–18.

Cools, E., and Bellens, K. (2012). The onion model: Myth or reality in the field of individual differences psychology? *Learning and Individual Differences, 22*(4), 455–462.

Cools, E., and Evans, C. (Eds) (2009). Using styles for more effective learning. *Multicultural Education and Technology Journal,* March, 5–16.

Cooper, C. (2012). Learning styles, academic achievement and personality – and the elephant in the room. *Presented at ELSIN conference,* June 26–28, Cardiff, Wales, UK.

Cossart, L., and Fish, D. (2005). *Cultivating a thinking surgeon. New perspectives on clinical teaching, learning and assessment.* Shrewsbury: tfm Publishing Ltd.

Courey, S. J., Tappe, P., Siker, J., and LePage, P. (2013). Improved lesson planning with universal design for learning (UDL). *Teacher Education and Special Education, 36*(1), 7–27.

Cowan, J. K., and Creme, P. (2005). Peer assessment or peer engagement? Students as readers of their own work. LATISS: *Learning and Teaching in the Social Sciences, 2,* 99–119.

Craske, M. L. (1988). Learned helplessness, self-worth and attribution retraining for primary school children. *British Journal of Educational Psychology*, 58, 152–164.

Crell Centre for Research in Education and Lifelong Learning. Available online at https://crell.jrc.ec.europa.eu/?q=content/research-areas (accessed 30 July 2013).

Curry, L. (1983). An organisation of learning styles theory and constructs. Paper presented at the Annual Meeting of the American Educational Research Association, Montreal, Quebec, April 1–15.

Davies, P. (2006). Peer assessment: Judging the quality of students' work by comments rather than marks. *Innovations in Education and Teaching International, 43*, 69–82.

Davies, P., and Dunnill, R. (2008). 'Learning Study' as a model of collaborative practice in initial teacher education. *Journal of Education for Teaching, 34(1), 3–16.*

Day, C. (1999). *Developing teachers. The challenges of lifelong learning.* London: Falmer Press.

Day, C., and Mujtaba, T. Flores, M. A., and Viana, I. (2007). Effects of national policies on teachers' sense of professionalism: Findings from an empirical study in Portugal and in England. *European Journal of Teacher Education*, 30(3), 249–265.

Day, C., and Gu, Q. (2007). Variations in the conditions for teachers' professional learning and development: Sustaining commitment and effectiveness over a career. *Oxford Review of Education, 33*(4), 423–443.

Day, C. W., Kington, A., Stobart, G., and Sammons, P. (2006a). The personal and professional selves of teachers: stable and unstable identities. *British Educational Research Journal,* 32(4), 601–616.

Day, C., Stobart, G., Sammons, P., Kington, A., Gu, Q., Smees, R., and Mujtaba, T. (2006b). *Variation in teachers' work, lives and effectiveness.* London: DfES.

De Boer, A-L., du Toit, P. H., Scheepers, M. D., and Bothma, T. J. D. (2013). *Whole brain learning in higher education. Evidence-based practice.* Oxford: Chandos Publishing.

De Boer, J., Kommers, P. A. M., and de Brock, B. (2011). Using learning styles and viewing styles in streaming video. *Computers and Education, 56*, 727–235.

Deci, E. L. (1971). Effects of externally mediated rewards on intrinsic motivation. *Journal of Personality and Social Psychology, 18*, 105–115.

de Laat, M., and Simons, R-J. (2002). Collective learning: Theoretical perspectives and ways to support networked learning, *Vocational Training, European Journal, 27*, 13–24.

Demetriou, H., and Wilson, E. (2009). Synthesising affect and cognition in teaching and learning. *Social Psychology of Education, 12*, 213–232.

DeNisi, A., and Kluger, A. N. (2000). Feedback effectiveness: Can 360 degree appraisals be improved? *Academy of Management Executives, 14*, 129–139.

Des Jarlais, D. C., Lyles, C., Crepaz, N., and the Trend Group (2004). Improving the reporting quality of nonrandomized evaluations of behavioral and public health interventions: The TREND statement. *American Journal of Public Health, 94*, 361–366. Available online at http://www.cdc.gov/trendstatement/ (accessed 4 January 2013).

Desmedt, E., and Valke, M. (2004). Mapping the learning styles 'jungle': An overview of the literature based on citation analysis. *Educational Psychology, 24*(4), 445–464.

Dewey, J. (1897). My pedagogic creed. *The School Journal. LIV (3):* Jan 16–1897, 77–80. Online. Available HTTP http: www.infed.org/archives/e-texts/e-dew-pc.htm (accessed 10 March 2014).

Dewey, J. (1910). *How we think.* Boston, MA: D. C. Heath & Co. Publishers.

Dewey, J. (1916). *Democracy and education.* New York: Free Press.

Dewey, J. (1933). *How we think: a restatement of the relation of reflective thinking to the educative process.* Chicago, IL: Henry Regnery Co.

Dewey, J. (1938). *Logic: The theory of inquiry.* Troy, MN: Rinehart and Winston.

DfE (2011a). *Teachers' Standards.* Department for Education. Available online at http//:www.education.gov.uk/publications (accessed 11 November 2013).

DfE (2011b). Independent review of key stage 2 testing, assessment and accountability: Final report. Available online at https://www.gov.uk/government/publications/independent-review-of-key-stage-2-testing-assessment-and-accountability-final-report (accessed 12 January 2014).

DfES (2004). *A National Conversation about Personalised Learning*. Available online at www.standards.dfes.gov.uk/personalisedlearning (accessed 12 May 2013).

DfES (2005). *White Paper: Higher standards, better schools for all*. London: Department for Education and Skills.

DfES (2006). *Making good progress. How can we help every pupil to make good progress at school*. London: Department for Education and Skills.

DFES/AfL (2008). *The Assessment for Learning Strategy*. Department for children, schools and families. Available online at https://www.education.gov.uk/publications/eOrderingDownload/DCSF-00341-2008.pdf (accessed 12 January 2014).

Dias, D., and Sá, M. J. (2014). The impact of the transition to HE: Emotions, feelings and sensations. *European Journal of Education, 49*(2), 291–303.

Diseth, A. (2011). Self-efficacy, goal orientations and learning strategies as mediators between preceding and subsequent academic achievement. *Learning and Individual Differences, 21*(2), 191–195.

Donche, V., De Maeyer, S., Coertjens, L., Van Daal, T., and Van Petegem, P. (2013). Differential use of learning strategies in first-year higher education: The impact of personality, academic motivation, and teaching strategies. *British Journal of Educational Psychology, 83*(2), 238–251.

Dubinsky, J. M., Roehrig, G., and Varma, S. (2013). Infusing neuroscience into teacher professional development. *Educational Researcher, 43*(6), 317–329.

Duckworth, A. L., Peterson, C., Matthews, M. D., and Kelly, D. R. (2007). Grit: Perseverance and passion for long-term goals. *Journal of Personality and Social Psychology, 92*(6), 1087–1101.

Dunlosky, J., Rawson, K. A., Marsh, E. J., Nathan, M. J., and Willingham, D. T. (2013). Improving students' learning with effective learning techniques: Promising directions from cognitive and educational psychology. *Psychological Science in the Public Interest, 14*(1), 4–58.

Dunn, R., Dunn, K., and Price, G. E. (1989). *Learning Styles Inventory*. Lawrence, KS: Price Systems.

Dunn, R., Griggs, S. A., Olson, J., Beasley, M., and Gorman, B. S. (1995). A meta-analytic validation of the Dunn and Dunn model of learning-style preferences. *The Journal of Educational Research, 88*, 353–362.

Dvir, N., and Avissar, I. (2013). *Constructing a critical professional identity among teacher candidates during service learning*. Professional Development in Education. Available online at http://dx.doi.org/10.1080/19415257.2013.818573

Dweck, C. S. (1986). Motivational processes affecting learning. *American Psychologist,* 41, 1040–1048.

Dweck, C. S. (2006). *Mindset: The new psychology of success*. New York: Random House.

Dweck, C. S. (2007). Boosting achievement with messages that motivate. *Education Canada, 47*(2), 6–10.

Dweck, C. S. (2012). *Mindset: How you can fulfil your potential*. Constable and Robinson Limited.

Eaves, M. (2011). The relevance of learning styles for international pedagogy in higher education. *Teachers and Teaching: Theory and Practice,* 17(6), 677–691.

Ecclestone, K. (2007). Resisting images of the 'Diminished Self': The implications of emotional well-being and emotional engagement in education policy. *Journal of Education Policy, 22*(4), 455–70.

Educational Broadcasting Corporation. Object based learning. Available online at http://schools.cbe.ab.ca/b101/pdfs/inquirybasedlearning.pdf (accessed 4 January 2014).

Educause (2012). Educause learning initiative 7: Things you should know about...flipped classrooms. Available online at http://net.educause.edu/ir/library/pdf/eli7081.pdf (accessed 3 May 2014).

Ekebergh, M. (2007). Lifeworld-based reflection and learning: A contribution to the reflective practice in nursing and nursing education. *Reflective Practice, 8*(3), 331–343.

Elkjaer, B. (2009). Pragmatism: A learning theory for the future. In K. Illeris (Ed.) *Contemporary theories of learning* (pp. 74–89). London: Routledge.

Ellis, R. A., Goodyear, P., Prosser, M., and O'Hara, A. (2006). How and what university students learn through online and face-to-face discussion: conceptions, intentions and approaches. *Journal of Computer Assisted Learning, 22*, 244–256.

Ellström, P-E (2001). Integrating learning and work: Conceptual issues and critical conditions. *Human Resource Development Quarterly, 2001, 12*(4), 421–435.

ELSIN: Education, Learning, Styles, Individual differences Network (ELSIN). Available online at http://www.elsinnetwork.com (accessed 10 June 2013).

Enfield, M., and Stasz, B. (2011). Presence without being present: Reflection and action in a community of practice. *Journal of the Scholarship of Teaching and Learning, 11*(1), 108–118.

Engeström, Y. (1987). *Learning by expanding: An activity theoretical approach to developmental research*. Helsinki: Orienta-Konsultit.

Engeström, Y. (2009). Expansive learning: Toward an activity-theoretical reconceptualisation. In K. Illeris (Ed.), *Contemporary learning theories* (pp. 53–73). London: Routledge.

Entwistle, N. J., McCune, V., and Walker, P. (2001). Conceptions, styles and approaches within higher education: analytic abstractions and everyday experience. In R. J. Sternberg and L. F. Zhang (Eds), *Perspectives on thinking, learning, and cognitive styles* (pp. 103–136). Mahwah, NJ, Erlbaum.

Entwistle, N., and Ramsden, P. (1983). *Understanding student learning*. London: Croom Helm.

Epstein, D. (2013). *The Sports Gene. What makes the perfect athlete*. New York: Penguin Group.

Eraut, M. (1994a). The acquisition and use of educational theory by beginning teachers.' In G. Harvard, and Hodkinson, P. (Eds), *Action and reflection in teacher education* (pp. 69–88). New Jersey: Ablex Publishing Corporation.

Eraut, M. (1994b). *Developing professional knowledge and competence*. London: Routledge Falmer.

Eraut, M. (2000). The intuitive practitioner: A critical overview. In: T. Atkinson and G. Claxton G. (Eds) *The intuitive practitioner* (pp. 253–268). Berkshire: Open University Press.

Eraut, M. (2004a). Transfer of knowledge between education and the workplace. In: Expertise development: The transition between school and work (pp. 53–73). Heerlen: Open University, The Netherlands. Available online at http://www.ou.nl/Docs/Expertise/OTEC/Publicaties/els%20 boshuizen/deel3.pdf (accessed 6 December 2013).

Eraut, M. (2004b). Transfer of knowledge between education and workplace settings. In Rainbird, H., Fuller, A., and Munro, A. (Eds) *Workplace learning in context* (pp. 201–221). London: Routledge.

Eraut, M. (2004c). Editorial: the practice of reflection. *Learning in Health and Social Care*, 3(2), 47–52.

Eraut, M. (2008). How professionals learn through work. Draft 1 / 22/04/08 Surrey: Surrey Centre for Excellence in Professional Training and Education. University of Surrey. Available online at http://surreyprofessionaltraining.pbworks.com/f/How+Professionals+Learn+through+Work.pdf (accessed 20 November 2013).

Ericsson, K. A., Krampe, R. T., and Tesch-Romer, C. (1993). The role of deliberate practice in the acquisition of expert performance. *Psychological Review, 100*, 363–406.

ESRC (2001–2006). Learntolearn. Economic and Social Research Council. Available online at http://www.learntolearn.ac.uk/ (accessed 30 July 2013).

Evans, C. (2003). *The relationship between the cognitive style(s) and preferred teachers' style(s) of PGCE students*. Unpublished thesis, University of Durham.

Evans, C. (2004). Exploring the relationship between cognitive style and teaching. *Educational Psychology, 24*(4), 509–531.

Evans, C. (2012a). Making formative assessment and feedback processes and practices explicit. Symposium. The European Conference on Educational Research, 18–21 September 2012, Cadiz, Spain.

Evans, C. (2012b). The emotional dimension of feedback. Linking multiple perspectives on assessment. 28–31 August 2012, EARLI SIG 1 Assessment and Evaluation, Brussels, Belgium.

Evans, C. (2013a). Styles in practice: a research perspective. Presentation at ELSIN conference, June 18–20, Legoland, Billund, Denmark.

Evans, C. (2013b). Making sense of assessment feedback in higher education. *Review of Educational Research, 83(1), 70–120.*

Evans, C. (2013c). Enhancing assessment feedback practice. EMERGe (Exeter Medical Education Research Group, 11 September 2013, University of Exeter.

Evans, C. (2014). Exploring the use of a deep approach to learning with students in the process of learning to teach. In D. Gijbels, V. Donche, J. T. E Richardson, and J. Vermunt (Eds), *Learning patterns in higher education. Dimensions and research perspectives* (pp. 187–213). London and New York: Routledge.

Evans, C. (2015). Students' perspectives on the role of peer feedback in supporting learning. *Journal of Cognitive Education and Psychology.*

Evans, C., and Cools, E. (2009). The use and understanding of style differences to enhance learning. *Reflecting Education, 5*(2), 1–18.

Evans, C., and Cools, E. (2011). New directions with styles research: Applying styles research to educational practice. *Learning and Individual Difference Journal, 21*(3), 249–254.

Evans, C., and Graff, M. (Eds) (2008). Exploring Style: Enhancing the capacity to learn? (Special Issue) *Education and Training, 50*(2), 93–103.

Evans, C., and Kozhevnikov, M. (Eds) (2011). Styles of practice: How learning is affected by students' and teachers' perceptions and beliefs, conceptions and approaches to learning. *Research Papers in Education, 26*(2), 133–148.

Evans, C., and Kozhevnikov, M. (2013). *Styles of practice in higher education: Exploring approaches to teaching and learning.* London: Routledge book series.

Evans, C., Richardson, J. T., and Waring, M. (2013). Field independence: A critique and a reinterpretation. *British Journal of Educational Psychology, 83*(2), 210–224.

Evans, C., and Sadler-Smith, E. (Eds) (2006). Learning styles. *Education and Training, 48* (2 and 3), 77–84.

Evans, C., and Vermunt. J. (2013). Styles, approaches and patterns in student learning. *British Journal of Educational Psychology, 83*(2), 185–195.

Evans, C., and Waring, M. (2006). Towards inclusive teacher education: Sensitising individuals to how they learn. *Educational Psychology, 26*(4), 499–518.

Evans, C., and Waring, M. (2007). Using the CSI in educational settings. In L. M. Lassen, L. Boström, and H. H. Henrik Knoop, (Eds), *Laeringoglaeringsstile om unikkeogfaellesveje I paedagogikken*[Promoting learning and learning styles of unique and common ways of teaching methods](pp. 103–122). Denmark: Dansk PsykolgiskForlag.

Evans, C., and Waring, M. (2008). Trainee teachers' cognitive styles and notions of differentiation. *Education and Training, 50*(2), 140–154.

Evans, C., and Waring, M., (2009). The place of cognitive style in pedagogy: Realising potential in practice. In L. F. Zhang and R. J. Sternberg (Eds)*Perspectives on Intellectual Style.* (pp 169–208). New Jersey:Springer.

Evans, C., and Waring, M. (2011a). Enhancing feedback practice: A personal learning styles pedagogy approach. In S. Rayner and E. Cools (Eds), *Style differences in cognition, learning, and management: Theory, research and practice* (pp. 188–203). New York: Routledge.

Evans, C., and Waring, M. (2011b). Student teacher assessment feedback preferences: the influence of cognitive styles and gender. *Learning and Individual Differences Journal,* 21(3), 271–280.

Evans, C., and Waring, M. (2011c). Exploring students' perceptions of feedback in relation to cognitive styles and culture. *Research Papers in Education, 26*(2), 171–190.

Evans, C., and Waring, M. (2011d). How can an understanding of cognitive style enable trainee teachers to have a better understanding of differentiation in the classroom *Educational Research for Policy and Practice, 10,* 149–169.

Evans, C., and Waring, M. (2012). Application of styles in educational instruction and assessment. In L. F. Zhang, R. J. Sternberg, and S. Rayner (Eds)*The Handbook of Intellectual Styles* (pp. 297–330). New York: Springer.

Evans, C., and Waring, M., (Forthcoming 2015). Using an informed understanding of styles to enhance learning in 21st Century learning environments. In R. Wegerif, J. Kaufman, and L. Liu (Eds) *Routledge Handbook of Research on Teaching and Thinking.* London: Routledge.

Evans, L. (2002). What is teacher development? *Oxford Review of Education, 28*(1), 123–137.

Evans, L. (2008a). Professionalism, professionality and the development of education professionals. *British Journal of Educational Studies*, 56(1), 20–38.

Evans, L. (2008b). Author produced version of Professionalism, professionality and the development of education professionals. *British Journal of Educational Studies*, 56(1), 20–38. Available online at http://eprints.whiterose.ac.uk/4077/ (accessed 10 June 2013).

Evans, L. (2010). Teacher professional development in England: A critical perspective on current issues and priorities. In V. – R Ruus, and E. -S., and Sarv. (Eds), Eestiõpetaja ja õpetajahariduseõppekavad 21. Saj and ialgul [Teacher education in Estonia and European teacher education curricula at the beginning of the 21st century]. Tallin, Estonia: University of Tallin.

Evans, L. (2011). The 'shape' of teacher professionalism in England: Professional standards, performance management, professional development and the changes proposed in the 2010 White Paper. *British Educational Journal, 37*(5), 851–870.

Evans, L. (2013). The professional status of educational research: Professionalism and developmentalism in twenty-first-century working life. *British Journal of Educational Studies, 61*(4), 471–490.

Evetts, J. (2003). The sociological analysis of professionalism: Occupational change in themodern world. *International Sociology 18*(2), 395–415.

Evetts, J. (2006). Short note: The sociology of professional groups: New directions. *Current Sociology, 54*, 133–143.

Evetts, J. (2012). *Professionalism in turbulent times: Changes, challenges and opportunities*. Propel International Conference, Stirling, Scotland, 9–11 May 2012.

Exeter Mindfulness Network. Available online at http://www.exeter-mindfulness-network.org/ (accessed 14 May 2014).

Falchikov, N., and Goldfinch, J. (2000). Student peer assessment in higher education: A meta-analysis comparing peer and teacher marks. *Review of Educational Research, 70*, 287–322.

Fan, W., Zhang, L-F., and Watkins, D. (2010). Incremental validity of thinking styles in predicting academic achievements: An experimental study in hypermedia learningenvironments. *Educational Psychology, 30*(5), 605–623.

Felder, R. M., and Silverman, L. K. (1988). Learning and teaching styles in college science education. *Journal of Engineering Education*, 78(7), 674–681.

Ferla, J., Valcke, M., and Schuyten, G. (2009). Student models of learning and their impact on study strategies, *Studies in Higher Education*, 34(2), 185–202.

Finlay, L. (2008). *Reflecting on 'reflective practice'. PBPL paper 52. A discussion paper prepared for PBPL CETL.* Open University: Practice-based professional learning centre. Available online at http://www.open.ac.uk/pbpl. (accessed 3 December 2013).

Flanagan, J. (1954). The critical incident technique. *Psychological Bulletin, 51(4)*, 1–33.

Fleming, N. D., and Mills, C. (1992). Not another inventory, rather a catalyst for reflection. *To Improve the Academy, 11*, p. 137.

Fook, J. (2006). Beyond reflective practice: Reworking the 'critical' in critical reflection. Keynote for 'Professional lifelong learning: beyond reflective practice', 3 July 2006, Standing Conference on University Teaching and Research in the Education of Adults (University of Leeds), 1–14.

Fook, J., White, S., and Gardner, F. (2006). Critical reflection: A review of contemporary literature and understandings. In White, S., Fook, J., and Gardner, F. (Eds), *Critical reflection in health and social care* (pp. 3–20). Maidenhead: Open University Press.

Fowler, E. (2013). Changing the learning landscape. Using blogs to support reflection. Available online at www.heacademy.ac.uk/resources/detail/cll/Workshop_materials (accessed 19 March 2014).

Foucault, M. (1980). *Power/knowledge: Selected interviews and other writings 1972–1977*. Brighton: Harvester.

Freire, P. (1972). *Pedagogy of the oppressed*. Harmondsworth: Pengiun.

Fried, L. (2011). Teaching teachers about emotional regulation in the classroom. *Australian Journal of Teacher Education, 36*(3), 117–127.

Fullan, M. (1993). *Change forces: Probing the depths of educational reform*. London: The Falmer Press.

Fullan, M. (1999). *Change forces: The sequel.* London: The Falmer Press.

Fund, Z. (2010). Effects of communities of reflecting peers on student-teacher development including in-depth case studies. *Teachers and Teaching: Theory and Practice, 16*, 679–701.

Furlong, J. (2000a). Intuition and the crisis in teacher professionalism In: T. Atkinson and G. Claxton G. (Eds) (2000). *The intuitive practitioner* (pp. 15–31). Berkshire: Open University Press.

Furlong, J. (2000b). *Higher education and the new professionalism of teachers: Realising the potential of partnership.* A discussion paper. London, SCOP/CVCP.

Furnham, A. (2012). Intelligence and intellectual styles. In L. F. Zhang, R. J. Sternberg, and S. Rayner, (2012). *Handbook of Intellectual Styles* (pp. 173–192). New York: Springer.

Furnham, A. (2014). Relax: Mindful managers will save the office's living dead. *The Sunday Times*, 11 May 2014, Appointments, p. 2.

Fyrenius, A., Wirell, S., Silén, C. (2007). Student approaches to achieving understanding approaches to learning revisited. *Studies in Higher Education, 32*(2), 149–65.

Gagné, R. M. (1985). *The conditions of learning and theory of instruction* (4th ed.). New York: CBS College Publishing.

Gagnon, G. W., and Collay, M. (2006). *Constructivist learning design.* California: Corwin Press.

Gale, R. A. (2006). Fostering integrative learning through pedagogy. Integrative Learning Project. Carnegie Foundation for the Advancement of Teaching and the Association of American Colleges and Universities. Available online at http://gallery.carnegiefoundation.or/ilp (accessed 6 May 2014).

Galloway, D., Rogers, C., Armstrong, D., Leo, E., and Jackson, C. (1998). *Motivating the difficult to teach.* London: Longman.

Galton, F. (1883). *Inquiries into human faculty and its development.* London: Macmillan.

Gardner, H. (2009). Reflections on my works and those of my commentators. In B. Shearer (Ed.), *MI at 25* (pp. 113–120). New York: Teachers College Press.

Gardner, R. W., Holzman, P., Klein, G., Linton, H., and Spence, D. (1959). Cognitive Control: a study of individual differences in cognitive behaviour. *Psychological Issues*, 4, Monograph 4.

Gardner, R. W., Jackson, D. N., and Messick, S. J. (1960). Personality organization in cognitive controls and intellectual abilities. *Psychological Issues, 2*(4).

Gardner, H. (2003). *Frames of mind. The theory of multiple intelligences.* New York: Basic Books. (Original work published1983.)

Ghaye, T. (2000). Into the reflective mode: Bridging the stagnant moat. *Reflective Practice, 1(1)*, 5–9.

Ghaye, T., and Lillyman S. (2000). *Reflection: Principles and practice for health care professionals.* Wiltshire: Mark Allen.

Ghinea, G., and Chen, S. Y. (2003). The impact of cognitive styles on perceptual distributed multimedia quality. *British Journal of Educational Technology, 34*(4), 393–406.

Gibbs, G. (1988). *Learning by doing: A guide to teaching and learning methods.* Oxford: Further Education Unit, Oxford Polytechnic.

Gibbs, G., and Simpson, C. (2004). Conditions under which assessment supports students' learning. *Learning and Teaching in Higher Education, 1*, 3–31.

Gielen, S., Dochy, F., and Onghena, P. (2011). An inventory of peer assessment diversity. *Assessment and Evaluation in Higher Education, 36*, 137–155.

Gijbels, D., Coertjens, L., Vanthournout, G., Struyf, E., and Van Petegem, P. (2009). Changing students' approaches to learning: A two-year study within a university teacher training course. *Educational Studies* 35(5), 503–513.

Gijbels, D., Donche, V., Richardson, J. T. E., and Vermunt, J. (2014). *Learning patterns in higher education. Dimensions and research perspectives.* EARLI Book Series. London and New York: Routledge.

Gijbels, D., Segers, M., and Struyf, E. (2008). Constructivist learning environments and the (im)possibility to change students' perceptions of assessment demands and approaches to learning. *Instructional Science, 36*, 431–443.

Gijbels, D., van de Watering, G., Dochy, F., and van den Bossche, P. (2006). New learning environments and constructivism: The students' perspective. *Instructional Science, 34*, 213–226.

Gilbert, C. (2007). *2020 Vision*, a report to the Secretary of State on behalf of the Teaching and Learning in 2020 Review Group. London: OFSTED.

Gilbert, L., Whitelock, D., and Gale, V. (2011). *Synthesis report on assessment and feedback with technology enhancement*. Southampton: Electronics and Computer Science EPrints.

Gipps, C. (2002). Sociocultural perspectives on assessment. In G. Wells and G. Claxton (Eds), *Learning for life in the 21st century* (pp. 73–83). Oxford: Blackwell.

Gipps, C. (2008). Socio-cultural aspects of assessment. In H. Wynne (Ed.), *Student assessment and testing* (vol. 1, chapter 8, pp. 252–291). Thousand Oaks, CA: Sage.

Giroux, H. (1988). *Teachers as intellectuals: Toward a critical pedagogy of learning*. Granby, MA: Bergin and Garvey.

Giroux, H. (1993). Paulo Freire and the politics of postcolonialism. In P. McLaren and P. Leonard (Eds), *Paulo Freire: A critical encounter* (pp. 177–188). New York: Routledge.

Giroux, H. A. (2007). Introduction: Democracy, education, and the politics of critical pedagogy. In P. M., McLaren, and J. L, Kincheloe (Eds)*Critical Pedagogy: Where Are We Now?* (pp. 1–5*)*. New York: Peter Lang.

Giroux, H. A., (2011). *On Critical Pedagogy*. London: Continuum.

Gladwell, M. (2008). *Outliers: The story of success*. New York: Little, Brown and Company.

Gladwell. M. (2013). *Complexity and the ten-thousand-hour rule*. Available online at http://www.newyorker.com/online/blogs/sportingscene/2013/08/psychology-ten-thousand-hour-rule-complexity.html (accessed 20 September 2013).

Goldacre, B. (2013). *Building evidence into education*. Available online at https://www.gov.uk/government/publications/test-learn-adapt-developing-public-policy-with-randomised-controlled-trials (accessed 20 July 2013).

Goswani, U. (2006). Neuroscience and education: From research to practice. *Nature Reviews Neuroscience*, 2–7.

Graff, M., and Evans, C. (Eds) (2008). Cognitive Styles in Practice. *The Psychology of Education Review, 32*(1), March.

Graham, I. W. (1995). Reflective practice: Using the action learning group mechanism. *Nurse Education Today 15*(1), 28–32.

Greenwood, J. (1998). The role of reflection in single and double loop learning. *Journal of Advanced Nursing, 27*, 1048–1053.

Grennon Brooks, J., and Brooks, M. G. (1993). *In search of understanding: The case for constructivist classrooms*. Alexandria, VA: Association for Supervision and Curriculum Development.

Gregorc, A. F. (1982). *Gregorc Style Delineator*. Maynard, MA: Gabriel Systems.

Grigorenko, E. L., and Sternberg, R. J. (1995). Thinking styles. In D. Saklofske and M. Zeidner (Eds), *International handbook of personality and intelligence* (pp. 205–229). New York: Plenum Press.

Gross, J. J. (2001). Emotion regulation in adulthood: Timing is everything. *Current Directions in Psychological Science, 10*, 214–219.

Grossman, P., Hammerness, K., and McDonald, M. (2009) Redefining teaching, re-imagining teacher education, *Teachers and Teaching: Theory and Practice, 15*(2), 273–289.

Grushka, K., Hinde-McLeod, J., and Reynolds, R. (2005). Reflecting upon reflection: Theory and practice in one Australian university teacher education program. *Reflective Practice, 6*(1), 239–246.

Guthrie, E. R. (1935). *The psychology of learning*. New York: Harper and Row.

Habermas, J. (1971). *Towards a rational society*. London:Heinemann.

Habermas, J. (1972). *Knowledge and human interest*. Trans. J. J. Shappiro. London: Heinemann.

Habermas, J. (1974). *Theory and practice*. Trans. J. Viertel, London: Heinmann.

Habermas, J. (1978.) *Knowledge and human interests*. London: Heinemann.

Hallahan, D. P., Kauffman, J. M., and Pullen, P. C. (2009). *Exceptional learners: An introduction to special education* (13th ed.). Boston, MA: Pearson Education.

Handal, B., and Herrington, A. (2004). On being dependent or independent in computer based learning environments. *E-Journal of Instructional Science and Technology*, 7, (2). Available online at http://www.ascilite.org.au/ajet/e-jist/docs/vol7_no2/default.htm. (accessed 10 January 2010).

Handley, K., Price, M., and Millar, J. (2008). *Engaging students with assessment feedback. Final report for FDTL project 144/03.* Available online at http://www.brookes.ac.uk/aske/documents/FDTL_FeedbackProjectReportApril2009.pdf (accessed 10 January 2011).

Hardaker, G., Jeffery, A., and Sabki, A. A. (2011). Learning styles and personal pedagogy. In S. Rayner and E. Cools (Eds), *Style differences in cognition, learning, and management: Theory, research and practice* (pp. 207–223). New York, NY: Routledge.

Hargreaves, A. (1994). *Changing teachers, changing times: Teachers' work and culture in the postmodern age.* London, New York, and Toronto: Cassell, Teachers' College Press, and University of Toronto Press.

Hargreaves, A. (1995). Development and desire: A post-modern perspective. In T. R. Guskey and M. Huberman (Eds), *Professional development in education: New paradigms and perspectives.* (pp. 9–34). New York: Teachers College Press.

Hargreaves, A. (2001). Emotional geographies of teaching. *The Teachers College Record, 103*(6), 1056–1080.

Hargreaves, A., and Goodson, I. (1996). Teachers' professional lives: aspirations and actualities. In I. Goodson and A. Hargreaves (Eds) *Teachers' professional lives.* London: Falmer.

Hargreaves, D. H. (1994). The new professionalism: The synthesis of professional and institutional development. *Teaching and Teacher Education, 10* (4), 423–438.

Hargreaves, D. (1996). *Teaching as a research-based profession: Possibilities and prospects.* The Teacher Training Agency Annual Lecture, 1996. London: Teacher Training Agency.

Hargreaves, D. (2000). Four ages of professionalism and professional learning. *Teachers and Teaching: History and Practice, 6*(2), 151–182.

Hargreaves, D., Beere, J., Swindells, M., Wise, D., Desforges, C., Goswami, U., Wood, D., Horne, M., and Lownsbrough, H. (2005). *About learning: Report of the Learning Working Group.* London: DEMOS.

Hargreaves, E. (2005). Assessment for learning? Thinking outside the (black box). *Cambridge Journal of Education, 35*(2), 213–224.

Hargreaves, J. (2004). So how do you feel about that? Assessing reflective practice. *Nurse Education Today*, 24(3), 196–201.

Hascher, T. (2010). Learning and emotion: Perspectives for theory and research. *European Educational Research Journal, 9*(1), 13–28.

Hastings, W. (2010). Expectations of a pre-service teacher: implications of encountering the unexpected. *Asia-Pacific Journal of Teacher Education, 38*(3), 207–219.

Hatano, G. (1997). Learning arithmetic with an abacus. In T. Nunes and P. E. Bryant (Eds), *Learning and teaching mathematics: An international perspective* (pp. 209–231). Hove: Psychology Press/Erlbaum.

Hatano, G., and Miyake, N. (1991). What does a cultural approach offer to research on learning? *Learning and Instruction, 1*, 273–281.

Hattie, J. (2004). *The power of feedback: What does feedback mean, and how can it be understood and enhanced in classrooms.* Presentation at ESRC Seminar Series: Effective Educational Interventions, July 8–2004, University of Newcastle, Newcastle, UK.

Hattie, J. (2012). *Visible learning for teachers. Maximizing impact on learning.* London and New York: Routledge.

Hattie, J., and Timperley, H. (2007). The power of feedback. *Review of Educational Research*, 77, 81–112.

Hattie, J., and Yates, G. C. R. (2014). *Visible learning and the science of how we learn.* London: Routledge.

Hatzipanagos, S., and Warburton, S. (2009). Feedback as dialogue: Exploring the links between formative assessment and social software in distance learning. *Learning Media and Technology, 34,* 45–59.

Hawkins, R., and Woolf, H. (n.d.). Available online at http://www2.wlv.ac.uk/celt/Projects/historians_reflect/Greater_Manchester_AHP-HCS_Life_Long_Learning_Project_Team.pdf (accessed 10 December 2013).

Hay, D. B. (2010). Prizewinning essays (vol. 1). Higher Education Research Network. London: King's Learning Institute, King's College, London. Available online at https://www.kcl.ac.uk/study/learningteaching/kli/research/hern/hernjvol1.pdf (accessed 19 March 2014).

Hayward, G., Hodgson, a., Johnson, J., Oancea, A., Pring, R., Spours, K., Wilde, S., and Wright, S. (2005). *Annual Report of the Nuffield Review of 14–19 Education and Training*. Oxford: University of Oxford Department of Educational Studies.

Heikkilä, A., and Lonka, K. (2006). Studying in higher education: students' approaches to learning, self regulation, and cognitive strategies. *Studies in Higher Education, 31*(1), 99–117.

Heilbronn, R., and Yandell, J. (2011). *Critical practice in teacher education*. London: Institute of Education, University of London.

Helsby, G. (1995). Teachers' construction of professionalism in England in the 1990s. *Journal of Education for Teaching, 21*(3), 317–332.

Hendry, G. D., Bromberger, N., and Armstrong, S. (2011). Constructive guidance and feedback for learning: The usefulness of exemplars, marking sheets and different types of feedback in a first year Law subject. *Assessment and Evaluation in Higher Education, 36*, 1–11.

Hendry, G. D., Heinrich, P., Lyon, P., Barratt, A., Simpson, J., Hyde, S., Gonsalkorale, S., Hyde, M., and Mgaith, S. (2005). Helping students understand their learning styles. Effects on study self-efficacy, preferences for group work, and group climate. *Educational Psychology, 25*, 395–407.

Hewitt, J., and Scardamalia, M. (1998). Design principles for distributed knowledge building processes. *Educational Psychology Review, 10*(1), 75–96.

Hiebert, J., Carpenter, T. P., Fennema, E., Fuson, K., Human, P., Murray, H., Olivier, A., and Wearne, D. (1996). Problem solving as a basis for reform in curriculum and instruction. The case of mathematics. *Educational Researcher, 25*(4), 12–21.

Higgins, S., Hall, E., Baumfield, V., Moseley, D. (2005). *A meta-analysis of the impact of the implementation of thinking skills approaches on pupils*. London: EPPI-Centre, Social Science Research Unit, Institute of Education, University of London. Available online at https://eppi.ioe.ac.uk/cms/Default.aspx?tabid=339 (accessed 14 January 2014).

Higgins, S., Katsipataki, M., Kokotsaki, D., Coleman, R., Major, L. E. and Coe, R. (2013). *The Sutton Trust – Education endowment foundation teaching and learning toolkit*. London: Education Endowment Foundation. Available online at http://educationendowmentfoundation.org.uk/index.php/toolkit (accessed 5 May 2014).

Higgs, J., and Hunt, A. (1999). Rethinking the beginning practitioner: 'the interactional professional', in J. Higgs and H. Edwards (Eds), *Educating beginning practitioners: Challenges for health professionals* (pp. 10–18). Oxford: Butterworth-Heinemann.

Higgs, J., and Titchen, A. (2001). *Professional practice in health, education and the creative arts*. Oxford: Blackwell.

Hill, D. (n.d.) Critical reflection in early childhood education: a framework for personal and professional empowerment. University of Auckland. New Zealand. Available online at https://www.google.co.uk/#q=Hill+critical+reflection (accessed 19 March 2014).

Hinton, C., Miyamoto, K., and della Chiesa, B. (2008). Brain research, learning and emotions: Implications for education research, policy and practice. *European Journal of Education, 43*(1), 87–103.

Hobbs, V. (2007). Faking it or hating it: Can reflective practice be forced? *Reflective Practice, 8*(3), 405–417.

Hodgkinson, G. P., Herriot, P., and Anderson, N. (2001). Re-aligning the stakeholders in management research: lessons from industrial, work and organizational psychology. *British Journal of Management, 12*, Special Issue, S41-S48.

Hodgkinson, G. P., and Sadler-Smith, E. (2003). Complex or unitary: A critique and empirical reassessment of The Cognitive Style Index. *Journal of Occupational and Organisational Psychology,* 76, 243-68.

Holzman, P. S. (1954). The relation of assimilation tendencies in visual, auditory, and kinaesthetic time error to cognitive attitude of levelling and sharpening. *Journal of Personality, 22*, 375–394.

Hong, J. Y. (2010). Pre-service and beginning teachers' professional identity and its relation to dropping out of the profession. *Teaching and Teacher Education, 26*, 1530–1543.

Hounsell, D. (2007). Towards more sustainable feedback to students. In D. Boud and N. Falchikov (Eds), *Rethinking assessment in higher education* (pp. 101–113). London: Routledge.

Hounsell, D., McCune, V., Hounsell, J., and Litjens, J. (2008). The quality of guidance and feedback to students. *Higher Education Research and Development, 27*, 55–67.

Howard-Jones, P. (2010). *Introducing neuroeducational research.* London and New York: Routledge.

Hoyle, E. (1975). Professionality, professionalism and control in teaching. In V. Houghton, R Mc Hugh, and C. Morgan. (Eds) *Management in Education: The Management of Organisationsand Individuals* (pp. 314–320). London: Ward Lock Educational in association with Open University Press.

Hoyrup, S., and Elkjaer, B. (2006). Reflection: Taking it beyond the individual. In D. Boud, P. Cressey, and P. Docherty (Eds), *Productive reflection and learning at work* (pp. 29–42). London: Routledge.

Huber, M. T., Brown C., Hutchings, P. Gale, R., Miller, R., and Breen, M. (Eds) (2007). *Integrative learning: Opportunities to connect.* Public report of the integrative learning project sponsored by the Association of American Colleges and Universities and The Carnegie Foundation for the Advancement of Teaching. Available online at http://www.gallery.carnegiefoundation.org/ilp (accessed 10 January 2013).

Huitt, W. G. (2013). *Ed psych interactive.* Available online at http://www.edpsycinteractive.org/materials/elecfile.html (accessed 1 May 2014).

Hull, C. L. (1951). *Essentials of behavior.* New Haven, CT: Yale University Press.

Ifanti, A. A., and Fotopoulopou, V. S. (2011). Teachers' perceptions of professionalism and professional development: A case study in Greece. *World Journal of Education, 1*(1), 40–51.

Illeris, K. (2007). *How we learn. Learning and non-learning in schools and beyond.* London: Routledge.

Illeris, K. (Ed.) (2009). *Contemporary learning theories.* London: Routledge.

Institute for Learning. Available online at http://www.ifl.ac.uk/publications/challenging-professional-learning (accessed 14 January 2014).

International Centre for Educators' Learning Styles. Available online at http://www.icels-educators-for learning.ca/index.php?option=com_content and view=article and id=54and Itemid=73 (accessed 12 January 2014).

Issitt, I. M. (2000). Critical professionals and reflective practice: The experience of women practitioners in health, welfare and education. In J. Batsleer and B. Humphries (Eds), *Welfare, exclusion and political agency* (pp. 116–133). London: Routledge.

Ixer, G. (2000). 'Assessing reflective practice.' *Journal of Practice Teaching in Social Work and Practice, 2*(3), 19–27.

Ixer, G. (2003) Developing the relationship between reflective practice & social work values. *Journal of Practice Teaching*, 5(1), 7–22.

Jackson, A., and Davis, G. (2000). *Turning points 2000: Educating adolescents in the twenty-first century.* New York: Teachers College Press.

Jakhelln, R. (2011). Early career teachers' emotional experiences and development – a Norwegian case study, *Professional Development in Education, 37*(2), 275–290.

James, M. (2006). Learning how to learn, in classrooms, schools and networks. *Research Papers in Education*, 21(2), 101–234.

James, M. (2006). Assessment, teaching and theories of learning. In Gardner, J. (Ed.) *Assessment and learning* (pp. 47–60). London, Sage.

James, M., and Pedder, D. (2006). Beyond method: Assessment and learning practices and values. *The Curriculum Journal*, 17(1), 109–138.

James, M., and Pollard, A. (2006). *Improving Teaching and Learning in Schools: A TLRP Commentary.* London, TLRP.

Jarvis, P. (2009). Learning to be a person in society: Learning to be me. In K. Illeris (Ed.), *Contemporary theories of learning* (pp. 21–34). London: Routledge.

Jaworski, B. (1993). *Constructivism and teaching – The socio-cultural context.* Available online at http://www.grout.demon.co.uk/Barbara/chreods.htm? (accessed 4 December 2013).

Jay, J. K. and Johnson, K. L. (2002). Capturing complexity: A typology of reflective practice for teacher education. *Teaching and Teacher Education, 18*, 73–85.

Jensen, K. (2007). The desire to learn: An analysis of knowledge seeking practices among professionals. *Oxford Review of Education, 33*(4), 489–502.

Johns, C. (1994). A philosophical basis for nursing practice. In C. Johns (ed.) *The Burford NDU model: Caring in practice*. Oxford: Blackwell Scientific Publications.

Johns, C. (2000). *Becoming a reflective practitioner*. Oxford: Blackwell.

Johns, C. (2002). *Guided reflection: Advancing practice*. Oxford: Blackwell Publishing.

Johns, C. (2006). *Engaging reflection in practice: A narrative approach*. Oxford: UK: Blackwell Publishing.

Johns, C. (2007). Reflective practice, effective practice. *Reflections on Nursing Leadership*. Online. Available HTTP 10/1/08 http://www2.nursingsociety.org/RNL/3Q_2007/features/feature3.html (accessed 10 March 2014).

Johnstone, A. H. (1997). Chemistry teaching, science or alchemy? *Journal of Chemical Education, 74*, 262–8.

Jones, M. M., and McLean, K. J. (2012). Personalising learning in teacher education through the use of technology. *Australian Journal of Teacher Education, 37*(1), 75–92.

Joughin, G. (2009). The hidden curriculum revisited: A critical review of research into the influence of summative assessment on learning. *Assessment and Evaluation in Higher Education, 35*, 335–345.

Jung, C. G. (1923). *Psychological types*. New York: Harcourt Brace.

Kagan, J. (1965). Individual differences in the resolution of response uncertainty. *Journal of Personality and Social Psychology, 2*, 154–160.

Kagan, J. (1966). Reflection-impulsivity: The generality and dynamics of conceptual tempo. *Journal of Abnormal Psychology, 71*, 17–24.

Kagan, J. Rosman, B. L., Day, D., Albert, J., and Phillips, W. (1964). Information processing in the child: Significance of analytic and reflective attitudes. *Psychological Monographs, 78*(1), No. 578.

Karagiannopoulou, E., and Christodoulides, P. (2005). The impact of Greek university students' perceptions of their learning environment on approaches to studying and academic outcomes. *International Journal of Educational Research, 43*(6), 329–350.

Kavale, K. A., Hirshoren, A., and Forness, S. R. (1998). Meta-analytic validation of the Dunn and Dunn model of learning-style preferences: A critique of what was Dunn. *Learning Disabilities Research and Practice, 13*, 75–80.

Keating, D. P., and Hertzman, C. (1999). Modernity's paradox, in: D. P. Keating and C. Hertzman (Eds), *Developmental health and the wealth of nations: social, biological and educational dynamics* (pp. 1–17). New York: The Guilford Press.

Keesee, G. S. (2012). Teaching and learning resources. Available online at http://teachinglearningresources.pbworks.com/w/page/19919565/Learning%20Theories (accessed 4 January 2014).

Kek, M., and Huijser, H. (2011). Exploring the combined relationships of student and teacher factors on learning approaches and self-directed learning readiness at a Malaysian university. *Studies in Higher Education, 36*(2), 185–208.

Kelchtermans, G. (2009). Who I am in how I teach is the message: Self-understanding, vulnerability and reflection. *Teachers and Teaching: Theory and Practice, 15*(2), 257–272.

Keller, J. M., and Deimann, M. (2012). Motivation, volition, and performance. In R. A. Reiser and J. V. Dempsey (Eds), *Trends and Issues in Instructional Design and Technology* (3rd ed.). Boston: Pearson Education.

Kelly, P. (2006). What is teacher learning? A socio-cultural perspective. *Oxford Review of Education, 32*(4), 505–519.

Kim, H. S. (1999). Critical reflective inquiry for knowledge development of nursing practice. *Journal of Advanced Nursing, 29*(5), 1205–12.

Kim, M. (2009). The impact of an elaborated assessee's role in peer assessment. *Assessment and Evaluation in Higher Education, 34*, 105–114.

Kirton, M. J. (1976). Adaptors and innovators, a description and measure. *Journal of Applied Psychology*, 61, 622–629.

Klein, G. S. (1951). A personal world through perception. In R. R. Blake and G. V. Ramsey (Eds), *Perception: An approach to personality* (pp. 328–355). New York, MY: Ronald Press.

Klein, G. S., Gardner, R. W. and Schlesinger, N. J. (1962). Tolerance for unrealistic experience: A study of the generality of a cognitive control. *British Journal of Psychology*, 53, 41–55.

Klein, P. D. (2003). Rethinking the multiplicity of cognitive resources and curricular representations: alternatives to 'learning styles' and 'multiple intelligences'. *Journal of Curriculum Studies, 35*(1), 45–81.

Knight, P., and Yorke, M. (2003). *Assessment, learning and employability*. Maidenhead: SRHE/Open University Press.

Koffka. K. (1922). Perception: An introduction to the Gestalt-theorie. *Psychological Bulletin, 19*, 531–585.

Köhler, W. (1939). *The place of value in a world full of facts*. London: Kegal Paul, Trench, Trubner and Co. Ltd.

Kolb, A. Y., and Kolb, D. A. (2005). *The Kolb Learning Style Inventory – Version 3.1: 2005 technical specifications*. Boston, MA: Haygroup.

Kolb, D. A. (n.d.). On experiential learning. Available online at http://infed.org/mobi/david-a-kolb-on-experiential-learning/ (accessed 3 March 2014).

Kolb, D. A. (1971). *Individual learning styles and the learning process*. Working Paper 535–71. MIT Sloan School of Management, Cambridge, MA: MIT Sloan School of Management.

Kolb, D. A. (1976). *Learning style inventory. Technical manual*. Boston, MA: Institute for Development Research.

Kolb, D. A. (1984). *Experiential learning. Experience as the sources of learning and development*. Englewood Cliffs, NJ: Prentice Hall.

Kolb, D. A., and Fry, R. (1975). Toward an applied theory of experiential learning. In C. Cooper (Ed.), *Theories of group process*. London: John Wiley.

Kolloffel, B. (2012). Exploring the relation between visualizer-verbalizer cognitive styles and performance with visual or verbal learning material. *Computers and Education, 58*(2), 697–706.

Kolsaker, A. (2008). Academic professionalism in the managerialist era: A study of English universities. *Studies in Higher Education*, 33 (5), 513–525.

Koopman, M., Den Brok, P. Beijaard, D., and Teune, P. (2011). Learning processes of students in pre-vocational secondary education: Relations between goal orientations, information processing strategies and development of conceptual knowledge. *Learning and Individual Differences, 21*(4), 426–431.

Korthagen, F. A. J. (2005). The organization in balance: Reflection and intuition as complementary processes. *Management Learning, 36*, 371–387.

Koschmann, T. (1999). *Toward a dialogic theory of learning: Bakhtin's contribution to understanding learning in settings of collaboration*. Paper presented at the CSCL'99, Palo Alto, 1999.

Kosnik, C., and Beck, C. (2009). *Priorities in teacher education: The 7 key elements of pre-service preparation*. New York: Routledge.

Kosslyn, S., and Miller, W. (2013). *Top brain, bottom brain: Surprising insights*. New York: Simon and Schuster. Available online at http://topbrainbottombrain.blogspot.co.uk/ (accessed 17 January 2014).

Kozhevnikov, M. (2007). Cognitive styles in the framework of modern psychology: toward an integrated framework of cognitive style. *Psychological Bulletin, 133*, 464–481. Available online at http://nmr.mgh.harvard.edu/mkozhevnlab/wp-content/uploads/pdfs/cognitive_styles2007.pdf (accessed 20 April 2014)

Kozhevnikov, M., Evans, C., and Kosslyn, S. (2014). Cognitive style as environmentally-sensitive individual differences in cognition: A modern synthesis and applications in education, business and management. *Psychological Sciences in the Public Interest, 15(1), 3–33.*

Kozhevnikov, M., Kozhevnikov, M., Yu, C. J., and Blazhenkova, O. (2013). Creativity, visualization abilities, and visual cognitive style. *British Journal of Educational Psychology, 83*, 196–209.

Krapp, A. (2005). Basic needs and the development of interest and intrinsic motivational orientations. *Learning and Instruction 15*, 381–395.

Kuncel, N. R., Hezlett, S. A., and Ones, D. S. (2004). Academic performance, career potential, creativity, and job performance: Can one construct predict them all? *Journal of Personality and Social Psychology, 86*, 148–161.

Kuyken, W., Weare, K., Ukoumunee, O. C., Vicary, R., Motton, N., Burnett, R., Cullen, C., Hennelly, S., and Huppert, F. (2013). Effectiveness of the mindfulnessin schools programme: Non-randomised controlled feasibility study. *The British Journal of Psychiatry, 9203*(2), 126–131.

Kyndt, E., Dochy, F., Struyven, K., and Cascallar, E. (2011). The perception of workload and task complexity and its influence on students' approaches to learning: A study in higher education. *European Journal of Psychology of Education, 26*(3), 393–415.

Lalley, J. P., and Gentile, J. R. (2009). Adapting instruction to individuals: Based on the evidence, what should it mean? *International Journal of Teaching and Learning in Higher Education, 20*(3), 462–475.

Lam, A. (2000). Tacit knowledge, organisational learning and societal institutions: An integrated framework. *Organisational Studies, 21*(3), 487–513.

Lamote, C., and Engels, N. (2010). The professional development of student teachers' professional identity. *European Journal of Teacher Education, 33*(1), 3–18.

Landrum, T. J., and McDuffie, K. A. (2010). Learning styles in the age of differentiated instruction. *Exceptionality, 18*(1), 6–17.

Larrivee, B. (2000). Transforming teaching practice: becoming the critically reflective teacher. *Reflective Practice, 1*(3), 293–307.

Lasky, S. (2005). A sociocultural approach to understanding teacher identity, agency and professional vulnerability in a context of secondary school reform. *Teaching and Teacher Education, 21*, 899–916.

Lave, J. (1993). The practice of learning. In S. Chaiklin and J. Lave (Eds), *Understanding practice: perspectives on activity and context* (pp. 3–32). Cambridge: Cambridge University Press.

Lave, J. (2009). The practice of learning. In K. Illeris (Ed.), *Contemporary learning theories* (pp. 200–208). London: Routledge.

Lave, J., and Wenger, E. (1991). *Situated learning: Legitimate peripheral participation*. Cambridge: Cambridge University Press.

Leach, J., and Moon, B. (Eds) (1999). *Learners and pedagogy*. London: Paul Chapman Publishing.

Leach, J., and Moon, B. (2008). *The power of pedagogy*. London: Sage.

Leadbeater, C. (2003). *Personalisation through participation*. London: Demos.

Leadbeater, C. (2005). *The shape of things to come: Personalised learning through collaboration*. Available online at http://www.innovationunit.org/sites/default/files/The%20shape%20of%20things%20to%20come.pdf (accessed 20 July 2007).

Leo, E., and Galloway, D. (1994). A questionnaire for identifying behavioural problems associated with maladaptive motivational style. *Educational and Child Psychology, 11*(2), 91–99.

Leonard, N. H., Scholl, R. W., and Kowalski, K. B. (1999). Information processing style and decision making. *Journal of Organizational Behaviour, 20*, 407–420.

Leonardo, Z. (2004). Critical social theory and transformative knowledge: The functions of criticism in quality education. *Educational Researcher, 33*(6), 11–18.

Leontiev, A. N. (1981). *Problems of the development of mind*. Moscow: Progress Press.

Leung, D. Y. P., and Kember, D. (2003). The relationship between approaches to learning and reflection upon practice. *Educational Psychology, 23*(1), 61–71.

Lewin, K. (1935). *A dynamic theory of personality*. New York: McGraw-Hill.

Lewin, K. (1951). *Field theory in social science; selected theoretical papers*. New York: Harper and Row.

Liu, N. F., and Carless, D. (2006). Peer feedback: The learning element of peer assessment. *Teaching in Higher Education, 11*, 279–290.

Livingston, K. (2014). Teacher educators: Hidden professionals. *European Journal of Education, 49*(2), 218–232.

Loftus, S., and Higgs, J. (2010). Researching the individual in workplace research. *Journal of Education and Work, 23*(4), 377–388.

Lombardi, M. M. (2007). *Authentic learning for the 21st century: An overview*. ELI paper 1. Available online at http://www.educause.edu/library/resources/authentic-learning-21st-century-overview (accessed 6 September 2013).

Lortie, R. (1975). *Schoolteacher*. Chicago, IL: University of Chicago Press.

Lovat, T., Dally, K., Clement, N., and Toomey, R. (2011). Values pedagogy and teacher education: Re-conceiving the foundations. *Australian Journal of Teacher Education, 36*(7), 31–44.

Loyens, S. M. M., Rikers, R. M. J. P., and Schmidt, H. G. (2007). Students' conceptions of distinct constructivist assumptions. *European Journal of Psychology of Education, 12,* 179–199.

Loyens, S. M. M., Rikers, R. M. J. P., and Schmidt, H. G. (2008). Relationships between students' conceptions of constructivist learning and their regulation and processing strategies. *Instructional Science, 36,* 445–462.

Lucas, P. (2012). *Critical reflection. What do we really mean?* Australian Collaborative Education Network (ACEN Inc). Available online at http://acen.edu.au/2012conference/wp-content/uploads/2012/11/92_Critical-reflection.pdf. (accessed 10 May 2013).

L2L: Learning how to learn. Available online at http://www.open.edu/openlearn/education/learning-how-learn/content-section-0 (accessed 10 August 2013).

Mackenzie, C. (2002). Critical reflection, self-knowledge, and the emotions. *Philosophical Explorations,* 5(3), 186–206.

Macnamara, B. N., Hambrick, D. Z., and Oswald, F. L. (2014). Deliberate practice and performance in Music, Games, Sports, Education, and Professions. A meta-analysis. *Psychological Science, 25*(8), 1608–1618.

Martin, S. (2010). Teachers using learning styles: Torn between research and accountability? *Teaching and Teacher Education: An International Journal of Research and Studies, 26*(8), 1583–1591.

Marton, F. (1975). On non-verbatim learning: I. Level of processing and level of outcome. *Scandinavian Journal of Psychology, 16,* 273–279.

Marton, F., Dall'Alba, G., and Beaty, E. (1993). Conceptions of learning. *International Journal of Educational Research, 19,* 277−300.

Marton, F., and Saljö, R. (1976). On qualitative differences in learning, outcome and process. *British Journal of Educational Psychology, 46,* 4–11.

Mayer, R. E. (2009). Advances in applying the science of learning and instruction to education. *Psychological Science In The Public Interest, 9*(3), i-ii.

Mayer, R. E. (2011). Does style research have useful implications for educational practice? *Learning and Individual Differences, 21*(3), 319–320.

Mayer, R. E., and Moreno, R. (2003). Nine ways to reduce cognitive load in multimedia learning. *Educational Psychologist, 38*(1), 43–52.

McClure, P. (2004). Making practice-based learning work: Reflection on practice. School of Health Sciences, University of Ulster: FDTL Phase 4, project no 174/02. Available online at http://cw.routledge.com/textbooks/9780415537902/data/learning/8_Reflection%20in%20Practice.pdf (accessed 3 March 2014).

McCune, V., and Entwistle, N. (2011). Cultivating the disposition to understand in 21st century university education. *Learning and Individual Differences, 21*(3), 303–310.

McJackson. Resources relating to differentiation. Available online at http://mcjackson.iweb.bsu.edu/ (accessed 5 May 2014).

McLaren, P. M., and Kincheloe, J. L. (2007). (Eds) *Critical pedagogy: Where are we now?* New York: Peter Lang.

McManus, J. (2011). *A new wave of sensation: the critical role emotions play in critical reflection.* Presentation OLKC Making Waves conference, 12–14 April, 2011, Hull: Hull University Business School Available online at https://www.yumpu.com/en/document/view/15636241/a-new-wave-of-sensation-the-critical-role-emotions- and at http://www2.warwick.ac.uk/fac/soc/wbs/conf/olkc/archive/olkc6/papers/id_252.pdf (accessed 10 March 2014)

McTighe, J., and Brown, J. (2005). Differentiated instruction and educational standards: Is détente possible? *Theory into Practice, 44*(3), 234–244.

Menaker, E. S., and Coleman, S. L. (2007). Learning styles again: Where is empirical evidence? Interservice Industry Training: Simulation and Education Conference (I/ITSEC), Paper no. 7426. The sixteenth mental measurements yearbook. Available online at http://www.unl.edu/buros. (accessed 3 March 2013).

Merrill, M. D. (1994). *Instructional design theory*. Englewood Cliffs: Educational Technology Publications.

Messick, S. (1970). The criterion problem in the evaluation of instruction: Assessing possible, not just intended, outcomes. In: M. C. Wiltrock and D. E. Wiley (Eds). *The evaluation of instruction: Issues and Problems*. New York, MY: Holt, Rinehart and Winston.

Messick, S. (1976). Personality consistencies in cognition and creativity. In S. Messick (Eds), *Individuality in learning* (pp. 4–23). San Francisco: Jossey-Bass.

Messick, S. (1984). The nature of cognitive styles: Problems and promise in educational practice. *Educational Psychologist, 29*, 121–136.

Mezirow, J. (1990). *Fostering critical reflection in adulthood. A guide to transformative and emancipatory learning. How critical reflection triggers transformative learning*. Available online at http://www.ln.edu.hk/osl/conference2011/output/breakout/4.4%20[ref]How%20Critical%20Reflection%20triggers%20Transformative%20Learning%20-%20Mezirow.pdf

Mezirow, J. (1991). *Transformative dimensions of adult learning*. San Francisco: Jossey Bass. Mezirow, J. (2000). Learning to think like an adult. Core concepts of transformation theory. In J. Mezirow and associates, *Learning as transformation: Critical perspectives on a theory in progress* (pp. 3–33). San Francisco: Jossey Bass.

Micari, M., and Light, G. (2009). Reliance to independence: Approaches to learning in peer-led undergraduate science, technology, engineering, and mathematics workshops. *International Journal of Science Education, 31*(13), 1713–1741.

Miller, A. (1987). Cognitive styles: An integrated model. *Educational Psychology*, 7: 251–268.

Mindfulness in Schools. Available online at http://mindfulnessinschools.org/; http://mindfulnessinschools.org/research/research-evidence-mindfulness-schools-project/ (accessed 14 May 2014).

Minear, M., and Shah, P. (2006). Sources of working memory deficits in children and possibilities for remediation. In S. J. Pickering (Ed.), *Working memory and education* (pp. 274–298). Oxford: Academic Press.

Moore, A. (2000). Teaching and learning. *Pedagogy, curriculum and culture*. London: Routledge.

Moran, A. (2009). Can a competence or standards model facilitate an inclusive approach to teacher education? *International Journal of Inclusive Education, 13*(1), 45–61.

Morgan, C., and Morris, G. (1999). *Good teaching and learning: Pupils and teachers speak*. Philadelphia, PA: Open University Press.

Mortimore, P. (Ed.) (1999). *Understanding pedagogy and its impact on learning*. London: Paul Chapman Publishing Ltd.

Moskvina, V., and Kozhevnikov, M. (2011). Determining cognitive styles: Historical perspective and directions for further research. In S. Rayner, and E. Cools (Eds), *Style differences in cognition, learning, and management: Theory, research and practice* (pp. 19–31). New York: Routledge.

Mutton, T., Burn, K., and Hagger, H. (2010). Making sense of learning to teach: Learners in context. *Research Papers in Education, 25*(1), 73–91.

Myers, I. B. (1976). *Introduction to type*. Palo Alto, CA: Consulting Psychologist Press.

Myers, I. B. (1978). *Myers-Briggs Type Indicator*. Palo Alto, CA: Consulting Psychologists Press.

Myers, I. B., and McCaulley, M. N. (1985). *Manual: A Guide to the Development and Use of the Myers-Briggs Type Indicator*, Palo Alto, CA: Consulting Psychologist Press.

Myers, I. B., McCaulley, M. N., Quenk, N., and Hammer, A. (1998). *Manual: A guide to the development and use of the Myers-Briggs Type Indicator* (3rd Ed.). Palo Alto, CA: Consulting Psychologist Press.

Nasser-Abu Alhija, F., and Barbara Fresko, B. (2010). Socialization of new teachers: Does induction matter? *Teaching and Teacher Education, 26*(8), 1592–1597.

Nationmaster.com encyclopedia. Available online at http://www.nationmaster.com/encyclopedia/Critical-social-theory (accessed 4 January 2014).

NCSL (National College for School Leadership) (2004). *Personalised Learning* Special LDR Supplement, Nottingham: NCSL.

New Zealand Education Ministry. Available online at http://assessment.tki.org.nz/Assessment-in-the-classroom/Readings-on-formative-assessment (accessed 10 July 2013).

Newcombe, N. S., and Stieff, M. (2012). Six myths about spatial thinking. *International Journal of Science Education, 34*(6), 955–971.

Niaz, M., Aguilera, D., Maza, A., and Liendo, G. (2002). Arguments, contradictions, resistances and conceptual change in students' understanding of atomic structure. *Science Education, 86*, 505–525.

Nicol, D. (2008). *Transforming assessment and feedback: Enhancing integration and empowerment in the first year*. Scotland: Quality Assurance Agency.

Nicol, D., and Macfarlane-Dick, D. (2004). *Rethinking formative assessment in HE: A theoretical model and seven principles of good feedback practice*. Available online at http://www.heacademy.ac.uk/assets/York/documents/ourwork/assessment/web0015_rethinking_formative_assessment_in_he.pdf (accessed 10 August 2011).

Nicol, D. J., & MacFarlane-Dick (2006). Formative assessment and self-regulated learning: A model and seven principles of good feedback practice. *Studies in Higher Education, 31*, 199–218.

Nieto, S., (2001). Critical pedagogy, empowerment and learning. In J., Collins, K., Insley, and J., Soler, (2001) (Eds)., *Developing Pedagogy: Researching Practice* (pp. 39–49). London: Paul Chapman Publishing and OU Press.

Nielsen, T. (2012). A historical review of the styles literature. In L. F. Zhang, R. J. Sternberg, and S. Rayner (2012). *The handbook of intellectual styles* (pp. 21–46). New York. NY: Springer.

Nixon, J., Martin, J., Mc Keown, P., and Ranson, S. (1997). Towards a learning profession: Changing codes of occupational practice within the new management of education. *British Journal of Sociology of Education, 18*(1), 5–28.

Noddings, N. (1992). *The challenge to care in schools: An alternative approach to Education*. NewYork, NY, Teachers College Press.

Nordlund, M. (2003). *Differentiated instruction: Meeting the educational needs of all students in your classroom*. Lanham, MD: Scarecrow Press.

Nosal, C. S. (1990). Psychologicznemodeleumyslu [Psychological models of mind]. Warsaw, Poland: PWN.

Nussbaum, J., and Novick, S. (1982). Alternative frameworks, conceptual conflict and accommodation. Toward a principled teaching strategy. *Instructional Science, 11*, 183–200.

O'Brien, M. (2002). *New pedagogies in the knowledge society: Why this challenge is an epistemological one*. AARE International Conference 2002, 2–6 December Brisbane, Australia.

O'Brien, T. (2000). Providing inclusive differentiation. In P. Benton and T. O'Brien (Eds), *Special needs and the beginning teacher*. London: Continuum.

O' Brien, T., and Guiney, D. (2001). *Differentiation in teaching and learning principles and practice*. London and New York: Continuum.

OECD (2007). *Understanding the brain: The birth of a learning science*. Paris, OECD Publishing). Available online at http://www.oecd.org/site/educeri21st/40554190. (accessed 12 January 2014).

OECD (2010). PISA 2009 results: Learning to learn – Student engagement, strategies and practices (Vol. III). Available online at http://dx.doi.org/10.1787/9789264083943-en (accessed 10 January 2012).

OECD (2013). *Synergies for Better Learning: An international perspective on evaluation and assessment*. Available online at http://www.oecd.org/education/school/oecdreviewonevaluationandassessmentframeworksforimprovingschooloutcomes.htm. Further information available: http://www.oecd.org/edu/school/Synergies%20for%20Better%20Learning_Summary.pdf. (accessed 10 December 2013).

Ofsted (2012). *Initial Teacher Education (ITE) inspection handbook*. Manchester: The Office for Standards in Education, Children's Services and Skills. Available online at www.ofsted.gov.uk/resources/120028 (accessed 9 September 2013).

Ofsted (2013). The framework for school inspection. Manchester: The Office for Standards in Education, Children's Services and Skills. Available online at www.ofsted.gov.uk/resources/120100 (accessed 9 December 2013).

Orlich, D., Harder, R., Callahan, R., Trevisan, M., and Brown, A. (2004). *Teaching strategies: A guide to effective instruction* (7th ed.). Boston, MA: Houghton Mifflin.

Orsmond, P., Merry, S., and Callaghan, A. (2004). Implementation of a formative assessment model incorporating peer and self-assessment. *Innovations in Education and Teaching International, 41*, 273–290.

Overton, T. L., and Potter, N. M. (2011). Investigating students' success in solving and attitudes towards context-rich open-ended problems in chemistry. *Chemistry Education, Research and Practice, 12*, 294–302.

Ozgen, K., Tataroglu, B., and Alkan, H. (2011). An examination of multiple intelligence domains and learning styles of pre-service mathematics teachers: Their reflections on mathematics education. *Educational Research and Reviews, 6*(2), 168–181.

Packer, M. J., and Goicoechea, J. (2000). Sociocultural and constructivist theories of learning: Ontology, not just epistemology. *Educational Psychologist, 35*(4), 227–241.

Paivio, A. (1971). *Imagery and verbal processes*. Oxford: Holt, Rinehart & Winston.

Paivio, A. (1986). *Mental representations: A dual coding approach*. Oxford: Oxford University Press.

Paivio, A. (2006). *Mind and its evolution: A dual coding theoretical approach*. London: Routledge.

Paivio, A., and Csapo, K. (1973). Picture superiority in free recall: Imagery or dual coding? *Cognitive Psychology, 5*, 176–206.

Parker, P., and Baughan, P. (2009). Providing written assessment feedback that students will value and read. *International Journal of Learning, 16*, 253–262.

Parsons, T. (1937). Remarks on education and the professions. *International journal of ethics, 47*(3), 365–369.

Pashler, H., McDaniel, M., Rowher, D., and Bjork, R. (2009). Learning styles: concepts and evidence. *Psychological Science in the Public Interest, 9*, 105–119.

Pavlov, I. P., and Anrep, G. V. (1927). *Conditioned reflexes*. London: Oxford University Press.

Pearce, J., and Morrison, C. ((2011) Teacher identity and early career resilience: Exploring the links. *Australian Journal of Teacher Education, 36*(1), Article 4.

Pedder, F., James, M., and MacBeath, J. (2005). How teachers value and practise professional learning. *Research Papers in Education, 20*(3), 209–243.

Pekrun, R. (2006). The control-value theory of achievement emotions: Assumptions, corollaries, and implications for educational research and practice. *Educational Psychology Review, 18*, 315–341.

Penney, D., and Waring, M., (2000). The Absent Agenda. Pedagogy and Physical Education. *Journal of Sport Pedagogy, 6*(1), 4–37.

Perera, N. C. (2011). *Constructivism, social constructivism and situated cognition: A sliding scale*. Available online at http://nishancperera.com/2011/01/31/constructivism-social-constructivism-and-situated-cognition-a-sliding-scale-by-nishan-perera/ (accessed 17 January 2014).

Perks, P., Prestage, S., and Edwards, A. (2005). Learning objectives: in a sociocultural activity system are they tools or rules? In D. Hewitt and A. Noyes (Eds), *Proceedings of the sixth British Congress of Mathematics Education* held at the University of Warwick, pp. 120–127. Available online at www.bsrlm.org.uk. (accessed 6 November 2013).

Perry, W. G., Jr. (1970). *Forms of intellectual and ethical development in the college years: A scheme*. New York: Holt, Rinehart, and Winston); reprinted November 1998: Jossey-Bass.

Perry, W. G., Jr. (1981). "Cognitive and ethical growth: The making of meaning", in Arthur W. Chickering and Associates, *The modern American college* (pp. 76–116). San Francisco: Jossey-Bass.

Peterson, E. R., Deary, I. J., and Austin, E. J. (2003). The reliability of Riding's Cognitive Styles Analysis test. *Personality and Individual Differences, 34*(5), 881–891.

Peterson, E., Brown, G. T. L., and Earl Irving, S. (2010). Secondary school students' conceptions of learning and their relationship to achievement. *Learning and Individual Differences, 20*, 167–176.

Peterson, E. R., Rayner, S. G., and Armstrong, S. J. (2009a). Researching the psychology of cognitive style and learning style: Is there really a future? *Learning and Individual Differences*, 19, 518–523.

Peterson, E. R., Rayner, S. G., and Armstrong, S. J (2009b). *Herding cats: In search of definitions of cognitive styles and learning styles*. ELSIN Newsletter, an international forum, Winter 2008–2009.

www.elsinnews.com, 10–12. ELSIN Newsletter, An International Forum, Winter 2008–2009, 10–12. Available online at http:// elsinnetwork.com/images/newsletters/2008elsinnewsletter.pdfm (accessed 20 August 2014).

Pettigrew, T. F. (1958). The measurement and correlates of category width as a cognitive variable. *Journal of Personality, 26*, 532–544.

Pham, H. L. (2012). Differentiated instruction and the need to integrate teaching and practice. *Journal of College Teaching and Learning, 9*(1), 13–20.

Piaget, J. (1952). *The origins of intelligence in children*. New York: International Universities Press.

Pintrich P. R. (2004). A conceptual framework for assessing motivation and self-regulated learning in college students. *Educational Psychology Review 16*(4), 385–407.

Pintrich, P. R., Smith, D. A., Garcia, T., and McKeachie, W. J. (1991). *A manual for the use of theMotivated Strategies for Learning Questionnaire (MSLQ)*. Technical report No. 91-B-004. Ann Arbor: University of Michigan.

Plucker, J. A. (Ed.) (2013). *Human intelligence: Historical influences, current controversies, teaching resources*. Available online at http://www.intelltheory.com http://www.intelltheory.com (accessed 6 January 2014).

Pollard, A. (Ed.) (2002). *Reflective teaching. Effective and evidence-informed professional practice*. London: Continuum.

Pollard, A. (Ed.) (2010). *Professionalism and pedagogy: A contemporary opportunity*. A commentary by TLRP and GTCE. London: TLRP. Available online at http://www.tlrp.org/pub/documents/TLRPGTCEProf and Pedagogy.pdf (accessed 10 September 2013).

Pollard, A. (Ed.) (2014). *Reflective teaching in schools*. London: Bloomsbury.

Pollard, A., and James, M. (Eds), (2004). *Personalised Learning, a Commentary by the Teaching and Learning Research Programme*. London: Economic and Social Research Council.

Poulson, L. and Wallace, M. (Eds) (2004). *Learning to read critically in teaching and learning*. London: Sage.

Prain, V., Cox, P. Deed, C., Dorman, J., Edwards, D., Farrelly, C., Keeffe, M., Lovejoy, V., Mow, L., Sellings, P., Waldrip, B., and Yager, Z (2013). Personalised learning: Lessons to be learnt. *British Educational Research Journal, 39*(4), *654–676*.

Price, M., Handley, K. Den Outer, B., and Millar, J. (2007). *Report on case studies conducted for the FDTL5 project: Engaging students with assessment feedback*. Available online at https://mwbrooked.ac.uk/display/eswaf?Case+Studies. (accessed 10 January 2009).

Price, M., Handley, K., Millar, J., and O'Donovan, B. (2010). Feedback: All that effort but what is the effect? *Assessment and Evaluation in Higher Education, 35*, 277– 289.

Prosser, M. (2004). A student learning perspective on problem-based learning. *European Journal of Dental Education, 8*, 51–58.

Purdie, N., and Hattie, J. (2002). Assessing students' conceptions of learning. *Australian Journal of Educational and Developmental Psychology, 2,* 17−32.

Putnam, R. (2000). *Bowling alone: the collapse and revival of American community*. New York: Simon and Schuster.

Puurula, A., and Löfström, E. (2003). Development of professional identity in SMEs. Paper presented at the Annual Meeting of the American Educational Research Association, Chicago, IL.

Pykett, J. (2010). Personalised governing through behaviour change and re-education. PSA Conference Paper, Edinburgh.

Quinn, F. M. (2000). Reflection and reflective practice. In C. Davies, L. Finlay and A. Bullman (Eds), *Changing practice in health and social care (pp. 81–90)*. London: Sage.

Raelin, J. A. (2001). Public reflection as the basis of learning. *Management Learning, 32*(1), 11–30.

Ramaprasad, A. (1983). On the definition of feedback. *Behavioral Science, 28*(1), 4–13.

Rayner, S. (2000). Reconstructing style differences in thinking and learning: Profiling learning performance. In R. Riding and S. Rayner (Eds), *International perspectives on individual differences. Volume 1: Cognitive styles* (pp. 115–180). Stamford, Connecticut: Ablex.

Redmond, B. (2004). *Reflection in Action: Developing reflective practice in health and social care services.* Aldershot: Ashgate Publications.

Renzulli, J. S., and Sullivan, E. E. (2009). Learning styles applied: Harnessing students' instructional style preferences. In L. F. Zhang and R. Sternberg (Eds), *Perspectives on the nature of intellectual styles* (pp. 209–232). NewYork, NY: Springer.

Research Centre for Learning to Learn. Available online at http://www.ncl.ac.uk/cflat/about/Learningtolearnresearch.htm (a accessed 30 September 2013).

Resnick, L. B. (1994). Situated rationalism: Biological and social preparation for learning. In L. A. Hirschfeld and S. A. Gelman (Eds). *Mapping the mind,* (pp. 474–494). New York: Cambridge University Press.

Reynolds, M., and Vince, R. (Eds) (2004). *Organizing reflection.* London: Ashgate.

Riding, R. J. (1991). *Cognitive Styles Analysis.* Birmingham: Learning and Training Technology.

Riding, R. J. (2000). Cognitive style: A strategic approach for advancement. In R. J. Riding and S. G. Rayner (Ends), *International Perspectives on Individual Differences. Volume 1: Cognitive Styles* (pp. 365–377). Stamford, CT: Able.

Riding, R., and Cheema, I. (1991). Cognitive styles—an overview and integration. *Educational Psychology, 11,* 193–216.

Riding, R., and Rayner, S. (1998). *Cognitive styles and learning strategies: Understanding style differences in learning and behaviour.* London: David Fulton.

Riegler, A. (2003). *The key to radical constructivism.* Available online at http://www.univie.ac.at/constructivism/key.html (accessed 10 January 2014).

Riener, C., and Willingham, D. (2010). The myth of learning styles. *Change, 42* (5), 32–35.

Ritter, L. (2007). Unfulfilled promises: How inventories, instruments and institutions subvert discourses of diversity and promote commonality. *Teaching in Higher Education, 12*(5 and 6), 569–579.

Rittschof, K. A. (2010). Field dependence-independence as visuospatial and executive functioning in working memory: Implications for instructional systems design and research. *Education Technology Research and Development, 58,* 99–114.

Rogoff, B. (1990). *Apprenticeship in thinking: Cognitive development in social context.* New York: Oxford University Press.

Rohrer, D., and Pashler, H. (2012). Learning styles: where's the evidence? *Medical Education, 46,* 630–635.

Rosenfeld, M., and Rosenfeld, S. (2011). Illustrating a complementary paradigm for styles research: From a third-person to a second-person perspective. In S. Rayner and E. Cools (Eds), *Style differences in cognition, learning, and management: Theory, research and practice* (pp. 143–159). New York: Routledge.

Ruddock, J., Brown, N., and Hendry, L. (2006). *Personalised learning and pupil voice. The East Sussex project.* Report. London: Department for Education and Skills.

Rust, C., O'Donovan, B., and Price, M. (2005). A social constructivist assessment process model: How the research literature shows us this could be best practice. *Assessment and Evaluation in Higher Education, 30,* 231–240.

Rutter, L. (2009). *Theory and practice within HE professional education courses: Integration of academic knowledge and experiential knowledge.* In 6th LDHEN Symposium 2009: The Challenge of Learning Development., 6–7 April 2009, Bournemouth University. (Unpublished).

Rychly, L., and Graves, E. (2012). Teacher characteristics for culturally responsive pedagogy. *Multicultural Perspectives, 14*(1), 44–49.

Sachs, J. (2003). Teacher Professional Standards: Controlling or developing teaching? *Teachers and Teaching: Theory and Practice, 9*(2), 175–186.

Sadler, D. R. (1989). Formative assessment and the design of instructional systems. *Instructional Science, 18,* 119–144.

Sadler, R. D. (2005). Interpretations of criteria-based assessment and grading in higher education. *Assessment and Evaluation in Higher Education, 30*(2), 175–194.

Sadler, D. R. (2010). Beyond feedback: Developing student capability in complex appraisal. *Assessment and Evaluation in Higher Education, 35*, 535–550.

Sadler-Smith, E. (2009). A duplex model of cognitive style. In L. F. Zhang and R. J. Sternberg (Eds), *Perspectives on the nature of intellectual styles* (pp. 3–28). Heidelberg: Springer.

Sadler-Smith, E. (2012). Metacognition and styles. In L. F. Zhang, R. J. Sternberg, and S. Rayner (Eds), *The handbook of intellectual styles* (pp. 153–172). New York: Springer.

Sadler-Smith, E., and Shefy, E. (2004). The intuitive executive: Understanding and applying 'gut feel' in decision-making. *Academy of Management Executive, 18*(4), 76–91.

Säljö, R. (1979a). Learning about learning. *Higher Education, 8*, 443−451.

Säljö, R. (1979b). *Learning from the learner's perspective. I: Some common sense conceptions (Rep. No. 76).* Göteborg, Sweden: University of Goteborg, Institute of Education.

Salomon, G. (Ed.) (1993). *Distributed cognitions. Psychological and educational considerations.* Cambridge: Cambridge University Press.

Salomon, G. (1994). *Interaction of media, cognition, and learning.* Hillsdale, NJ: Erlbaum.

Salomon, G., and Perkins, D. N. (1998). Individual and social aspects of learning. *Review of Research in Education, 23*, 1–24.

Sammons, P., Day, C., Kington, A., Gu, Q., Stobart, G., and Smees, R. (2007). Exploring variationsin teachers' work, lives and their effects on pupils: Key findings and implications from a longitudinal mixed-method study. *British Educational Research Journal, 33*(5), 681–702.

Santrock, J. W. (2006). *Educational psychology.* New York: McGraw Hill.

Saxe, G. B. (1991). *Culture and cognitive development: Studies in mathematical understanding.* Hillsdale, NJ: Erlbaum.

Schmeck, R. R. (Eds), (1988). *Learning strategies and learning styles.* New York and London: Plenum Press.

Schön, D. (1983). *The reflective practitioner: How professionals think in action.* London: Temple Smith.

Schön, D. A. (1987). Edu*cating the reflective practitioner.* San Francisco, CA: Jossey-Bass.

Schön, D. (Ed.) (1991). *The reflective turn. Case studies in and on educational practice.* New York: The Teachers College Press.

Schön, D. (1996). *The reflective practitioner: How professionals think in action.* Aldershot: Arena Ashgate.

Schwartz, B. (2013). The paradox of choice on TED. Available online at http://www.ted.com/speakers/barry_schwartz (accessed 10 May 2014).

Scott, C. (2010). The enduring appeal of "learning styles". *Australian Journal of Education, 54*(1), 5–17.

Scott, D., Hughes, G., Evans, C., Burke, P. J., Walter, C., and Watson, D. (2014). *Learning transitions in higher education.* London: Palgrave.

Scott, D., and Usher, R. (2011). *Researching education.* London and New York: Continuum.

Sebba, J., Brown, N., Steward, S., Galton, M., James, M., Celentano, N., and Boddy, P. (2007). *An investigation of personalised learning approaches used by schools.* Sussex: University of Sussex and DfES.

Segers, M., Gijbels, D., and Thurlings, M. (2008). The relationship between students' perceptions of portfolio assessment practice and their approaches to learning. *Educational Studies, 34*(1), 35–44.

Segers, M., and DeGreef, M. (2011). Transformational learning: The perspective of J. Mezirow In F. Dochy, D. Gijbels, M. Segers and P. Van Den Bossche, *Theories of learning for the workplace* (pp. 37–51). London and New York: Routledge.

Segers, M., and Van de Haar, S. (2011). The experiential learning theory: D. Kolb and D. Boud. In F. Dochy, D. Gijbels, M. Segers and P. Van Den Bossche, *Theories of learning for the workplace* (pp. 52–65). London and New York: Routledge.

Seifert, T. (2004). Understanding student motivation. *Educational Research, 46*(2), 137–149.

Sfard, A. (1998). On two metaphors for learning and the dangers of choosing just one. *Educational Researcher, 27*(2), 4–13.

Shandomo, H. M. (2010). The role of critical reflection in teacher education. *School-University Partnerships, 4*(1) (Spring), 101–113. Available online at http://files. eric.ed. gov/fulltext/ EJ915885. pdf (accessed 3 March 2014).

Shanks, R., Robson, D., and Gray, D. (2012). New teachers' individual learning dispositions: A Scottish case study. *International Journal of Training and Development, 16*(3), 183–199.

Sharp, J. G., Bowker, R., and Byrne, J. (2008). VAK or vak-ous? Towards the trivialisation of learning and the death of scholarship. *Research Papers in Education, 23*(3), 293–314.

Sharp, P., Ainslie, T., Hemphill, A., Hobson, S., Merriman, C., Ong, P., and Roche, J. (2006). Making problem-based learning work: Mentoring. A resource for those who facilitate placement learning. School of Health and Social Care, Oxford Brookes University. Available online at http://www.inclentrust.org/uploadedbyfck/file/compile%20resourse/new-resourse-dr_-vishal/Practice-Based%20learning.pdf (accessed 3 March 2014).

Shulman, L. (1999). Taking learning seriously. *Change, 31*(4), 10–17.

Shulman, L. (2005). The signature pedagogies of the professions of Law, Medicine, Engineering, and the Clergy: Potential lessons for the education of teachers. Presented at the Maths Science Partnership (MSP) Workshop: 'Teacher education for effective teaching and learning'. Hosted by the National Research Council's Centre for Education, February 6–8, 2005, Irvine, California.

Signorini, P., Wiesemes, R., and Murphy, R. (2009). Developing alternative frameworks for exploring intercultural learning: A critique of Hofstede's cultural differences model. *Teaching in Higher Education, 14*(3), 253–264.

Silén, C., and Uhlin, L. (2008). Self-directed learning – A learning issue for students and faculty. *Teaching in Higher Education, 13*(4), 461–75.

Simon, H. A., and Chase, W. G. (1973). Skill in chess. *American Scientist, 61*, 394–403.

Skinner, B. F. (1953). *Science and human behaviour.* New York: Macmillan.

Sluijsmans, D. M. A., Brand-Gruwel, S., and Van Merrienböer, J. J. G. (2002). Peer assessment training in teacher education: Effects on performance and perceptions. *Assessment and Evaluation in Higher Education, 27*, 443–454.

Smith, E. (2011). Teaching critical reflection. *Teaching in Higher Education, 16*(2), 211–223.

Smith, M. K. (2003). Learning theory. In *The encyclopedia of informal education.* Available online at http://infed.org/mobi/learning-theory-models-product-and-process/ (accessed 29 December, 2013). (Original work published1999.)

Smyth, J. (1987). *Educating teachers: Changing the nature of pedagogical knowledge.* Lewes: Falmer Press.

Smyth, J. (1989). Developing and sustaining critical reflection in teacher education. *Journal of Teacher Education, 40*(2), 2–9.

Smyth, J. (1992). Teachers' work and the politics of reflection. *American Educational Research Journal,* 29(2), 267–300.

Smyth, J. (1993). Reflective practice in teacher education. *Australian Journal of Teacher Education, 18*(1). Available online at http://dx.doi.org/10.14221/ajte.1993v18n1.2 (accessed 17 August, 2014).

Snow, R. E., and Lohman, D. F. (1984). Toward a theory of cognitive aptitude for learning from instruction. *Journal of Educational Psychology, 76*, 347–376.

Snyder, W. M., and Wenger, E. (2004). Our world as a learning system: A communities-of-practice approach. In M. L. Conner, and J. G. Clawson (Eds). *Create a learning culture: Strategy, practice, and technology* (pp. 35–58). Cambridge: Cambridge University Press.

Soja, E. W. (1996). *Thirdspace: Journeys to Los Angeles and other real-and-imagined places.* Oxford: Blackwell.

Solvie, P., and Sungur, E. (2012). Teaching for success: Technology and learning styles in preservice teacher education. Contemporary issues in technology and teacher education. *CITE Journal, 12*(1), 6–40.

St. Clair-Thompson, H., Overton, T., and Botton, C. (2010). Information processing: A review of implications of Johnstone's model for science education. *Research in Science and Technological Education, 28*(2), 131–148.

Stamovlasis, D., and Tsaparlis, G. (2005). Cognitive variables in problem-solving: A nonlinear approach. *International Journal of Science and Mathematics Education, 3*, 7–32.

Stanford Encyclopedia of Philosophy. Available online at http://plato.stanford.edu/entries/critical-theory/ (accessed 10 January 2014).

Steffe, L. P., Cobb, P., and von Glasersfeld, E. (1988). *Construction of arithmetical meanings and strategies.* New York: Springer-Verlag.

Stein, D. (2000). *Myths and realities no. 7. Teaching critical reflection.* The Ohio state University: Centre on Education and Training for Employment. ERIC Clearinghouse on Adult, Career, and Vocational Education.

Sternberg, R. J. (1996). Matching abilities, instruction, and assessment: Reawakening the sleeping giant of ATI. In I. Dennis and P. Tapsfield (Eds)*Human abilities: Their nature and measurement* (pp. 167–181). Mahwah, NJ: Erlbaum.

Sternberg, R. J. and Grigorenko, E. L. (1997). Are cognitive styles still in style? *American Psychologist,* 52, 700–712.

Sternberg. R. J., and Wagner, R. K. (1992). *Thinking styles inventory.* Unpublished manual, Yale University.

Sternberg, R. J., and Zhang, L. F. (Eds) (2001). *Perspectives on thinking, learning, and cognitive styles.* Mahwah, NJ: Erlbaum.

Stewart, W. (2012). Think you've implemented Assessment for Learning? *Times Educational Supplement Magazine,* 13 July 2012. Available online at http://www.tes.c.uk/article.aspx?storycide= 6261847 (accessed 14 July 2012).

Stipek, D. (1998). *Motivation to learn. From theory to practice.* Massachusetts: Allyn and Bacon.

Strijbos, J. W., and Sluijsmans, D. (2010). Unravelling peer assessment: Methodological, functional, and conceptual developments. *Learning and Instruction, 20,* 265–269.

Struyven, K., Dochy, F., Janssens, S., and S. Gielen (2006). On the dynamics of students' approaches to learning: The effects of the teaching/learning environment. *Learning and Instruction 16*(4), 279–294.

Subban, P. (2006). Differentiated instruction: A research basis. *International Education Journal,* 7(7), 935–947.

Sweller, K., van Merrienböer, J. G., and Paas, F. G. (1998). Cognitive architecture and instructional design. *Educational Psychology Review, 10,* 251–296.

Syed, M. (2010). *Bounce: The myth of talent and the power of practice.* New York: HarperCollins Publishers.

Tatto, T. (2013). *International Policy and Practice in Teacher Education: The Role of Research,* Paper Commissioned for the ERA-RSA Inquiry, London: BERA.

TDA (Training and Development Agency for Schools) (2007a) *Professional Standards for Teachers,* London: TDA publications.

TDA (2007b). Qualified teacher status. *Professional standards for teachers.* London: The Training and Development Agency for Schools. Available online at www.tda.gov.uk.standards (accessed 10 December 10–2013).

Tertiary education research database. Available online at http://hdl.voced.edu.au/10707/69027 (accessed 12 January 2014).

Thiessen, D. (2000). A skilful start to a teaching career: A matter of developing impactful behaviors, reflective practices, or professional knowledge? *International Journal of Educational Research, 33,* 515–537.

Thirteen ed. Available online at http://www.thirteen.org/edonline/concept2class/constructivism/index_sub5.html (accessed 10 January 2014).

Thomas, G. (2013). A review of thinking and research about inclusive education policy, with suggestions for a new kind of inclusive thinking. *British Educational Research Journal, 39*(3), 473–490.

Thomas, P. R., and McKay, J. B. (2010). Cognitive styles and instructional design in university learning. *Learning and Individual Differences, 20*(3), 197–202.

Thompson, N. (1995). *Theory and practice in health and social welfare.* Buckingham: OpenUniversity Press.

Thompson, N. (2000). *Theory and practice in human services.* Buckingham: OpenUniversity Press.

Thorndike, E. L. (1903). *Educational Psychology.* New York: Lemcke and Buechner.

TLRP: Learning how to learn – in classrooms, schools and networks 2001–2005. Teaching and learning research programme. Available online at http://www.tlrp.org/proj/phase11/phase2f.html

Tolman, E. C. (1932). *Purposive behavior in animals and men.* New York: Century.

Tomlinson, C. A. (1997). *Differentiation of instruction in mixed ability classrooms*, Idaho Council for Exceptional Children State Conference, Sun Valley, ID. Available online at http://www.gifted.uconn.edu/siegle/epsy373/Tomlinson.htm (accessed 25 April 2007)

Tomlinson, C. A. (1999). *The differentiated classroom: Responding to the needs of all learners*. Alexandria, VA: Association for Supervision and Curriculum Development.

Tomlinson, C. (2003). *Fulfilling the promise of the differentiated classroom: Strategies and tools for responsive teaching*. Alexandria, VA: Association for Supervision and Curriculum Development.

Tomlinson, C. A. (2005). *Differentiated Instruction as a way to achieve equity and excellence in today's schools, building inclusive schools: A search for solutions*. Conference Report Canadian Teachers' Federation Conference, November 17–19–2005, Ottawa, Ontario, 19–21.

Tomlinson hot topic (2009). Available online at http://mcjackson.iweb.bsu.edu/ (accessed 5 May 2014).

Tomlinson, C. Brighton, C., Hertberg, H., Callahan, C. M., Moon, T. R., Brimijoin, K., Conover, L. A., and Reynolds, T. (2003). Differentiating instruction in response to student readiness, interest, and learning profile in academically diverse classrooms: A review of the literature. *Journal for the Education of the Gifted, 27*(2/3), 119–145.

Topping, K. J. (1998). Peer assessment between students in college and university. *Review of Educational Research, 68*, 249–276.

Topping, K. J. (2010). Methodological quandaries in studying process and outcomes in peer assessment. *Learning and Instruction, 20*, 339–343.

Torrance, H. (2007). Assessment 'as' learning? How the use of explicit learning objectives, assessment criteria and feedback in post-secondary education and training can come to dominate learning. *Assessment in Education: Principles, Policy and Practice, 14*, 281–294.

Transition Consciousness. Available online at http://transitionconsciousness.wordpress.com/2013/11/16/guest-article-iain-mcgilchrist-replies-to-stephen-kosslyn-and-wayne-miller-on-the-divided-brain (accessed 17 January 2014).

Tripp, D. (1993). *Critical incidents in teaching: Developing professional judgement*. Oxford: Routledge Falmer.

Tripp, D. (1994). Teachers' lives, critical incidents and professional practice. *Qualitative Studies in Education*, 7(1), 65–76.

Tseng, S. C., and Tsai, C. C. (2010). Taiwan college students' self-efficacy and motivation of learning in online peer assessment environments. *Internet and Higher Education, 13*, 164–169.

Tudge, J., and Scrimsher, S. (2003). Lev S. Vygotsky on education: A cultural-historical, interpersonal, and individual approach to development. In B. J. Zimmerman and D. H. Schunk (Eds), *Educational psychology: A century of contributions* (pp. 207–228) Mahwah, NJ: Erlbaum.

Turner, J. E., and Husman, J. (2008). Emotional and cognitive self-regulation following academic shame. *Journal of Advanced Academics, 20*(1), 138–173.

Tynjälä, P. (1997). Developing education students' conceptions of the learning process in different learning environments. *Learning and Instruction*, 7, 277–292.

Tynjälä, P. (1999). Towards expert knowledge? A comparison between a constructivist and a traditional learning environment in the University. *International Journal of Educational Research, 33*, 355–442.

University of California, Berkeley. *Teaching guide for graduate student instructors*. Available online at http://gsi.berkeley.edu/teachingguide/theories/learning-chapter.pdf (accessed 20 December 2013). Ure, C. (2009) *Reforming teacher education: a developmental model for program design and pedagogy*. Unpublished report, London: Institute of Education.

Van Boxtel, C. (2000). Collaborative concept learning: Collaborative learning tasks, student interaction and the learning of physics concepts. Utrecht, The Netherlands: Universiteit Utrecht.

Van den Bossche, P., and Beausaert, S. (2011). The reflective practitioner: D. Schön In F. Dochy, D. Gijbels, M. Segers and P. Van Den Bossche *Theories of learning for the workplace* (pp. 79–86). London and New York: Routledge.

Van der Pol, J., Van den Berg, B. A. M., Admiraal, W. F., and Simons, R. P. J. (2008). The nature, reception, and use of online peer feedback in higher education. *Computers and Education, 51*, 1804–1817.

Van der Zwet, J., Zwietering, P. J., Teunissen, P. W., van der Vleuten, C. P. N., and Scherpbier, A. J. J. A. (2011). Workplace learning from a socio-cultural perspective: Creating developmental space during the general practice clerkship. *Advances in Health Science Education, 16*, 359–373.

Van Merrienböer, J., and Sweller, J. (2005). Cognitive load theory and complex learning: Recent developments and future directions. *Educational Psychology Review* 17, 147–77.

Van Zundert, M., Sluijsmans, D. M. A., and Van Merrienböer, J. J. B. (2010). Effective peer assessment processes: Research findings and future directions. *Learning and Instruction, 20*, 3270–3279.

Verloop, N. (2003). De leraar [The teacher]. In J. Lowyck, andN. Verloop (Eds), *Onderwijskunde: eenkennisbasisvoor profession* [Educational sciences: a knowledge base for professionals] (pp. 195–248). Groningen: Wolters-Noordhof.

Verloop, N., Van Driel, J., and Meijer, P. (2001). Teacher knowledge and the knowledge base of teaching, *International Journal of Educational Research, 35*(5), 441–461.

Vermunt, J. D. (1994). *Inventory of Learning Styles (ILS) in higher education.* Tilburg, The Netherlands: Tilburg University, Department of Educational Psychology.

Vermunt. J. D. (1996). Metacognitive, cognitive and affective aspects of learning styles and strategies: A phenomenographic analysis. *Higher Education, 31*, 25–50.

Vermunt, J. D. (1998). The regulation of constructive learning processes, *British Journal of Educational Psychology*, 68, 149–71.

Vermunt, J. D. (2007). The power of teaching-learning environments to influence student learning. *British Journal of Educational Psychology* Monograph Series II, 4, 73–90.

Vermunt, J. D. (2013). *Teacher learning and student learning: are they related?* Inaugural lecture given at the University of Cambridge, Faculty of Education, on 22nd May 2013. Available online at http://sms.cam.ac.uk/media/1497678 (accessed 20 July 2013).

Vermunt, J. D., and Endedijk, M. (2011). Patterns in teacher learning in different phases of the professional career. *Learning and Individual Differences, 21*(3), 294–302.

Vermunt, J. D., and Verloop, N. (1999). Congruence and friction between learning and teaching. *Learning and Instruction, 9,* 257–280.

Visser, B. A., Ashton, M. C., and Vernon, P. A. (2006). Beyond g: Putting multiple intelligences theory to the test. *Intelligence 34*, 487–502.

Vogel-Walcutt, J. J., Gebrim, J. B., Bowers, C., Carper, T. M., and Nicholson, D. (2011). Cognitive load theory vs. constructivist approaches: Which best leads to efficient, deep learning? *Journal of Computer Assisted Learning, 27*, 133–145.

Vosniadou, S. (1996). Towards a revised cognitive psychology for new advances in learning and instruction. *Learning and Instruction, 6*, 95–109.

Vygotsky, L. S. (1986). *Thought and language.* Cambridge, MA: MIT Press.

Vygotsky, L. S. (1978). *Mind in society.* The development of higher psychological processes. Cambridge, MA: Harvard University Press.

Vygotsky, L. S. (1997). *The collected works of L. S. Vygotsky, Vol. 4: The history of the development of higher mental functions (R. W. Rieber,* Vol. Ed; M. J. Hall, Trans.). New York: Plenum Press. (Original work published 1941.)

Wall Street Journal: A new map of how we think: Top brain/bottom brain. Available online at http://online.wsj.com/news/articles/SB10001424052702304410204579139423079198270 (accessed 17 January 2014).

Wallace, M., and Wray, A. (2011). *Critical reading and writing for postgraduates* (2nd ed.). London: Sage.

Wallach, M. A. (1962). Active-Analytical vs. Passive-Global cognitive functioning. In S. Messick and J. Ross (Eds), *Measurement in Personality and Cognition.* New York: Wiley.

Waring, M., and Evans, C. (2010). *A consideration of physical education student teachers' feedback-seeking behaviours from a cognitive styles perspective.* Paper presented at the 15th European Learning Styles Information Network (ELSIN) conference, June 28–30, Aveiro, Portugal.

Watkins, C., and Mortimore, P. (1999). Pedagogy: What do we know? In P. Mortimore, (Ed.) *Understanding pedagogy and its impact on learning.* (pp. 1–19). London: Paul Chapman Publishing.

Watson, J. B. (1913). Psychology as the behaviorist views it. *Psychological Review, 20,* 158–177.

Weaver, M. R. (2006). Do students value feedback? Student perceptions of tutors' written responses. *Assessment and Evaluation in Higher Education, 31,* 379–394.

Webb, M., and Jones, J. (2009). Exploring tensions in developing assessment for learning. *Assessment in Education, 16,* 165–184.

Webb, R., Vulliamy, G., Hamalainen, S., Sarja, A., Kimonen, E., and Nevelainen, R. (2004). A comparative analysis of primary teacher professionalism in England and Finland. *Comparative Education, 40*(1), 83–107.

Wenger, E. (1998). *Communities of practice. Learning, meaning, and identity.* Cambridge: Cambridge University Press.

Wenger, E. (2000). Communities of practice and social learning systems. *Organization,* 7, 225–246.

Wenger, E. (2009). A social theory of learning. In K. Illeris (Ed.). *Contemporary learning theories* (pp. 209–218). London: Routledge.

Wenger, E. (2010). Knowledgeability in landscapes of practice: From curriculum to identity. Keynote address at SRHE Annual Research Conference 2010, Wales, 14–16 December.

Wertsch, J. (1991). *Voices of the mind: A Sociocultural approach to mediated action.* Cambridge, MA: Harvard University Press.

What is Theatre of the Oppressed? In *Tree of the Theatre of the Oppressed.* The Forum Project. Available online at http://theforumproject.org/whatisto/> (accessed 15 March 2014).

Whitty, G. (2001). Teacher professionalism in new times. In D. Gleeson and C. Husbands (Eds). *The performing school* (pp. 159–173). London: Routledge.

Wiliam, D. (2011). What is assessment for learning? *Studies in Educational Evaluation, 37,* 3–14.

Wiliam, D., and Thompson, M. (2008). Integrating assessment with instruction: What will it take to make it work? In C. A. Dwyer (ed.), *The future of assessment: Shaping teaching and learning* (pp. 53–82), Mawah, NJ, Erlbaum.

Willingham, D. T. (2005). Visual, auditory, and kinaesthetic learners need visual, auditory, and kinaesthetic instruction? *American Educator,* Spring 2005, 31–35.

Willis, J. (2009). Assessment for learning a sociocultural approach. In P. Jeffery (Ed.) *Proceedings of: Changing climates: Education for sustainable futures.* Australian Association for Research in Education (AARE), Queensland, Australia: Kelvin Grove. Available online at http://ocs.sfu.ca/aare/index.php/AARE_2008/AARE/paper/view/348/94 (accessed 4 December 2013).

Wilson, A., Akerlind, G., Walsh, B., Stevens, B., Turner, B., and Shield, A. (2013). Making 'professionalism' meaningful to students in higher education. *Studies in Higher Education, 38*(8), 1222–1238.

Wilson, E., and Demetriou, H. (2007). New teacher learning: Substantive knowledge and contextual factors. *The Curriculum Journal, 18*(3), 213–229.

Wilson, K., and Fowler, J. (2005). Assessing the impact of learning environments on students' approaches to learning: Comparing conventional and action learning designs. *Assessment and Evaluation in Higher Education, 30*(1), 87–101.

Wilkins, C. (2011). Professionalism and the post-performative teacher: New teachers reflect on autonomy and accountability in the English school system. *Professional Development in Education, 37*(3), 389–409.

Wilson, A., Akerlind, G., Walsh, B., Stevens, B., Turner, B., and Shield, A. (2013). Making 'professionalism' meaningful to students in higher education. *Studies in Higher Education, 38*(8), 1222–1238.

Winch, C., Oancea, A., and Orchard, J. (2013). *The contribution of research to teachers' professional learning,* Paper Commissioned for the BERA-RSA Inquiry, London: BERA.

Witkin, H. A., Dyk, R. B., Faterson, H. F., Goodenough, D. R., and Karp, S. A. (1962). *Psychological differentiation.* New York: Wiley.

Witkin, H. A. (1964). Origins of cognitive style. In C Sheerer. (Ed.), *Cognition: Theory, research, promise* (pp. 172–205). New York: Harper and Row.

Witkin, H. A., Lewis, H., Hertzman, M., Machover, K., Meisener, P., and Wapner, S. (1954). *Personality through perception.* New York: Harper.

Wood, D. (1998). *How children think and learn.* Malden, MA: Blackwell Publishing.

Woods, P., and Jeffrey, B. (2002). The reconstruction of primary teachers' identities. *British Journal of Sociology of Education, 23*(1), 89–106.

Yang, Y-F., and Tsai, C-C. (2010). Conceptions of and approaches to learning through online peer assessment. *Learning and Instruction, 20*(1), 72–83.

Yang, M., and Carless, D. (2013). The feedback triangle and the enhancement of dialogic feedback processes. *Teaching in Higher Education,* 18(3), 285–297.

Yates, G. C. R. (2000). Applying learning style research in the classroom: Some cautions and the way ahead, (pp. 347–364). In R. J. Riding and S. G. Rayner (Eds), *International perspectives on individual differences, Volume 1 Cognitive Styles.* Stamford, CT: Ablex.

Ylonen, A., and Norwich, B. (2013). The Lesson Study process: How it works and what it offers. Lessons from a development and research project in England. *International Journal of Lesson and Learning Study, 2*(2), 137–154.

Zeichner, K. M., and Liston, D. P. (1996). *Reflective teaching: An introduction.* Mahwah, NJ: Erlbaum.

Zhang, L. F. (2011). The developing field of intellectual styles: four recent endeavours. *Learning and Individual Difference, 21*(3), 311–318.

Zhang, L. F. (2013). *The malleability of intellectual styles.* New York: Cambridge University Press.

Zhang, L. F., and Sternberg, R. J. (2005). A threefold model of intellectual styles. *Educational Psychology Review, 17* (1), 1–53.

Zhang, L. F., and Sternberg, R. J. (2006). *The nature of intellectual styles.* Mahwah, NJ: Erlbaum.

Zhang, L. F., and Sternberg, R. J. (Eds) (2009). *Perspectives on the nature of intellectual styles.* New York: Springer

Zhang, L. F., Sternberg, R. J., and Rayner, S. (Eds) (2012). *Handbook of intellectual styles: Preferences in cognition, learning and thinking.* New York: Springer.

Zull, J. E. (2002). *The art of the changing brain.* Sterling, Virginia, USA: Stylus.

Index

f refers to figures, *t* refers to tables

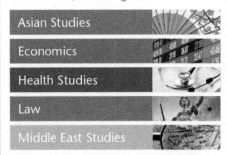